# Kurt Weill's America

# Kurt Weill's America

NAOMI GRABER

OXFORD
UNIVERSITY PRESS

## OXFORD
### UNIVERSITY PRESS

Oxford University Press is a department of the University of Oxford. It furthers
the University's objective of excellence in research, scholarship, and education
by publishing worldwide. Oxford is a registered trade mark of Oxford University
Press in the UK and certain other countries.

Published in the United States of America by Oxford University Press
198 Madison Avenue, New York, NY 10016, United States of America.

This volume is published with the generous support of the General Publications Fund of
the American Musicological Society, supported in part by the National Endowment for
the Humanities and the Andrew W. Mellon Foundation.

Library of Congress Cataloging-in-Publication Data
Names: Graber, Naomi, author.
Title: Kurt Weill's America / Naomi Graber.
Description: New York : Oxford University Press, 2021. |
Includes bibliographical references and index.
Identifiers: LCCN 2020040831 (print) | LCCN 2020040832 (ebook) |
ISBN 9780190906580 (hardback) | ISBN 9780190906603 (epub)
Subjects: LCSH: Weill, Kurt, 1900–1950—Criticism and interpretation. |
Music—Political aspects—History—20th century. |
Opera—United States—20th century. | United States—In opera.
Classification: LCC ML410.W395 G73 2021 (print) |
LCC ML410.W395 (ebook) | DDC 782.1/159—dc23
LC record available at https://lccn.loc.gov/2020040831
LC ebook record available at https://lccn.loc.gov/2020040832

DOI: 10.1093/oso/9780190906580.001.0001

1 3 5 7 9 8 6 4 2

Printed by Sheridan Books, Inc., United States of America

*To Zack, with love and gratitude.*

# Contents

# Acknowledgments

I have had the great fortune of being part of a vast network of professionals, mentors, and friends who have helped me throughout this process. First and foremost, I cannot express enough gratitude to Tim Carter, who has guided this project since its days as a dissertation, and who has patiently read and reread drafts over the years. His attention to detail and keen insight have informed this work at every stage, and I would not be the scholar I am today without his generous attention and guidance. Kim H. Kowalke kindly read long passages, and offered significant critiques that pushed me to probe deeper into every aspect of Weill's career, especially in regard to the years before 1935 and *Street Scene*. I am also indebted to Sally Bick for her thoughts on U.S. modern music communities and their relationship to Hollywood; Elissa Harbert for her insights on the intersections of history, nationalism, and musical theatre; Susan Thomas for her critiques on issues of gender and sexuality; and to the anonymous reviewers at Oxford University Press for their counsel. Conversations with Stephen Hinton, Elmar Juchem, Annegret Fauser, Arianne Quinn Johnson, Dan Blim, Jake Cohen, Emily MacGregor, and many other scholars also profoundly shaped the work. Finally, my musical theatre cohort within the Society for American Music is an inspiration.

This book would not be possible without the tireless work and guidance of librarians and archivists throughout the country. I owe Dave Stein of the Kurt Weill Foundation a great debt of thanks for his enthusiasm and help navigating their vast archival collection. He pointed me in directions I would never have considered, and shared with me far too much material to include in a single book. Richard Boursy at the Beinecke Rare Book and Manuscript Library at Yale University was similarly generous with his time and expertise. At the Library of Congress, conversations with and advice from Mark Horowitz and Janet McKinney helped shape the project, and they graciously allowed me access to uncatalogued parts of the Gershwin Collection. Louise Hilton and Rachael Bernstein of the Margaret Herrick Library and Jim Kuhn and Richard B. Watson at the Harry Ransom Center also provided indispensable assistance.

A number of institutions have also supported this project. A research and travel grant from the Kurt Weill Foundation funded much of my archival work, and a fellowship from the Willson Center for the Humanities and Arts at the University of Georgia allowed me much-needed time to write. My colleagues at the UGA, especially Dale Monson, Pete Jutras, David Haas, and Jean Kidula, have been supportive throughout this process, and I have benefited tremendously from their advice. At Oxford University Press, Norm Hirschy has been patient with my troubles as a novice author, and has provided invaluable critique along the way. Shalini Balakrishnan expertly guided this project through production, and Elizabeth Bortka's careful proofreading has saved me numerous headaches.

I would not be who I am today with the support of friends and family. I am a proud member of the Frank, Graber, and (more recently) Sheffield clans: three large, loving families who are always up in each other's Facebook pages, cheering each other on. My grandparents and Auntie nurtured early interests in opera and Broadway, and my parents Mark Graber and Julia Frank instilled in me a love of Judaism, history, politics, literature, theatre, and music, all evident in this book. They are the best sounding boards a young academic could ask for. Although my husband Zack only officially joined the family toward the end of this process, he has been by my side since before I discovered Kurt Weill. Whether from hundreds of miles away or right next to me, his love and support have sustained me body and soul. I can only hope to be as good a partner to him as he has been to me. It is to him that this book is dedicated.

# Abbreviations

| | |
|---|---|
| ERP | Elmer Rice Papers. Harry Ransom Research Center, University of Texas, Austin. |
| FLP | Fritz Lang Papers. Special Collections #40, Louis B. Mayer Library, American Film Institute, Los Angeles, CA. |
| *KWE* | Kurt Weill Edition. |
| *KWH* | Drew, David. *Kurt Weill: A Handbook*. Berkeley: University of California Press, 1987. |
| *KWiE* | Kowalke, Kim H. *Kurt Weill in Europe*. Ann Arbor: UMI, 1979. |
| GS2 | Weill, Kurt. *Musik und Musikalisches Theater: Gesammelte Schriften. Mit einer Auswahl von Gespächen und Interviews.* Expanded and revised edition. Edited by Stephen Hinton and Jürgen Schebera. Mainz: Schott, 2000. |
| LOC/FTP | Federal Theatre Project Collection. Library of Congress, Music Division, Washington DC. |
| LOC/Gershwin | George and Ira Gershwin Papers. Library of Congress, Music Division, Washington, DC. |
| LOC/GT | Gershwin Trust Collection. Library of Congress, Music Division, Washington, DC. |
| MAC | Maxwell Anderson Collection. Harry Ransom Research Center, University of Texas, Austin. |
| NARA/FTP | Federal Theatre Project Collection. National Archives and Records Administration, Record Group 69, College Park, MD. |
| NYPL | New York Public Library, Schwartzman Building, Fifth Avenue at 42nd Street, New York, NY. |
| *NYT* | *New York Times* |
| ODP | Olin Downes Papers, Series 1. MS 688.series. Hargrett Rare Book and Manuscript Library, the University of Georgia Libraries. |
| *W-Fam* | Weill, Kurt. *Briefe an die Familie, 1914–1950*. Edited by Lys Symonette and Elmar Juchem. Stuttgart: J.B. Metzler, 2000. |
| WLA | Weill–Lenya Archive, MSS 30, The Papers of Kurt Weill and Lotte Lenya, Irving S. Gilmore Music Library, Yale University, New Haven, CT. |

WLL(e)          Weill, Kurt and Lotte Lenya. *Speak Low (When You Speak*
                *Love): The Letters of Kurt Weill and Lotte Lenya*. Edited
                and translated by Kim H. Kowalke and Lys Symonette.
                Berkeley: University of California Press, 1996.
WLRC            Weill-Lenya Research Center, New York, NY.
WPD(e)          Farneth, David, with Elmar Juchem and Dave Stein. *Kurt*
                *Weill: A Life in Pictures and Documents*. Woodstock,
                NY: Overlook, 2000.
WUE             Weill, Kurt. *Briefwechsel mit der Universal Edition*. Edited by
                Nils Grosch. Stuttgart: J.B. Metzler, 2002.

# Introduction

On the 9 March 1941 episode of the NBC radio program *I'm an American!*, composer Kurt Weill waxed enthusiastic about the United States: "I think it is this kinship of the spirit which brings America its new citizens from all lands. Those who come here seeking the freedom, justice, opportunity, and human dignity they miss in their own countries are already Americans before they come." Still, Weill worried about complacency, reminding listeners that "the greatest danger to the human race is indifference," and that people "are much too ready to forget what a precious thing it is to be able to live their own lives and they don't know what they would lose if their way of life would be destroyed." To counter this impulse, he hoped to "show on the stage what it really means to be free" and to "show it in simple terms so that it can reach everybody." Weill proposed to continue the aesthetic work he had begun in Germany, suggesting that the "musical play," which he defined as "a form of theater which combines the elements of drama, musical comedy, ballet and opera," was best suited to this purpose.[1]

Weill's vision of America here embodies both his hopes and fears for the nation. (Throughout this book, I use "America" to refer to the culture—both real and imagined—of the United States. I use "United States" or "U.S." to refer to the political entity.) This represents a consistent part of the composer's career, for as Hermann Danuser and Hermann Gottschewski observe, Weill "explored *Amerikanismus* as centrally in his Weimar period as he did Americanism in his New York Period."[2] Kim H. Kowalke further notes that Weill's America was more complex than his Brechtian collaborations indicate; the composer associated jazz (or at least the European version of jazz) with modernization, transnationalism, and urbanization, and at times considered it a potential source for the renewal of German music.[3] Kowalke also

---

[1] "I'm an American! Interview with Kurt Weill," NBC Blue Network, 9 March 1941, available at http://www.kwf.org/pages/wt-im-an-american.html.
[2] Hermann Danuser and Hermann Gottschewski, foreword to *Amerikanismus, Americanism, Weill: Die Suche nach kultereller Identität in der Moderne* (Schliengen: Edition Argus, 2003), 7.
[3] See Kurt Weill, "A Note Concerning Jazz" (1929), trans. in *KWiE*, 497–98.

*Kurt Weill's America.* Naomi Graber, Oxford University Press (2021). © Oxford University Press.
DOI: 10.1093/oso/9780190906580.003.0001

notes that, after Weill's immigration to the United States on 10 September 1935, the composer actively celebrated America, particularly during the war years, when he hailed its ideals of freedom and democracy as a restorative to a world gone mad.[4] While this could be the defensive posture of an immigrant, private correspondence reveals the sentiments were genuine; returning to the United States after his only trip abroad in 1947, Weill wrote to Maxwell Anderson, "wherever I found decency and humanity in the world, it reminded me of America."[5] Still, he was critical of his adopted homeland when it failed to live up to those ideals, especially before and after the war. Moreover, in this interview Weill also makes clear that his commitments to innovative and socially engaged musical theatre remained consistent.

This book continues on the path laid out by Danuser, Gottschewski, and Kowalke. As Weill's notions of the vices and virtues of America deepened, his critiques and analyses changed in significant and intriguing ways. The idea of America can serve as a prism through which we can view all the various facets and contradictions of Weill's transnational life. Examining Weill's output through his engagement with America reveals a composer adept at navigating the uneven and ever-changing ground of the first half of the twentieth century.

## Rethinking Assimilation

Although Weill argued for some continuity between his German and U.S. careers, scholars perceived a split, represented in what David Drew calls the "two Weills" problem. In the 1980 *New Grove Dictionary of Music and Musicians*, Drew wrote that Weill had "done away with his old creative self in order to make way for a new one. The pre-1934 composer had been acutely conscious of his roots and responsibilities as a German artist in postwar society" who measured "his talents and achievements against those of the most eminent of his German contemporaries, Paul Hindemith." But after 1940, Drew claimed that Weill's "only roots were those he had now established in the U.S.A., and that his responsibilities were to the American musical stage in its popular form. The composer whom he now saw as his chief rival was Richard Rodgers." This post-1940 Weill was inferior to the pre-1934

---

[4] Kim H. Kowalke, "Kurt Weill's *Amerika*/America," in *Amerikanismus, Americanism, Weill,* ed. Danuser and Gottschewski, 10.

[5] Kurt Weill to Maxwell Anderson, 22 June 1947, MAC, Series "Misc." Folder "Weill, Kurt."

modernist, rendering him "one of music's great 'might-have-beens.' "[6] Drew summarized a line of thought that had been building since late in Weill's career, when the composer's contemporaries accused him of pandering to U.S. audiences and abandoning his artistic integrity.[7] Ernst Krenek, for example, wrote that Weill's U.S. works were marked with "the mundane sentimentality and the, if at all, circumspect irony of the Broadway manner," such that "he descended in our eyes below the level of his tradition and his earlier works."[8] Although J. Bradford Robinson rewrote the passage for the 2001 edition of *Grove*, this debate still dogs scholarship on the composer.

The roots of Weill's posthumous reputation lay in part with Theodor W. Adorno, who as Kowalke and Stephen Hinton observe, is a "key figure" in the composer's posthumous reception.[9] Weill's bifurcation owes much to Adorno's declaration that "Every intellectual in emigration is, without exception, mutilated, and does well to acknowledge it to himself, if he wishes to avoid being cruelly apprised of it behind the tightly closed doors of his self-esteem." This mutilation precludes the possibility of transformative art: "Between the reproduction of his own experience under the monopoly of mass culture, and impartial, responsible work yawns an irreconcilable breach."[10] Drew's account of Weill's shifting feelings of obligation from interwar Germany to U.S. popular theatre brings to mind Adorno's question of whether or not it is possible to be a socially "responsible" artist within American mass culture.

Much recent scholarship challenges these views, recognizing continuities in Weill's career.[11] Hinton takes a psycho-analytic approach, declaring that Weill was an "other-directed composer," one whose career was shaped

---

[6] David Drew, "Kurt Weill," in *The New Grove Dictionary of Music and Musicians*, ed. Stanley Sadie (London: Macmillan, 1980) 20: 307, 309.

[7] See Kim H. Kowalke, "Kurt Weill, Modernism, and Popular Culture: *Offentlichkeit als Stil*," *Modernism/Modernity* 2, no. 1 (1995): 28–29.

[8] Ernst Krenek, "America's Influence on Its Émigré Composers" (1959), trans. in *Perspectives of New Music* 8, no. 2 (1970): 115. For more posthumous reception of Weill, see Tamara Levitz, "Putting Kurt Weill in His Historical Place: The *New Grove* Articles," *Kurt Weill Newsletter* 20, no. 2 (2002): 5.

[9] Kowalke, "Kurt Weill, Modernism, and Popular Culture," 29–34; Stephen Hinton, *Kurt Weill: The Threepenny Opera* (Cambridge, UK: Cambridge University Press, 1990), 182–86.

[10] Theodor W. Adorno, *Minima Moralia: Reflections on a Damaged Life* (1951), trans. E.F.N Jephcott (London: Verso, 2005), 33. On Drew's debt to Adorno, see Levitz, "Putting Kurt Weill in His Historical Place," 7, and Stephen Hinton, *Weill's Musical Theater: Stages of Reform* (Berkeley: University of California Press, 2012), 231.

[11] For a summary of these arguments, see Claire Taylor-Jay, "The Composer's Voice? Compositional Style and Criteria of Value in Weill, Krenek, and Stravinsky," *Journal of the Royal Musical Association* 134, no. 1 (2009): 91–99.

by the guidance of his collaborators and the influence of the public.[12] He also points out that Weill never abandoned the teachings of his mentor Ferruccio Busoni, and that he consistently engaged with issues of music-theatrical form.[13] Michael H. Kater observes that Weill rarely differentiated between "light" and "serious" music, and even in Europe strove to reach, as Weill put it, "as large a circle of listeners as possible," constantly simplifying his style in the process.[14] Kowalke similarly notes that Weill always wrote for his audience, adopting an attitude of "*Öffentlichkeit*" ("openness" or "public-facing"), as opposed to the *Einsamkeit* ("loneliness") that Adorno valued in Arnold Schoenberg's music.[15] Kowalke also observes significant structural, expressive, and even stylistic continuities in Weill's creative output.[16] According to bruce d. mcclung, Weill even had a signature musical "thumbprint," a melodic formula of a major second followed by a minor third (or its reverse).[17]

Weill scholars are not alone in facing the question of how to approach post-immigration compositional change, yet Weill has become emblematic of the discussion; Danuser and Gottschewski note that interpretation of Weill's life and works is bound up with "the general question of cultural studies in the first half of the twentieth century," given that the composer's career raises significant issues regarding the interactions of Jewish, German, and American identities.[18] As Lydia Goehr observes, musicologists tend to place German migrant composers of the 1930s and 1940s on the spectrum of assimilation and resistance.[19] Sometimes, the latter is endowed with moral superiority, which is read as heroic cultural preservation in the face of philistine American audiences. Failure, conversely, becomes something heroic, an individual's strength to pursue one's own goals without succumbing to the lure of material concerns. Claudia Mauer Zenck, for example, writes that while one genuine "masterpiece," *Lamentations*, did come out of Ernst Krenek's experiences in the United States, "in his symphonic music, however,

[12] Stephen Hinton, "Hindemith and Weill: Cases of 'Inner' and 'Other' Direction," in *Driven into Paradise: The Musical Migration from Nazi Germany to the United States*, ed. Reinhold Brinkmann and Christoph Wolff (Berkeley: University of California Press, 1999), 261–78.

[13] Hinton, *Weill's Musical Theater*, 15ff.

[14] Kurt Weill, "A Note Concerning *Das Berliner Requiem*" (1929), trans. in *KWiE*, 504. Michael H. Kater, *Composers of the Nazi Era: Eight Portraits* (Oxford, UK: Oxford University Press, 2000), 84–85.

[15] Kowalke, "Kurt Weill, Modernism, and Popular Culture," 30.

[16] Kowalke, "Kurt Weill, Modernism, and Popular Culture," 41–52.

[17] bruce d. mcclung, *Lady in the Dark: Biography of a Musical* (Oxford, UK: Oxford University Press, 2007), 67–68.

[18] Danuser and Gottschewski, foreword to *Amerikanismus, Americanism, Weill*, 7.

[19] Lydia Goehr, "Music and Musicians in Exile: The Romantic Legacy of a Double Life," in *Driven into Paradise*, ed. Brinkmann and Wolff, 66–91.

he seems to have succumbed to the temptation of making concessions to the general public."[20] The reverse can also be true; resisters can be seen as ungrateful, while assimilators are praised for finding something "universal" in their art (as Weill on many occasions publicly aspired to do). Sabine Feisst notes this trend in Schoenberg scholarship; the composer is often painted as elitist for refusing to adapt. But she also notes that he is sometimes seen as too accommodating to U.S. culture.[21]

Changes to an immigrant composer's idiomatic writing are scrutinized because, as Claire Taylor-Jay observes, contemporary scholarship still owes much to nineteenth- and twentieth-century romantic and high modernist aesthetics, which emphasize the transcendent potential of compositional voices, rendering suspicious any radical stylistic shift caused by external factors.[22] Furthermore, as Brigid Cohen notes, musicological historiography often relies on "nation-centered" frameworks, in which "traditional genealogies of influence and style" are "bound up with ideas of national inheritance of expression."[23] Within such frameworks, "Notions of exile work in the service of national canons, because the very idea of exile casts displacement primarily in relation to the lost homeland."[24] Tamara Levitz and Nils Grosch note that this is especially problematic for Weill, whose Öffentlich orientation means that his U.S. works do not fit neatly into the historiography of German music.[25] Indeed, many composers have stylistic periods, but those of Weill, Krenek, Schoenberg, and many others seem problematic because these shifts result from something other than autonomous personal development. Rather, immigration seems to have forced their hands.

The root of Weill's troubled reception comes from the fact that musicology as a field places a high value on artistic autonomy.[26] For Weill especially, this

---

[20] Claudia Mauer Zenck, "Challenges and Opportunities of Acculturation: Schoenberg, Krenek, and Stravinsky in Exile," in *Driven into Paradise*, ed. Brinkmann and Wolff, 180.

[21] See the first chapter of Sabine Feisst, *Schoenberg's New World: The American Years* (Oxford, UK: Oxford University Press, 2011).

[22] Taylor-Jay, "The Composer's Voice?" 86–87.

[23] Brigid Cohen, *Stefan Wolpe and the Avant-Garde Diaspora* (Cambridge, UK: Cambridge University Press, 2012), 14.

[24] Cohen, *Stefan Wolpe and the Avante-Garde Diaspora*, 16. See also Kowalke, "Formerly German," 38–39.

[25] Levitz, "Putting Kurt Weill in His Historical Place," 9; Nils Grosch, "'Gewohntes zu überdenken': Der andere Blick auf Musik in der Migration und im Exil," *Österreichische Musikzeitschrift* 72, no. 2 (2017): 30–35.

[26] Sarah Whitfield, "'Next You're Franklin Shepard Inc.?' Composing the Broadway Musical—A Study of Kurt Weill's working Practices," *Studies in Musical Theatre* 10, no. 2 (2016): 170. This has also been a principle concern for the KWE. See Harsh, Selk et al. "Guide for Volume Editors. of the Kurt Weill Edition," 3, available online at https://www.kwf.org/media/edguide.pdf.

view has roots in Adorno's thought. In his obituary of Weill, Adorno wrote that Weill was not a "composer" (*Komponisten*), but a "music director" (*Musikregisseur*), who "made a virtue of his limited creativity by subordinating it to other purposes—artistic in some cases, but also political." By *Musikregisseur*, he meant one who writes music for the vagaries of all-ready existing criteria, including the demands of musical theatre.[27] Given Weill's lifelong devotion to musical theatre, he always worked in collaboration with other professionals, and his working process involved cooperation and negotiation with various conventions and institutions. Adorno did find value in this role; in the 1930s he wrote, "The shock with which Weill's compositional practice overexposes common compositional means, unmasking them as ghosts, expresses alarm about the society within which they have their origin," and that "Weill's music is today the only music of genuine social polemic impact, which it will remain as long as it resides in the height of its negativity."[28] But when Weill ceased to "subordinate" his "limited creativity" to political purposes or to greater talents (which for Adorno meant Brecht), composition became a mere "test of skill" in pleasing the public.[29] This reflects Adorno's musical and cultural values more than Weill's. Adorno argued that composers (rather than "music directors") must "surrender all alleged connections and obligations which stand in the way of freedom of movement of individual expressions" as such connections were "the reflection of an 'agreement' of bourgeois society with the psyche of the individual which is now renounced by the suffering of the individual," an ideal he found fulfilled in the free atonal music of Arnold Schoenberg.[30] In this light, Weill's collaborative work could be valuable, but only in the negative, revealing the contradictions in that "agreement" between "bourgeois society" and the individual, but not transcending them. Such a negative formulation could never achieve the individual expression that marked true progress.[31] These values have been extended to many collaborative mediums in contemporary

---

[27] Hinton, *Weill's Musical Theater*, 13–15; Kowalke, "Kurt Weill, Modernism, and Popular Culture," 55.

[28] Theodor W. Adorno, "On the Social Situation of Music" (1932), trans. Wes Blomster and Richard Leppert in Theodor W. Adorno, *Essays on Music*, ed. Richard Leppert (Berkeley: University of California Press, 2002), 409.

[29] Theodor W. Adorno, "Kurt Weill" (1950), in *Theodor W. Adorno: Gesammelte Schriften*, vol. 18, ed. Rolf Tiedemann and Klaus Schultz (Frankfurt am Main: Suhrkamp, 1984), 544–45.

[30] Adorno, "On the Social Situation of Music," 398.

[31] Weill's neoclassical tendencies and debt to Stravinsky also played a role in Adorno's evaluation; the critic characterized neoclassicism as "regressive" in contrast to Schoenberg's "progressive" style. For a summary of these debates, see Tamara Levitz, *Modernist Mysteries: Perséphone* (Oxford, UK: Oxford University Press, 2012), 18–20.

scholarship, including filmmaking. For example, Dorothy Lamb Crawford writes that in Hollywood, "the conditions of studio work demanded a great degree of adaptability. One must ask, given the humiliations and frustrations they experienced: how did those composers who stayed to earn their livings manage to save their artistic identities and achieve their own goals?"[32] Crawford equates "adaptability" with humiliation and an inability to control one's artistic identity. At the heart of these evaluations are two related assumptions: high culture and personal identity are both monolithic, and they are at their most authentic when allowed to develop autonomously, without foreign or popular influence.

But such autonomy is a myth; cultural and aesthetic evolutions are always informed by external stimuli. Michel Espagne and Michaël Werner's notion of "cultural transfer" offers an alternative framework. They acknowledge the importance of both collaboration and national style while bypassing the value structure of high modernism. They observe that notions of "influence" dominate ideas of cultural interaction, where "strong" cultures induce "weaker" cultures to change.[33] To circumvent notions of "influence," Espagne and Werner highlight the importance of reception, national and international networks, and the specific situations of individual border-crossings.[34] Cultural transfer recognizes that, whenever cultural practices cross boundaries, the receiving culture reshapes them.[35] Jonathan O. Wipplinger uses the metaphor of a prism, noting that the ways cultures reshape foreign materials and practices are rarely a "mirror image of internal concerns," but "more akin to that of prismatic refraction."[36] This is particularly applicable to musical theatre, which has long been a transnational phenomenon. Donizetti's *Lucia di Lammermoor* underwent significant revisions in Paris, and the story of Weber's *Der Freischütz* (1821) migrated to Broadway as *The Black Crook* in 1866 via the British author

---

[32] Dorothy Lamb Crawford, *A Windfall of Musicians: Hitler's Émigrés and Exiles in Southern California* (New Haven, CT: Yale University Press, 2009), 166.

[33] Michel Espagne and Michaël Werner, "La Construction d'une Référence Culturelle Allemande en France Genèse et Histoire (1750–1914)," *Annales, Histoire, Science Sociales* 42, no. 4 (1987): 970.

[34] Espagne and Werner, "La Construction," 984–86. See also Annegret Fauser and Mark Everist, Introduction to *Music, Theater, and Cultural Transfer: Paris 1830–1914*, ed. Annegret Fauser and Mark Everist (Cambridge, UK: Cambridge University Press, 2009), 6.

[35] Michel Espagne and Michaël Werner, "Deutsch-Französischer Kulturtransfer im 18. und 19. Jahrhundert: Zu einem neuen interdisziplinären Forschungsprogramm des. C.N.R.S.," *Francia* 13 (1985): 510.

[36] Jonathan O. Wipplinger, *The Jazz Republic: Music, Race, and American Culture in Weimar Germany* (Ann Arbor: University of Michigan Press, 2017), 5.

Charles Barras and U.S. producer William Wheatley, absorbing a French ballet troupe in the process.[37]

While Espagne and Werner mostly examine how ideas, styles, and practices change according to national context, their paradigm can be extended to explore how immigrants adapt to new cultures and new cultures adapt to immigrants. I use this framework to take up Tamara Levitz's challenge to "describe all of Weill's works within their individual historical contexts, without seeking to elevate one culture above another."[38] I also build on Raymond Knapp's observation that the musical is a continually evolving art form, "both accommodating changes in American culture and society, and in turn, helping to shape their development in profound ways."[39] The same can be said about Weill. As he adapted to America, he also adapted American styles to suit his goals, both political and aesthetic. One could hardly call *Johnny Johnson* (1936), *Lady in the Dark* (1941), *Street Scene* (1947), *Down in the Valley* (1948), *Love Life* (1948), or *Lost in the Stars* (1949) typical Broadway musicals.

Acknowledging the complex web of adaptation and cultural transfer also helps us to gain an better understanding of the multifaceted nature of the "receiving" culture. To speak of a single culture ignores the myriad of different classes, races, institutions, and artistic movements that make up nations and states. Assumptions regarding the superiority of an identity unbound by popular or external cultural factors do the United States a disservice given how the national conversations about commercial culture, class, race, ethnicity, gender, and the country's place in the international community have defined the terms of artistic engagement.[40] This is especially true for Broadway. As Knapp observes, the meeting of national and international styles serves as "a fairy-tale account of the birth of the American musical," speaking to deep-seated notions of the heterogeneous nature of American culture.[41]

---

[37] Rebecca Harris-Warrick, "*Lucia* goes to Paris: A Tale of Three Theaters," *Music, Theater, and Cultural Transfer*, ed. Fauser and Everist, 195–227; Raymond Knapp, *The American Musical and the Formation of National Identity* (Princeton, NJ: Princeton University Press, 2005), 20–23.

[38] Levitz, "Putting Kurt Weill in his Historical Place," 9.

[39] Knapp, *The American Musical and the Formation of National Identity*, 3. See also John Bush Jones, *Our Musicals, Ourselves: A Social History of the American Musical Theatre* (Waltham, MA: Brandeis University Press, 2003).

[40] See especially Annegret Fauser, *Sounds of War: Music in the United States during World War II* (Oxford, UK: Oxford University Press, 2013); Charles Hiroshi Garrett, *Struggling to Define a Nation: American Music and the Twentieth Century* (Berkeley: University of California Press, 2008); Jeffrey Melnick, *A Right to Sing the Blues: African Americans, Jews, and American Popular Song* (Cambridge, MA: Harvard University Press, 1999); David Savran, *Highbrow/Lowdown: Theatre, Jazz and the Making of the New Middle Class* (Ann Arbor: University of Michigan Press, 2009).

[41] Knapp, *The American Musical and the Formation of National Identity*, 23.

As Elizabeth Craft notes, multiple generations have used this quality of the musical to "write a broad range of immigrant groups into cultural citizenship, especially during fraught periods in which their belonging within the nation was contested."[42] But as Bruce Kirle observes, the musical also attests to the "messiness of American identity," revealing the hopes and dreams of a future society unfettered by racial, gender, and ethnic divisions, yet simultaneously reinforcing those boundaries in the present with artificial happy endings that reveal the herculean effort it takes to transcend differences.[43]

Recognizing this heterogeneity reveals that assimilation and resistance are a set of non-mutually exclusive options for an individual within vast networks of possibilities. Immigrants simultaneously assimilate into some communities and resist others. Adorno's skepticism toward mass culture resembles positions within the U.S. academy, and in turn, he shaped the course of U.S. musicology and critical theory.[44] Weill, conversely, fell in with the theatrical communities of the Group Theatre, the Federal Theatre Project, and the Playwrights Producing Company, all of whom hoped to harness the power of mass culture for social good.

Weill's devotion to musical theatre makes him especially vulnerable to devaluations based on the politics of autonomy. Musical theatre, and Broadway especially, is a profoundly collaborative endeavor, requiring cooperation between composers, lyricists, book writers, directors, orchestrators, dance arrangers, choreographers, set and lighting designers, builders, actors, singers, dancers, musicians, stage hands, publishers, and marketing teams.[45] Broadway shows also go through a rigorous process of revision before

---

[42] Elizabeth Titrington Craft, "Becoming American Onstage: Broadway Narratives of Immigrant Experiences in the United States" (PhD diss., Harvard University, 2014), 1.

[43] Bruce Kirle, *Unfinished Business: Broadway Musicals as Works-in-Progress* (Carbondale: Southern Illinois University Press, 2005), 2.

[44] Peter U. Hohendahl, "The Displaced Intellectual? Adorno's American Years Revisited," *New German Critique* 59 (1992): 93–94.

[45] As this relates to Weill, see Sarah Whitfield, "Kurt Weill: The 'Composer as Dramatist' in American Musical Theatre Production" (PhD diss., Queen Mary, University of London, 2010), and "'Next You're Franklin Shepard Inc.?'" Numerous other publications on the Broadway musical have addressed this subject, particularly in relationship to the music: Bruce Kirle, *Unfinished Business*; Dominic McHugh, "'I'll Never Know Exactly Who Did What': Broadway Composers as Musical Collaborators," *Journal of the American Musicological Society* 68, no. 3 (2015): 605–52; and Part V of Raymond Knapp, Mitchell Morris, and Stacy Wolf, eds., *The Oxford Handbook of the American Musical* (Oxford, UK: Oxford University Press, 2015). Studies of individual shows also address this issue. See particularly Tim Carter, *Oklahoma! The Making of an American Musical* (New Haven: Yale University Press, 2007); Carol Oja, *Bernstein Meets Broadway: Collaborative Art in a Time of War* (Oxford, UK: Oxford University Press); Paul R. Laird, "How to Create a Musical: The Case of *Wicked*," in *The Cambridge Companion to the Musical*, 3rd edition, ed. William A. Everett and Paul R. Laird (Cambridge, UK: Cambridge University Press, 2017), 11–45.

(and sometimes even after) opening night during rehearsals and previews. Contributors may be replaced, or outside professionals may be brought in to offer their expertise. Songs are written for particular stars and replaced when those stars refuse to sing them, and aspects of the production can shift with the political winds or on the basis of cash flow. Working methods also vary by individual, which may help or hinder collaboration. Weill, for example, preferred to have the lyrics in hand before he began composing, which presented difficulties in his working relationship with Ira Gershwin, who previously contributed the words only after his brother George had composed the tunes.[46] Consequently, it becomes difficult to speak of an "author" of a Broadway show; the final production is the result of a mix of ideas that have developed in dialogue with one another.[47]

This process proved especially attractive to Weill, who as an "other-directed" composer (to use Hinton's terminology), valued the collaborative process. As Sarah Whitfield observes, Adorno's idea of a *Musikregisseur* is not entirely an insult, despite the fact that it is often construed as such.[48] This opens the possibly of reading Weill as a "collaborative practitioner who used music as his medium" and who "brought the process of composing into the rehearsal room."[49] For Whitfield, it is the idea of "composer" that is limiting, and *Musikregisseur* "enables the recognition of the full range of Weill's activities."[50] I build on Hinton and Whitfield's ideas, emphasizing collaborative networks as key to the final productions. While Weill usually served as his own orchestrator and dance arranger, and so had more control over the score than many of his contemporaries, he valued the input of his lyricists, book writers, directors, and show doctors, and made an effort to seek out the most prestigious playwrights and lyricists of the era on both sides of the Atlantic. I follow Levitz in acknowledging that, in any venture with multiple authors, each brings their own aesthetics and agendas to the table.[51] Rarely did Weill agree wholeheartedly with his creative partners, although their goals were often not mutually exclusive—for example, Weill appears to have

---

[46] mcclung, *Lady in the Dark*, 48.

[47] See Whitfield, "Kurt Weill," 27–30. Sally Bick observes a similar phenomenon in films of the era in *Unsettled Scores: Politics, Hollywood, and the Film Music of Aaron Copland & Hanns Eisler* (Urbana: University of Illinois Press, 2019), ix–x.

[48] Whitfield, "Kurt Weill," 69–71.

[49] Whitfield, "Kurt Weill," 71. The *KWE* similarly acknowledges "the possibility of positive textual development through production and performance," which informs its editorial guidelines. Harsh, Selk et al., "Guide for Volume Editors," 3.

[50] Whitfield, "Kurt Weill," 71.

[51] Levitz, *Modernist Mysteries*, 17, 25–26.

cared little about psychoanalysis and more about dramaturgy in *Lady in the Dark*. At other times, the composer worked at cross-purposes with his partners. The spectacle produced by Max Gordon for *The Firebrand of Florence* contradicted Weill's idea for a more intimate production, for example, and he and Franz Werfel clashed throughout the writing of *The Eternal Road*.[52] Throughout this book, I highlight not only Weill's contributions to his shows, but also his creative partners'.

While much of Weill's personal archive from his time in Europe is lost, a great deal of evidence from his time in the United States survives. These sources provide a window into Weill's collaborative process, revealing how he negotiated both U.S. culture and the demands of his creative partners. Like most Broadway shows, Weill's U.S. works were constantly in flux, going through several different versions in rehearsals, try-outs, previews, Broadway runs, and national tours. Although each libretto, score, and set of sketches provides a unique snapshot of single moment in the life of a continually evolving production, I condense the creative process into a series of discrete stages for clarity. Where there is archival evidence to document to the process through which ideas were retained, discarded, or transformed, or simple logical leaps can be made, I credit the individuals involved. But given that Weill's working process often involved in-person or telephone communication, I rely mostly on the opening night productions (though there are some exceptions) in my analysis to describe how these shows both reflect and attempt to shape culture without attributing these views to specific individuals. This is not to say I treat these opening night productions as authoritative versions of the shows; many continued to evolve on tour, or as stars came and went.[53] Instead, I adopt the *Kurt Weill Edition*'s strategy of treating each production as an "event," with ties to a specific time, place, and presumed audience.[54]

Returning to the "two Weills" conundrum, Taylor-Jay asks, "why is it not possible simply to let the 'multiplicities' of Weill's style be?" As she acknowledges, "The music is still, ultimately, divisible into two distinct styles."[55]

---

[52] On *Firebrand*, see the introduction to Edwin Justus Mayer, Ira Gershwin, and Kurt Weill, *The Firebrand of Florence: Broadway Operetta in Two Acts*, ed. Joel Galand, *KWE*, Series I, Volume 18 (New York: Kurt Weill Foundation for Music/European American Music, 2002), 30. On *The Eternal Road*, see Guy Stern, "The Road to *The Eternal Road*," in Kim H. Kowalke, ed., *A New Orpheus: Essays on Kurt Weill* (New Haven, CT: Yale University Press, 1986), 279–84.

[53] Kirle, *Unfinished Business*, 11–14.

[54] Harsh, Selk et al., "Guide for Volume Editors," 3–4.

[55] Taylor-Jay, "The Composer's Voice?" 93, 96.

Weill himself acknowledged that change, discouraging a production of *Mahagonny* at the Festival Internazionale di Venezia in 1948 because it was "very much an expression of the decade after the first world war."[56] Throughout this book, I highlight both continuities and discontinuities in Weill's career, accounting for Kirle's "messiness" of identity, both in terms of Weill himself, but also the values his shows espouse, which sometimes represent Weill's own beliefs, but often do not. His shifting understanding of what it means to be an American—and to work toward a better America—affords scholars an opportunity to study the ways immigrants both adapt to new cultural situations, and the ways their new culture adapts to them.

## Political Theatre

One continuity in Weill's career is his commitment to socially engaged theatre. *Pace* Drew, U.S. musical theatre during this era was not just entertainment, and Richard Rodgers did not simply compose pop songs; *Babes in Arms* (1937) argues for liberal, multicultural democracy, and *South Pacific* (1949) for racial equality.[57] Broadway also hosted many kinds of musical theatre, including spectacles like the *Ziegfeld Follies* (1907–1931, 1934, 1936), topical revues like *Pins and Needles* (1937–1940), and more experimental operatic productions like *Porgy and Bess* (1935) and Benjamin Britten's *The Rape of Lucretia* (1947, Broadway 1948). Weill's competition with Rodgers was not just about who could write the most popular show, but about who could write the most innovative, politically relevant one; his racially charged and similarly tragic *Lost in the Stars* appeared the same year as *South Pacific*, one of his many attempts to outdo Rodgers.

More broadly, Adorno and (to a lesser extent) Drew dismiss the modernist and political potential of American musical theatre because they judge the genre in terms of a high modernist agenda, which dismisses the potential of mass culture to produce social change (although, as noted earlier, "negative" use of mass culture could reveal contradictions). Such a formulation has extended to Weill's career as a whole. For example, Derek B. Scott in *The Cambridge History of Twentieth-Century Music* says

---

[56] Kurt Weill to F. Ballo, 29 December 1948, WLA, Box 47 Folder 2.
[57] On liberal democracy in *Babes in Arms*, see Chapter 3 of Andrea Most, *Making Americans: Jews and the Broadway Musical* (Cambridge, MA: Harvard University Press, 2004). On South Pacific, see Jim Lovensheimer, *South Pacific: Paradise Rewritten* (Oxford, UK: Oxford University Press, 2010).

The "Moritat" from *Die Dreigroschenoper* can be used to illustrate Weill's ambiguous position as a composer for the stage. The song can be heard as an example of Weimar political satire, in a context of *Neue Sachlichkeit* ("new objectivity") and experimental theatre. Yet Bobby Darin's version "Mack the Knife" (1959) occupies quite a different position; it's bowdlerized gruesomeness becomes "tongue-in-cheek," it reaches for hit-parade success as an American popular song, and falls comfortably into the lower-status category of easy-listening. The argument may be extended to explain the lower-status category of Weill's New York works as compared to his Berlin works.[58]

Scott does not explain how an argument regarding a version of a Berlin song made almost ten years after Weill's death may be extended to his music written in the drastically socially and politically different U.S. of the 1930s and 1940s. Rather, he simply assumes that the popular music of the U.S. is by definition apolitical and musically conservative, and therefore "lower-status."

But as Crispin Sartwell observes, the political uses of any aesthetic are constrained by "the culture from which it emerges and the discourses in which it appears."[59] Different cultures adopt different aesthetics to convey political ideas, so that even if a work is obviously political, its ideas may fail to resonate for aesthetic reasons, or its politics may not be legible for audiences unfamiliar with the aesthetic codes. Adorno acknowledges that Weill's polemic practice comes from manipulating conventions to expose problems in "the society within which they have their origin." If, as Hinton claims, Weill's style is characterized by irony and a "richness of topical allusion," the composer necessarily relies a shared body of cultural signifiers for effect.[60] As Kowalke notes, Adorno and Weill's other European detractors missed the subtleties in Weill's U.S. works because they are unfamiliar with U.S. theatrical conventions and traditions.[61] Indeed, liberal and Leftist artists adopted different aesthetics on opposite sides of the Atlantic. In the United States, they tended to appeal to the "American Dream," that is, the idea that hard work can lead to a comfortable middle-class life, as opposed to the more

---

[58] Derek B. Scott, "Other Mainstreams: Light Music and Easy Listening, 1920–70," in *The Cambridge History of Twentieth-Century Music*, ed. Nicholas Cook and Anthony People (Cambridge, UK: Cambridge University Press, 2004), 323.

[59] Crispin Sartwell, *Political Aesthetics* (Ithaca, NY: Cornell University Press, 2010), 7.

[60] Hinton, *Weill's Musical Theater*, 33.

[61] Kowalke, "Formerly German," 38–39.

broadly revolutionary ideals that permeated Europe.[62] (There are notable exceptions, including the Brechtian Marc Blitzstein.) Thus, in Germany, Weill and his contemporaries drew on the stylized, unsentimental, occasionally cynical aesthetics of *Neue Sachlichkeit* to condemn the bourgeoisie. In the United States, Leftists opted not to attack the system as whole, but rather, to reveal and remove the barriers to class mobility. Consequently, they drew from naturalism and sentimental melodrama.

A comparison between Brecht's *Mother* (originally *Die Mutter*, 1931, Broadway 1935) and Clifford Odets's *Waiting for Lefty* (1935) illustrates these different approaches to political theatre. Both draw on modernist theatrical techniques, directly addressing the audience and using nonlinear, episodic narratives. But the ways the two playwrights employed these techniques are diametrically opposed. In *Mother*, actors step out of character to narrate the most dramatic events, preventing the audience from becoming emotionally involved. Conversely, in *Waiting for Lefty*, a corrupt official speaks to the audience as if they were members of the union. Actors scattered throughout the theatre help the audience experience the drama with immanent urgency. In *Mother*, the protagonist Pelagea walks other characters through logical, objective defenses of Marxism, while Odets wrote emotionally charged scenes of wives losing respect for their husbands because they cannot stand up for themselves, and young men unwilling to marry because they cannot afford a family. *Waiting for Lefty* was one of the most successful Leftist plays of the decade while *Mother* left U.S. critics cold. Critics found the overt didacticism of *Mother* insulting. James T. Farrell of the *Partisan Review* felt that "the simplicity of the play is overstressed and it is fair to assume that Brecht, in insisting on this kind of an adaptation of his play for an American audience, was simply indulging himself."[63] Still, the production had done relatively well with German working-class audiences in 1931.[64] Conversely, Harold Clurman recalled that at the premiere of *Waiting for Lefty*, "deep laughter, hot assent, a kind of joyous fervor seemed to sweep the audience toward the stage."[65] In the United States of the 1930s, appeals to emotion

---

[62] Eric Salehi, "No Brecht-fest in America: Revisiting the Theatre Union's 1935 Production of *The Mother*," *Onstage Studies* 21 (1998): 82.

[63] Quoted in Salehi, "No Brecht-fest in America," 81–82.

[64] Laura Bradley, *Brecht and Political Theatre: The Mother Onstage* (Oxford, UK: Oxford University Press, 2006), 54.

[65] Harold Clurman, *The Fervent Years: The Group Theatre and the '30's* (New York: Da Capo, 1983), 148.

did not preclude politics; rather, emotions were the vehicle through which messages were most effectively delivered.[66]

Weill's first works in the United States show him becoming increasingly aware of these differences. *Johnny Johnson* and *You and Me* (1938) made some efforts toward U.S. styles, but relied primarily on stylized satire and overt didacticism. Both left U.S. audiences confused; one reviewer called *You and Me* "the weirdest cinematic hash I ever saw."[67] For his political theatre to be effective, Weill realized he needed a different approach, telling Margaret Arlen of WCBS that "American audiences are much more receptive to emotions in the theatre."[68] He also realized that showing the connections between personal tragedy and contemporary issues worked better for Americans than abstract political lessons. As he told the *New York Times*, in *Lost in the Stars*, by showing the moral "in terms of the personal tragedies of these two men, we are able to say all that we want to say, and we never do have to declare what the message is."[69] The production affected *New York Times* reviewer Brooks Atkinson, who wrote "You can answer a political argument. But there is no answer to this recognition of the value of purity of character in a bewildering and frightened society."[70]

## Kurt Weill's America

Weill lived through a turbulent period in U.S. history. From afar, he witnessed the free-wheeling 1920s give way to the devastation of the Great Depression. When he arrived, the United States was beginning to recover from the stock-market crash, and the efforts of President Franklin D. Roosevelt's New Deal were beginning to bear fruit. But a conservative backlash followed Roosevelt's landslide victory in 1936. Nevertheless, the increasing certainty of war with Germany and an inexperienced political opponent helped Roosevelt win

---

[66] For a discussion of the nuances and roots of these differences, see Ilka Saal, "Vernacularizing Brecht: The Political Theatre of the New Deal," in *Interrogating America through Theatre and Performance*, ed. William W. Demastes and Iris Smith Fischer (New York: Palgrave Macmillan, 2007), 101–19.

[67] "The Current Cinema," *New Yorker*, 11 June 1938, 62.

[68] "WCBS Presents Margaret Arlen," broadcast 7 January 1950, available at https://www.kwf.org/pages/wt-wcbs-presents-margaret-arlen.html.

[69] Harry Gilroy, "Written in the Stars: Composer Kurt Weill and Playwright Maxwell Anderson Air Views on Racial Harmony in Latest Collaboration," *NYT*, 30 October 1949, available at https://www.kwf.org/pages/kw-further-reading.html#enginterviews.

[70] Brooks Atkinson, "Musical Tragedy is Put Together from Paton Novel About South Africa," *NYT*, 6 November 1949, X1.

a historic third term in 1940. The war years saw the nation unite against European fascism, and industrial production rose to meet the demands of the armed forces, ending the Depression. With Roosevelt's death in 1944, the more moderate Harry S. Truman became president, and the New Deal coalition dissolved with his reelection in 1948. Meanwhile, the newly resurgent Right commenced a purge of suspected communists, resulting in the jailing of the Hollywood Ten, the advent of the blacklist, and the hearings before the House Committee on Un-American Activities.

Throughout this tumultuous period, numerous issues emerged, were swept aside, and re-emerged. The New Deal provoked a national conversation about public and private economic responsibilities whose terms shifted with both the onset and the end of the war. While racism and civil rights figured prominently in the political discourse of the 1920s and 1930s, such issues were downplayed during the early 1940s as America attempted to present a united front, only to resurface later in the decade. Appropriate levels of immigration to the United States were hotly debated in the lead-up to World War II, but vanished from the discourse soon thereafter. The isolationist movement of the late 1920s and early 1930s began to fade into reluctant support of the Allies later in the decade, but the attack on Pearl Harbor in December 1941 changed U.S. sentiment overnight.

During this decade and a half, Broadway professionals of all stripes worked through these issues. As Knapp observes, "the American musical had a jump start in acquiring the specific capacity and implicit charge of projecting a mainstream sense of 'America'—of what America was, what it was not, and what it might become."[71] As such, the twentieth-century Broadway musical (and Hollywood film) became a staging ground for immigrant and marginalized cultures to negotiate their identities as Americans.[72] As an outsider-turned-insider, Weill presents a unique voice in this period.[73] He quickly diagnosed some of America's issues—the nation's difficult relationship with immigration, for example. Still, especially early in his career, he struggled with the subtleties of others, such as the complexities of racism. He kept up

[71] Knapp, *The American Musical and the Formation of National Identity*, 8. See also Jones, *Our Musicals, Ourselves*.

[72] Along with those works already cited, see Jeffrey Magee, *Irving Berlin's American Musical Theatre* (Oxford, UK: Oxford University Press, 2012); Michael Rogin, *Blackface, White Noise: Jewish Immigrants in the Hollywood Melting Pot* (Berkeley: University of California Press, 1996).

[73] I borrow this formulation from Peter Gay, who highlights the importance of political, ethnic, religious, and artistic "outsiders" to the culture of the Weimar Republic, seeking solutions to immanent problems through aesthetic means. *Weimar Culture: The Outsider as Insider* (New York: W. W. Norton, 1968), 7–8ff. See also Elizabeth Craft "Becoming American Onstage," 17–19.

with certain aspects of American culture, while others left him behind. He participated wholeheartedly in the folk music movement of the late 1930s and mid-1940s, but his frustrations with Hollywood led him to focus mostly on Broadway, although he expressed desire to return to film as late as 1946.[74] With the opening of Rodgers and Hammerstein's *Oklahoma!* (1943) and the advent of the "integrated" musical, Weill felt his own efforts in combining song, dance, and spectacle in the previous decade deserved more credit.

In order to capture the nuances of Weill's shifting tactics and aesthetics, this book is arranged only roughly according to chronology. Instead, I highlight how Weill's approach to themes, issues, and styles changed with context. As single shows encompass many different ideas, often these themes appear in multiple chapters, even if the broader section is dedicated to analysis of another issue. Chapter 1 explores Weill's initial encounters with *Amerikanismus* in the Weimar Republic. Jazz, or at least the idea of jazz, came to symbolize both the good and bad aspects of America and, more importantly, the "Americanization" of German culture. Weill was ambivalent about jazz. He spoke of it as a source of renewal for German culture, yet the idea of America and the urban alienation it could represent also allowed him to critique that culture. Weill also saw in the United States a potential market, particularly beginning in 1933. However, several factors made it difficult for him to gain a foothold in the United States, including trends in contemporary U.S. modern music circles and the increasing political tension with Germany.

Chapter 2 explores Weill's early attempts to adapt his European ideas for American audiences in *Johnny Johnson* (1936) and the film *You and Me* (1938). Both projects combine experimental techniques from both sides of the Atlantic with stereotypically American subject matter: small-town war heroes in *Johnny Johnson* and gangster melodrama in *You and Me*. But even though a variety of experimental movements—including a strain of expressionism—had taken root in the United States in the 1920s and 1930s, *Johnny Johnson* and *You and Me* failed to resonate with their intended audiences.

Several other projects from the late 1930s saw him taking on the challenge of writing in American musical idioms in ways that he carried over into the 1940s. This is the subject of Chapter 3. Weill first showed interest in U.S. folk styles with *One Man from Tennessee* (1937) and *Railroads on Parade*

---

[74] Kurt Weill, "Music in the Movies," *Harper's Bazaar* 8, no. 9 (1946), available at https://www.kwf.org/pages/kw-further-reading.html#engwritings1.

(1939, rev. 1940), then returned to these idioms after the war with *Down in the Valley* (1948). In this, Weill was part of a broader trend in U.S. modern music that sought to find a unique, autochthonous national style in folk culture. This is clear in *One Man from Tennessee*, which uses Leftist language to address contemporary political issues, although problems with the libretto doomed the project. *Railroads on Parade* represents a major step forward for the composer, as the score incorporates folk material in a way that U.S. audiences understood and appreciated. It also represents Weill's willingness to work within the political center, which coincided with mounting tensions with Germany. After the war (and his naturalization), Weill returned to folk idioms with *Down in the Valley*, which draws on some of the same musical and theatrical language as *One Man from Tennessee*, but in a drastically different cultural context.

Chapter 4 explores how the national conversation about immigration shifted as the Great Depression gave way to World War II. This is apparent in two works that concern the "origin story" of America: *Knickerbocker Holiday* (1938), a satire about old Dutch New York, and *Where Do We Go from Here?* (1945), a patriotic film that revisits important moments in U.S. history. Whereas *Knickerbocker Holiday* paints America as vulnerable to the same kind of fascism that had taken hold in Europe, *Where Do We Go from Here?* holds up the nation as a bastion of freedom and democracy. Correspondence indicates that both Weill and the Office of War Information may have had one eye on European audiences, given that the film premiered after the surrender of Germany. Weill again tried to feel out the international market with *The Firebrand of Florence* (1945), but that proved to be the greatest professional miscalculation of his U.S. career.

Chapter 5 concerns the changing norms of gender and sexuality over the course of the 1940s in *Lady in the Dark* (1941), *One Touch of Venus* (1943), and *Love Life* (1948). The first two are escapist pieces, linking the notion of fantasy with an idealized feminine figure, but the onset of war changed the terms of that ideal. These two shows were Weill's greatest Broadway successes during his lifetime. The third, *Love Life*, built on the innovations of *You and Me*, *Lady in the Dark*, and *One Man from Tennessee* to trace 150 years of U.S. history through one married couple, using interscene vaudeville numbers to illuminate the lessons of the narrative. Although influential to Broadway creatives of the 1960s and 1970s, in its own time *Love Life* was a disappointment. This chapter also traces Weill's evolving relationship with the musicals of Rodgers and Hammerstein. Although a tremendous success, *Lady in the*

*Dark* was overshadowed by *Oklahoma!* and documents around *One Touch of Venus* show Weill trying to respond quickly. *Love Life* counters the integration revolution of *Oklahoma!* with its self-consciously Brechtian separation of elements.

The last chapter explores Weill's relationship to race and ethnicity, particularly his Jewish heritage. Although *The Eternal Road* (1937) premiered in the United States, it was initially conceived with European audiences in mind. Thus, Weill's score draws on both German and Jewish musical styles and forms in order to prove that—despite Nazi declarations—the two identities were not in conflict. But anti-Semitism was on the rise in the United States in the late 1930s, and after *The Eternal Road*, Weill preferred to emphasize his German rather than Jewish heritage. During the war, Weill returned to Jewish themes with several pageants written by Ben Hecht, and in 1946, he wrote his first Jewish characters for the mainstream Broadway stage in *Street Scene* (1947), which (among other things) explores the place of Jews within a multicultural community. Weill's last large-scale work, *Lost in the Stars* (1949), represents the culmination of Weill's lifelong passion for racial equality, which he tried to address as early as 1939 with *Ulysses Africanus*, but that musical was abandoned. *Lost in the Stars* also hearkens back to *The Eternal Road* in both form and style, aligning it with emergent conceptions of "Judeo-Christian" identity.

Where possible, musical examples have been taken from published sources, although I have silently edited them for clarity and consistency. A significant portion of Weill's music remains either unfinished or unpublished. If no published source exists, Weill usually produced a piano-vocal score (or had one copied), which serves as the basis for the relevant musical example. Occasionally more than one version of a piece survives, in which case I have used my judgment as to which transmits the best reading. Throughout, I have silently realized Weill's idiosyncratic notations for repeated notes and measures, and added punctuation to the text for consistency. Occasionally, Weill indicated which orchestral instrument plays each of the lines, which I have also omitted for clarity.

Weill was never merely a happily assimilated immigrant. After his arrival, he set to work using musical theatre to correct the injustices he observed, even as he declared (and most likely felt) ardent patriotism. Weill remained committed to socially engaged theatre during his tenure in the United States, putting his persistent and insistent optimism to work, helping to shape a better future—both aesthetic and social—for his adopted homeland.

# 1

# Weill's America, America's Weill

In 1944, nine years after he arrived in the United States, Kurt Weill told
*New Yorker* magazine, "In every age and part of the world, there is a place
about which fantasies are written." He continued: "In Mozart's time it was
Turkey. For Shakespeare it was Italy. For us in Germany, it was always
America."[1] But just as Shakespeare's Italy and Mozart's Turkey were part of
broader trends in Renaissance London and Emperor Joseph II's Vienna,
Weill's ideas of America were bound up with the culture of the Weimar
Republic. Following the abdication of Emperor Wilhelm II and the November
Revolution in 1918, and then the Dawes Plan in 1924, Hollywood films, jazz
(or something called jazz), sports, automobiles, and other U.S. products became part of the daily life. Within this field of cultural and political tensions,
the idea of "America" served as a proxy for larger questions about modernity,
democracy, capitalism, and mass culture. Some embraced *Amerikanismus*
("Americanism") as sign that Germany had at last entered the transnational
culture of modernity. In economic terms, America also represented a potential market for German films, music, and art. Others were not so sanguine.
For communists, America signified the excesses and miseries of capitalism,
while conservatives felt that the new parliamentary government, associated
with America through ideas of democracy, negated something deep within
the German soul.

Weill's attitude toward America and *Amerikanismus* varied according to
his collaborators and his aesthetic goals for individual projects. His ideas
formed within two specific contexts: the avant-garde artists collective the
*Novembergruppe*, which he joined in the early 1920s, and then the broader
ideas of *Neue Sachlichkeit* ("New objectivity" or "New matter-of-factness")
that developed in the second half of the decade. Even within these communities, attitudes toward America were inconsistent. In his writings,
Weill praised jazz for its originality and innovative potential, but his

---

[1] "Pensacola Wham," *New Yorker*, 10 June 1944, available online at https://www.kwf.org/pages/wt-
pensacola-wham.html.

*Kurt Weill's America*. Naomi Graber, Oxford University Press (2021). © Oxford University Press.
DOI: 10.1093/oso/9780190906580.003.0002

compositions betray a more ambivalent engagement with broader ideas of *Amerikanismus*.

Weill's European understanding of America, along with the realities of the United States, set the stage for his post-immigration professional life. The composer's reputation for idiosyncratic ideas of America and jazz preceded his arrival, coloring his initial U.S. reception and professional possibilities. Caught between several different strands of musical modernism, all of which sought to distance themselves from central Europe, Weill found himself with few options among U.S. modern music communities, and so quickly turned toward Broadway. Still, the reasons Weill and other European immigrants of that generation had trouble finding a foothold within U.S. modern music circles deserve scrutiny, and speak to the challenges they faced in trying to earn a living in the United States.

## Weill before America

In the early 1920s, Germans began to speak of *Amerikanismus*, which contemporary journalist Rudolf Kayser noted was an undefinable term, yet still encompassed "the basic character" of the era.[2] As Jonathan O. Wipplinger and Nils Grosch observe, *Amerikismus* represented a way of processing modernity rather than any specific cultural practice or product, and contemporary German thinkers recognized that *Amerikanismus* had little to do with the United States.[3] Rather, America became a Janus-faced "doppelgänger" (to use Kim H. Kowalke's word), reflecting Germany's hopes and fears for its own cultural future.[4] Some Germans hoped for the political modernity and economic efficiency that the myth of America embodied.[5] America also signified cultural youthfulness unburdened by the centuries of bloody history that seemed to weigh down Europe.[6] However, despite the terminology,

---

[2] Quoted in Nils Grosch, *Die Musik der Neue Sachlichkeit* (Stuttgart: J.B. Metzler, 1999), 150.

[3] Grosch, *Die Musik der Neue Sachlichkeit*, 150–51; Jonathan O. Wipplinger, *The Jazz Republic: Music, Race, and American Culture in Weimar Germany* (Ann Arbor: University of Michigan Press, 2017), 68–74, 79.

[4] Kim H. Kowalke, "Kurt Weill's *Amerika*/America," in *Amerikanismus, Americanism, Weill: Die Sucher nach kultureller Identität in der Moderne*, ed. Hermann Danuser and Hermann Gottschewski (Schliengen: Argus, 2003), 12–13.

[5] Alexander Schmidt-Gernig, "'Amerikanismus' als Chiffres des modernen Kapitalismus. Zur vergleichenen Kulturkritik im Deutschland der Weimarer Republik," in *Amerikanismus, Americanism, Weill*, ed. Danuser and Gottschewski, 56.

[6] Richard Herzinger, "Der 'Amerikanismus' in den Deutungsmustern linker und rechter Modernekritik," in *Amerikanismus, Americanism, Weill*, ed. Danuser and Gottschewski, 93, 95; Susan C. Cook, *Opera for a New Republic: The Zeitopern of Krenek, Weill, and Hindemith* (Ann Arbor: UMI, 1988), 87.

many "American" cultural artifacts came to Germany through France or England rather than directly from the United States.[7] Indeed, even before American mass culture was widely available, avant-gardes in Swiss and French dada movements incorporated signifiers of America into their works, a practice which came to Germany through figures like Richard Huelsenbeck and George Grosz.[8] Thus, *Amerikanismus* also represented Germany's entry into a broader international political, economic, and artistic community. Still, some looked aghast on America's detective novels and Hollywood films, which they felt were corrupting the youth and preventing them from absorbing their own German culture.[9] A number of censorship laws were introduced shortly following the Dawes plan, aimed at curbing this influence.[10]

Soon after Weill arrived in Berlin in 1918, he began an association with the *Novembergruppe*, officially joining in 1922, soon after the group began admitting musicians.[11] The *Novembergruppe* took its name from the November Revolution, and sought to unite modernist art and progressive politics, a goal Weill pursued for his entire adult life. As the November Revolution had upended the political order, given rise to modern democracy, and paved the way for Germany's participation in broader European culture, the *Novembergruppe* declared that "renewed contact with like-minded people of all countries is our duty" and that "the future of art and the gravity of the present moment force all of us revolutionaries of the spirit (expressionists, cubists, futurists) into mutual agreement" in order to "achieve the closest possible relationship between the people and art."[12] Similar trends permeated the broader culture, as the abstract art of the previous generation was falling out of favor. In 1925, Gustav Hartlaub, the director of the Mannheim Art Gallery, curated an exhibit of young German artists who favored clear figuration and sober distance rather than expressionism's abstraction and subjectivity. To call attention to this difference, Hartlaub called the exhibit "The

[7] John Willett, *Art and Politics in the Weimar Period: The New Sobriety, 1917-1933* (New York: Pantheon, 1979), 33; Wipplinger, *The Jazz Republic*, 24–29, 31–32; Cook, *Opera for a New Republic*, 82–84.

[8] On the relationship between America, dada, and Germany, see Willett, *Art and Politics in the Weimar Period*, 28–33. On jazz, dada, and Germany, see Wipplinger, *The Jazz Republic*, 32–33.

[9] Schmidt-Gernig, " 'Amerikanismus' als Chiffres des modernen Kapitalismus," 51–59.

[10] Eric D. Weitz, *Weimar Germany: Promise and Tragedy* (Princeton, NJ: Princeton University Press, 2007), 139–40.

[11] On Weill's association with the *Novembergruppe*, see KWiE, 32–34.

[12] "November Group Circular" (1918), trans. in *The Weimar Republic Sourcebook*, ed. Anton Kaes, Martin Jay, and Edward Dimendberg (Berkeley: University of California Press, 1994), 477.

*Neue Sachlichkeit.*" He featured several artists from the *Novembergruppe*, including Grosz and Otto Dix, along with others who had moved in dada, constructivist, and surrealist circles in the previous decade.[13] In these works, he wrote, "We see the distinctions more clearly: the timely, coldly verificational bent of a few, and the emphasis on that which is objective and the technical attention to detail on the part of all of them."[14] Hartlaub divided the artists in the exhibit into two groups, the "verists" or "left-wing," and "classicists." The former "tears the objective from the world of contemporary facts and projects current experience in its tempo and fevered temperature," while the latter "searches more for the object of *timeless* validity to embody the eternal laws of existence in the artistic sphere."[15]

Although initially only a description of painting, *Neue Sachlichkeit* became a watchword for young artists and musicians in the 1920s, but it was characterized by a constellation of styles and ideas rather than a unified aesthetic.[16] These painters, photographers, architects, and musicians emphasized clarity, balance, function, and craft.[17] They painted, composed, built, and wrote with broad audiences in mind rather than the small circle of patrons and colleagues who supported modernism and the avant-garde in the previous decade. Often, this required incorporating elements of mass culture—movies, music, and popular novels, many from the United States—into their work. Showing the world in the harsh light of objective reality further required artists to relinquish subjectivity and express universal truths. Such a renunciation meant abandoning the search for new forms and means of expression, as they might imbue works with individuality and impede broad comprehensibility. *Neue Sachlichkeit* was also associated with America. In some cases, such as Krenek's *Jonny spielt auf* (1927), America is the emblem

---

[13] Willett, *Art and Politics of in the Weimar Period*, 112.

[14] Gustav Hartlaub, "Introduction to 'New Objectivity': German Painting since Expressionism" (1925), trans. in *The Weimar Republic Sourcebook*, ed. Anton Kaes et al., 492.

[15] Hartlaub, "Introduction to 'New Objectivity,'" 492, emphasis in the original. See also Steve Plumb, *Neue Sachlichkeit 1918–33: Unity and Diversity of an Art Movement* (Amsterdam: Rodopi, 2006), 11–13, 48–49; Stephen Hinton, "Aspects of Hindemith's *Neue Sachlichkeit*," *Hindemith-Jahrbuch* 14 (1985): 25–27 and Stephen Hinton, "Weill: *Neue Sachlichkeit*, Surrealism, and Gebrauchsmusik," in *A New Orpheus: Essays on Kurt Weill*, ed. Kim H. Kowalke (New Haven, CT: Yale University Press, 1986), 62–63.

[16] Hinton, "Weill: *Neue Sachlichkeit*, Surrealism, and Gebrauchsmusik," 62–63.

[17] On the characteristics of *Neue Sachlichkeit*, see Hinton, "Aspects of Hindemith's *Neue Sachlichkeit*," 25–31. Plumb, *Neue Sachlichkeit 1918–33*, 36–54. Willett, *Art and Politics in the Weimar Period*, 106, 112–17; Peter Gay, *Weimar Culture: The Insider as Outsider* (New York: W.W. Norton, 1968), Kindle Edition.

of modernity and the future; the piece ends with the chorus singing, "The new world comes gloriously sailing across the sea and by dancing inherits old Europe."[18] Others used America to evoke ideas of efficiency and precision, as in the case of the novels and poetry of Lion Feuchtwanger, or alleged primitiveness and lack of inhibitions or cultural hierarchies in works like Hermann Hesse's *Der Steppenwolf* (1927), although such evocations were often ambivalent.[19]

In terms of music, critics and composers associated with *Neue Sachlichkeit* observed a renewed appreciation for line, depersonalization and despiritualization, and musical evocations of the urban and the mechanical.[20] Although many musicians and critics felt ambivalent about the term itself, composers drew on its styles and aesthetic attitudes. Even though he rejected the term *Neue Sachlichkeit*, Krenek still advocated for "assenting to everyday aims" and efforts to "create an art, particularly an art of the musical theater, which will fit the enlarged society as earlier art fitted the limited society— in other words, to find a basis for an art that the general public could enter into and assimilate."[21] The concept of *Gebrauchsmusik* ("music for use") owes much to the *neue sachliche* ideal that artists should seek out a broad audience.[22] There were many definitions of the idea, although all touch on the combination of quality and accessibility. For Hindemith, *Gebrauchsmusik* meant writing music for "musical laypeople," that is, highly trained amateurs, to perform in order to bring musicians and their audiences into closer contact.[23] These he distinguished from musical "dilettantes," who listened to music merely for pleasure. Rather, he classified these laypeople as those who played for themselves rather than others, and lamented the "preoccupation with things that are out of the way," the pursuit of "musical directions incapable of development," the cultivation of "strange or outdated instruments," and "an exaggerated sense of history," at the expense of quality music for this market.[24] Rather, he hoped to produce simple, well-crafted music written

---

[18] Translated in Alan Lareau, "Jonny's Jazz: From *Kabarett* to Krenek," in *Jazz and the Germans*, ed. Michael J. Budds (Hillsdale, NY: Pendragon, 2002), 59.

[19] Marc A. Weiner, *Undertones of Insurrection: Music, Politics, and the Social Sphere in the Modern German Narrative* (Lincoln: University of Nebraska Press, 1993), 134–39; Willett, *Art and Politics of in the Weimar Period*, 98–99.

[20] Hinton, "Weill: *Neue Sachlichkeit*, Surrealism, and *Gebrauchsmusik*," 63–66.

[21] Ernst Krenek, "New Humanity and Old Objectivity" (1931), trans. in *The Weimar Republic Sourcebook*, ed. Kaes et al., 586–87.

[22] Hinton, "Weill: *Neue Sachlichkeit*, Surrealism, and *Gebrauchsmusik*," 78–81.

[23] Hinton, "Aspects of Hindemith's *Neue Sachlickeit*," 46–79.

[24] Paul Hindemith, "Forderungen an den Laien" (1930), in *Paul Hindemith: Aufsätze, Vorträge, Reden*, ed. Giselher Schubert (Zürich: Atlantis Musikbuch, 1994), 43.

for specific contexts and ensembles. Hanns Gutman pursued similar goals, reproaching composers who wrote music that was "self-willed to the point of incomprehensibility." However, he proposed a neoclassical solution: a return to the economic structures of the pre-romantic era. Before Beethoven, Gutman wrote, "one composed upon receiving a commission," therefore, "J.S. Bach, with the conscientiousness of a respectable artisan, wrote his works in conformity with the requirements of the ecclesiastical year. And even in Mozart's time the idea of composing a piece out of the blue without any occasion for it would have been completely absurd." Still, this orientation toward the public did not detract from the quality of the music: "Bach's cantatas, [and] Mozart's sonatas are utilitarian without therefore being any less artistic."[25] Later, Weill echoed these sentiments, lionizing Bach for rendering the difference between utility and quality "inseparable" (unnzertrennlich).[26]

The neue sachliche imperative of widespread appeal and public acceptance necessitated using a popular musical language, which often meant jazz.[27] What Germans in the 1920s knew as jazz arose through a series of musical cross-cultural and interracial encounters, and referred to almost any music featuring syncopated dance rhythms, a series of instrumental timbres (particularly saxophone and banjo), and an improvisatory performance style.[28] (For the purposes of this chapter, I use "jazz" to refer to this style for the sake of simplicity.) In the 1910s and 1920s, most Germans thought of jazz as a dance style rather than as music, which first came to Germany through bands (mostly English and French) in the occupied territories in and around the Rhineland, and which arrived in Berlin around 1921.[29] After 1924, traveling revues like Sam Wooding's Chocolate Kiddies gained popularity in Berlin and throughout Europe.[30] Weill's wife Lotte Lenya remembered the two of them seeing Josephine Baker, and listening to records by Sophie Tucker and the Revelers

[25] Hanns Gutman, "Music for Use" (1929), trans. in The Weimar Republic Sourcebook, ed. Kaes et al., 580.

[26] Kurt Weill, "Bekenntis zu Bach" (1930), in GS2, 101.

[27] On the appeal of jazz, see Cook, Opera for a New Republic, 87–88, and Lareau, "Jonny's Jazz."

[28] Wipplinger, The Jazz Republic, 13–14ff; J. Bradford Robinson, "Jazz Reception in Weimar Germany: In Search of a Shimmy Figure," in Music and Performance during the Weimar Republic, ed. Bryan Gilliam (Cambridge, UK: Cambridge University Press, 1994), 119; Nils Grosch, "Facetten des Amerikanismus in Die Sieben Todsünden," in Amerikanismus, Americanism, Weill, ed. Danuser and Gottschewski, 272–73; Pamela Potter, Most German of the Arts: Musicology and Society from the Weimar Republic to the End of Hitler's Reich (New Haven, CT: Yale University Press, 1998), 20.

[29] Wipplinger, The Jazz Republic, 24–29, 31–32.

[30] Robinson, "Jazz Reception in Weimar Germany," 113–14; Frank Tirro, "Jazz Leaves Home: The Dissemination of 'Hot' Music to Central Europe," in Jazz and the Germans, ed. Budds, 61–82; Wipplinger, The Jazz Republic, 51–53.

later in the 1920s.[31] The first recordings came to Germany mostly through white artists such as Paul Whiteman and Al Jolson.[32] Jazz also flourished in sheet music and instruction manuals for composition. Bandleaders could acquire British or U.S. arrangements with written-out "improvised" solos, and instructional booklets with tips on adapting jazz for German audiences.[33]

These manuals described a music suited to the *neue sachliche* aesthetic. Alfred Baresel, a conservatory professor and music journalist, advocated in the composition manual *Das Jazz-Buch* for a *Kunstjazz* that could speak to contemporary audiences.[34] He wrote that jazz was a music from which "all romantic prettiness" had been stripped, leaving behind an "elementary and refined" music that "corresponded almost exactly to our modern mindset," and called it "Gebrauchsmusik."[35] Baresel also compared the way jazz had entered the art music world to the way dance rhythms had entered into more cultivated styles in previous generations: "No man of taste danced socially to Bach's courantes and gavottes, to Haydn's, Beethoven's, and Mozart's minuets, to Schubert's Ländlern, Chopin's waltzes and mazurkas. But long-forgotten dancers and popular musicians created these meaningful musical forms long before they were taken over by 'serious' art. Should not ragtime and blues undergo a similar refining?"[36] Here, Baresel echoes Gutman's neoclassical rhetoric.

Although Weill's European library is lost, he likely owned at least some of the composition manuals that circulated in Berlin, given that his surviving U.S. library includes several similar English-language books, and some of his European jazz writing resembles examples in those manuals.[37] Like Baresel, he distinguished between popular jazz and its uses in modern music circles, writing that elements of jazz "form firm, indispensable components of musical structure," but that "they can no longer appear in the form of jazz, as dance music, but rather, in transformation."[38] Like Baresel and Gutman, the composer put a neoclassical spin on this concept, telling the *New York World-Telegram* in 1935, "In all times, the dance has had an effect on music. It was so with Bach, Chopin, Beethoven, Schumann and others. They took the popular

[31] Kowalke, "Kurt Weill's *Amerika*/America," 13.
[32] Robinson, "Jazz Reception in Weimar Germany," 116.
[33] Robinson, "Jazz Reception in Weimar Germany," 120–21, 123–25.
[34] Robinson, "Jazz Reception in Weimar Germany," 124–25.
[35] Alfred Baresel, *Das Jazz-Buch* (Leipzig: Zimmerman, 1926), 5, 7.
[36] Baresel, *Das Jazz-Buch*, 7.
[37] Robinson, "Jazz Reception in Weimar Germany," 128–29.
[38] Kurt Weill, "A Note Concerning Jazz" (1929), trans. in *KWiE*, 497 (translation adapted).

dance music of their or other days and lifted it into the region of art."[39] In this sense, jazz was a way of bypassing the excesses of Wagnerian romanticism, and could offer fresh musical materials to a culture looking to enter modernity, while still retaining links to its history. The baroque, classical, and early romantic eras represented the heyday of German culture through Bach, Mozart, and Beethoven (three composers who often appear in Weill's German writings). Just as they adapted popular forms, these figures reasoned, so could modern composers.

Jazz also represented difference, upon which Germans projected both fears and hopes for the nation.[40] As Kowalke observes, "The jazzband became a hyperbolic representation of American otherness, collapsing not only music and dance, but 'primitive' and 'modern,' 'African' and 'American' into a single metaphor."[41] Writer and feminist Alice Gerstel's article "*Jazzband*" published in *Die Aktion* in February 1922 captures the heady mix of pleasure, politics, and primitivism that jazz represented.[42] For Gerstel, jazz represented "the genius of the eclectic, the cocktail of mixed souls, the recklessness of puppets on a string, the passion of a people condemned to death." In this jazz band, "a Negro sits behind the mystical instrument," as

[h]is thick lips press on the mouth of the trumpet, in his eyes he holds a sly and melancholy smile, meanwhile there is a drum roll, a blow on the tambourine, a stroke on the bell. Next to him a pale adventurer strums chords on a balalaika—the sound as monotonous as a debate in Parliament—and the violinist, the third in the devilish trio, occupies no fixed place but skips, fiddle under his chin, among the skipping couples, and plays sweet cantilenas for the ladies and rakish trills under their skirts.

She evokes not only contemporary stereotypes of blackness (thick lips and a sly smile), but also Russian timbres (the balalaika) and Latin genres (the cantilena). Indeed, she concludes: "But sometimes out of the drumbeat whirlpool and the trumpet blasts comes the mighty rhythm of the *Internationale*." For Gerstel and others, the revolutionary potential of jazz lay in its ability

---

[39] R.C.B., "Kurt Weill Has Secured a Niche of His Own at 35," *New York World-Telegram*, 21 December 1935, available online at https://www.kwf.org/pages/wt-kurt-weill-has-secured-niche.html. See also *KWiE*, 103–4, 116.

[40] Weiner unpacks this idea in German literature of the period in *Undertones of Insurrection*, 121–34.

[41] Kowalke, "Kurt Weill's *Amerika*/America," 13.

[42] The essay is reprinted in *The Weimar Republic Sourcebook*, ed. Kaes et al., 554–55.

to speak across class, national, and racial lines. Jazz was modern, heterogeneous, yet primitive: modern in its rhythmic vitality and motoric drive; but primitive in the affects it had on listeners. Baresel wrote that the rhythm was "familiar to us in our era of speedways and motorcycles. It excites us without pause, like the primitive drumbeat does the ecstatic ritual dancer."[43]

Critiques of the *Neue Sachlichkeit* and jazz often took the form of unfavorable comparisons to America. Conservative journalist (and future Nazi propagandist) Adolf Halfeld disdained the "new, American objectivity" and its superficial culture: "Californian fruit growers have succeeded in raising pineapples, melons, and grapefruit that far exceed their natural size—but they also robbed them of their heaven-sent fragrance and aroma. And thus it is everywhere in this instrumental culture."[44] In this light, American objectivity and economic rationalization sapped the life from culture, rendering it shallow and trite. Adolf Weissmann wrote that jazz was the "embodiment of the mechanization of music, divested of anything emotional or romantic," and Hans Pfitzner argued, "It is the jazz-foxtrot-flood, the musical expression of Americanism, this danger to Europe" which "kills the *soul*."[45] Others saw jazz as an insidious weapon of the Allies to tear down German culture.[46]

Weill's adult career coincides with the rise of these cultural movements and pressures. Under the direction of Ferruccio Busoni, Weill pursued a musical language that reflected the qualities he admired in his teacher's compositions: "a synthesis of all stylistic tropes of recent decades, a new, restrained, slag-free [*schlackenreinen*] art."[47] His first large-scale success, the one-act opera *Der Protagonist* ("The Protagonist," 1926) had a libretto by formerly expressionist playwright Georg Kaiser, and complex, contrapuntal music to match. Elements of a lighter style are evident in the pantomime sections, which owe much to Busoni's *Arlecchino* (1916).[48]

---

[43] Baresel, *Das Jazz-Buch* 5. On the relationship between jazz and technology, see Jürgen Arndt, "Tango und Technik: Kurt Weills Rezeption des '*Amerikanismus*' der Weimar Republik," in *Musik der zwanziger Jahre*, ed. Werner Keil, with Kerstin Jaunich and Ulrike Kammerer (Hildesheim: Georg Olms, 1996), 44. On jazz, technology, and the primitive, see Wipplinger, *The Jazz Republic*, 44–46.

[44] Adolf Halfeld, "America and the New Objectivity" (1928), trans. in *The Weimar Republic Sourcebook*, ed. Kaes et al., 408.

[45] On Weissman, see Alexander Rehding, "On the Record," *Cambridge Opera Journal* 18, no. 1 (2006): 79; on Pfitzner, see Weiner, *Undertones of Insurrection*, 51, 63–67, quote on 65, emphasis in the original.

[46] Wipplinger, *The Jazz Republic*, 25–26, 33–37.

[47] Kurt Weill, "Busoni and Modern Music" (1925), trans. in *KWiE*, 462 (translation adapted).

[48] Stephen Hinton, *Weill's Musical Theater: Stages of Reform* (Berkeley: University of California Press, 2012), 64.

The premier in Dresden established the composer's presence in the German operatic world. Soon after, Weill began building on that new, simplified musical language, reflecting *neue sachliche* ideals: clean lines, restrained emotions, and the integration of art and community, sometimes signified with *Amerikanismus*. Two pieces hint at this new musical language: *Der neue Orpheus* ("The New Orpheus," 1926) and the one-act opera *Royal Palace* (1927), both with texts by surrealist poet Ivan Goll.[49] This new style emerged in full with the *Mahagonny Songspiel* (1927), a "scenic cantata" comprising six songs: five with texts from Bertolt Brecht's *Die Hauspostille* ("Manual of Piety"), and one new, also by Brecht. The piece represented the beginning of Weill's fruitful, sometimes contentious partnership with Brecht, whose texts the composer set in seven additional large-scale works: *Die Dreigroschenoper* ("The Threepenny Opera," 1928), *Das Berliner Requiem* ("The Berlin Requiem," 1928), *Der Lindberghflug* ("Lindbergh's Flight," 1929), *Happy End* (1929), *Aufstieg und Fall der Stadt Mahagonny* ("The Rise and Fall of the City of Mahagonny," an expanded and reworked version of the *Songspiel*, 1930), *Der Jasager* ("The Yes-Sayer," 1930), and *Die sieben Todsünden* ("The Seven Deadly Sins," 1933). All but two of them— *Das Berliner Requiem* and *Der Jasager*—confronted the contemporary politics of Germany using *Amerikanismus*, even if (like *Die Dreigroschenoper*) they were set elsewhere.

In November 1924, Weill began writing for the weekly periodical *Der deutsche Rundfunk*, and his essays and reviews there and elsewhere shed light on his aesthetic and political thinking. In his writing, he characterized jazz as a source of renewal. Like many of the German composers of his generation, he sought to "withdraw as much as possible from the sphere of influence of Richard Wagner," who represented a moribund, nineteenth-century German operatic tradition.[50] One way to accomplish this was incorporating music from New World mass culture and jazz, which represented not the "towering personalities who stand above time," but rather "the instinct of the masses."[51] Jazz was "the healthiest, most vigorous expression of art, which due to its popular origin, immediately became an international folk music of the broadest consequence," and was thus the *lingua franca* (so to speak) of the

---

[49] *KWiE*, 281. Hinton identifies *Der neue Orpheus* as the work that first signals Weill's interest in *Neue Sachlichkeit* in "Weill: *Neue Sachlichkeit*, Surrealism, and *Gebrauchsmusik*," 82.
[50] Kurt Weill, "New Opera" (1926), trans. in *KWiE*, 464.
[51] Kurt Weill, "Dance Music" (1926), trans. in *KWiE*, 473.

transnational musical community.[52] "Every evening," Weill opined, "London offers jazz music from the Hotel Savoy, Rome from the Hotel di Russia," and that "the Berlin radio too must incorporate the performance of first-rate dance music as a permanent institution."[53]

But while Weill's writings on jazz take on a laudatory tone, the way he incorporated its elements into his compositions reveals a more complex engagement with the style. His earliest uses of jazz are confined to short moments, where the style illustrates class or racial difference. Jazz is also associated with technology in these early works. The first clear use occurs in the film sequence of *Royal Palace*, where jazz represents both modernity and a decadent "otherness."[54] Typical ragtime textures and rhythms combine with a slinky saxophone melody to accompany a film depicting a suitor's promise of wealth, luxury, and novel experiences, linking jazz with technology (through the film itself) and glamorous exoticism. This reflects the librettist Goll's exoticist view of America; the poet praised the "primitive" nature of black dance, writing of the *Revue nègre*, "This was the dance of the Egyptians, the whole of antiquity, of the Orient."[55] Jazz appears again in *Der Zar lässt sich photographieren* (1927, libretto by Kaiser), first as a foxtrot accompanying the Tzar's entrance, and then in the "Tango-Angèle," which plays on an onstage phonograph as the Tzar and the False Angèle dance. Again, jazz represents modernity, albeit ironically, as it accompanies the Tzar, who wants to be up-to-date despite his antiquated politics.[56] The "Tango" represents the ways music and technology interact; the gramophone itself, with its clicks, hisses, and tinny timbres, becomes another instrument in the ensemble.[57] Similarly, *Der Lindberghflug*—a radio cantata based on Charles Lindbergh's transatlantic flight—uses the American protagonist, introduced with a hint of the dotted foxtrot rhythm, to represent technological modernity, albeit with much less ambivalence. The medium—radio—also speaks to the associations of jazz and technology.

---

[52] Weill, "A Note Concerning Jazz," 497 (translation adapted). On jazz as a source of renewal and a corrective to European opera, especially in Krenek's works, see Grosch, *Die Musik der Neue Sachlichkeit*, 149–50.

[53] Weill, "Dance Music," 474.

[54] Dane Heuchemer, "American Popular Music in Weill's *Royal Palace* and Krenek's *Jonny Spielt Auf*: Influences and Usage," in *Jazz and the Germans*, ed. Budds, 105.

[55] Ivan Goll, "The Negroes are Conquering Europe" (1926), trans. in *The Weimar Republic Sourcebook*, ed. Kaes et al., 559.

[56] Cook, *Opera for a New Republic*, 139.

[57] Arndt, "Tango und Technik," 48, 51; see also Weiner, *Undertones of Insurrection*, 121.

Weill's prose writing also incorporates *neue sachliche* themes, most obviously in the fact that he consistently argued for an "objective" music, as opposed to the "subjective" expressionist style. This new objective style required a *"departure from individualistic artistic principles,"* replaced by "clarity of language, precision of expression, and simplicity of feeling."[58] Especially after he met Brecht, the composer's writing took on a socially conscious point of view, although he rarely advocated for a particular politics beyond a broad liberal humanism. Weill advocated using musical theatre to elucidate the relationship between objects, or between people and objects.[59] His concept of "gestic" music embodies these ideas: "We find gestic music wherever a process relating men to one another is presented musically in a naïve manner."[60] Weill's concept of gestic music (which differed from Brecht's) owes much to Busoni, who argued that music should not imitate or illustrate the emotional thrust of the libretto, but should provide a new perspective.[61] Allusions to popular genres provide reference points for the audience, enabling them to relate onstage action to broader themes; the stilted melodrama in *Die Dreigroschenoper* shows Polly and Macheath to be nothing more than stock characters, revealing the emptiness of the story, and the "Moritat" and "Surabaya-Johnny" (both blues) connect the subject of the text with the gangster archetype. Weill cited two of Busoni's favored composers, Bach and Mozart, along with Offenbach and Bizet, as the composers who successfully wrote gestic music.[62] Weill also searched for something universal in art, praising baroque and classical composers, as well as contemporary neoclassicists like Stravinsky, for their anti-romantic, timeless sensibility. He also argued for a balance between topicality and timelessness, writing that "the intellectual and emotional matrices which music can depict" have "remained fundamentally the same for centuries."[63]

---

[58] Kurt Weill, "Shifts in Musical Composition" (1927), trans. in *KWiE*, 478–79, emphasis in the original.

[59] See Plumb, *Neue Sachlichkeit 1918–33*, 64, for this idea's roots in *Neue Sachlichkeit*.

[60] Kurt Weill, "Concerning the Gestic Character of Music" (1929), trans. in *KWiE*, 492 (translation adapted).

[61] Joy H. Calico, *Brecht at the Opera* (Berkeley: University of California Press, 2008), Kindle Edition. See also Michael Morley "'Suiting the Action to the Word': Some Observations on *Gestus* and *Gestische Musik*," in *A New Orpheus*, ed. Kowalke, 187. On the differences between Brecht and Weill's concept of gestus, see Calico, *Brecht at the Opera*, Kindle Edition, and Kim H. Kowalke, "Singing Brecht vs. Brecht Singing: Performance in Theory and in Practice," in *Music and Performance in during the Weimar Republic*, ed. Gilliam, 82–88.

[62] The inclusion of Offenbach and Bizet, who both wrote primarily in French, also reflects Busoni's preference for Latin rather than Aryan composers. See Weiner, *Undertones of Insurrection*, 39–41.

[63] Kurt Weill, "Zeitoper" (1928), trans. in *KWiE*, 483.

Weill was also interested in another operatic phenomenon linked with *Neue Sachlichkeit*: *Zeitoper*, or "topical opera," which, as Hermann Danuser and Herbert Gottschewski note, often incorporated elements of *Amerikanismus*.[64] The term arose in connection with Krenek's *Jonny spielt auf*, which combined modernist, popular, and neoclassical styles to depict the modernization/Americanization of European culture.[65] Subsequent pieces like Hindemith's *Neues vom Tage* (1929) and Stefan Wolpe's *Zeus und Elida* (1927) purported to reflect the experience of modernity on the operatic stage, combining the comedy, satire, quotidian subject matter, and the class-based politics of *opera buffa* with a modern musical language and an urban sensibility, often invoking dance music, jazz, and other popular styles.[66]

Although Weill did compose one true *Zeitoper* (*Der Zar lässt sich photographieren*), he objected to the term on the grounds that it was too facile and did not represent contemporary life: "People took the 'tempo of the twentieth century,' combined it with the much-praised 'rhythm of our time' and, for the rest, limited themselves to the representation of sentiments of past generations."[67] In what was likely a jab at *Neues vom Tage*, he wrote that contemporary opera should present its ideas "in a more enduring, more significant form than the newspaper would probably be capable of offering."[68] Still, Weill adhered to some of the principles, particularly the idea that opera should comment on contemporary life. But for him, that engagement with modernity meant more than simply reproducing its trappings. Opera should represent the world not as "a photograph, but as mirror reflection. In most cases, it will be a concave or convex mirror, which reproduces life in a magnification or reduction appropriate to how it appears in reality." In this sense, "Stravinsky's *Oedipus Rex* is no less a mirror of our time than, for example, Chaplin's *The Gold Rush*."[69] For Weill, opera was a tool to dissect and analyze modern life, rather than a simple aesthetic experience. Indeed, Weill's operas deal in metaphor, with time and space often out-of-joint with one another, like the fairy tale world of *Der Silbersee* or the fact that *Mahagonny*—ostensibly set in Alabama—more resembles contemporary German ideas of Chicago. While these inconsistencies are often attributed to Weill's (and Brecht's) ignorance of U.S. geography, they also highlight the metaphorical

---

[64] Danuser and Gottschewski, Foreword to *Amerikanismus, Americanism, Weill*, 7.
[65] Grosch, *Die Musik der Neuen Sachlichkeit*, 153.
[66] Cook, *Opera for New Republic*, 4–5, 125.
[67] Weill, "Zeitoper," 482.
[68] Kurt Weill, "Topical Opera" (1929), trans. in *KWiE*, 510.
[69] Weill, "Zeitoper," 482–83.

nature of these spaces, distorting the culture and politics of Weill's Berlin to bring the important issues to the forefront, and to keep the audience off-balance, and therefore critically engaged. Weill's music reflects this distorted reality. Following Busoni, Weill advocated for a return to eighteenth-century ideals, based on the notion (shared by Gutman) that it represented a time when musical theatre was more deeply embedded in its broader culture, as opposed to the "splendid isolation" of opera aimed at elite audiences in 1920s Berlin.[70] To this eighteenth-century structure, Weill also often added elements of *Amerikanismus*, especially jazz. This combination of baroque and jazz forms and techniques mirrors the distorted time and space of the setting, reinforcing the idea that these stories take place both nowhere/no-when and everywhere/every-when simultaneously.

*Die Dreigroschenoper* exemplifies many of these ideas. The work is a modern retelling of John Gay's *The Beggar's Opera* (1728), as translated by Brecht's assistant Elisabeth Hauptmann with a libretto by Bertolt Brecht (with liberal borrowings from François Villon and Rudyard Kipling).[71] Weill retained the format of the original, writing individual songs connected by passages of dialogue. Instead of eighteenth-century tunes, he substituted foxtrots, tangos, and melodramas, along with the occasional chorale and operetta finale. There is an element of the baroque as well, as Weill's use of dance music also echoes the sicilianos, sarabandes, and allemandes in eighteenth-century musical theatre.[72] The more pervasive influence of jazz in this piece is likely the influence of Hauptmann, who collected and translated magazines, recordings, and newspapers for Brecht, and who wrote most of the libretto for the follow-up to *Die Dreigroschenoper*, *Happy End*.[73] Evidence suggests that neither Hauptmann or Weill felt that either piece had any relationship to the real United States; Hauptmann said that the story of *Happy End* included a "not uninteresting portion of the concept of America," and Weill's writing on *Die Dreigroschenoper* mostly concerns musical structures and styles rather than politics.[74]

*Die Dreigroschenoper* represents Weill's hope for renewal; he called it a "prototype" of a new form for musical theatre.[75] In this way, *Die*

---

[70] Kurt Weill, "Correspondence about *Die Dreigroschenoper*" (1929), 487. See also Kurt Weill, "The Future of Opera in America," *Modern Music* 14, no. 4 (1937): 183–88.

[71] On the various authors of *Die Dreigroschenoper*, see Stephen Hinton, ed., *Kurt Weill: The Threepenny Opera* (Cambridge, UK: Cambridge University Press, 1990), 9–12.

[72] *KWiE*, 116.

[73] Patty Lee Parmelee, *Brecht's America* (Columbus: Ohio State University Press, 1981), 4, 55, 199.

[74] Quoted in Parmelee, *Brecht's America*, 199.

[75] Weill, "Correspondence about *Die Dreigroschenoper*," 487.

*Dreigroschenoper* reflects the Weimar-era interest in montage, in which artists would combine fragments of cultural detritus (in the case of sculptors of
the Bauhaus, literally) into something new and modern. As Brigid Cohen has
observed, Weimar-era artists felt montage represented the artistic ability to
"salvage what might seem irredeemable in the world and transfigure it," in
the process, realizing "an optimistic vision of rebuilding society and culture
from the very fragments that remain from, and testify to, its devastated history."[76] The juxtaposition of jazz-inflected musical styles and operetta-esque
structure was crucial to the composer's hopes for a renewal of German opera.
He described the process of writing the piece as revelatory:

> This reversion to a primitive operatic form brought with it a far-reaching
> simplification of musical language. It was a question of writing music that
> could be sung by actors, that is, by musical amateurs. But what appeared in-
> itially to be a limitation proved to be a huge asset in the course of the work.
> Only the realization of a comprehensible, palpable melodic structure made
> possible what was achieved in *Die Dreigroschenoper*, the creation of a new
> genre of musical theatre.[77]

These sentiments align with Weill's idiosyncratic concept of *Gebrauchsmusik*.
Initially, he saw potential in Hindemith's ideas that *Gebrauchsmusik* could
appeal to a broader audience while retaining artistic quality. But he remained
wary of Hindemith's focus on educated musical laypeople, writing in 1927
that "it remains to be seen [whether] this youthful movement is not restricted too much to certain circles of people to create the actual basis for
a renewal of musical appreciation or even for the formation of a people's
art." Indeed, Weill was more concerned with expression and audience,
rather than performers, as Hindemith was. After 1928, Weill's concept of
*Gebrauchsmusik* grew to include political aims (if not a specific political program). While this tendency in Weill's music is often linked to his association
with Brecht, it predates their collaboration, stemming also from the ideals of
the *Novembergruppe* and from Busoni, who argued that music should make
people "think" rather than "believe."[78] In 1929, Weill defined *Gebrauchsmusik*
as that which was "capable of satisfying the musical needs of broader levels of

---

[76] Brigid Cohen, *Stefan Wolpe and the Avant-Garde Diaspora* (Cambridge, UK: Cambridge
University Press, 2012), 86.

[77] Weill, "Correspondence about *Die Dreigroschenoper*," 488 (translation adapted).

[78] On Busoni, see Weiner, *Undertones of Insurrection*, 50, 56.

the population without giving up artistic substance," and "expressing simple human emotions and actions," and that "reproduces the natural condition of man."[79] He admitted that there might be some confusion, that "with the use of elements of jazz, simple, easily comprehensible melodies originate which superficially produce a more or less strong resemblance to the melodies of 'light' music." However, he chided critics for overlooking the fact that

> the effect of this music is not catchy, but instead rousing; that the intellectual bearing of this music is thoroughly serious, bitter, accusing, and in the most pleasant cases still ironic; that neither the poetry of this music nor the form of the music itself would be conceivable without the vast background of an ethical or social nature on which it is based.[80]

It is this aspect of Weill's *Gebrauchsmusik* that Theodor Adorno acknowledged in his review of *Die Dreigroschenoper*. As Jonathan O. Wipplinger observes, Adorno wrote about the score in terms of montage, acknowledging that it borrowed "much color" from jazz, and appealed to broad audiences because "everyone can sing the new melodies" and "the thoroughly homophonic framework is quite audible to amateur ears."[81] The nominally tonal language was "loosened up with jazz," in line with contemporary aesthetic trends: "The functional links between the chords may [. . .] be severed, because that's what one likes doing in the New Objectivity." Like Weill, Adorno felt that the superficial resemblance to popular music carried a polemical thrust. But the montage for Adorno did not indicate possibilities for renewal, but rather, it led to a sense of resignation. The combination of jazz and more "classical" styles becomes a mode of deconstruction and reconstruction through which the composer "pieces together the debris of empty phrases shattered by time. The harmonies, the fatal diminished seventh chords, the chromatic alternations of diatonic melodic steps, the *espressivo* that expresses nothing— they sound false to us." He declared the work was "*Gebrauchsmusik*" that "may be enjoyed today as an enzyme" that revealed

[79] Kurt Weill, "Opera—Where To?" (1929), trans. in *KWiE*, 506. For a detailed reading of this important essay, see Stephen Hinton, "The Idea of *Gebrauchsmusik: A Study of Musical Aesthetics in the Weimar Republic (1919-1933) with Particular Reference to the Works of Paul Hindemith* (New York: Garland, 1989), 83–85, and "Weill: *Neue Sachlichkeit*, Surrealism, and Gebrauchsmusik," 71–74.

[80] Weill, "Opera—Where To?" 507.

[81] Theodor Weisengrund-Adorno, "*The Threepenny Opera*" (1929), trans. by Stephen Hinton in *The Threepenny Opera*, ed. Hinton, 129–34. On the language of montage, see Wipplinger, *The Jazz Republic*, 72–73.

the barrenness of past operatic culture. Adorno adds a Marxist component to Weill's position on accessibility, polemic, and its relationship to jazz, and the critic felt that the public misunderstood the piece, missing its critique and taking it for light entertainment.[82] But the underlying idea that jazz sonorities and structures could be "thoroughly serious, bitter, accusing, and in the most pleasant cases still ironic" links the composer's position with the critic's. For both Weill and Adorno, the ironic combination of jazz and opera reveals the latter to be moribund, but for the composer, it also points toward possibilities for renewal.

Adorno's Marxist interpretation view aligns with Brecht's, who found in America a fascinating yet corrupt embodiment of unchecked capitalism. Although set in London, the Chicago-style gangsters and jazz-inflected score gestures at broader ideas of ostensibly American-style economic exploitation. The success of *Die Dreigroschenoper* likely owes something to the match between the jazz-inflected musical style and the view of America as a land of capitalist excess, even if Weill never held such a view.

If *Die Dreigroschenoper* drew on ballad opera and operetta, *Aufstieg und Fall der Stadt Mahagonny* adapted baroque and classical-era *opera seria*. With its narrator and plethora of choruses and chorales interrupting and commenting on the action, *Mahagonny* also bears a resemblance to a Handel oratorio or a Bach Passion. There are further parallels between the piece and the structure of *Die Zauberflöte*, a favorite of Weill's, which also includes moments in which characters turn toward the audience to impart moral lessons. Weill connected Mozart with sacred choral genres, advocating for a return to " 'theater music' (in the Mozartean sense)," and noting that "this altered fundamental attitude can lead to a junction with the form of the oratorio."[83] If, in *Die Driegroschenoper*, jazz was an international modern musical language and a call to arms against a crumbling operatic tradition, in *Aufstieg und Fall der Stadt Mahagonny*, jazz more clearly represents America specifically, although this America had less to do with the United States than with what America represented to Brecht and the German Left.

The opera serves as a cautionary tale about the dangers of commodification and consumerism, allegorically showing how a society can crumble under the weight of unbridled capitalism. Weill and Brecht used America in much the same way as Handel uses the biblical Middle East: as a set of familiar signifiers

---

[82] Hinton critiques this position and its legacy in *The Threepenny Opera*, 181–92.
[83] Weill, "Zeitoper," 484.

that allow for commentary on contemporary issues. Just as librettist Charles Jennens used King Belshazzar and ancient Babylon as a metaphor for King George II in Handel's *Belshazzar* (1745), in *Mahagonny*, America stands for larger, dehumanizing forces at work in Germany, and has very little to do with the United States as a political entity.[84] Ironizing the religious sensibility of the oratorio and Passion was important to Brecht, who often drew on religiously inflected genres to make clear his didactic intent.[85] Indeed, the approaching hurricane is reminiscent of the biblical natural disasters that God visits upon wicked cities.[86] The "biblical" nature of *Mahagonny* was also important to Weill, who wrote that his opera was "topical" in "the same way as the biblical stories of the prodigal son, the banquet, and the adulterous woman are," and that the "history of the city" was "in that sense a 'biblical' event already" given that "Mahagonny, like Sodom and Gomorrah, falls on account of the crimes, licentiousness and the general confusion of its inhabitants."[87] The idea of America as equivalent to the biblical Middle East or the ancient world was popular in the Weimar Republic; architect Erich Mendelssohn (another member of the *Novembergruppe*) made Babylon a theme of his photographic book on America, which was an important influence on Brecht.[88] Goll captured the ambivalence of attitudes toward jazz, writing, "Some say it is the rhythm of Sodom and Gomorrah. . . . Why should it not be from paradise? In this case, rise and fall are one."[89] The mock-religious sensibility extends to Weill's other *Amerikanismus*-infused collaborations with Brecht, from the Christian premise of *Die sieben Todsünden* to the satirical apotheosis of "Hosiannah Rockerfeller," the finale of *Happy End*.

Acknowledging Weill's debt to eighteenth-century opera and oratorio also clarifies the composer's cautioning against "Wild-West or Cowboy romanticism" in productions of *Mahagonny*. Weill likely realized that his depiction of America might be read through the lens of the popular late-nineteenth-century German view of the New World as an exciting frontier populated by

[84] On *Belshazzar*, see Ralphe P. Locke, *Musical Exoticism: Images and Reflections* (Cambridge, UK: Cambridge University Press, 2009), 95.

[85] This is particularly true for the *Lehrstück*; see Stephen Hinton, "*Lehrstück*: Aesthetics of Performance," in *Music and Performance during the Weimar Republic*, ed. Gilliam, 61–66. Hinton has also observed biblical allusions in *Die Dreigroschenoper*. See *The Threepenny Opera*, 187–88.

[86] Parmelee, *Brecht's America*, 105.

[87] Kurt Weill, "Concerning the Premiere of the Opera *Mahagonny*" (1930), trans. in *KWiE*, 519. The final quote is trans. in Parmelee, *Brecht's America*, 177. See also Willett, *Art and Politics in the Weimar Period*, 153–54.

[88] Parmelee, *Brecht's America*, 69–75.

[89] Goll, "The Negroes are Conquering Europe," 559, ellipses in the original.

exotic peoples, exemplified in the popular novels of Karl May, or something akin to Puccini's *La fanciulla del West* (1910).[90] But Weill aimed to create a "modern classical art," which would form "the most complete opposition to Romantic art."[91] This included eschewing the romantic use of exotic places to explore the pleasures and anxieties related to sensuality and barbarism. Instead, Weill opted for a more baroque conception of "elsewhere" as a place of myth, where archetypal figures can be used to impart lessons to present-day audiences. In this sense, Weill's statement in 1944 that he wrote fantasies "about" America is misleading; these fantasies may be set in some place resembling America, but they are really "about" modernity and the human condition.

The multi-faceted and ambivalent feelings that *Amerikanismus* represented in 1920s Germany made for a remarkable range of signifiers that Weill deployed for many different purposes. Weill's America was thus anything he wanted it to be: an emblem of modernity, a transnational nexus, or the biblical landscape of a morality play. In this light, Weill used America in the same way that he used Japan in *Der Jasager*, the mythical land of Urb in *Die Bürgschaft* ("The Pledge," 1932), the fairy-tale landscape of *Der Silbersee* (1933), and the tropics in *A Kingdom for a Cow* (1935): as a space in which universal moral lessons might be imparted.

## Coming to the United States

Weill knew that as useful as the concept of America was, the real United States posed serious and difficult challenges. He saw it at first as a potentially lucrative market, and when the political situation in Germany began to worsen, as a potential haven. Weill began think about U.S. audiences in 1928, when he proposed to arrange *Der Zar lässt sich photographieren* for a chamber performance there.[92] But Hans Heinsheimer, his contact at his publisher Universal Edition (UE), cautioned him against it on that grounds that German composers often had trouble drawing audiences in the United States, and Weill dropped the matter.[93] As early as 1931, Weill sensed that

[90] Glenn Watkins, *Pyramids at the Louvre: Music, Culture, and Collage from Stravinsky to the Postmoderns* (Cambridge, MA: Harvard University Press, 1994), 90–94.
[91] Quoted in Hinton, *Weill's Musical Theater*, 54–55, emphasis in the original.
[92] *WUE*, 111.
[93] *WUE*, 121.

Germany might not remain safe for much longer, and he proposed a production of *Die Bürgschaft* in Philadelphia, writing to UE that "in the present conditions in Central Europe, it will in any case be good to gain more ground than before with my work in the big centers of foreign countries, particularly in the United States."[94] Heinsheimer discouraged this as well, arguing that the only way the work could be successful in the United States was to be embraced in Europe first.

Still, Weill's music did precede his arrival in the United States. The first performance appears to have been a short run of *The Magic Night*, an adaptation of *Zaubernacht* (1922), that played at the Garrick Theatre on 27 December 1925, which was well-received, but not widely noticed.[95] The second was at a small private concert at pianist E. Robert Schmitz's Pro-Musica Society on 29 January 1927, directed by Eugene Goossens and Darius Milhaud, which included Weill's violin concerto.[96] The concerto was performed once again on 28 March 1930 by Fritz Reiner and the Cincinnati Symphony Orchestra, with concert master Emil Heermann playing the solo. Reviews were poor, with Samuel T. Wilson of *Musical America* likening the work to a "hive of angry bees."[97] Leopold Stokowski's radio broadcast of *Der Lindberghflug* on 5 April 1931 followed, which received mostly positive notices. Critics found the novelty appealing, with the *Minneapolis Star* reporting that it was composed "in ultra-modern symphonic form."[98]

The performance of *Der Lindberghflug* may have given Weill the confidence to try for a larger-scale introduction to the United States; in 1932, he began to think about a U.S. performance of *Die Dreigroschenoper*.[99] The opportunity presented itself in early 1933, when John Krimsky and Gifford Cochran mounted a production in New York as *The 3-Penny Opera*. Weill had high hopes for the project, and even planned to travel to the United States to be present if the premiere was a success, but UE again discouraged him from making the journey.[100] Weill may have been interested in

---

[94] *WUE*, 304.
[95] See Elmar Juchem, Introduction to Kurt Weill, *Zaubernacht*, ed. Elmar Juchem and Andrew Kuster, KWE, Series I, Volume 0 (New York: Kurt Weill Foundation for Music/European American Music Corporation, 2008), 16–17.
[96] "Season, 1926–1927," *Pro-Musica Quarterly* 4, no. 4 (1926): 51.
[97] Introduction to Kurt Weill, *Music with Solo Violin*, ed. Andreas Eichhorn, KWE, Series II, Volume 2 (New York: Kurt Weill Foundation for Music/European American Music Corporation, 2010), 19.
[98] "'Lindbergh's Flight' to Feature Program by Philadelphians," *Minneapolis Star*, 4 April 1931, 29.
[99] *WUE*, 393.
[100] *WUE*, 462.

traveling because he sensed conditions in Germany were worsening. He decided against the New York trip on 15 March, but left Germany merely a week later on 22 March, arriving in Paris the next day.[101] Meanwhile, Heinsheimer believed (erroneously) that modern music circles in the United States would support the production, and promised to contact new music societies in New York City.[102] For his part, Weill knew that some cultural translation was necessary, and reminded UE that the score was "not jazz-music in the American sense, but rather, an entirely unique, new sound." He also suggested they market the piece as part of the "process of liberating" German music.[103]

However, the performance was not a success. The increasing trend toward fascism in Germany made many U.S. audiences wary of German culture. In this light, the decision to market *The 3-Penny Opera* as a "continental success" likely did not help matters.[104] After a try-out in Philadelphia, the production opened on Broadway in April 1933, and played for only a week and half. Robert Garland of the *Pittsburgh Press* wrote that the opening-night audience seemed determined not to like it, and that it was "as humorless as Hitler," although he did note that the Nazis had tried to suppress the piece.[105] Weill was devastated, and called the affair "tragic" and "catastrophic."[106] He maintained that the failure was due to a poor translation.[107] Moving forward, Weill and UE hesitated to have any more of his German works performed in the United States. Alfred Kalmus at UE hoped that, even though the production had failed, the "Moritat" could become a hit on its own, but Weill discouraged it, and Heinsheimer similarly turned away several inquiries about putting *Mahagonny* on Broadway.[108]

Shortly after *The 3-Penny Opera* closed in April 1933, Lehman Engel conducted the U.S. premier of *Der Jasager* at the Henry Street Settlement School, an appropriate venue given that Weill and Brecht intended the piece to both instill basic musical skills and spark discussion about the value of

[101] *WUE,* 462.
[102] *WUE,* 459.
[103] *WUE,* 460–61.
[104] "Display Ad," *NYT,* 7 April 1933, 22.
[105] Robert Garland, "Nose-Thumbing 'Three-Penny Opera' Fails to Impress New York," *Pittsburgh Press,* 21 April 1933, 30.
[106] *WUE,* 468.
[107] Kim H. Kowalke, "*The Threepenny Opera* in America," in *Kurt Weill: The Threepenny Opera,* ed. Hinton, 81.
[108] *WUE,* 483–84, 490.

"acquiescence," although it is not clear if such a discussion took place.[109] As with *The 3-Penny Opera*, critics reviewed the piece with contemporary German politics in mind. Even though the Nazis had denounced both Weill and Brecht, the reviewer for the *New York Times* wrote that "recent events in the Reich perhaps explain somewhat why a piece whose ideology combines devotion to an abstract virtue with personal callousness has achieved such popularity there."[110]

The reception of both showed Weill that U.S. audiences would not respond well to his German innovations. He remained based in Louveciennes (a suburb of Paris) for the remainder of 1933 and all of 1934, although he traveled extensively, visiting his parents in Czechoslovakia and vacationing in Italy.[111] There, he also saw Lenya (even though they were officially divorced) and Caspar Neher (the designer for many of his Brechtian collaborations and librettist of *Die Bürgschaft*) and his wife Erika (with whom Weill was involved romantically). Professional obligations also took him to Rome, London (for *A Kingdom for a Cow*), and to Salzburg (for *The Eternal Road*). In January of 1935, he relocated to London to oversee *A Kingdom for a Cow*, but after its poor reception, moved back to France in July. After that, he split time between Louveciennes and Salzburg, where he continued to work on *The Eternal Road*. When the premiere for that piece was set for early 1936 in New York, Weill once again made plans to cross the Atlantic. On 4 September 1935, he and Lenya, having reconciled, boarded the S.S. *Majestic*, arriving in New York on 10 September.

Weill faced numerous challenges upon his arrival in the United States. His professional aspirations were complicated by the reputation that preceded him. Seen primarily by the mainstream press as a high modernist, and a German one at that, popular audiences were wary of him. At first he sought to gain a foothold within U.S. new-music communities like the League of Composers. But he found little success there either, finding those groups hostile to Germans for aesthetic, if not political reasons. Thus, when he applied for citizenship in the United States in 1937 (before achieving success), he still bore the weight of both his own cultural background and his previous reputation.

---

[109] "Henry St. Children Mark Anniversary," *NYT*, 24 April 1933, 12.
[110] N.H., "Music: Settlement Gives Opera," *NYT*, 26 April 1933, 13.
[111] This account of Weill's movements between 1933 and 1935 is distilled from *WLL(e)*, 79–191.

## The United States before Weill

The reasons Weill eventually found a professional home on Broadway are complex, and owe much to Weill's finances and aesthetic goals, as Kowalke has observed.[112] But they are also partially rooted in his pre-1935 reputation in the United States. Although many of Weill's European contemporaries despaired over the lack of support for modern music in the United States (Paul Hindemith felt that audiences in New York were "abnormally dopey"), this belies the presence of a flourishing modern-music community in the first half of the twentieth century.[113] New York of the 1920s and 1930s was home to the International Composer's Guild (ICG) and the League of Composers, while Pro-Musica and the New Music Society supported modernist composers on the West Coast.[114] But while these organizations seemed ideal places for modernist immigrant composers to find professional support, in practice they proved unreliable, particularly for Weill. During the 1920s and into the 1930s, the battle lines of U.S. modernism were drawn between ultra-modernist experimentation (exemplified by the ICG and Henry Cowell on the West Coast) and the students and followers of Nadia Boulanger's French neoclassicism (the League). While these lines owed more to rhetoric than compositional practice, Weill's self-consciously popular style seemed derivative of both Stravinsky and Gershwin to American ears, and did not fit into either category, though it more closely resembled the League's aesthetics than the ultra-modernist's.[115] Furthermore, anxiety over Europe's influence on U.S. music meant that German composers in particular were often denied access to professional networks and audiences. Aaron Copland and Roger Sessions—two members of the League—established a concert series for new U.S. compositions, as the Pan-American Association

---

[112] Kim H. Kowalke, "Formerly German: Kurt Weill in America," in *A Stranger Here Myself: Kurt Weill Studien*," ed. Kim H. Kowalke and Horst Edler (Hildescheim: Georg Olms, 1993), 43–47.

[113] Paul Hindemith, *Selected Letters of Paul Hindemith*, ed. and trans. By Geoffrey Skelton (Binghamton, NY: Vail-Ballou, 1995), 172. For other examples of composers who were frustrated with audiences and infrastructure in the United States, see Ehrhard Bahr, *Weimar on the Pacific: German Exile Culture in Los Angeles and the Crisis of Modernism* (Berkeley: University of California Press, 2007), 273; Lydia Goehr, "Music and Musicians in Exile: The Romantic Legacy of a Double Life," in *Driven into Paradise: The Musical Migration from Nazi Germany to the United States*, ed. Christoph Wolff and Reinhold Brinkmann (Berkeley: University of California Press, 1999), 72–73.

[114] On the modern music organizations of the United States in the 1920s and 1930s, see Carol Oja, *Making Music Modern: New York in the 1920s* (Oxford and New York: Oxford University Press, 2000), 178–87.

[115] Oja, *Making Music Modern*, 179. See also Kowalke, "Formerly German," 40–42.

of Composers (formed in the late 1920s), sought to renew ties among the western hemisphere as a show of cultural strength against Europe.[116] In the 1930s, a renewed focus on folk music on the neoclassical side left Weill scrambling to learn a new musical language.

Initially, Weill's music was judged in these circles against the backdrop of a 1920s high modernism that defined itself in opposition to mass culture. With the advent of the Great Depression, several sectors of the U.S. avant-garde experienced a political awakening, and many were attracted to the ideals of Communist Party of the United States of America (CPUSA).[117] In the early 1930s, the CPUSA still answered to Moscow's Communist International (Comintern), which had entered the "Third Period" of Party cultural policy. The designation "Third Period" comes from Nikolai Bukharin's report to the Comintern's Sixth World Congress in 1928, in which he divided the post-Revolution world into three chronological stages, culminating in the collapse of global capitalism. Feeling that this collapse was imminent, Leftist avant-gardes in the United States in the early 1930s attempted to distance themselves from commodity culture by experimenting with transgressive and taboo forms and subjects.[118]

Because of Weill's association with the *Neue Sachlichkeit*, he gained a reputation as a neoclassicist (even though he likely would not have used that term), and those initially most interested his music primarily came from the League. Weill's name does not appear at all in the ICG's *Eolian Review*, and only once in *Pro-Musica Quarterly* (to announce the U.S. premiere of the violin concerto), but his music was hotly debated in the pages of the League's journal *Modern Music*, and people associated with the League often wrote about Weill in other academic periodicals and in the mainstream press. The League's interest in Weill aligned with their general aesthetic agenda. The organization split from the ICG in 1923 ostensibly to pursue a broader variety of modernisms and distance itself from the "bizarre element of experiment" in the Guild, intending to cultivate a simpler, more accessible musical language

---

[116] Oja, *Making Music Modern*, 178.

[117] Stuart D. Hobbs, *The End of the American Avant-Garde* (New York: New York University Press, 1997), 19–25; Michael Denning, *The Cultural Front: The Laboring of American Culture in the Twentieth Century* (London: Verso, 1997), 28–29.

[118] Walter Kalaidjian, *American Culture Between the Wars: Revisionary Modernism and Postmodern Critique* (New York: Columbia University Press, 1993), 59–61; Richard A. Reuss with JoAnne C. Reuss, *American Folk Music and Left Wing Politics, 1927–1957* (Lanham, MD: Scarecrow, 2000), 39–40; Elizabeth B. Crist, *Music for the Common Man: Aaron Copland during the Depression and War* (Oxford, UK: Oxford University Press, 1999), 17–19.

(goals that generally aligned with Weill's).[119] The anti-Semitic undertones of some of the ICG's rhetoric also played a role.[120] The League also professed a more internationalist bent in the 1920s.[121] When the ICG disbanded in 1927, the League became the most prominent organization dedicated to modern music on the East Coast, and shaped the tastes of U.S. new music audiences.

Between 1927 and 1935, a variety of opinions regarding Weill's music appeared in *Modern Music*, all reflecting biases of the authors and the changing dynamics of U.S. new-music culture. Weill's music fared better among reviewers who had a strong connection to German-speaking countries, who often praised his fusing of modernist and popular styles. Germans like Gutman, Heinsheimer, and Alfred Einstein promoted their fellow countryman, and wrote positively about his music, admiring his ability to keep opera accessible to the public while remaining innovative; Gutman praised *Die Dreigroschenoper's* "singularly happy style suggested by American popular music without the use of its percussive beat."[122] George Antheil believed that *Die Dreigroschenoper* could even provide a model for reviving popular opera in the United States on Broadway.[123] But Weill's use of popular styles also left him open to accusations of pandering, particularly from contributors who had no strong connection to Germany. In his review of *Die Dreigroschenoper*, Nikolai Lopatnikoff wrote, "Comparison with Stravinsky's epoch-making *L'histoire du soldat* is inevitable; but Stravinsky denied himself the ultimate compromise, the yielding of his individuality to the demands of the musical 'customers,' preserving intact the artistic entity of his music."[124] These objections were especially prominent in the criticism of more politically minded members of the community. Marc Blitzstein wrote that

> [s]uccess has crowned Kurt Weill, with his super-bourgeois ditties (stilted *Otchi Tchornayas* and *Road-to-Mandalays*) harmonized with a love of distortion and dissonance truly academic; the "sonx" go over, the "modernisms" get sunk. This is real decadence: the dissolution of a

---

[119] Quoted in David Metzer, "The League of Composers: The Initial Years," *American Music* 15, no. 1 (1997): 55.

[120] Rachel Mundy, "The 'League of Jewish Composers' and American Music," *Musical Quarterly* 96, no. 1 (2013): 50–99.

[121] Metzer, "The League of Composers," 56–57.

[122] Hans Gutman "Young Germany, 1930," *Modern Music* 7, no. 2 (1930): 9; See also Hans Heinsheimer, "Youth Leaves the Vanguard," *Modern Music* 9, no. 1 (1931): 5; Alfred Einstein, "German Opera, Past and Present," *Modern Music* 11, no. 2 (1934): 71.

[123] George Antheil, "Wanted—Opera by and for Americans," *Modern Music* 7, no. 4 (1930): 11–12.

[124] Nikolai Lopatnikoff, "New Life in Berlin," *Modern Music* 6, no. 4 (1929): 26.

one-time genuine article, regurgitated upon an innocent public, ready, perhaps even ripe to learn.[125]

This rhetoric resonates with Third Period ideals (aligning with Blitzstein's
politics, if not the League's in general); in the early part of the decade, some
parts of the League felt that Weill's apparent capitulation to bourgeois
standards of popular music rendered it unworthy of the label "modernism,"
foreshadowing the debates over his posthumous reputation.

In other quarters, Weill faced explicit criticism on the grounds of his
German heritage in ways that resembled the U.S. reception of *The 3-Penny
Opera* and *Der Jasager*. Critics who wrote for both *Modern Music* and the
mainstream press often took this view. W.H. Haddon Squire wrote in the
*Christian Science Monitor* that *A Kingdom for a Cow* "could only have been
written by a modern German and I cannot imagine it finding acceptance
among any but modern Germans."[126] Herbert Peyser wrote in the *New York
Times*, "As for taking *Mahagonny* seriously and solemnly—well, you have to
be a German to understand that."[127] Weill was caught in a double bind. His
use of jazz would always be read as derivative. However, to write in a more
typically Austro-German style would render him either too conventional or
too foreign for U.S. audiences, both within and outside of new music circles.
Thus, Weill's German heritage was perhaps the greatest impediment when
he arrived in the United States, and in several of his first English-language
interviews and writings, he made sure to note that he had left Germany behind, and that the parting was mutual.[128]

Several political and cultural changes just before Weill's arrival also had
an impact on his reputation. In 1934, partly as a response the rise of the
Nazis in Germany and a desire to unify the Left, the Comintern began to
encourage the CPUSA to ally with a broad range of Leftist movements, even
if they were not explicitly communist.[129] As part of this move toward more
inclusivity, the Comintern also encouraged artists to harness folk and mass
culture for political purposes, a reversal of the previous focus on the avant-
garde. In the United States, this shift toward a broader alliance gave rise to the

---

[125] Marc Blitzstein, "Popular Music—An Invasion: 1923–1933," *Modern Music* 10, no. 2
(1933): 101, emphasis in the original. *Óči čjórnye* ("Dark Eyes") is a sentimental Russian ballad.
[126] W.H. Haddon Squire, "Kurt Weill's Cow," *Christian Science Monitor*, 3 August 1935, 6.
[127] Herbert Peyser, "Berlin Hears *Mahagonny*," *NYT*, 10 January 1932, X8.
[128] See, for example, N.S., "Kurt Weill's New Score," *NYT*, 27 October 1935, available online at
http://www.kwf.org/pages/wt-kurt-weills-new-score.html.
[129] Crist, *Music for the Common Man*, 18–19.

Popular Front, a cultural bloc that included hard-line Marxists, New Dealers, feminists, older 1920s progressives, and civil-rights workers, as well as anti-fascist movements born in the wake if the Spanish Civil War, among other similar groups.[130] Later in the decade, as the horrors of Stalin's government were made public, the U.S. Left drifted further away from the Comintern and began to strengthen ties with autochthonous institutions, while still retaining its populist political focus.

The rise of the Popular Front in 1935 had a crucial impact on the U.S. careers of immigrants like Weill, although it was not always positive. As part of the renewed interest in folk culture, modern composers rethought their methods of creating American music. The roots of this movement appear as early as 1932, when Copland wrote,

> A true musical culture never has been and never can be solely based upon the importation of foreign artists and foreign music, and the art of music in America will always be essentially a museum art until we are able to develop a school of composers who can speak directly to the American public in a musical language which expresses fully the deepest reactions of the American consciousness to the American scene.[131]

Anything that hinted at European music was seen as a contamination, and was to be avoided.[132] Copland still drew on European models—especially Eisler—in his thinking about the revolutionary potential of music, but in terms of sound, he sought to develop something that would speak to American audiences.[133] In 1939, Virgil Thomson wrote, "Just as the United States is going to have to absorb a goodly number of German composers in these next years, France is already having already to absorb and educate a very considerable body of German listeners," continuing that the task is "a tedious job too," because the Germans "think they are so right about music, are so proud of their bad taste and so ostentatious in expressing it."[134] As Krenek wrote in 1959, "the emigrant composers, as victims of oppression, were received with open arms and given war assurances of readiness to help. But even without their being told so directly, they could feel that in regard to their

---

[130] Denning, *The Cultural Front*, 4–21.
[131] Aaron Copland, "The Composer and His Critic," *Modern Music* 9, no. 4 (1932): 144.
[132] Metzer, "The League of Composers," 56–57. See also Chapter 2 of Crist, *Music for the Common Man*.
[133] Crist, *Music for the Common Man*, 15, 43–44.
[134] Virgil Thomson, "More from Paris," *Modern Music* 16, no. 2 (1939): 105.

professional situation people would have been happier had they not been forced to come."[135]

These attitudes had financial implications. As the 1930s wore on, the League began to favor Americanist projects. Writing retrospectively in the late 1940s, Claire Reis and Marion Bauer, both heavily involved with the administration of the League, touted the success of productions like Douglas Moore's *The Devil and Daniel Webster* (1938), Ernst Bacon's *A Tree on the Plains* (1942), and collaborations with the Ballet Caravan, including Virgil Thomson's *Filling Station* (1937), Copland's *Billy the Kid* (1938), and Elliot Carter's *Pocahontas* (1939) (along with one composition by an immigrant: Benjamin Britten's *Paul Bunyan* in 1941).[136] In contrast, the League's earliest theatrical performances had showcased European works:; Stravinsky's *The Rite of Spring* (1913), *L'histoire du soldat* (1918), *Les noces* (1923), and *Oedipus Rex* (1927), Manuel de Falla's *El retablo de Maese Pedro* (1923), Schoenberg's *Die glückliche Hand* (1913), Prokofiev's *Le pas d'acier* (1926), and Shostakovich's *Lady Macbeth of the Mtsensk District* (1934) were all mounted by 1935.[137] Similarly, most of the awards and commissions from the Composers' Fund (which the League established in 1926), started to go to composers with established U.S. reputations (even if some, like Leo Ornstein, were foreign-born).[138]

In the late 1920s and early 1930s, jazz increasingly fell out of fashion in these circles as well, as many felt it had become too commercial.[139] But the denigration of jazz's commercialism masked more subtle reasons for the "folkloric" turn in U.S. modernism. For one, whiter genres like Appalachian folk music and cowboy songs signaled a new American masculinity that deflected attention away from homosexuality, particularly given the associations between jazz and sexual outsiders.[140] Furthermore, for many white U.S. audiences, jazz meant Louis Armstrong, but also Irving Berlin, George Gershwin, and Al Jolson, and its associations with urban life contributed to insidious notions of rootless, cosmopolitan Jews. Gentiles like Virgil Thomson and Henry Cowell, as well as Russian Jews like Lazare Saminsky,

---

[135] Ernst Krenek, "America's Influence on Its Émigré Composers," (1959), trans. in *Perspectives of New Music* 8, no. 2 (1970): 113.

[136] Marion Bauer and Claire R. Reis, "Twenty-Five Years with the League of Composers," *Musical Quarterly* 34, no. 1 (1948): 8–9.

[137] Bauer and Reis, "Twenty-Five Years," 7–8.

[138] Bauer and Reis, "Twenty-Five Years," 10.

[139] Crist, *Music for the Common Man*, 4, 23; Beth E. Levy, *Frontier Figures: American Music and the Mythology of the American West* (Berkeley: University of California Press, 2012), 298.

[140] Levy, *Frontier Figures*, 302.

began to associate Copland's eclectic jazziness as evidence of his "cosmopolitanism" that at best was inauthentic, and at worst, was a "Jewish menace to our artistic integrity," to quote Daniel Gregory Mason.[141] In this light, the accusations of pandering and sentimentality leveled at Weill take on additional significance: not for nothing did Virgil Thomson evoke anti-Semitic stereotypes in purporting to admire Weill's "super-banal and super-sensitive debasement of late-German chromatic melody," and his "consistent and determined cult of extreme weakness" in *Die Dreigroschenoper* and *Mahagonny*.[142] Weill's music—steeped in Europeanized jazz—was thus too Jewish and too German for U.S. modern music circles. Indeed, early in his U.S. career, Weill tried his hand at writing the kind of folkloric music that was gaining popularity in the League (particularly apparent in *One Man from Tennessee* from 1937), but he only succeeded in the more commercial context of the World's Fair with *Railroads on Parade* (1939, rev. 1940).

All these factors played into Weill's first real failure after his arrival: a concert of his music performed by Lottie Lenya, sponsored by the League, on 17 December 1935, which was coolly received. After that, Weill ceased searching for work within the East Coast new-music communities. But even if the League did not provide financial or direct professional support for Weill, it did serve as a network through which other connections might be made. For example, Harold Clurman of the Group Theatre was Copland's cousin, and several other figures associated with the League were involved with Weill's later projects, including Olin Downes, Lehman Engel, and Hans Heinsheimer, who had immigrated to the United States after the *Anschluss* in 1938.

In this light, the Popular Front also had several potential advantages for Weill. His existing commitment to mixing modernism and mass culture made him an appealing collaborator in broader Popular Front circles (if not new-music ones), and former critics like Blitzstein began to see Weill in a new light. By 1936, Blitzstein declared Weill "hasn't changed, I have," and he praised *Johnny Johnson* as containing some of Weill's best music:

> It is soft-voiced music—but there is a message there. Velvet propaganda—as he calls it, poison. Danger exists—but not always. You get this danger to

[141] Levy, *Frontier Figures*, 301–2. The Mason quote (reprinted in Levy) comes from Daniel Gregory Mason, *Tune In, America: A Study of Our Coming Musical Independence* (New York: Alfred A. Knopf, 1931), 160. Mason quotes himself from ten years before. On jazz and Jewishness, see also Jeffrey Paul Melnick, *A Right to Sing the Blues: African Americans, Jews, and American Popular Song* (Cambridge, MA: Harvard University Press, 1999), 26–27, 46–48.

[142] Virgil Thomson, "In the Theatre," *Modern Music* 14, no. 2 (1937): 104–5.

best advantage when Brecht is the poet; he hits hard, clean, sharp jabs to the chin with his texts. These, underpinned by Weill's nostalgic, inconsolably sad music have a compelling effect which I have just got 'round to.[143]

Blitzstein's newfound admiration for Weill's honeyed method of delivering Brecht's hard-hitting propaganda is in line with the general embrace of more populist aesthetics across the Left-wing spectrum in the later 1930s.

Moreover, the diversity of politics, styles, and methods within the Popular Front gave Weill options. While he was most famous for his work with Brecht, his politics were less defined than his partner's, and the aesthetic and political diversity of the Popular Front enabled him to pursue more centrist projects, particularly after his application for citizenship in 1937. He initially began work with the radical Group Theatre, then moved into the more moderate anti-fascist circles of Hollywood, then collaborated with the New Dealers in the Federal Theatre Project. In these groups, he found a very different attitude toward jazz, Jewishness, and the relationship between Europe and the United States. This range of ideas gave Weill plenty of grist for his compositional mill, allowing him the freedom to explore what he could be to American.

---

[143] Marc Blitzstein, "Weill Scores for *Johnny Johnson*," *Modern Music* 14, no. 1 (1936): 44–45.

# 2

# Shifting Paradigms

## Experiments in German and U.S. Alchemy

When Weill arrived in the United States on 10 September 1935, he encountered a nation clawing its way out of the Great Depression. With the collapse of the stock market on in September and October 1929, the deep-seated trust in the free market that had driven U.S. culture from Reconstruction through the Jazz Age seemed misplaced, and the accompanying turmoil forced the population to redefine what it meant to be an American.[1] Even amid the troubled economy, Weill had some advantages; his interest in mixing Leftist politics and popular forms resonated with the Popular Front, an emerging cultural bloc of artists, intellectuals, and activists who sought to use mass culture to advocate for populist Leftist ideals (see the previous chapter). The United States also offered Weill a chance to continue his experiments with stylization and abstraction in musical theatre; with the first experimental plays of Eugene O'Neill and Elmer Rice, critics proclaimed the advent of American expressionist drama, although the works of O'Neill and his followers resembled the *Neue Sachlichkeit* theatre of Germany as much as the expressionists.[2] A version of expressionism closer to that of the German movement thrived in Hollywood, where the previous generation of German-speaking immigrants also brought their techniques to the United States. This community gave Weill a chance to put his ideas about music and film to the test for the first time.

In two of his earliest U.S. efforts, Weill continued to balance innovation with accessibility as he had in Europe, while now also trying to learn the different aesthetic demands of U.S. markets. The work he produced with the Leftist Group Theatre, *Johnny Johnson*, was Weill's first project conceived entirely with U.S. audiences in mind, yet still bears traces of Weill's connections

---

[1] David M. Kennedy, *Freedom from Fear: The American People in Depression and War, 1929–1945* (Oxford, UK: Oxford University Press, 1999), 10.
[2] David Savran, *Highbrow/Lowdown: Theater, Jazz, and the Making of the Middle Class* (Ann Arbor: University of Michigan Press, 2009), 151–53.

*Kurt Weill's America.* Naomi Graber, Oxford University Press (2021). © Oxford University Press.
DOI: 10.1093/oso/9780190906580.003.0003

to *Neue Sachlichkeit* circles, along with elements of both U.S. experimental and conventional shows. After Weill and the Group cut ties, the composer collaborated with German immigrant director Fritz Lang on what they hoped would be a hard-hitting film version of a Brechtian *Lehrstück*. But in both projects, stylization and didacticism sit uncomfortably within frameworks drawn from Broadway and Hollywood. Ultimately, neither proved the success Weill had hoped.

## The Group Theatre

Although Weill came to the United States to work on *The Eternal Road*, by winter of 1935–36 he realized that project would not likely earn him money or recognition in the short term. In order to establish himself, Weill turned to the types of communities that had supported him in Europe: Left-leaning modernists. Weill had some connections with the League of Composers, but after their tepid reception of a concert of his music, he began to look elsewhere. René Blum offered him a commission for the Ballet Russes de Monte Carlo in 1936, but the idea came to nothing. Eugene Meyer, the publisher of the *Washington Post*, was willing to finance a ballet on the subject of Weill's choice, and the composer got so far as choosing Franz Wedekind's *The Empress of Newfoundland* before the idea collapsed.[3] By the end of the year, Weill began looking for more commercial opportunities, writing to his publishers at Heugel on 31 January 1936 that he was in talks to do something with Ben Hecht and Charles MacArthur, and that both Paramount and MGM had expressed interest. He also mentioned a prospective project with Group Theatre, which Weill called "the youngest and most modern theatre in New York."[4] With the Group and playwright Paul Green, Weill wrote *Johnny Johnson*, his first American-style "play with music," which opened in November 1936, and closed shortly thereafter. However, *Johnny Johnson* was revived by another Popular Front organization, the Federal Theatre Project (FTP), which mounted successful productions in Los Angeles and Boston in May 1937.[5]

---

[3] On the Blum and Meyer commissions, see *KWH*, 397.

[4] *WPD*(e), 163.

[5] Unless otherwise noted, my account of *Johnny Johnson* is drawn from the Introduction to Paul Green and Kurt Weill, *Johnny Johnson: A Play with Music in Three Acts*, ed. Tim Carter, KWE, Series I Volume 13 (New York: Kurt Weill Foundation for Music/European American Music Corporation, 2012).

The Group originated within the Theatre Guild, a company dedicated to "serious" drama, including classics, nineteenth- and twentieth-century European fare, and new American plays.[6] The Group formed in 1931 when Guild play reader Harold Clurman, actor-director Lee Strasberg, and casting director Cheryl Crawford grew dissatisfied with the Guild's hierarchical practices and elitist aesthetics, and started their own company. They envisioned a collaborative group of actors and playwrights confronting the problems of modernity with a psychological realism based in the acting methods of Konstantin Stanislavsky. Their first production, Paul Green's *The House of Connolly*, opened in September 1931 to favorable reviews. In 1935, the Group had their greatest triumph with Clifford Odets's *Waiting for Lefty*, followed by Odets's successful *Awake and Sing!* the same year. But the success was short-lived. The Group opened the following season with Nellie Child's *Weep for the Virgins* and Odets's *Paradise Lost*, neither of which impressed critics. Furthermore, success had masked internal tensions within the Group. Crawford resented being assigned to second-tier projects like *Virgins*, Strasberg worried about his diminishing role, and Clurman's tempestuous relationships with Odets and actor Stella Adler began to erode morale. The Group also had trouble finding material; promised scripts from Odets and John Howard Lawson failed to materialize, and nothing else seemed appropriate.[7]

This was the situation in late 1935, when Weill met Clurman and other members of the Group. Crawford, eager for the Group to expand into musical theatre, suggested a collaboration between Weill and Paul Green. The project seemed like a good fit for all involved. A fiercely progressive Southerner, Green won the Pulitzer Prize in 1927 for *In Abraham's Bosom*, and served as a professor in the philosophy department of the University of North Carolina at Chapel Hill, where he lived most of the year. Green also had connections with Germany, having spent 1928–1929 overseas on a Guggenheim fellowship, where he recalled being inspired by *Die Dreigroschenoper*'s mix of music and drama, if not its subject matter, writing, "The people were a sorry lot, but there was something about the way the music and the story mixed together that I liked."[8] While in Berlin, Green encountered Russian director Alexei

---

[6] My summary of the formation of the Group is drawn from Wendy Smith, *Real Life Drama: The Group Theatre and America, 1931–1940* (New York: Vintage, 1990).

[7] Smith, *Real Life Drama*, 248.

[8] Paul Green, "Symphonic Outdoor Drama: A Search for New Theatre Forms," in Paul Green, ed., *Drama and the Weather: Some Notes and Papers on Life and the Theatre* (New York: French, 1958), 14.

Granowsky, who encouraged Green to develop his notions of "symphonic drama," a form of theatre that favored folkloric imagery, pantomime, music, and movement rather than dialogue.[9] Like Granowsky, Weill had worked closely with Max Reinhardt, which may have also made him an attractive to Green as a collaborator. Furthermore, Weill's last German projects, *Die Bürgschaft* and *Der Silbersee*, both incorporated folkloric elements, a key aspect of Green's Granowsky-inspired "symphonic drama."

Furthermore, Broadway had become more hospitable to experimental drama during the previous decade and a half, beginning in earnest with Eugene O'Neill's *The Emperor Jones* (1920) and *The Hairy Ape* (1922), both of which critics labeled "expressionist." The movement gained speed with productions like Elmer Rice's *The Adding Machine* (1923), John Howard Lawson's *Processional* (1925), and Sophie Treadwell's *Machinal* (1928).[10] Although U.S. authors denied any direct German influence, they described a style that resembled European theatre, although not necessarily expressionism. Elmer Rice laid out his conception in a letter to the *New York Times* in 1923:

> The author attempts not so much to depict events faithfully as to convey to the spectator what seems to him their inner significance. To achieve this end the dramatist often finds it expedient to depart entirely from objective reality and to employ symbols, condensations and a dozen devices which, to the conservative, must seem arbitrarily fantastic.[11]

Although Rice's emphasis on the "inner significance" and rejection of "objective reality" seems to align with German conceptions of expressionism, other aspects of U.S. playwrights' conception of the term more resembled *Neue Sachlichkeit*. All of these U.S. plays incorporate mass culture (particularly the vaudevillian *Processional*) in ways anathema to expressionism, but an important part of the *Neue Sachlichkeit* aesthetic. They take a sober, at times cynical position on reality, rather than the transcendent yearning of German expressionist drama.

[9] See Tim Carter, "Celebrating the Nation: Kurt Weill, Paul Green, and the Federal Theatre Project (1937)," *Journal of the Society for American Music* 5, no. 3 (2011): 305–7.

[10] On the expressionist background of these plays, see Part II of Julia A. Walker, *Expressionism and Modernism in the American Theatre: Bodies, Voices, Words* (Cambridge, UK: Cambridge University Press, 2005).

[11] Quoted in Mardi Valgemae, *Accelerated Grimace: Expressionism in the American Drama of the 1920s* (Carbondale: Southern Illinois University Press, 1972), 63.

Green admired O'Neill deeply, who in turn supported Green. O'Neill's Provincetown players mounted *In Abraham's Bosom* in 1926, and in 1967, Green told Mardi Valgemae that the pantomimic sequences toward the end of that play were inspired by *The Emperor Jones* as well as German expressionism.[12] Meanwhile, the Theatre Guild began to import expressionist drama from Germany like Georg Kaiser's *From Morn to Midnight* (first U.S. production 1922) and Ernst Toller's *Man and the Masses* (first U.S. production 1924), with mixed success. The achievements of O'Neill, Rice, Treadwell, Lawson, and to a lesser extent, the Theatre Guild productions, may have given Green and the Group reason to believe a highly experimental drama might be financially successful.

In early April 1936, Green and Weill decided to write an anti-war drama inspired in part by Georg Büchner's *Woyzeck*, the film *Der Hauptmann von Koepenick*, Green's own experiences in the army, and most importantly, *The Good Soldier Schweik*, a novel by Czech author Jaroslav Hašek adapted for the stage by Brecht and director Erwin Piscator in 1929 (it is unclear whether they were inspired by the novel or the play).[13] Meanwhile, the Group accepted a suggestion from Milton Shubert, of the prominent producing dynasty, and agreed to mount Piscator's adaptation of Theodore Dreiser's *An American Tragedy*, which exemplified the director's take on epic theatre.[14] The directors were skeptical of the show's didactic nature. Clurman felt it was "schematic in a cold way that to my mind definitely went against the American grain," but "nevertheless technically intriguing and capable of being fashioned into a novel type of stage production."[15] The play, directed by Strasberg, premiered as *The Case of Clyde Griffiths* in March, and ran for only nineteen performances; the Group hoped the production would continue, but could not agree to terms with Shubert.[16]

[12] Valgemae, *Accelerated Grimace*, 51–52, 56–59.

[13] Paul Green, *A Southern Life: Letters of Paul Green, 1916–1981*, ed. Laurence G. Avery (Chapel Hill: University of North Carolina Press, 1994), 684. Helen Krich Chinoy and John Herbert Roper both cite the play rather than the novel as the primary influence, but none of the primary sources are clear. See Helen Krich Chinoy, *The Group Theatre: Passion, Politics, and Performance in the Depression Era*, ed. Don. B. Wilmeth and Milly S. Barranger (New York: Palgrave Macmillan, 2013), 122, and John Herbert Roper, *Paul Green: Playwright of the Real South* (Athens: University of Georgia Press, 2003), 161. Green almost certainly saw the stage version, as I discuss later in this chapter.

[14] On the production of *The Case of Clyde Griffiths*, see Chinoy, *The Group Theatre: Passion*, 118–22, and Harold Clurman, *The Fervent Years: The Group Theatre & the 30s* (1975; reprint New York: Da Capo, 1983), 174–76. Smith, *Real Life Drama*, 249, 255–58.

[15] Clurman, *The Fervent Years*, 174.

[16] "News of the Stage," *NYT*, 31 March 1936, 16.

In early May, Crawford and Weill came down to Chapel Hill for a week to discuss the details of the new project, and Weill began the music. The story follows Johnny Johnson, an idealist tombstone maker who goes to fight in World War I to protect democracy and impress his sweetheart Minnie Belle, who is also being courted by the businessman Anguish Howington. After witnessing the senselessness of war, Johnny is wounded defending a young German sniper and sent to an army hospital. Determined to end the fighting, Johnny takes his message of peace to the commanders, eventually resorting to dosing the generals with laughing gas to engineer a ceasefire. He is declared insane and consigned to a lunatic asylum, diagnosed with "peace monomania." Johnny ends the show as a peddler, as Minnie Belle marries Howington.

In June, Weill, Green, and the company agreed to provide entertainment for hotel guests in Connecticut while they honed their new season, including *Johnny Johnson*. But while Crawford championed the project, Clurman and Strasberg were less enthusiastic.[17] Clurman was initially slated to direct, but felt overmatched by the material, so Strasberg (who generally won praise for his "expressionistic" staging of *Clyde Griffiths* despite otherwise mixed reviews) took over in September.[18] Meanwhile, crucial aspects of sets and costumes went relatively unnoticed, and the designs left the company surprised and somewhat dismayed when they were finally revealed. They had pictured something small and picturesque, and instead received a monumental set, which required late adjustments to blocking.

After several under-rehearsed previews, the show opened on 19 November 1936. Reviewers generally supported the Group's efforts to fuse music, drama, and politics into a new form of theatre, but they felt that *Johnny Johnson* did not quite come together. Brooks Atkinson of the *New York Times* wrote that *Johnny Johnson* was "part good and part bad since new forms cannot be created overnight. There are many interludes in Mr. Green's work when both the satire and the idealism wither away to restless emptiness."[19] Similarly, Stirling Bowen of the *Wall Street Journal* wrote that the novelty of the project made for a rocky premiere: "A play like this, unique in quality, does not lend itself

[17] On the difficulties facing the Group Theatre during the production of *Johnny Johnson*, see Smith, *Real Life Drama*, 265–82.

[18] See, for example, J.P.B, "The Theatre: Creatures of Circumstance," *Wall Street Journal*, 17 March 1936, 8; Brooks Atkinson, "The Play: Group Theatre in a Skeletonized Version of Dreiser's *An American Tragedy*," *NYT*, 14 March 1936, 10.

[19] Brooks Atkinson, "The Play: *Johnny Johnson* Opens a New Season for the Group Theatre," *NYT*, 20 November 1936, 26.

readily to smooth and fully rounded performance."[20] Others praised the play's experimental quality, comparing it favorably with the work of O'Neill. "About once every so often some playwright-iconoclast other than Eugene O'Neill kicks over the traces and starts trail-blazing for new phases of dramatic expression" wrote Ralph W. Carey in the *Hartford Courant* review of *Johnny Johnson*, "Just now it is Paul Green."[21] An anonymous interviewer for the *Brooklyn Daily Eagle* observed that Green's "ability to fuse his dramas with both thoughtful issues of discussion and the theatrical dressings of light and sound" was second only to O'Neill's.[22] Weill's music largely went over well when mentioned at all. The production closed on 16 January 1937 after thirty-six performances.

*Johnny Johnson* was given new life by the FTP and its leader Hallie Flanagan. Created in 1935 as a branch of the WPA (Works Progress Administration, later renamed Works Projects Administration), the FTP was tasked with promoting U.S. theatrical culture and putting theatre professionals back work. Flanagan attended a performance of *Johnny Johnson* and saw possibilities in the show's anti-war theme (in line with President Roosevelt's recent pronouncements), experimental form, and large number of speaking roles.[23] On 18 December, she wrote to Green, whose plays were in the FTP's repertory, inquiring about the possibilities of a production. After consulting Weill, Green responded enthusiastically. The FTP mounted two productions in 1937, one in Boston which ran for twenty performances (25 May through 19 June) and another in Los Angeles, which ran for thirty-three (28 May through 4 July). The Los Angeles production restored much of the material cut by the Group, bringing it much closer to Green and Weill's original vision. Both productions featured sets and costumes more appropriate to the scale of the story, and both were relatively well-received. The *Los Angeles Times* noted that the premiere was "warmly acclaimed" and later called Weill's music "a highlight."[24]

---

[20] Stirling Bowen, "The Theatre: Simpleton Paradoxically Wise," *Wall Street Journal*, 23 November 1936, 13.

[21] Ralph W. Carey, "Among the New York Theatres," *Hartford Courant*, 6 December 1936, 50.

[22] "The Week," *Brooklyn Daily Eagle*, 19 September 1937, 31.

[23] See the "Address before the Inter-American Conference for the Maintenance of Peace, Buenos Aires, Argentina," 1 December 1936, available online at Gerhard Peters and John T. Woolley, *The American Presidency Project*. https://www.presidency.ucsb.edu/documents/address-before-the-inter-american-conference-for-the-maintenance-peace-buenos-aires.

[24] "Historical Drama Next at Playhouse," *Los Angeles Times*, 6 June 1937, C4, and "Historical Play Staged by Federals," *Los Angeles Times*, 20 June 1937, C4.

Weill learned important lessons about U.S. show business with *Johnny Johnson*. Among other concerns, Weill expected the show would help make his name as a U.S. theatre composer, and he realized that usually meant writing a hit song that could be separated from the show and sold as sheet music. Weill hoped that "Johnny's Song" would become that number, and so he and Green wove it into important moments of the story. The idea was not new; many previous musical comedies, revues, and film musicals used such recurring songs to unify an otherwise disparate score, which could also be used in marketing and promotion.[25] However, problems arose when Weill realized Green's politicized lyrics did not work outside of the show. Consequently, the composer had his publisher commission new lyrics from Edward Heyman: "To Love You and to Lose You." Green objected, but eventually was forced to accept a combination of his lyrics and Heyman's.[26] Even within the show, the song's moralizing did not work. Johnny sings the song as a street vendor, a figure who, as Stirling Bowen wrote, "has been pretty thoroughly discredited by the debauchees of sentimentality."[27] Having the moral sung at all may have alienated some audiences. Bowen also observed, "*Johnny* is supposed to be one of our indigenous Americans. And we are not a singing people."[28] Mainstream U.S. audiences were more used to seeing high-stakes moral dilemmas worked out in non-singing theatre; with a few notable exceptions, musical theatre usually implied fun and frivolity, not stoic ethical lessons.

Weill was also frustrated with the marketing of "Johnny's Song." He blamed the song's lackluster commercial performance on his publisher Chappell, whom he thought failed to promote it properly. He wrote to Max Dreyfus at Chappell on 20 December 1936:

> Here is a musical play running in its fifth week, with growing success, after an excellent, partly sensational reception. The music was better received by critics and audiences than any music on Broadway in this season. The audience simply loves the show. There are between 8 and 12 curtains every night, and people are humming the music in leaving the theater (which is, I think, internationally the best test for the success of a music [*sic*]). And

---

[25] Jeffrey Magee, *Irving Berlin's American Musical Theatre* (Oxford, UK: Oxford University Press, 2012), 107–15; Katherine Spring, *Saying It with Songs: Popular Music and the Coming of Sound to Hollywood Cinema* (Oxford, UK: Oxford University Press, 2013), 98–111.

[26] Carter, Introduction to *Johnny Johnson*, 17.

[27] Bowen, "The Theatre," 13.

[28] Bowen, "The Theatre," 13.

yet it seems not possible to have these songs sung over the radio, played in dance orchesters [*sic*], in nightclubs, on records etc.[29]

Weill exaggerated the show's success (a tactic he often employed in his business negotiations), but his frustration with his publishers appears genuine. Several other songs from Johnny Johnson were published as sheet music, including "Mon Ami, My Friend," and "Oh, the Rio Grande" (also sometimes called the "Cowboy Song") but none did well enough to satisfy Weill. Still, the composer learned an important lesson about U.S. show business, and in almost all his later projects he made sure to include songs he believed might become breakaway hits without alteration, and Weill often closely monitored which stars recorded them. He also rarely set the moral of the story to a separable popular song, although there are exceptions late in his career ("Lonely House" from *Street Scene* and "Lost in the Stars" from *Lost in the Stars*).

## Competing Paradigms

The Group understood that *Johnny Johnson* combined several different theatrical modernisms. Crawford wrote to Green in April 1936, "We all think it's a fine idea for an American anti-war comedy in almost revue style."[30] Designer Donald Oenslager recalled,

> Through three acts and thirteen scenes, Green and Weill's script took off in diverse directions. The first act, with its sentimental scenes on the home front, required poetic realism to establish the nostalgia of preparations for war. The second act, with its scenes of fantasy on the battlefront, employed expressionism to present the distorted harmonies of war. In one scene the mouths of three cannon appeared [*sic*] above the soldiers sleeping in a dugout and complained to the audience that their iron could have been better used for machines or plowshares, "but you decreed that we just kill." The third act, with its scenes of comic satire in a psychiatric hospital, required distorted settings to reflect their mad unreality. Finally, Johnny

---

[29] WLA, Box 47 Folder 3.
[30] WLRC, Series 47 Folder "Crawford, Cheryl."

became a pathetic pedlar [sic], dispensing toys to children along a street symbolically leading nowhere.[31]

Along with comedy, revue, poetic realism, expressionism, and satire, elements of epic theatre and the broader *Neue Sachlichkeit* movement also inform *Johnny Johnson*. But the failure of *Clyde Griffiths*, particularly critics' disdain for the narrator and overt politics, necessitated some rethinking of epic paradigms, even if the staging had been well-received.

Still, even if the Group knew they were facing a challenge, in the end they did not always rise to meet it. Green was more familiar with drama than comedy (in May, Crawford felt the need to "impress it on you too deeply—that I am sure the best way for you to approach this is lightly. You should have a slogan in your workroom which says 'Have fun—enjoy yourself.'"), and had never written a play that included so much music.[32] Weill was still learning U.S. theatrical conventions, and had trouble blending these ideas together.

Three different musical theatre paradigms exist side-by-side in *Johnny Johnson*, and attempts to combine them are not always successful. There are elements of typical operetta and revue, as well as epic theatre.[33] (In practice, many works of musical theatre combined these paradigms, and the lines between them are often ill-defined. However, separating them for heuristic purposes in this context illuminates some of the miscalculations in *Johnny Johnson*.) In the revue paradigm, music gives stars a chance to sing, dance, or otherwise show off their skills, regardless of whether the songs make sense dramatically. In the operetta paradigm, music is a vehicle for emotional expression, or moves the story forward. In Weill's epic paradigm (which is slightly different than Brecht's and Piscator's), music "elucidates the events on stage" and "prescribes a definite attitude for the actor," eliminating "any doubt or misunderstanding about the respective incident."[34]

---

[31] Donald M. Oenslager, *The Theatre of Donald Oenslager* (Middletown, CT: Wesleyan University Press, 1978), 68. Bruce Kirle also observes *Johnny Johnson's* debt to expressionism in *Unfinished Business: Broadway Musicals as Works-in-Progress* (Carbondale: Southern Illinois University Press, 2005), 98.

[32] WLRC, Series 40 Folder "Crawford."

[33] I am adapting these paradigms from Kirle, *Unfinished Business*, 15–16. For my purposes, "operetta" and "musical comedy" are the same; for Kirle, they differ in style, but not significantly in dramaturgy, although musical comedies are more likely to be star vehicles than operettas.

[34] Kurt Weill, "Concerning the Gestic Character of Music" (1929), trans. in *KWiE*, 492. On the differences between Weill's and Brecht's conception of epic theatre, see Stephen Hinton, *Weill's Musical Theater: Stages of Reform* (Berkeley: University of California Press, 2012), 139–48. Weill, for example, never wrote anything that disparaged emotional involvement, and in his post-Brecht career,

There are some moments in *Johnny Johnson* that resemble contemporary Broadway shows, which mostly worked within the revue and operetta paradigms. The "Cowboy Song," for example, is indebted to specialty numbers that were meant to be sold separately as sheet music to promote the show. Such songs were often framed—as that song is—as diegetic performances, and indeed, this was one of the songs the publishers made available as sheet music. The show begins like an operetta, in which characters sing to express themselves or move the story forward in songs that are inseparable from the plot, such as the opening sequence ("Over in Europe" and "Democracy Advancing"). There are other moments in *Johnny Johnson* that echo vaudeville acts. The comic banter between Johnny and the sergeant in Act I, Scene 4, resembles popular soldier sketches (compare the drill scene in the Abbott and Costello film *Buck Privates* from 1941), although Green adds a bitter satirical twist that is absent in most versions of the routine. In many musical comedies and comic operettas of the era, Act I ends with a comedic sequence, sometimes a chase. The second act of *Johnny Johnson* (which has three acts rather than two), appears as if it will end in that fashion. In Scene 5, Johnny doses the Allied high command with laughing gas so that they inadvertently declare peace, and a dance number breaks out ("The Dance of the Generals"). Johnny, pretending to be a general, relays the order to suspend the war in Scene 6 ("The Battle"). The music of these two numbers employs the tropes of a comic chase. The inebriated generals gleefully singing "We'll All be Home for Christmas," and the high clarinets doubling the "reveille"-like passage in the trumpets at the beginning of "The Battle," and xylophone interjections later in that piece are typical comic touches. "Song of the Guns" and other moments like it constitute numbers in the epic paradigm, in which a pause in the narrative allows the authors to elucidate the political or social consequences of the situation in song. The two most obviously epic numbers—"The Song of the Goddess" and the "Song of the Guns"—both comment on the action, reinforcing the experimental aspects of the play, and allow Green and Weill to shift the register from semi-realism to a fantasy.

Several other experimental paradigms also inform *Johnny Johnson*, particularly German expressionism and *Neue Sachlichkeit*, along with U.S. expressionism. Given their broad nature and the overlap among these styles, it is difficult to untangle exactly what influence resulted in individual aspects

often encouraged his collaborators to put more focus on the romantic and human elements of their stories.

of the play. For example, the combination of modernist and popular theatre might be attributed to either *Neue Sachlichkeit* or U.S. expressionism. In expressionist plays (both U.S. and German), characters are named symbolically or according to their job, such as the American everyman Yank in *The Hairy Ape*, or in Ernst Toller's Friedrich in *Der Wandlung* ("Transfiguration," 1919), which is phonetically similar to *Frieden* (peace).[35] Such stock figures also appeared in the *Neue Sachlichkeit* works of George Grosz.[36] The characters' names in *Johnny Johnson* are similarly overly generic, indicating a series of types rather than individual characters. Indeed, Green chose the name "Johnny Johnson" after learning that it was the most common name in the U.S. army during World War I.[37] Naming the German sniper "Johann" further emphasizes the everyman status of these two characters, and highlights his essential sameness with Johnny, despite their different nationalities. The episodic form of *Johnny Johnson* echoes both the German and U.S. expressionist interest in the medieval "station play," in which an everyman character visits stations (often based on Stations of the Cross), and at each one faces and overcomes a challenge.[38] Green even referred to the project as "a sort of morality play, an *Everyman* if you will," referencing the famous medieval drama.[39] Weill also argued that epic theatre should be "a stepwise *sequence of situations*," as demonstrated in *Mahagonny*, which he similarly called "a sequence of '*morality pictures of the twentieth century*.'"[40]

*Johnny Johnson* also might owe something to two European directors: Alexei Granowsky and Erwin Piscator. Green met Granowsky in Berlin in 1929, when the director was there with the Moscow-based State Jewish Theatre. The playwright admired Granowsky's production of I.L. Peretz's *A Night in the Old Marketplace*, which he lauded as "a grotesque, tragic carnival, with hardly any dialogue or spoken words, nearly all pantomime, dance, and musicalized action. It, too, dealt with decay and death, but with such verve and even comic satire that a sense of liveliness and zest

[35] Renate Benson, *German Expressionism: Ernst Toller and Georg Kaiser* (London: Macmillan, 1984), 23.

[36] Steve Plumb, *Neue Sachlichkeit 1918–1933: Unity and Diversity of an Art Movement* (Amsterdam: Brill Academic, 2006), 20.

[37] Carter, Introduction to *Johnny Johnson*, 25.

[38] On the "station play" framework in Expressionist drama, see Brenda Murphy, "Plays and Playwrights: 1915–1945," in *The Cambridge History of American Theatre, Volume Two: 1870–1945*, ed. Don B. Wilmeth and Christopher Bigsby (Cambridge, UK: Cambridge University Press, 1999), 294. On *Johnny Johnson* as a station play, see Kirle, *Unfinished Business*, 98.

[39] Green, *A Southern Life*, 684.

[40] Kurt Weill, "Foreword to the Production Book of the Opera *Aufstieg und Fall der Stadt Mahagonny*" (1930), trans. in *KWiE*, 514–15, emphasis in the original.

spilled over from the footlights."[41] Green recalled a later conversation with Granowsky in which the latter claimed, "Mine is first a musical theatre, last a musical theatre" because music helped to "go right to the heart of your dramatic matter, to reach the inner meaning and symbolism of the story you have to tell, to make it immediately available to the audience."[42] According to Green, Granowsky encouraged him to pursue similarly experimental folk drama based on U.S. subjects. Along with *Tread the Green Grass* (1929) and *Roll, Sweet Chariot* (1934), Green thought of *Johnny Johnson* as an early attempt at symphonic drama, writing "I tried this sort of symphonic drama a couple of other times on Broadway. Once the cool loyal judgement of Cheryl Crawford, the enthusiasm of Harold Clurman and the Group Theatre, the fine direction of Lee Strasberg and the resilient and theaterwise music of Kurt Weill—all helped to mend matters." Still, he recalled, "they were not enough," and the production "was marked down as a failure," even though "the critics' circle gave it a tombstone vote of confidence for its obituary."[43] The "sentimental" and "nostalgia"-filled first act, and the long stretches without dialogue toward the end of the second point to Granowsky's influence. Indeed, *Johnny Johnson* was at various times called "a legend," "a fable," and "a fantastic drama."[44]

Also in attendance the evening Green met Granowsky in Berlin was Erwin Piscator, the celebrated director of *The Good Soldier Schweik*, which featured projections designed by George Grosz, whom Weill knew from his days in the *Novembergruppe*.[45] Green likely saw this production, as he remembered attending shows at the *Volksbühne* during its run.[46] Piscator was also well known to the Group Theatre. Clurman and Strasburg met him on separate occasions during trips to Moscow in 1935.[47] Piscator combined the grotesque, a sense of emotional distance, and allegorical subjects with sharp political satire, bringing *Neue Sachlichkeit* to the

[41]  Green, "Symphonic Outdoor Drama," 17.

[42]  Green, "Symphonic Outdoor Drama,"18–19.

[43]  Paul Green, "Symphonic Drama," in *Dramatic Heritage*, ed. Paul Green (New York: Samuel French, 1953), 23. On *Tread the Green Grass*, see Roper, *Paul Green*, 128. On *Roll, Sweet Chariot*, see Green, "Symphonic Outdoor Drama," 27–30.

[44]  Carter, Introduction to *Johnny Johnson*, 25.

[45]  John Willett, *Art and Politics in the Weimar Period: The New Sobriety, 1917–1933* (New York: Pantheon, 1978), 115, 151.

[46]  Green, "Symphonic Outdoor Drama," 14.

[47]  John Willett, *The Theatre of Erwin Piscator: Half a Century of Politics in Theater* (London: Eyre Methuan, 1978), 24, 146. Crawford may have also met Piscator, as she was in Moscow at the same time as Clurman, but she does not mention it in her memoirs.

theatre. In the wake of World War I, many of these dramas took pacifist stances, which may have made the style appealing to Green when he came to write his anti-war play.

The European influence on *Johnny Johnson* is best illustrated in the sequence of scenes that ends Act II, after the comic sequence with the generals. When Johnny's effort to stop the war fails, two masses of bodies appear onstage, leading to

> A series of flashes—by the light of bursting shells. The orchestra is now an organ playing the stately chant music of a church prayer, while in a nebulous circle of light at the extreme right front of the stage an AMERICAN PRIEST is seen standing above the members of his congregation who are bowed in prayer, and while at the left front a GERMAN PRIEST likewise stands above his praying flock.

Both priests intone the same prayer in different languages ("In the Time of War and Tumult") as a series of images appear onstage: "two squads of horrible creatures in gas masks," "two men fighting—an American and a German, with bare fists choking and strangling each other," "a squad of German soldiers holding up their hands in surrender. An American on his belly in the foreground with a machine gun mowing them down." Amid this chaos, Johnny, now clad in only "a torn piece of cloth tied around his middle" and "marked with sweat and powder burns," comes across the dead body of his German friend Johann ("In No-Man's Land").[48] He is arrested and transported back to the States as the curtain falls ("Johnny's Homecoming: Reminiscence").

The themes of this sequence recall the drawings of Otto Dix and George Grosz, two artists Weill knew through his time in the *Novembergruppe*. Weill and Grosz moved in the same circles in Berlin, as the artist, like the composer, collaborated with George Kaiser and Ivan Goll.[49] Grosz's *Maul halten und weiter dienen* ("Shut Up and Carry On," 1910) depicts a crucified Christ in combat boots and a gas mask, evoking an image similar to the sniper Johann hiding in a statue of Christ in *Johnny Johnson*.[50] The collusion of corrupt government, military, and medical establishments evident

---

[48] Green and Weill, *Johnny Johnson*, ed. Carter, 274.
[49] Willett, *Art and Politics in the Weimar Period*, 85.
[50] Plumb, *Neue Sachlichkeit, 1918–1933*, 95.

in this sequence (which is preceded by Johnny in a hospital room) might hearken back to Grosz's *Kriegsverwendungsfähig* ("Fit for active service," 1918, Figure 2.1), which depicts a doctor proclaiming a skeleton fit for duty, observed by German officials.

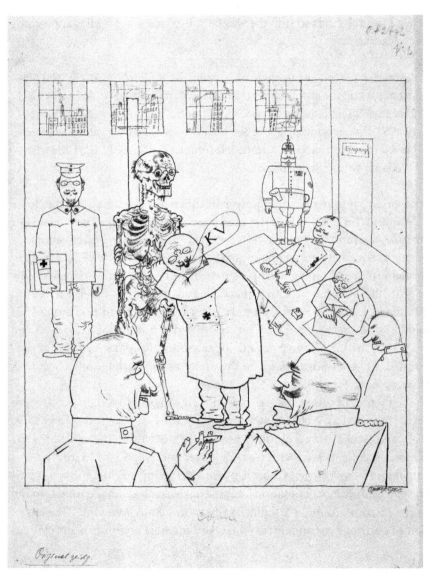

**Figure 2.1** George Grosz, "Fit for Active Service" (Kriegsverwendungsfähig) (1918). Ink on Paper, 20" × 14 3/8". A Conger Goodyear Fund. © VAGA at ARS, NY. Digital Image © The Museum of Modern Art/Licensed by SCALA/Art Resource, NY.

The sequence includes a great deal of music and action, but very little dialogue, suggesting Green may have had in mind Granowsky's "symphonic drama." The use of projections to depict the battle recalls Piscator's (and Brecht's) similar use of film, and the overlapping recitation in "In the Time of War and Tumults" of a sermon in German and English might have been inspired by a famous moment in Piscator's production of *Rasputin* (1927), in which the kaiser, the tzar, and the emperor of Austria recite nearly identical speeches simultaneously to emphasize their sameness, despite being political enemies.[51] Strasberg was certainly familiar with the technique from *Clyde Griffiths*. Willard Keefe of the *Washington Post* excoriated the politics of the production but praised unique staging; in a moment of "extraordinary penetration and power," the trial scene depicted "On the one side of the stage the laboring masses [that Clyde] deserted yell for his head. Opposite, in more cultured tones, the monied masters he strove to join upraise the same cry."[52]

The entire end-of-act sequence, from the comic scene with the generals to the tragedy of the battle and its aftermath, illustrates what Weill and the Group were trying to accomplish, and why it did not always work. While the comedy of the previous sequence with the drugged generals vanishes in the middle of "The Battle," other end-of-act conventions of Broadway shows still operate, including the reprise of several earlier numbers; snatches of "Democracy Advancing," "The Song of the Goddess," and the melody that becomes "Johnny's Song" are all present. Weill and Green, both well-versed in Brecht's notions of "estrangement," likely intended the sequence to be a de-familiarized version of the conventional end-of-act number, turning something comforting and predictable into something strange and disturbing (although they tried to elicit an emotional response, which is antithetical to Brecht's style of epic theatre). But critical reaction to this sequence shows that it misfired, illuminating some of the ways the paradigms clashed. Stirling Bowen called the scene "awkwardly out of key and comparatively pointless."[53] While U.S. audiences exposed to O'Neill and others may have been used to rapid changes of scene, the sudden shifts in emotional register proved more difficult to process. But epic theatre relies on "awkward" shifts of tone and strange juxtapositions of ideas to keep audiences in a critical frame of mind. Although Weill, unlike Brecht, often wanted audiences to empathize with his characters,

[51] Christopher Innes, "Piscator's *Rasputin*," *Drama Review* 22, no. 4 (1978): 93.
[52] Willard Keefe, "Group Theater Is Flayed for Warping Story," *Washington Post*, 29 March 1936, AA1.
[53] Bowen, "The Theatre," 13.

in his German works, he often juxtaposed tragic and comic moments in order to jolt audiences out of emotional complacency, a strategy that did not work as well in the United States. Brooks Atkinson also singled out this sequence as particularly jarring and weak, observing that "*Johnny Johnson* breaks away into confusion when Mr. Green pushes his theme too far into fantasy—in the scene with the high command, for example, when Johnny leaves the sphere of the natural man and becomes a world savior."[54] But because Green hoped that the everyman figure would eventually redeem the world, the power of *Johnny Johnson* relies on the title character becoming that "world savior." The blend of fantasy, symbol, and realism—common in straight plays—did not work in the context of the musical.

While *Johnny Johnson* was only a modest success at best for Weill, it proved crucial to advancing his career. The show convinced critics like Atkinson that Weill had the potential to push the boundaries of the Broadway musical, even if they agreed that *Johnny Johnson* was a flawed experiment. More importantly, in the short term, Weill made professional connections that allowed him to get his foot in the door of American show business. Although he abandoned several other projects with both the Group and the Federal Theatre Project, he used those connections to find other more satisfying and lucrative opportunities. His first step after *Johnny Johnson* was to try his luck in Hollywood.

## Weill Goes West

Like many European immigrants of the 1930s, Weill hoped to find work in the film industry. He had several reasons to be optimistic about his chances. By 1937, the film industry was already transnational; in the early 1920s, major Hollywood studios began "talent raids" of Europe, luring away the biggest stars and directors to maintain their dominance in the international film market.[55] While the advent of sound film made it difficult for foreign actors to find work, German-speaking directors such as Ernst Lubitsch, Willem Dieterle, and (briefly) F.W. Murnau flourished, and formed the core of a continental community that already existed when Weill immigrated.

[54] Atkinson, "The Play," 26.
[55] Gerd Gemünden, *Continental Strangers: German Exile Cinema, 1933–1951* (New York: Columbia University Press, 2014) 5.

Furthermore, by the 1930s the film industry was home to a strong Popular Front presence.[56]

Soon after he left Germany, Weill considered coming to the United States to work with Josef von Sternberg and Marlene Dietrich in Hollywood. On 4 March 1934, while he was still in France working on *Der Kuhhandel*, he wrote to Lenya, "I think one can only say yes to this, no? Sternberg and Marlene and six months of work—that doesn't come up often."[57] But just over week later, the opportunity vanished. On 13 March, Weill wrote Lenya, "I'm afraid this beautiful project has gone the way of all flesh," and "I thought they were using those tactics to keep me hanging. But now, after a week without news, I believe the whole thing has fallen through."[58] Weill's time on the West Coast was marked with all the hope, disappointment, bewilderment, and ego that he expressed to Lenya. In the end, he only composed three original commercial movie scores: *The River is Blue* (1937; unused), *You and Me* (1938), and *Where Do We Go from Here?* (1945). He also composed one noncommercial film, *Salute to France* (1944), as part of the war effort. Three of his musicals were also adapted for film—*Lady in the Dark* (1944), *Knickerbocker Holiday* (1944), and *One Touch of Venus* (1948)—but they left him frustrated.

Still, like many immigrants, Weill was also well paid for his efforts on the West Coast, even if his products were left on the cutting-room floor. His initial contact with Hollywood came through the Group Theatre. Although his score for the resulting film was not used, Weill was paid $7,500 for his efforts.[59] After internal strife tore the Group apart, Weill collaborated with German director Fritz Lang on *You and Me*, for which he earned $10,000.[60] In contrast, Weill earned only about $3,168 from his annual stipend from his publisher Heugel until 1936, and the royalties from *The Eternal Road* came to $3,474.71 for the first month and never reached that peak again. Weill's multiple letters to the financial team in charge of that project indicate that he may never have received a substantial portion of his money, or may not have received any at all.[61]

---

[56] Saverio Giovacchini, *Hollywood Modernism: Film and Politics in the Age of the New Deal* (Philadelphia: Temple University Press, 2001), 10ff.

[57] *W-LL(e)*, 115.

[58] *W-LL(e)*, 120.

[59] Sarah Whitfield, "Kurt Weill: The 'Composer as Dramatist' in American Musical Theatre Production" (PhD diss., Queen Mary, University of London, 2010), 166.

[60] *W-LL(e)*, 237.

[61] Whitfield, "Kurt Weill," 148, 152.

Weill first arrived in Hollywood as part of a subset of the Group Theatre who, after the financial failure of *Johnny Johnson*, went to the West Coast to try to recoup their losses (and to solve some of personal troubles that had plagued them).[62] Harold Clurman struck a deal with independent producer Walter Wanger to cast members of the company in a film about the Spanish Civil War. Clifford Odets was to write the script, Weill was to compose the score, and Lewis Milestone was to direct. Odets finished his draft of the film, called *Castles in Spain* and then *The River is Blue*, and Weill produced a complete piano score, but Odets and Milestone then left the project, and Wanger decided that Werner Janssen was better suited to score the new film, which was eventually released as *Blockade* in 1938. Weill, frustrated with the internal politics of the Group and Wanger, turned to his fellow immigrants for his next Hollywood effort, eventually finding a collaborator in Fritz Lang.

Lang frequently claimed that he had become so famous that in 1933 Joseph Goebbels invited him to take over the German film industry and offered Lang the title of "honorary Aryan," which Lang refused, leaving for France the next day. In reality his departure was carefully planned, and driven mostly by the financial lure of Paris.[63] After making one film in French (*Liliom*, 1934), he came to the United States on an invitation from David O. Selznick.[64] Once in Hollywood, Lang began directing stories about the nature of law and order with a trilogy of "social problem" films, each with a different studio, and each starring Sylvia Sidney.

The social problem film arose in 1934 after the Motion Picture Association of America began strictly to enforce the Production Code, making it difficult to produce the politically minded gangster films like *Little Caesar* (1931), *The Public Enemy* (1931), and *Scarface* (1932). While Hollywood progressives argued that these films revealed the seedy underbelly of capitalism, the office of the Production Code insisted they glamorized an immoral lifestyle. In response, the same actors, directors, and writers channeled their consciences into movies about the failures of the justice system and the oppressive effects of poverty and unemployment.[65] Lang was relatively happy

---

[62] The following account of Weill's early Hollywood career and his work on *The River is Blue* is taken from Naomi Graber, "Kurt Weill's *The River is Blue*: 'Film-Opera' and Politics in 1930s Hollywood," *Journal of the Society for American Music* 11, no. 3 (2017): 317–23.

[63] Tom Gunning, *The Films of Fritz Lang: Allegories of Vision and Modernity* (London: British Film Institute, 2000), 8–10.

[64] Anton Kaes, "A Stranger in the House: Fritz Lang's *Fury* and the Cinema of Exile," *New German Critique* 89 (2003): 39.

[65] Guiliana Muscio, *Hollywood's New Deal* (Philadelphia: Temple University Press, 1997), 71.

with his first social problem film, *Fury* (1936), but was dismayed that MGM pressured him into changing the ending. He intended to end with an impassioned speech about the nature of justice, but the studio insisted on a kiss between the romantic leads.[66] Lang switched to Wanger's independent studio for *You Only Live Once* (1937), but disliked Alfred Newman's score, which he thought was too romantic for his gritty story.[67] Wanger, meanwhile, had become an admirer of Mussolini, so Lang went to Paramount for *You and Me*.[68]

The story of *You and Me* originated in 1936 as script for a romantic comedy by Norman Krasna (the author of the original script for *Fury*). Two former convicts who work as department store clerks, Joe and Helen, fall in love and marry. Joe tells Helen about his time in prison, but Helen keeps her previous incarceration a secret. Eventually, Joe finds out and leaves her, but on the day their baby is born, the pair reconcile. Krasna wrote two screenplays based on this story, one completed on 25 August 1936, and a revised version completed on 13 January 1937.[69] Originally, George Wallace was slated to direct George Raft and Carol Lombard, but Wallace and Lombard dropped the project, so producer B.P. Schulberg invited Sidney.[70] Sidney suggested Lang as director, and Lang brought Weill onto the project.[71] At first glance, Lang and Weill were well-matched. Lang drew on Brechtian theatre for his German film, *M* (1931), especially in the casting of Peter Lorre, whom Brecht held up as an example of the epic style of acting.[72] Lang was also interested in adapting Brecht's theories of music and theatre to film, making Weill the natural choice for the score. Both hoped to speak to contemporary audiences; Lang told the *New York Herald Tribune* that he thought of cinema as a "means of conveying social messages" which could depict "people of today and the things that interest them or imprison them."[73] They also shared an interest in

[66] Gunning, *The Films of Fritz Lang*, 233–34.

[67] Gunning, *The Films of Fritz Lang*, 258.

[68] Charles Higham and Joel Greenberg, "Interview with Fritz Lang" (1969), reprinted in *Fritz Lang Interviews*, ed. Barry Keith Grant (Jackson: University of Mississippi Press, 2003), 105.

[69] These two screenplays, as well as all other drafts of the script for *You and Me*, survive in Paramount Pictures Scripts, Margaret Herrick Library, Academy of Motion Picture Arts and Sciences, Beverly Hills, CA, Series "Production Files."

[70] James Robert Parish with Steven Whitney, *The George Raft File: The Unauthorized Biography* (New York: Drake Publishers, 1973), 110–11.

[71] Nick Smedley, *A Divided World: Hollywood Cinema and Émigré Directors in the Era of Roosevelt* (Bristol, UK: Intellectual, 2011), 104.

[72] Gunning, *The Films of Fritz Lang*, 170, 181; Bertolt Brecht, "The Question of Criteria for Judging Acting" (1931), trans. in John Willett, ed. *Brecht on Theatre: The Development of an Aesthetic* (New York: Hill and Wang, 1957), 54–55.

[73] Quoted in Smedley, *A Divided World*, 92. See also Thomas Elsaesser, *Weimar Cinema and After: Germany's Historical Imaginary* (London: Routledge, 2000), 148.

the images, personas, and narratives of pulp fiction.[74] Lang also had an eye for fantasy, something Weill complained that Lewis Milestone (the initial director of *The River is Blue*) lacked.[75]

The first hint of a collaboration between Weill and Lang appeared on 17 April 1937, just as Weill began to doubt the viability of the Group's Spanish Civil War project. He told Lenya that he was beginning to lose faith in Hollywood, although he had the prospect of one intriguing project with Lang, "which would not be uninteresting."[76] Meanwhile, Lang collaborated with Virginia van Upp and Jack Moffit to write a darker version of the Krasna script, though neither Lang nor Moffit ultimately received screen credit.[77] This script included songs for Weill, with lyrics by Johnny Burke and Sam Coslow. This version, dated 12 December 1937, probably served as the initial shooting script given that it mostly matches the shooting schedule.[78]

Weill left Hollywood the following June to work on two projects for the Federal Theatre Project (*The Common Glory* and *One Man from Tennessee*), returning in December to honor his contract with Lang. During this trip, Weill composed most of the music for *You and Me*, and even recorded some of it, including the "Knocking Song,"[79] which was conceived by music supervisor Phil Boutelje (though Weill wrote the music).[80] He left for New York again in February 1938 (earlier than planned) to begin work on *Knickerbocker Holiday*, returning to Hollywood in April 1938 to oversee the rest of the recording, departing again in late May, leaving Lang to oversee the final revisions of the score.[81]

The collaboration was not a happy one. Weill accused Morros and Lang of "trying to twist things so that someone else would collaborate on the *score*, because time is so short. [. . .] The whole thing is so deeply immoral and vicious that it's impossible to retain any enthusiasm." He did add, however, that "the movie could turn out to be very good."[82] He also wrote that he enjoyed the recording process, despite personal frustrations. Lang resented

---

[74] Elsasser, *Weimar Cinema and After*, 149, 159.

[75] *W-LL(e)*, 204.

[76] *W-LL(e)*, 233.

[77] Smedley, *A Divided World*, 104.

[78] Fragments of the shooting schedule survive in FLP, Box 8 Folders 52 and 54.

[79] Boris Morros to Weill, 15 February 1938, WLA, Box 48 Folder 49.

[80] Lyrics for "Knocking Song," undated, FLP, Box 8 Folder 54. The sequence may have been inspired by the final scene of Ernst Toller's *Hoppla! Such is Life!*, which also features prisoners using a knocking language to communicate the death of a fellow inmate.

[81] Ralph W. Nelson to Fritz Lang, 2 February 1938, FLP, Box 8 Folder 53.

[82] *WLL(e)*, 258, emphasis in the original.

Weill for leaving, telling interviewers in 1969, "Weill left me in a lurch by going to New York where he had an offer to work with the Spewacks" (referring to *The Opera from Mannheim*, another unfinished project from the late 1930s).[83] In fact, Weill did not get along with West Coast immigrant communities in general.[84] During his time in Hollywood, Weill attended parties and salons with other immigrants, but he complained at length about the company in his correspondence with Lenya. After a concert by Otto Klemperer, Weill wrote, "In the greenroom with Klemperer was the wunderkind [Erich Wolfgang] Korngold grown old. I put on my haughtiest face and stayed for only two minutes. All of them are abundantly disgusting."[85] He spoke similarly of Salka and Bertold Viertel, whose home became a hub for the immigrant community. After his first party, he told Lenya, "He's an old fool, and she's a horrible witch. They won't see me again soon."[86]

Weill's disdain for this community may have had several roots. He was younger than the major figures of the German Los Angeles enclave (twenty-six years younger than Arnold Schoenberg, fifteen than Klemperer, and ten than Fritz Lang). The artistic products of this older generation in many ways represented the art Weill rebelled against; for example, even in Germany he had spoken out against Lang's *Metropolis* (1927) as a "superficial" attempt at topicality that still "holds meticulously to ideologies of past eras."[87] The younger Hollywood immigrants such as Korngold also wrote in a musical language Weill considered old-fashioned. As part of a younger generation, Weill may have also found it easier to adapt to the United States than his elders, and was impatient with their insistence European social customs.

The final film, released on 3 June 1938, stars Sylvia Sidney and George Raft as Helen and Joe Dennis, who work in a department store owned by Mr. Morris, a man who hires paroled convicts as a public service. They fall in love, but Helen's parole conditions prohibit marriage. Without telling either her parole officer or Joe, she marries anyway. Joe discovers her deception, leaves her, and returns to his criminal ways. However, just as he is about to rob Morris, Helen returns to explain to her estranged husband and his gang that crime does not pay, literally. Complete with blackboard and chalk, she breaks down the math of criminal activity, proving that legitimate employment is a

---

[83] Higham and Greenberg, "Interview with Fritz Lang," 105.

[84] Michael H. Kater, *Composers of the Nazi Era: Eight Portraits* (Oxford, UK: Oxford University Press, 2000), 66–67.

[85] *W-LL(e)*, 209.

[86] *W-LL(e)*, 205.

[87] Kurt Weill "Topical Theatre" (1929), trans. in *KWiE*, 511.

**Table 2.1**  Songs Weill composed for *You and Me*

| Song title | Alternate title | Lyricist |
| --- | --- | --- |
| Knocking Song[a] | Five Years Ain't So Long Knocking Scene | Sam Coslow |
| Romance of a Lifetime | — | Sam Coslow |
| Barbershop Quartet | — | Sam Coslow |
| The Right Guy[a] | — | Sam Coslow |
| The Song of the Lie[b] | — | Johnny Burke |
| Song of the Cash Register[a] | You Can't Get Something for Nothing | Sam Coslow |
| We're the Kind of People Who Sing Lullabies[b] | — | Johnny Burke |
| You Cannot Buy Love[c] | — | Unknown |
| Too Much to Dream | — | Sam Coslow |

[a] Appears in the final film.

[b] Does not appear in the final film, but was copied by the studio.

[c] The first page of this song is lost, so the original title and lyricist are unknown.

better path to wealth. Believing she has lost Joe forever, Helen disappears, but Joe tracks her down just as she is giving birth to their child, and all ends well. The plot is punctuated by expressionist montages accompanied by Weill's songs. "The Song of the Cash Register" opens the film, followed by "The Right Guy," during Helen and Joe's courtship in a nightclub. "The Knocking Song" plays over a flashback sequence of Joe and his gang in jail.

Although the film contains only three songs, Weill wrote nine in total (see Table 2.1), along with a several ideas for the underscore.[88] Some of the songs were clearly written to replace others. "You Cannot Buy Love," was likely replaced by "The Song of the Cash Register," given that they both concern what money can and cannot buy. Likewise, "Romance of a Lifetime" and the "Barbershop Quartet" may have been contenders for the slot eventually filled by "The Right Guy"—all three are romantic numbers that would be at home in the nightclub scene. "We're the Kind of People Who Sing Lullabies" was intended for Helen to sing after Joe leaves her, but was cut because Sidney did

[88] The music for *You and Me* survives in WLA, Box 33 Folders 457–59. Folder 457 is dedicated to several versions and sketches of the "Knocking Song" and "The Right Guy," well as the only complete copies of "The Barbershop Quartet," "Romance of a Lifetime," and a "Gigaboo" (probably meant as underscore for the nightclub scene). Folder 458 contains studio copies of the conductor's score, as well as the published version of "The Right Guy." Folder 459 contains sketches, as well as the music for "Too Much to Dream," and "You Cannot Buy Love." The cue sheet is in this final folder.

not want to sing.[89] "The Song of the Lie" (discussed in more detail later in this chapter) was filmed, but cut after the 18 May preview, possibly because Lang did not have the budget or time to re-edit the sequence to his satisfaction.[90] It is unclear where "Too Much to Dream" would have fit into the film.

The mix of gangster melodrama, romantic comedy, and German expressionism left critics befuddled and confused. Frank Nugent wrote that the film was "remarkably bad."[91] Initially, George Antheil expressed excitement for the film, writing in *Modern Music*, "What I've heard is in Weill's best style and if it's not barbarously cut upon the dubbing stage it will certainly prove a sensation in Hollywood and, very possibly, pave the way to better things for all composers."[92] But upon the film's release, he wrote, "I must register my keen disappointment with Kurt Weill's *You and Me*. This picture score I heard in part before production was completed and had 'gone out upon a limb for.' But the ultimate dubbing made it a drab affair indeed."[93] Weill, for his part, was deep into work on *Knickerbocker Holiday* by the time *You and Me* came out, and had all but disavowed the project.

## Expressionist-Gangster-Musical-Lehrstück

Like *Johnny Johnson*, *You and Me* draws on several different paradigms, some rooted in German film and some in Hollywood. It shares several themes with Lang's social problem films and the gangster melodramas of the early 1930s: the lure of crime, the closeness of criminal "families," and the justice system's lack of respect for its subjects. But the film is also interrupted with songs in the manner of a musical. *You and Me* opens with "The Song of the Cash Register" intoning, "You cannot get something for nothing," as the camera lovingly pans over all the things that money can buy: luxury, beauty, and so on. Later, as Joe and Helen watch a nightclub singer perform "The Right Guy," the scene shifts to a hazy depiction of the "waterfront dive, full of wretches and vagabonds" described in the song's opening, while Helen

---

[89] Roy Fjasted to Fred Leahy, 5 January 1938, FLP, Box 8 Folder 5.

[90] The scene appears on the fragments of shooting schedules cited earlier, but not in the final version of the film. See also "Cutting, Dubbing, and Printing Schedule," and letter from Boris Morros to Evelyn Winters, 6 June 1938, both FLP, Box 8 Folder 53.

[91] Frank S. Nugent, "The Screen in Review," *NYT*, 2 June 1938, 19.

[92] George Antheil, "On the Hollywood Front," *Modern Music* 15, no. 2 (January–February 1938): 117.

[93] George Antheil, "On the Hollywood Front," *Modern Music* 16, no. 1 (November–December 1938): 63.

ponders how the lyrics reflects her feelings for Joe: "They call him 'good for nothing' / He isn't much to see / But I've a funny feeling / He's the right guy for me."[94] "The Knocking Song" plays as Joe's criminal gang reminisce about the knocking language they used to communicate in prison. All three of these sequences draw on German expressionist cinematography; chiaroscuro lighting, composite shots, and distorted imagery echo the German expressionist technique of interweaving realistic sequences with more stylized scenes.[95] The film also resembles a Brechtian *Lehrstück* in the sequence in which Helen breaks down the math of crime versus honest money, methodically walking her "students" through the maxim that "crime doesn't pay."

Indeed, the overall structure of *You and Me* particularly resembles *Kuhle Wampe* (1932), with a screenplay by Brecht and music by Hanns Eisler. Both films are presented as straightforward "boy meets girl, boy loses girl, boy gets girl back" stories, interrupted by non-narrative montages that comment on the story or illuminate character motivations. Musical underscoring is mostly present in the montages only, enhancing the atmosphere of strangeness and fantasy in these moments. Both films also end with a long didactic sequence that stylistically breaks with the rest of the film. In *Kuhle Wampe* this is the scene on a train (directed by Brecht himself) in which characters of different classes debate the price of coffee, which is equivalent to Helen's lesson.

In *You and Me*, Weill put into practice some of the ideas he had developed in Germany regarding film music. In 1927, Weill wrote that film music should not be "illustrative," a term Weill associated with the Wagnerian practice of using music as leitmotives to stir the emotions and reinforce the plot. Rather, he argued, "We need an objective [*sachliche*], almost concert-like film music," aligning himself with the *Neue Sachlichkeit* impulse.[96] By that, Weill meant that the music should not function as a representation of a character's psychological state ("subjective" music), but should provide

---

[94] This song was published as sheet music and sold to promote the film. Lenya incorporated it into her nightclub act, but it never became popular.

[95] The term "expressionism" as applied to Weimar-era cinema is somewhat contentious. For a summary of the debates around this issue, see Dietrich Scheunemann, "Activating the Differences: Expressionist Film and Early Weimar Cinema," in *Expressionist Film: New Perspectives*, ed. Dietrich Scheunemann (Rochester, NY: Camden House, 2003), 1–32. However, given that U.S. audiences understood "expressionism" to be synonymous with "German" where film was concerned, I use the term in regard to *You and Me*.

[96] Kurt Weill, "Musikalische Illustration oder Filmmusik" (1927), in *GS2*, 438. On Weill's use of the term "illustrative" and its Wagnerian connotations in his writing, see Graber, "Kurt Weill's *The River is Blue*," 346–47.

more information about the situation, or should move the narrative forward (an idea he also applied to stage music).[97] To accomplish those goals, he suggested that "in musical talkies, not only can the characters sing, but also their environment: the objects in his room, the house, the city, the animals."[98] Weill's idea was not original; German legends and literature are rife with inanimate objects come to life (the Golem and clockwork doppelgangers in E.T.A. Hoffmann's stories) and sets that seem to have a personality, tropes which carried over to cinema.[99] Weill himself had also already employed this idea; in *Der Lindberghflug* (1929), the clouds and the fog try to lull Lindberg to sleep with a lullaby, and in *Johnny Johnson* with the "Song of the Guns" and "Song of the Goddess." *You and Me* gave Weill his first chance to employ this technique in film.

Comparing a moment in Lang's *Metropolis* (1927) to the opening of *You and Me* shows how Weill translated Lang's expressionist themes and imagery into music. Both *Metropolis* and *You and Me* explore humanity's relationship to machines, imbuing physical objects with uncanny life, illuminating the social forces acting on characters. *Metropolis* depicts the rise of technology interfering with the development of human intellect, as workers become either human sacrifices to machines, or little more than machines themselves. When the young patrician Freder stumbles into the undercity, he is horrified to find workers mechanically slaving away at their industrial jobs. When one of the machines explodes, Freder momentarily sees the contraption as the demon Moloch gobbling up workers. Thus, Lang anthropomorphizes an intimate object to make a political point, illustrating the character's internal struggle in external, visual terms.

The opening of *You and Me* employs the same technique, but with music instead of image. "The Song of the Cash Register" gives a voice and personality to the machine that controls the lives of the characters. This may not have been obvious to the audience since the title of the song does not appear in the film, but the shots of the cash register scattered throughout the sequence cement the association between the tune and machine. Later in the film, this musical connection allows the cash register to speak to the characters. After

---

[97] Here, he echoes some of the ideas put forward by Hanns Eisler and Theodor Adorno in *Composing for the Films*. See Sally Bick, *Unsettled Scores: Politics, Hollywood, and the Film Music of Aaron Copland and Hanns Eisler* (Urbana: University of Illinois Press, 2019), Kindle Edition.

[98] Weill, "Tonfilm, Opernfilm, Filmoper" (1930), in *GS2*, 112.

[99] Lotte Eisner, *The Haunted Screen: Expressionism in the German Cinema and the Influence of Max Reinhardt* (1952), trans. Roger Greaves (repr. Berkeley: University of California Press, 1973), 40, 101–9.

**Example 2.1** *You and Me,* "Song of the Lie."

Helen convinces the gang to abandon their lives of crime, a humbled Joe is left alone in the darkened department store. Determined to repair his relationship with Helen, he takes a bottle of perfume and starts out the door. But his flashlight falls on the cash register as music of the opening line of "The Song of the Cash Register" ("You cannot get something for nothing") sounds in the underscore. As if hearing the cash register's siren song, Joe realizes he must pay for the perfume, and the music takes a heroic turn as the character proudly completes his purchase.

In their original concept, Weill and Lang hoped to have other intimate objects comment on the ethics of the character's decisions. In a sequence that was later cut, Helen and Joe would take the subway to the "information bureau" in search of the procedure on quick marriages. During the ride, Joe would reveal to Helen that he thought of that moment as the start of a new life, while she tried to temper his expectations without revealing her secret. Shots of the subway were interspersed with the conversation, and "The Song of the Lie" (Example 2.1) was to play on the soundtrack:[100]

---

[100] According to the recording schedule, Marsha Hunt recorded the track for the film. "Recording Schedule," 5 May 1938, FLP, Box 8 Folder 52.

B-24 INSERT – THE ROLLING WHEELS
(*Over the rattling of the wheels and over the music we hear a voice—THE VOICE OF HELEN'S CONSCIENCE.*)

THE VOICE (*Sings the* "Song of the Lie"): What are you doing?
What are you doing?
With every word you speak

B-25 CLOSE-UP – HELEN LISTENING TO THE VOICE OF HER CONSCIENCE

Are you sincere?
Are you betraying
Someone who's praying?[101]

According to the screenplay, as mentioned, the song would have reappeared at key moments in the drama: a scene (later cut) at the information bureau in which Joe asks about quick marriages, and later when Joe draws out Helen's secret. Weill's setting, with its insistent, repeated-note triplet figure, reinforces the urgency of the situation. Here, the train becomes a literalized version of Helen's "train of thought," just as the cash register becomes the voice of Joe's conscience in the final scene.

These ideas and techniques owe much to Brecht, whose influence is more obvious in the original shooting script, which echoes *Die Dreigroschenoper* in implying that capitalism amounts to nothing more than organized theft, so one might as well participate in the legal institutions.[102] The shooting script makes clear that Mr. Morris (the head of the department store) and Mickey (the lead gangster) are equivalent figures. Originally, Mickey was introduced in his hideout, where he and his gang are running a department store of stolen goods:

MICKEY (*turns around*): Did they pay off?
BATH HOUSE (*Approaching the table he hands him a check.*): Sure. They want anything you got. Auto parts—clothes—canned goods—anything—
(*as Knucks passes by*) He better hurry up with them cans. They want to re-label them tonight.[103]

---

[101] Virginia Van Upp, *You and Me*, Paramount Pictures Scripts, Margaret Herrick Library, Academy of Motion Picture Arts and Sciences, Beverly Hills, CA, Series "Production Files," B-7-9.
[102] Smedley, *A Divided World*, 105.
[103] Van Upp, *You and Me*, D-1–2.

But the scenes which depict Mickey as the "bad" capitalist were cut before shooting began, and this facet of the script was mostly lost. A remnant of this theme remains in Helen's final monologue, when reminds the criminals, "There's always a boss on any job; you've simply traded Mr. Morris for another boss. But this one doesn't pay your wages in advance and get his profit afterward. This one takes his profits first, and you get what's left to divvy up among you." But the way the film stands, Helen's lesson only proves that the New Deal system (represented by Morris) is much better for the store employees than a life of crime. By cutting the scenes in which Mickey is clearly Morris's corrupt double, this subtlety is lost.

The self-consciously "arty" quality of You and Me likely did the film no favors. In the German-speaking world, anxieties over the place of film in the new media landscape ran high, as some filmmakers aspired to the status of "art," even as the new medium became increasingly integrated into mass consumer culture.[104] In this context, expressionist montages highlight the artificiality of standard continuity editing, and allowed the audience moments of contemplation.[105] But in Hollywood, narrative rather than image was king, and the desire to elevate film into the realm of highbrow art was not nearly as strong. Successful politically minded filmmakers (Frank Capra and Willem Dieterle for example) more seamlessly integrated commentary into film through narrative cohesion, which meant audiences did not know what to make of the strange "arty" moments of You and Me.

Understandably, this mix of genres, styles, and morals only left audiences confused, and many of the themes described previously emerge in the reviews. An anonymous reviewer from the New Yorker wrote that "to describe it as simply as possible, it is a naïve morality play with impressionistic Teutonic overtones by Fritz Lang and Kurt Weill."[106] The Variety reviewer opined "Lang tries to blend dramatic music with melodramatic action more than heretofore. It's a sort of Mercury theatre, by way of Marc Blitzstein–Orson Welles, with European flavoring, also. However, it's rather confusing."[107] As with Johnny Johnson, Weill and his collaborators miscalculated, asking audiences who were unused to radical shifts of mood and register to process many different styles. While German audiences, familiar with

---

[104] Elsaesser, Weimar Cinema and After, 64.
[105] Elsaesser, Weimar Cinema and After, 160.
[106] "The Current Cinema," New Yorker, 11 June 1938, 62.
[107] "You and Me," Variety, 8 June 1938, clipping available in Core Collection, Margaret Herrick Library, Academy of Motion Picture Arts and Sciences, Beverly Hills, CA, Folder "You and Me."

Brechtian irony or Kaiser's sudden shifts of tone, may have been better prepared to follow the arguments and ideas of both, U.S. audiences were left scratching their heads in both cases.

Weill never gave up on Hollywood; as late as 1946, he wrote that film was the future of musical theatre in America.[108] But even though he held out hope, he never achieved his goals of revolutionizing the musical film. This hope may have been doomed from the start given that Weill never committed fully to the film industry. Even while he was in Los Angeles, Weill maintained his relationship with the New York Popular Front theatre community, returning periodically to work on other projects. As he was working in Hollywood, he collaborated with Columbia University–based poet and playwright H.R. Hays, the pageant-maker Edward Hungerford, and most importantly, the celebrated mainstream playwright Maxwell Anderson. Overall, New York seemed to be a better fit for him, both professionally and aesthetically.

While *Johnny Johnson* and *You and Me* are very different, they share many of the same problems. In both, experimental theatrical or filmic traditions interrupt American melodramatic or slapstick moments. But Weill also learned that some aspects of thought and style were easier to transfer and translate. *Johnny Johnson* was Weill's first experiment with the "marriage trope," where a couple's issues mirror or become a metaphor for broader societal problems. Weill often used music to tell stories of individuals suffering under unjust economic circumstances or the rule of tyrannical governments. Beginning with *Johnny Johnson*, he adopted the American practice of telling that story using romantic metaphors. The businessman–everyman romantic rivalry that Weill first explored in *Johnny Johnson* appears in many of his later works, including *One Man from Tennessee, Knickerbocker Holiday, Down in the Valley*, and *Street Scene*. Weill also learned that much of his previous musical and visual language did not transfer well, but that formal principles could be adaptable. Both *Lady and the Dark* and *Love Life* are formally similar to *You and Me*, with non-narrative musical sequences interrupting the main story to provide commentary or clarify character motivation. The difference lies in the nature of those sequences. The interruptions of *You and Me* took the form of expressionist montages, but in *Lady in the Dark* and *Love Life* they draw from classic American vaudeville acts and theatrical

---

[108] Kurt Weill, "Music in the Movies," *Harper's Bazaar* 80, no. 9 (1946): available at https://www.kwf.org/pages/wt-music-in-the-movies.html.

traditions, and so were easier for audiences to understand. For Weill, form generally followed function, and so as he continued to search for his place in the U.S. theatre world, he abandoned the elements of his style that worked against his ultimate purpose: using musical theatre to speak to contemporary audiences about issues that mattered.

# 3

# For the People

## Folk music

Despite his lack of mainstream success, Weill was in a fairly good professional position by early 1937. Although *The Eternal Road* languished in financial troubles and the Group Theatre production of *Johnny Johnson* (1936) only played thirty-six performances, the latter had caught the attention of the Federal Theatre Project (FTP), which mounted successful versions in Los Angeles and Boston in May 1937.[1] Like the Group, the FTP was one of the many organizations that comprised part of the Popular Front, the loose bloc of politicians, artists, and intellectuals that drove a turn toward Leftist populism in the second half of the 1930s.

The Leftist turn in the mainstream accompanied an ideological shift "from a vanguard proletariat to an indigenous peoples' culture," as historian Robert Cantwell writes.[2] In 1935, Kenneth Burke called on the American Writer's Congress to replace the symbol of "the worker" in communist writing with the symbol of "the people." He argued that "the people" was a positive symbol that incorporated the ideal of a classless society, as opposed to the worker, a negative symbol which appealed only to sympathy.[3] Like the narrator of John La Touche and Earle Robinson's radio cantata *Ballad for Americans* (1939), the everyman represented the "everybody who's nobody" and the "nobody who's everybody."[4] During this period, historical figures, as well, were often

---

[1] Introduction to Paul Green and Kurt Weill, *Johnny Johnson: A Play with Music in Three Acts*, ed. Tim Carter, KWE, Series I, Volume 13 (New York: Kurt Weill Foundation/European American Music Corporation, 2012), 20–23.

[2] Robert Cantwell, *When We Were Good: The Folk Revival* (Cambridge, MA: Harvard University Press, 1996), 88.

[3] Kenneth Burke, "Revolutionary Symbolism in America: Speech by Kenneth Burke to American Writers' Congress, April 26, 1935," in *The Legacy of Kenneth Burke*, ed. Herman W. Simons and Trevor Melia (Madison: University of Wisconsin Press, 1989), 270; Michael Denning, *The Cultural Front: The Laboring of American Culture in the Twentieth Century* (London: Verso, 1997) 124–28. As Denning observes, "The People" was not a monolithic slogan of the era, but rather a concept that many different political and artistic movements—Left and Right—co-opted for their own ends.

[4] John La Touche, lyrics of "Ballad for Americans," performed by the New York City Labor Chorus, available at http://www.cpsr.cs.uchicago.edu/robeson/links/NYlabor.ballad.lyrics.html.

*Kurt Weill's America.* Naomi Graber, Oxford University Press (2021). © Oxford University Press.
DOI: 10.1093/oso/9780190906580.003.0004

portrayed as down-to-earth and relatively ordinary before they were called to greatness.[5] By 1942, vice president Henry Wallace had declared their epoch "The Century of the Common Man," echoed in Copland's *Fanfare for the Common Man.*[6]

The people and the everyman were represented by folk music. But art music communities were slow to embrace folk song. The center of Leftist compositional thought was the Composer's Collective, an affiliate of the Workers Music League and the Pierre Degeyter Club, which counted Aaron Copland, Charles Seeger, Marc Blitzstein, Elie Siegmeister, and Lehman Engel among its members.[7] Before 1935, such composers sometimes took a condescending tone toward folk music, with Nathan Nevins writing in 1932 that the folk-based songs of the Kentucky miners in the *Red Song Book* (not to be confused with the International Workers of the World's *Little Red Song Book*) were "immature" and "the result of an arrested development" caused by capitalist oppression.[8] Instead, they favored the modernist harmonic language and militant rhythms of Hanns Eisler, whose music many in the Collective saw as model for working-class composition.[9] But later, the Collective embraced both styles. In *Songs of the People*, published by the Collective in 1937, old favorites like Joe Hill's version of the folk ballad "Casey Jones," revised spirituals like "Join the Fight" (originally "Heav'n Boun' Soldier"), and even songs for children like "Old Man Banker Had a Plan" to the tune of "Old McDonald Had a Farm" sit side by side with translations of Eisler's "United Front," "Comintern," and "In Praise of Higher Learning," demonstrating that these composers had not abandoned their vision, but rather had opened up to mixing (or at least juxtaposing) the popular, the folk, and the modernist.

Although Weill was not part of the collective, he was influenced directly and indirectly by many who were, especially his friend Lehmen Engel. For Weill, folk music, ostensibly the music of "the people," posed increasingly interesting possibilities for American musical theatre, which he explored in

[5] Alfred Haworth Jones, "The Search for a Usable American Past in the New Deal Era," *American Quarterly* 23 (1971): 710–24.

[6] Elizabeth B. Crist, *Music for the Common Man: Aaron Copland during the Depression and War* (New York and Oxford, UK: Oxford University Press, 2005), 181–83.

[7] Crist, *Music for the Common Man*, 23.

[8] Quoted in Marc Endsley Johnson, "The Masses Are Singing: Insurgency and Song in New York City, 1929–1941" (PhD diss., City University of New York, 2003), 152; Richard A. Reuss with JoAnne C. Reuss, *American Folk Music and Left-Wing Politics, 1927–1957* (Lanham, MD: Scarecrow, 2000), 46.

[9] Johnson, "The Masses Are Singing," 195–99; Reuss and Reuss, *American Folk Music and Left-Wing Politics*, 48–49.

several arenas throughout his career. In his first years in the United States, he sustained an interest in plebian everyman characters, which first manifested in *Johnny Johnson*. After the success of the FTP's *Johnny Johnson*, Weill began two more projects with the FTP (and contemplated several others) but completed neither. The first was *The Common Glory*, a pageant celebrating the U.S. Constitution with a libretto by Paul Green, but Weill only composed one fragment before abandoning the project. However, Weill nearly finished the second, a biographical musical folk play about the life of Davy Crockett called *One Man from Tennessee* with a text by H.R. Hays (sometimes called *The Ballad of Davy Crockett*). *One Man from Tennessee* used the story of the famous congressman as a fable about the issues facing rural populations during the Great Depression. Both *The Common Glory* and *One Man from Tennessee* are linked to *Johnny Johnson* through their everyman heroes.

Although *One Man from Tennessee* floundered in development, this early encounter with the political uses of U.S. folk culture and folk music had profound implications for two of Weill's most popular works during his lifetime. The first was *Railroads on Parade*, a large-scale pageant about the history of the U.S. railroad industry that played at the 1939 and 1940 World's Fairs in New York. The second was *Down in the Valley*, a chamber opera that Weill wrote for a failed radio venture conceived by Olin Downes and Charles MacArthur in 1945, which he revised for amateur performance in 1948, and which became his most performed work during his lifetime. All three of these works—*One Man from Tennessee, Railroads on Parade*, and *Down in the Valley*—reveal Weill's increasingly sophisticated understanding of the political and aesthetic uses of folk music in the 1930s and 1940s. *One Man from Tennessee* combines the related traditions of the proletarian play and the folk play to draw attention to political crises facing the United States, albeit somewhat clumsily. *Railroads on Parade* shows the influence of a number of folksong-based film documentary scores such as Virgil Thomson's music for Pare Lorentz's *The Plow That Broke the Plains* (1937) and *The River* (1938), even though the pageant itself promoted private industry, while Lorentz and Thomson's films touted the virtues of New Deal public programs. *Down in Valley* returns to Depression-era political populism: Downes, MacArthur, Weill and librettist Arnold Sundgaard envisioned the project as a democratic folk opera that would herald a new age of American composition.

Weill's encounters with U.S. folk music occurred against the nation's shifting conception of its role in the world. In the 1930s, the national gaze remained firmly domestic, but the rise of fascism across the Atlantic became

increasingly difficult to ignore. With the advent of war in 1939, the nation's relationship to events in Europe came to the forefront of public consciousness. Thus *One Man from Tennessee* speaks solely to domestic matters, but *Railroads on Parade*, as part of the 1939–1940 World's Fair, constitutes a demonstration of American exceptionalism in an increasingly turbulent world. In *Down in the Valley*, Weill and his collaborators composed a piece they hoped would shore up those exceptional American values on the home front, but they also had one eye on Europe, as the United States took charge of rebuilding the Old World.

## Man of the People

The Leftist theatrical communities of the 1930s embraced folk music earlier than composers. Playwrights often incorporated folk songs into proletarian plays, including Samuel Ornitz's *In New Kentucky* (1932) and Albert Bein's *Let Freedom Ring* (1933) to emphasize the protagonist's connection to "the people." Folk songs were also a part of the larger folk drama movement that developed in the early 1930s. Led by figures like University of North Carolina professor Frederick Koch (a friend of Paul Green), the folk drama movement sought to depict the "legends, superstitions, customs, environmental vernacular of the common people."[10] Koch implied the genre might have political uses, writing that an appropriate subject might be "the tragic plight of refugees from the Dust Bowl of Texas" or "a tragedy of a copper-mining town of Arizona," among more traditional subjects like Abraham Lincoln, cowboys, outlaws, and even Davy Crockett.[11] The FTP took up this challenge, producing a number of historically minded folk plays, one of which was H.R. Hays's *The Ballad of Davy Crockett* (1936). Hallie Flanagan, in charge of the FTP, hoped to build on its success by making it a full-blown musical with Weill as the composer. The new project was called *One Man from Tennessee*.

*One Man from Tennessee* represents a continuation of Weill's penchant for using folk tales to comment on social and political problems, as he did

---

[10] Frederick H. Koch, "American Folk Drama in the Making," Introduction to *American Folk Plays*, ed. Frederick H. Koch (New York and London: D. Appleton-Century, 1939), xv. The Carolina Playmakers mounted a production of *Johnny Johnson* in October 1937, so he and Weill likely met at some point.

[11] Koch, "American Folk Drama in the Making," xiii.

in *Die Bürgschaft* (1931), which was based on a folk-tale-like parable by Herder, and *Der Silbersee* (1933), which was subtitled "ein Wintermärchen," or "a winter's fairy tale." The project transfers that impulse to a U.S. cultural context, reworking the story of the historical backwoodsman-turned-congressman to tackle the issue of rural homelessness and migration. The subject loomed large in the mind of the Depression-era United States as banks repossessed many of the farms in the South and West. The problem became so widespread that violence erupted in the middle of the country, where Iowa farmers attacked a sheriff and the agent of a New York mortgage company. In response, between 1932 and 1934, twenty-five state legislatures enacted moratoria on foreclosures.[12] The subject captured the imagination of many Popular Front writers, culminating in John Steinbeck's *The Grapes of Wrath*, published in 1939, based on articles he wrote for the *San Francisco Chronicle* in beginning in 1936.[13] These tensions also came out in popular culture, for example, Frank Capra's *Mr. Smith Goes to Washington* (1939) depicts an everyman figure in Congress fighting big business for local control of the land.

Weill was interested in such everyman figures, writing to Paul Green that he hoped they might write a story about "a kind of Johnny Johnson of 1776" in *The Common Glory*.[14] That idea seems to have extended to *One Man from Tennessee*, which portrays the folk hero as a simple backwoodsman who is inspired to fight for the little man. As the story begins, the young Crockett loses respect for his father when the latter cannot prevent the bank from reclaiming the property. Crockett then falls in love with Sarah, but her parents hesitate to bless their marriage, preferring the wealthy Job Spindle, who could save their farm (although they eventually consent to Crockett). Crockett goes to Congress to fight against land speculation, and dies at the Alamo rather than let bankers buy the land from Santa Anna.

The FTP began 1935 under the auspices of the New Deal's Works Progress Administration (WPA, renamed the Works Projects Administration in 1939). Led by former Vassar professor Hallie Flanagan, the FTP was charged with providing work for actors and stage professionals who had been left jobless by the Great Depression. By federal directive, the FTP could not compete

[12] Lee J. Alston, "Farm Foreclosure Moratorium Legislation: A Lesson from the Past," *American Economic Review* 74, no. 3 (1984): 446–47.

[13] The articles were later collected and published in John Steinbeck, *Their Blood Is Strong* (San Francisco: Simon J. Lubin Society of California, 1938).

[14] Kurt Weill to Paul Green, 13 October 1937, copy in Ronald Sanders Collection, NYPL, Box 21 Folder 2.

with commercial theatre, so Flanagan turned to classics and children's theatre, as well as experimental and socially conscious productions, even though it remained officially politically neutral. Above all, she called on playwrights to write "plays about Americans—in the settings, in the speech, in the manner of Americans."[15] *The Ballad of Davy Crockett* fulfilled many of these requirements. Its historical subject matter could be spun as "educational," and therefore outside of commercial theatre, another interest of the FTP. The FTP had mounted several similar productions, such as Mike Gold and Michael Blankfort's *Battle Hymn* (1936), which told the story of John Brown, which also fell under that "educational" mantle, and like the later *One Man from Tennessee*, employed a large narrative chorus (albeit speaking instead of singing).[16]

The Davy Crockett project had been part of the FTP for several years before Weill got involved. Hays's *The Ballad of Davy Crockett* opened at the Majestic Theatre in New York on 21 May 1936 and played for about 2,140 people over the course of nine performances, closing on 30 May.[17] Flanagan liked the production, saying it was "a very good show."[18] Hays's play included music, mostly in between scenes, as a fiddle and banjo player narrated off-stage events. Although no printed score survives for Hays's version, it is most likely that the tune for these interludes was a variation on the minstrel number "The Ballad of Davy Crockett," also sometimes called "Pompey Smash," a popular minstrel song that told the story of a black man named Pompey (a Jim Crow-like character) getting into a fight with the famous congressman. The song appeared in print throughout the 1920s and 1930s.

It remains unclear how Hays and Weill found each other, but Weill maintained a close relationship with the FTP throughout 1937. The composer's name appears frequently in inter-office correspondence throughout year, with a casual tone suggesting a fairly close relationship.[19]

---

[15] Federal Theatre Project, "The Prompter," December 1936, NARA/FTP, Folder "Exile."

[16] Hallie Flanagan called for innovations regarding choral speech in her address to the first production conference of the New York City Federal Theatre Unit in 1936; see "Highlights from the First Production Conference of the New York City Unit of the Federal Theatre Project," July 22–23, 1936, Library of Congress, Music Division, Washington DC Federal Theatre Project Collection (LOC/FTP), Box 1 Folder 1.1.9a.

[17] "Performance and Attendances of all Productions of the Federal Theatre Project of New York City," 11 November 1935 to 12 November 1938, NARA/FTP, Box 528 Folder "National Service Bureau."

[18] Hallie Flanagan to John McGee, 30 April 1936, NARA/FTP, Box 37 Folder "John McGee #4."

[19] See, for example, the letter quoted in Tim Carter, "Celebrating the Nation: Kurt Weill, Paul Green, and the Federal Theatre Project (1937)," *Journal of the Society for American Music* 5, no. 3 (2011): 316–17.

It was also in line with the FTP interest in helping refugee theatre professionals; on 22 March 1938, barely a month after Weill and his collaborators brought *One Man from Tennessee* to Flanagan, Pierre Loving of the translations department suggested that "the National Service Bureau publish a catalogue of Plays by Exiles (from non-democratic countries). Some of the greatest writers in the world are exiles today and have no access to a public owing to the censorship of their writings from their native countries."[20] The idea took off, and by the following July, the FTP had produced such a list, and had formed a Committee of Exiled Dramatists, which consisted of several political figures officially unaffiliated with the FTP, whose purpose was to promote works of foreign-born refugees.[21]

The pairing of Hays and Weill seemed ideal; Hays became interested in Brecht in 1935 when he saw the Theatre Union's production of *Mother*, and became a lifelong admirer and champion of the playwright, helping to bring him to the United States in 1940.[22] Three other people figure prominently in the early history of the Davy Crockett project: director Charles Alan, actor Burgess Meredith, and FTP producer Louis Simon. Weill knew Alan as the assistant director of *The Eternal Road* (1937), and Burgess Meredith had been involved with the 1933 U.S. production of *The 3-Penny Opera*, and had also tried out for *Johnny Johnson*.[23] Meredith and Weill attempted several collaborations, although they only managed to finish one project together: the radio cantata *The Ballad of the Magna Carta* (1940). Louis Simon, who had directed several regional productions for the FTP, served as the official point of contact between the creative team and Flanagan. Simon had worked with Max Reinhardt in Berlin and with Marc Blitzstein, either of whom could have made the connection between producer and Weill.[24] In September 1937, Weill wrote to his brother that work on the Davy Crockett project had begun in earnest.[25]

In his memoirs, Meredith recalled that he and Weill attempted to form the "Ballad Theatre" company, which would "produce plays in which a new

[20] Pierre Loving to Irwin Rubinstein, 22 March 1938, NARA/FTP, Box 39 Folder "Rubinstein, Irwin #1."

[21] LOC/FTP, Box 128 Folder 2.4.36.

[22] James K. Lyons, *Bertolt Brecht in America* (Princeton, NJ: Princeton University Press, 1980), 23. Hays later collaborated with Hanns Eisler on a Living Newspaper called *Medicine Show* in 1940.

[23] Burgess Meredith, *So Far, So Good: A Memoir* (Boston: Little, Brown, 1994), 58–9.

[24] Howard Pollack, *Marc Blitzstein: His Life, His Work, His World* (Oxford, UK: Oxford University Press, 2012), 53.

[25] Weill mentions working on *The Common Glory* and "other projects" to his brother on 4 September 1937, probably *One Man from Tennessee* given the timeline. *W-Fam*, 356.

musical form would be used. A chorus of singers, like a musical Greek chorus, would sing the story line, and the actors would go into action only when the mood was prescribed by the chorus."[26] *One Man from Tennessee* appears to be the only project to come out of that idea, although the choral narrative sections of *The Ballad of the Magna Carta* and *Down in the Valley* bear some resemblance to it. In December, just before Weill returned to Hollywood to work on *You and Me*, the *New York Times* announced that Weill, Alan, Meredith, and designer Robert Edmond Jones had formed a theatrical company financed by singer Libby Holman.[27] The first enterprise of this new group was to be a new version of *The Ballad of Davy Crockett* by H.R. Hays, with music by Kurt Weill; the second was to be a musical version (also composed by Weill) of Albert Bein's as yet unfinished proletarian play *Heavenly Express*. The inclusion of Bein's name hints at the political dimensions, although there is no other evidence that he was involved.[28] The same can be said of Jones and Holman, whose names do not appear in any other correspondence surrounding the idea.

Weill likely finished work on *One Man from Tennessee* while he was on the West Coast. On 21 February 1938, with Weill still in Los Angeles, Simon sent Flanagan a letter:

> The idea briefly and essentially is this: to set up a unit in New York that would be independent of the New York City Project, in order to produce a repertory of music-plays in a special style so that the social content of the plays would be correctly brought out. In order to achieve the distinction of style the unit would have to be governed by the combined forces of Weill, Alan, and me; being exclusively responsible to you, or to some one person mutually acceptable.[29]

He wrote that their first production would be *The Ballad of Davy Crockett*, and that they had several other projects in the works, including a new translation of *Die Dreigroschenoper*, a reworking of Offenbach's *Les contes d'Hoffmann* and *La Périchole*, Harold Smith's *Tell Us Democracy*, and possibly

---

[26] Meredith, *So Far, So Good*, 59. Meredith's memory was notoriously faulty by this point in his life, and some of the details that he describes as part of this Ballad Theatre project do not match *One Man from Tennessee*. For example, he remembers the chorus was to be *a cappella*.

[27] "Gossip of the Rialto," *NYT*, 5 December 1937, 213.

[28] *Heavenly Express* premiered in 1940 with music by Lehman Engel.

[29] Louis Simon to Hallie Flanagan, 18 February 1938, NARA/FTP, Box 24 Folder "General Correspondence 'S' #4."

a Paul Green play (probably *The Common Glory*). He also noted that the libretto for the Davy Crockett project was complete.

One full copy of the libretto survives, along with a short synopsis that details an intermediate stage between Hays's original play and the musical version.[30] The libretto of *One Man from Tennessee* contains twenty-two numbers, including incidental music (Table 3.1). Between Weill's sketches and an incomplete piano-vocal score in his hand (probably meant for rehearsal), music for eighteen of these numbers survives.[31]

Simon's letter also casts doubt on the authorship of the libretto, as he writes that "Weill and Alan have adapted Hoffman Hayes' [sic] *The Ballad of Davy Crockett*."[32] In a letter to Paul Green on 24 November 1937, Weill mentions Alan, writing that he and the director had "a very good collaboration [...] for the Davy Crockett-play,"[33] implying that Alan had some hand in the libretto. Weill also expressed frustration with Hays in a letter to Lenya on 15 May 1938, writing from Hollywood that "Hays has written a letter full of excuses; he hasn't worked on a single line of the play since I've been gone."[34] Most likely, Weill and Hays began working on the play sometime between early September and November 1937. Sometime in late November, Weill became frustrated with Hays, and turned to Alan for help around January 1938. Weill and Alan probably completed the surviving draft, and sent it on to Hays for approval and revisions, which he never completed to Weill's satisfaction.

The changes between *The Ballad of Davy Crockett* and *One Man from Tennessee* all speak to the needs and desires of the FTP. The most prominent dramaturgical change between Hays's original play and the new version is the presence of a chorus. Instead of a simple fiddler and a banjo player singing the narrative ballad between scenes, the synopsis describes "a group of poverty stricken hilly billys [sic] who play folk instruments and sometimes act bits which help the transitions, meaning, or the development of the story,"

[30] See H.R. Hays, *One Man from Tennessee*, WLRC, Series 20 Box D Folder 1938, and H.R. Hays and Kurt Weill, "Synopsis of *The Ballad of Davy Crockett*," WLRC, Series 20 Folder D2.
[31] The piano-vocal score resides in WLA, Box 2 Folder 21, and the sketches are in WLA, Box 2 Folder 20. Weill sketched music for "When the Summer Breezes Blow," and "A Mother Weeps," but never completed them. The sketches contain music for a discarded song called "I'll Cook the Corn and Taters," which "When the Summer Breezes Blow" eventually replaced, and the "Indian Battle." "Interscene IV," was probably dropped because it serves the same function as "All Goes Badly."
[32] David Drew dates *One Man from Tennessee* to January–April 1938 in *KWH*, 297. Simon might be incorrect as to the state of the work, but considering Weill mentions the project in early September 1937, it seems unlikely that he would still be working on it in April 1938, when he was back in Hollywood working on *You and Me*.
[33] Quoted in Carter, "Celebrating the Nation," 320 n55.
[34] *WLL(e)*, 269.

**Table 3.1** Summary of *One Man from Tennessee* by H.R. Hays

| Act | Scene | Action | Music |
|---|---|---|---|
| I | Prologue: A corner of the interior of the Alamo. | A band of musicians enters carrying the body of a man (1). They are approached by Job Spindle, who identifies the corpse as Davy Crockett and says the remains should be buried like any average soldier. The musicians reply that Crockett belongs to the people now, and they resolve to spread his legend. | 1. Opening March (orchestra) |
| | 1: An open spot in the woods. | Josh Hawkins sings about his life as a wanderer, echoed by the chorus (2). He and Crockett discuss Hawkins's plans to move to Texas. Crockett wants to go, but Hawkins discourages him. Crockett asks Hawkins about serving under Andrew Jackson. As Hawkins leaves, Crockett forlornly sings a verse of a folk song (3). | 2. "Oh I'm a Rolling Stone" (Josh and chorus) <br> 3. "Good-bye Josh" (Crockett) |
| | 2: Interior of the Crockett cabin. | Ma, Kate, and Billy (Crockett's mother and siblings) do chores (4) as Ma bemoans the fact that they might have to move again. Crockett enters, disconsolate over Hawkins's departure. The family tries to keep him from coming in, but forces the door. He announces that the Crocketts have three days to get off their land. When Crockett protests, the surveyor threatens to arrest him. Spurred by the surveyor's treatment, Crockett resolves to run away and live in the woods (5). | 4. "When the Summer Breezes Blow" (Ma) <br> 5. "Where the Green Pines Shadow the Ground" (Crockett and chorus) |
| | Interscene 1 | The chorus describes Crockett's life in the woods. | Interscene I |
| | 3: The same open space in the woods as Scene 1. | Job Spindle, a peddler, is lost in the woods and comes across Crockett. Spindle tries to sell him things, then tries to get Crockett to play Three Card Monte with a pea and three thimbles. Spindle says he needs a man to win so that other customers do not get discouraged. Crockett becomes angry and scares Spindle away when he threatens to clear people off the land. Crockett is visited by spirits who tell him about his destiny (6). | 6. "Song of the Trees" (chorus) |
| | Interscene 2 | The chorus describes how Crockett enlists with Jackson to fight Indians, but that Crockett is lonely without a home and a family. | Interscene II |

4: Sarah's House. A divided stage. To the left we see the interior of the cabin... To the right, the woods.

Sarah's mother (also "Ma") sings about how sad she is about losing her only daughter (7). Spindle flatters her in hopes of winning her daughter's hand. In the woods, Crockett courts Sarah. Sarah worries that her mother might make her marry Spindle because her family is about to lose their farm. Crockett resolves to talk to the family. Sarah's mother rejects him for Spindle and kicks Crockett out of the house, but he comes back in the window, appealing to Pa. Ma has none of it, so Crockett tries to impress her by asking her to dance (8). She is briefly charmed, but not for long. Crockett finally runs off with Sarah.

7. "A Mother Weeps" (Sarah's Ma)

8. "Look Your Partner Straight in the Eye" (Crockett)

Interscene 3

The chorus describes Crockett and Spindle's disparate lives.

5: A painted drop with large trees in the center. One side goes up and discloses Spindle perched on a stool in his office.

Spindle sings about his philosophy of life (9). Spindle, who now runs a newspaper, has a meeting with Alexander. Spindle hints that he might be generous with an elected official who will raise taxes on the foreign goods that impede on Spindle's trade. The two strike a deal.

Interscene III

9. "The Hand Is Quicker Than the Eye" (Spindle and chorus)

6: Interior of Crockett's home.

Edmonds attempts to convince Crockett to run for Congress. Crockett refuses. Sarah thinks running is a good idea, but Crockett ignores her and begins to sing about the woods (10). Sarah says she has a letter, and reads it to Crockett, telling him (with the help of the chorus), that Hawkins has died (11). With this new information, Sarah convinces Crockett to run for Congress (12).

10. "When the Summer Breezes Blow" (Crockett)

11. "Death of Josh Hawkins" (Sarah and chorus)

12. "Watch Out for Me" (Crockett, Sarah, and chorus)

7: The Tavern of Tusconville, Tennessee. A tavern right with a table and benches. A big tree left with an election platform. Rear drop shows Spindle's Emporium, Tusconville Torch [and the] Publisher and Bank of Tusconville.

Alexander, Spindle, and a carpenter prepare for Alexander's speech. Alexander begins to orate. Crockett enters with a procession and a band. He jumps up on a table opposite Alexander and begins campaigning. The crowd turns his way, Crockett and the crowd sing about the promise of his congressional career (13). They march off, leaving Spindle alone onstage, who echoes their song, but implies that he will buy Crockett the way he bought Alexander.

13. "When I'm in Congress" (Crockett and crowd)

(continued)

**Table 3.1** Continued

| Act | Scene | Action | Music |
|-----|-------|--------|-------|
| II | 8: A gilded room behind a box in a Washington Theatre. | The chorus sings about the perils of politics (14). A senator meets with Spindle, who is upset that the tariff bill has not past because Crockett has opposed it. Fanny and the senator's wife enter and distract the senator. All are opposed to Crockett's proposed land bill. Spindle vainly tries to convince the senator's wife to manipulate another senator into opposing Crockett's bill. Crockett enters and tries to pitch the land bill, but Spindle intervenes. Crockett tells his wife he will talk to the only man who will listen: Jackson. | 14. "Politics" (chorus and Fanny) |
| | Interscene 4 | The chorus describes Jackson as an old soldier who misses his home state of Tennessee. | Interscene IV (chorus) |
| | 9: Jackson's private office. | The chorus sings about how badly things are going (15). Crockett appeals to Jackson's memories of Tennessee, speaking to him as a comrade. Jackson notes that Crockett has opposed him, but seems ashamed. When Crockett implies that Vice President Van Buren is manipulating Jackson, the president becomes angry. Captain Morgan enters with bad news from the Alamo. Crockett urges Jackson to send aid, and Jackson appears sympathetic until Van Buren enters and convinces him otherwise. | 15. "All Goes Badly" (chorus) |
| | 10: Drop showing the outside of the White House. | Crockett and Sarah. They recognize that they never had a chance in Washington and resolve to go back to Tennessee. Crockett says that he must go to fight at the Alamo first, against Sarah's protestations (16). | 16. "I'm Not Living by the Clock" (Sarah and chorus). |
| | 11: Corner of the roof of the Alamo. | Crockett reprises Sarah's song. Crockett and the men wait for the Mexicans to attack. Spindle appears, saying he has cut a deal with Santa Anna to buy Texas as long as the Alamo surrenders. Crockett refuses. Crockett attacks the Mexicans, the rest of the soldiers following (17, 18). Spindle cowers in the ensuing battle. Crockett staggers onstage, wounded, and dies. Santa Anna approaches Spindle, who invites him to play the Three Card Monte thimble game. | 17. "Battle of the Alamo" (orchestra) <br> 18. "You Can See the Mexicans" (Chorus) |

giving the play the aura of a folk tale coming from "the people" (and aligning with the "Ballad Opera" idea described by Meredith). The chorus was a prudent addition on a practical level; it enabled the employment of more people. The issue of land repossession is also more emphasized in *One Man from Tennessee* than it is in Hays's original. Crockett's foil, the Yankee peddler Job Spindle, evolves in ways that highlight the politics of the new play. In the original *The Ballad of Davy Crockett*, he is merely a hapless sidekick, but in *One Man from Tennessee*, he becomes Crockett's nemesis. In the later version of their meeting scene, he tries to interest Crockett in a real estate partnership, which at first appeals to the backwoodsman. But when Crockett asks Spindle what they would do to people already living on the land, Spindle responds, "Squatters? We'll burn them off, easy as anything, if they make a fuss we'll get the soldiers." Crockett subsequently explodes: "Soldiers! Why you low snake in the grass!" and frightens Spindle into running away.[35] Spindle remerges as a rival for Sarah's hand, supports Crockett's political opponents, and tries to cheat Texans out of their land at the Alamo. This aligns the production with one of the FTP's most famous offerings: *One Third of a Nation* (1938), the Living Newspaper which took a similarly historical look at the problem of homelessness, albeit in an urban context. Flanagan reported that Weill had discussed *One Third of a Nation* with her at some point, though she does not provide further context.[36]

Making Spindle a villain also allowed the authors to set up the "marriage trope," that is, a popular formula for musicals in which "couples whose individual issues mirror or embody larger ones that turn out to be what the musical in question is 'really' about."[37] Sarah stands for the larger body politic, and must decide what kind of man she wants to become part of her family/country: Crockett, the man of the people, or the Spindle, the businessman. The businessman may make false promises or try dishonest tactics to win the affection of the people, but in the end the choice is clear; Leftist populism (Crockett) is the correct choice. A few scenes later, the people must make the same choice; either send Crockett or Spindle's handpicked candidate Alexander to Congress. Again, the choice is clear.

[35] Hays, *One Man from Tennessee*, 3-4–3-5.

[36] Hallie Flanagan, *Arena: The History of the Federal Theatre* (New York: Benjamin Blom, 1940), 222.

[37] Raymond Knapp, *The American Musical and the Formation of National Identity* (Princeton, NJ: Princeton University Press, 2005), 9.

Musically, Spindle and Crockett are differentiated in ways that resonate with Popular Front uses of folk music. Folksy pastiches paint Crockett as a man of the people, and jazzy Tin-Pan-Alley-type numbers characterize Spindle as a man of business.[38] Spindle has only one number: "The Hand Is Quicker Than the Eye," a song about deceit (Example 3.1). This makes him seem musically disconnected from The People, who see through his slippery personality. Spindle thus must resort to trickery and double-dealing to achieve his goals, while Crockett can be honest.

The title character, conversely, is associated with a variety of folk idioms. As in the original *The Ballad of Davy Crockett*, a recurring folk tune describes offstage events between scenes, although Weill wrote an original song for this version.[39] Weill's tune appears first in Josh Hawkins's (Crockett's uncle's) introductory song, "Oh, I'm a Rolling Stone," and then is used by the chorus to narrate the action in between scenes. The tune consists of a triadic, pentatonic melody, resembling some of the popular folk songs of the era (and was eventually reworked into "Nowhere to Go but Up" in *Knickerbocker Holiday* in 1938).

There is another recurring tune associated with Davy that also has ties to folk idioms, even though Weill borrowed it from the Tango-Habañera from *Marie Galante*. It first appears as the funeral march that opens the play, then is set to the words "Be sure you're right, then go ahead," in the song "Where the Green Pines Shadow the Ground."[40] Anyone in the audience familiar with the Davy Crockett legend would recognize these words as "Davy Crockett's motto," which had been part of the Davy Crockett song tradition since the man's lifetime.[41] In *One Man from Tennessee*, the young Crockett gets this motto from Josh in Scene 1. Hays (or Alan) reinforces the connection between the words and the tune by having Crockett state the motto just as he decides to run for office, only a few lines before he bursts into "Watch Out for Me," and the tune reappears in the accompaniment of that song's coda. Its last

---

[38] Reuss and Reuss, *American Folk Music and Left-Wing Politics*, 159.

[39] The songs are referred to as "Interscenes" in the libretto and "Hill Billy Narrative Songs" in the piano score. For the sake of simplicity, I use "Interscene."

[40] Examples from *One Man from Tennessee* come from the vocal score in WLA, Box 2 Folder 21. This tune appears several more times in Weill's music before *One Man from Tennessee*: in *Der Kuhhandel* (1934) as part of Juan and Juanita's farewell, and the end of *Johnny Johnson*'s "Song of the Goddess." The melody was finally published 1946 as "Youkali/Tango-Habañera" with lyrics by Roger Fernay.

[41] William R. Chemerka and Allen J. Wiener, *Music of the Alamo: From 19th Century Ballads to Big-Screen Soundtracks* (Houston: Bright Sky, 2008), 20, 61.

**Example 3.1** *One Man from Tennessee,* "The Hand Is Quicker Than the Eye."

**Example 3.1** *Continued*

appearance comes at the very end of the piece as "Battle of the Alamo," an instrumental passage that probably replaced "You Can See the Mexicans."

The fact that Crockett's tragic death is memorialized in a folk ballad reinforces his status as a Leftist folk hero. The folk ballad tradition was associated with Leftist causes in the late 1930s, with songs that celebrated important events and martyrs to the cause, including the Elie Siegmeister (under the name L.E. Swift) and Charles Abron song, "The Scottsboro Boys Shall Not Die," and Earl Robinson's and Alfred Hayes's "I Dreamed I Saw Joe Hill Last Night." Contemporary proletarian dramatists lionized their heroes through folk song, including the "Ballad of Kirk McClure" (the name of the fictional martyred union leader) written for Bein's *Let Freedom Ring*, and "John Brown's Body" used prominently in *Battle Hymn* (1936). Crockett is also associated with diegetic folk-like tunes throughout the show. During the courtship scene, he charms Sarah's mother by playing "Look Your Partner Straight in the Eye," a pastiche of fiddle tunes such as "Sourwood Mountain" (which Weill eventually used in *Down in the Valley*) and play songs like "Skip to my Lou."

*One Man from Tennessee* proved untenable for several reasons. Unfortunately for Weill and his collaborates, in early 1938 the FTP could not grant any unit complete artistic freedom. Flanagan wrote to her assistant director John McGee about the project: "Although the suggestion in Louis Simon's letter is impossible, I still think that he is a very good producer and Weill a very good composer, and I thought we should not lose an opportunity at something really exciting, particularly since Burgess Meredith has told me he wants to act in some of these operas."[42] The previous unit of the FTP allowed

---

[42]  Hallie Flanagan to John McGee, 24 February 1938, NARA/FTP Box 37 Folder "John McGee #1."

creative independence was John Houseman and Orson Welles's Project 891, which attempted to mount Blitzstein's *The Cradle Will Rock*. In the summer of 1937, the FTP abandoned *Cradle*, ostensibly because of budget cuts, but both Flanagan and Blitzstein believed that those cuts were made by anti–New Deal congressmen and senators who objected to *Cradle*'s political content.[43] After the commercial production of *Cradle* proved a great success, the FTP was left with all of the political fallout and none of the revenue. In early 1938, still recovering from the entire affair, Flanagan and McGee were in no position to offer similar autonomy to another unit, particularly not one that that wanted to produce plays or musicals with "social content." After it became clear that the FTP could not sponsor the Davy Crockett project, Weill chose not to continue with it, likely because, as he told Paul Green in 1941, he had never been satisfied with the libretto (although he did briefly hope to revive it after the success of Rodgers and Hammerstein's *Oklahoma!*).[44] Furthermore, some of Weill's folk song pastiches are unsophisticated and sound forced. In the end, *One Man from Tennessee* represents an interesting experiment and an important stepping-stone for Weill as he learned the sounds and idioms of his new country, but probably not a viable piece of musical theatre.

## Getting Railroads Back on Track

*Railroads on Parade: A Pageant Drama of Transport* was one of the most popular of Weill's works during his lifetime, at least in terms of the number of people who saw the production; the *New York Times* reported that least 3,000,000 saw it over the course of both seasons.[45] Weill wrote about forty minutes of music for this hour-long "Pageant Drama of Rail Transport," which played four times a day at the 1939 World's Fair, and then in a revised version at the 1940 season. The score consists of a mixture of folk songs and nineteenth-century popular styles, both quotations and pastiche. He also included one original number with modern popular aspirations, "Mile after Mile," which was distributed as sheet music to promote the pageant. This

[43] Pollack, *Marc Blitzstein*, 175.
[44] Carter, "Celebrating the Nation," 327 n66.
[45] "Mayor Gives Press a Few Tips at Fair," *NYT*, 20 August 1940, 22. In the 1940 season, the Eastern Railroad Presidents' Conference estimated that about 5.68% of fairgoers saw *Railroads on Parade* (about 1,023,000 people, reflecting the general drop in attendance), but there are no similar specific numbers available for 1939.

spectacular extravaganza featured a cast of about 250, along with live horses, and both historical and replica train engines parading across the five-and-a-half-acre stage.[46] Weill's librettist was Edward T. Hungerford (though Charles Alan wrote the lyrics for "Mile after Mile," and Buddy Bernier contributed additional lyrics for the commercial release), an eccentric train enthusiast who published numerous books on the railroad industry, and who served as the mastermind behind the project.

The 1939 World's Fair was a demonstration of American exceptionalism, a notion first articulated by John Winthrop in 1630, when he called for the emerging nation to be "a city upon a hill" given that "the eyes of all people are upon us."[47] The darkening situation in Europe made this a particularly important theme in 1939, and the guidebook to the Fair reminded patrons that "the American ideal has exerted wide and fruitful influence in the world."[48] The 1939 Fair demonstrated United States' leadership through technological and consumer innovation with the theme of the "World of Tomorrow." The "theme center" was a spherical building called the Perisphere, home to the "Democracity" diorama, which symbolized "humanity's age-old quest for knowledge, increased leisure and happiness."[49] Cultural critic Lewis Mumford emphasized the United States' spiritual and moral strength to use technology for good, contrasted against those who were "ready to make hell on earth and destroy our civilization unless the forces which are working in the other direction, on the side of a different order of society, become victorious."[50]

In 1939, the faltering railroad industry hoped to use this emphasis on technology and American exceptionalism to bolster their finances by highlighting the relationship between railroads and nationhood. Since the late 1910s, the industry had been in decline, in part because of competition from automobiles and then airplanes, but also due to generations of corrupt management.[51] In February 1937, the responsibility for the exhibit

---

[46] "'Iron Horse Opera' Groomed for Fair: *Railroads on Parade* Exhibit to Cost $2,500 a Day for Operating Expenses," *NYT*, 16 April 1939, 3.

[47] John Winthrop, "A Modell of Christian Charity" (1630), available online at https://www.mtholyoke.edu/acad/intrel/winthrop.htm.

[48] New York World's Fair 1939 Incorporated, *Official Guidebook: New York World's Fair: The World of Tomorrow, 1939*, 2nd ed. (New York: Exposition, 1939), 40.

[49] *Official Guidebook, 1939*, 45.

[50] Quoted in Marco Duranti, "Utopia, Nostalgia, and World War at the 1939–40 New York World's Fair," *Journal of Contemporary History* 41, no .4 (2006): 666.

[51] John F. Stover, *American Railroads*, 2nd ed. (Chicago, IL: University of Chicago Press, 1997), 97, 192.

passed from the Association of American Railroads to the Eastern Railroad Presidents Conference,[52] which had already retained Hungerford to direct their exhibit.[53] Hungerford likely became aware of Weill through *The Eternal Road* (1937); the two pageants share several members of the production team, including Weill, conductor Isaac Van Grove, director Charles Alan, and designer Harry Horner. Hungerford approached Weill in 1938 while the composer was in California (presumably working on *You and Me*).[54] This visit probably took place either in late April or early May 1938 given that Weill asked Lenya if she had received Hungerford's check in a letter of 5 May 1938.[55] Weill wrote most of the score in California, likely finishing around early June.

The production opened with the Fair on 10 April 1939 as part of the railroad pavilion, the largest single exhibit on the grounds, housing not only *Railroads on Parade*, but also a sizable working model railroad under the title "Railroads at Work" (which required a ten-cent admission and was retitled "Railroads in Action" in 1940), a large outdoor yard featuring historical and contemporary engines, and "Railroads in Building" (retitled "Building the Railroad" in 1940), a diorama explaining railroad construction.[56] The 1939 version of *Railroads on Parade* fit the "World of Tomorrow" theme: it tells the story of a British invention perfected by American ingenuity, which was used to tame the Wild West, and then provide modern comforts to discerning travelers. According to the souvenir program, the show presented "a sharp impression of this outstanding example of man's achievement in America."[57] The final two scenes before the epilogue emphasize the technological complexity of the railroad system, as mastered by the guiding hands of human operators. The sheer size of the production and the noise from the machines necessitated that the performers onstage lip-sync their parts, while the twenty-five-person orchestra, seventeen soloists, and large chorus produced

---

[52] The styling of this organization's name in the documents is inconsistent. The styling here is from the 1940 program, but in the 1939 program, they are called the Eastern Presidents' Conference, and in the 1940 guidebook, they are the Eastern Railroad Presidents' Conference.

[53] Maurice Mermey to Director of Exhibits and Concessions, 20 February 1937, World's Fair Collection, NYPL, Box 385 Folder 17.

[54] Edward Hungerford, *Setting History to Music* (Princeton, NJ: Princeton University Press, 1939), 11.

[55] *WLL(e)*, 262.

[56] These are visible in amateur footage of the Fair available at "1939 World's Fair—Railroad Exhibits," YouTube video, 10:59, posted 24 September 2012, https://www.youtube.com/watch?v=NySKJczYKUQ.

[57] *Bill of the Play: Railroads on Parade; a Pageant Drama of Transport*, 1939, author's personal collection.

the music and dialogue offstage, which was piped out over speakers to the audience.[58] It was also one of few attractions that had an entry fee. Patrons had to decide if it was worth the twenty-five-cent price of admission, or if they wanted to spend that money on another offering such as Billy Rose's famous water ballet *Aquacade* (forty cents) or Democracity (twenty-five cents).[59]

Several railroad companies made a major advertising push related to the Fair. Both the Pennsylvania Railroad and the Baltimore and Ohio Railroad advertised in the *Washington Post* offering special, all-inclusive World's Fair packages, along with plugging the pageant. Hungerford also arranged for several of the historical engines to make trips into local towns filled with people in historical costumes to advertise the show.[60] In the end, the advertising seems to have worked, and *Railroads on Parade* was one of the most popular attractions of the Fair.

But the advent of war in Europe on 1 September 1939, just a month before the Fair closed in October, caused the planning committee to rethink the theme for the following year. Isolationist sentiment in the United States remained strong through the end of 1940, and the Fair's new theme, "For Peace and Freedom," reflected that desire with a distinctly nostalgic bent; chairman Harvey D. Gibson offered visitors "a welcome as sincere and friendly as an old-fashioned county fair."[61] Instead of leadership through technological prowess guided by a strict moral compass, the United States of the 1940 Fair purported to keep the light of liberal democracy burning while Europe descended into madness. A new show called *American Jubilee* celebrated the nation by presenting a fantasy version of the Victorian Age with pastiches of nineteenth century popular music by Oscar Hammerstein and Arthur Schwartz, and the Soviet Pavilion was torn down to make room for the "American Common," a new theme center.[62] The new guidebook noted

---

[58] bruce d. mcclung, "Liner Notes to *Kurt Weill's Lost Recording of Railroads on Parade*," Transcription Records, 2012.

[59] "Facts About the Fair," *NYT*, 15 July 1939, 6 and "How Much it Costs," NYT, 5 May 1940, 140. The admission fee did not change between the two seasons for any of the attractions.

[60] "Old Train 'Speeds' on 16-Mile Trip: The J.W. Bowker: Old Wood-Burning Engine, Rides Again," *NYT*, 1 April 1939, 21.

[61] New York World's Fair 1940 Incorporated, *Official Guide Book: The World's Fair of 1940 in New York: For Peace and Freedom* (New York: Rogers–Kellogg–Stillson, 1940), 5. See also Duranti, "Utopia, Nostalgia, and World War," 674–75; Warren I. Susman, "The People's Fair: Cultural Contradictions of a Consumer Society," in *Dawn of a New Day: The New York World's Fair, 1939/40*, ed. Helen A. Harrison (New York: New York University Press, 1980), 21; Elizabeth A. Liebman, "Catherine Littlefield's Bicycle Ballet and the 1940 World's Fair," *Dance Chronicle* 36 (2013): 336–37, 341.

[62] On the politics of *American Jubilee*, see Liebman, "Catherine Littlefield's Bicycle," 341–43.

"Probably in no other country do the magic words—peace and freedom— mean as much as they do in America today. Within its boundaries you find the greatest variety of racial strains getting along with each other and living at peace."[63]

Weill and Hungerford reconfigured *Railroads on Parade* for the new theme (see Table 3.2 for a comparison). They dropped two scenes that showed the technical workings of the railroad, added several new ones set in the past, and shortened the opening. They also inserted a burlesque striptease for dancer Betty Garrett into the Pullman scene.[64] One new scene set in 1890 matched the new *American Jubilee*, as did the expanded Lincoln sequence, as the beloved president also now made an appearance in that production.[65] Lastly, several new engines were added to the parade.

The 1939 version is split into five acts and the 1940 version falls into four, but the pageant ran from beginning to end without pause. Both versions fall into roughly two parts. The first featured a succession of important technical developments in overland transport ending with the completion of the transcontinental railroad in 1869. The second part covered the history of the industry from the point of view of the passengers, starting in the 1870s and ending in 1940, with a score drawn from the sounds of the turn of the century: waltzes, parlor songs, and ragtime, mostly newly composed for the pageant, as well as a more modern-style pop song ("Mile after Mile") for the Pullman car scene.

The sources for *Railroads on Parade* are extensive, but incomplete. There is one surviving libretto, which mostly matches the 1939 program, although several scenes in it were dropped by the final version.[66] The most reliable outline of the show comes from the two souvenir programs sold at the Fair in both seasons, both of which contain a scene-by-scene breakdown of that year's version. Quite a bit of musical material survives as well. There are preliminary sketches, and two piano-vocal scores of the 1939 version, one in Weill's hand and one in a copyist's, although the latter lacks most of the second half.[67] These mostly match the libretto and each other, although there are some minor differences. There are also three alternate versions

[63] *Official Guide Book, 1940*, 14.

[64] mcclung, "Liner Notes."

[65] Liebman, "Catherine Littlefield's Bicycle Ballet," 341.

[66] Edward Hungerford, *Railroads on Parade: A Fantasia on Rail Transport*, typescript libretto, WLA, Box 29 Folder 407.

[67] The sketches reside in the WLA, Box 29 Folder 409. Weill's score is in Box 29 Folder 411 and the copyist's is in Box 29 Folder 412.

Table 3.2 *Railroads on Parade*, 1939 and 1940 versions compared

| 1939 Version | | | 1940 Version | | |
| --- | --- | --- | --- | --- | --- |
| Act | Scene and description of the action from the program | Music | Act | Scene and description of the action from the program | Music |
| | Prologue: Before the Coming of the Trains. | (no quotations) | | Prologue: The gradual unfolding of transport by water and land is shown with highway vehicles on the fore-stage and a medieval ship on the upper-stage. These in turn are followed by representations of very early locomotives—Stephenson's *Rocket* (1829) and John Stevens' engine built at Hoboken, New Jersey (1825). | (no quotations) |
| I | 1: "New York—Gateway of a New Empire" At the Battery in the city of New York upon the occasion of the formal opening of the Erie Canal—in the autumn of 1825. It is a time of great rejoicing. | "The British Grenadiers" | I | 1: "The First Railroad" A horse-car on the newly built railroad reaching from Boston to Providence is shown gaily making its way from Boston Town to Dedham Plain. | (no quotations) |
| II | 1: "The Stourbridge Lion" Honesdale, Pennsylvania, at the inner terminus of the Delaware and Hudson Canal in August, 1829. The steam locomotive makes its first appearance upon American soil. | "Low Bridge" "Casey Jones" | | 2: "The Stourbridge Lion" Honesdale, Pennsylvania, at the inner terminus of the Delaware and Hudson Canal in August, 1829. The steam locomotive makes its first appearance upon American soil. | "Low Bridge" "Casey Jones" |
| | 2: "The Iron Horses" Across the stage comes the slow parade of the pioneer engines of the American railroad. The *Best Friend of Charleston* (1830), of the South Carolina Railroad, is followed closely by the *DeWitt Clinton* (1831), of the Mohawk and Hudson Railroad. | "John Henry" "She'll Be Coming 'round the Mountain" | | 3: "The Iron Horses" Across the fore-stage moves the slow parade of the pioneer engines of the American railroad. First of all comes the *John Bull*, built by Robert Stephenson and Company, Newcastle-on-Tyne, England, for the Camden and Amboy Railroad in 1831 and brought to America and placed in service on that road in the fall of the same year. The *Best Friend of Charleston* (1830) of the South Carolina Railroad is followed closely by the *DeWitt Clinton* (1831) of the Mohawk and Hudson Railroad. | "John Henry" "She'll Be Coming 'round the Mountain" |

3: "The Tom Thumb"
At the inner harbor of Baltimore City in the spring of 1830. Alderman Peter Cooper, of New York, has devised a curious gadget for the new railroad through the Ohio. An interested spectator is Charles Carroll, of Carrollton.

"Heave Away" / "Whisky Johnny"[a] "Old Grey Mare" "Casey Jones" "This Train Is Bound for Glory"[b]

III

1: "The Overland Trail"
The scene is on the road to the West—in 1849. Gold has been discovered in California and there is a steady trek of wagons and coaches and men and women afoot and on horseback.

"Oh California"[c]

2: "Lincoln Rides the Railroad"
The scene is at a station on the Hudson River Railroad in February 1861. President-elect Abraham Lincoln is on his way to his inauguration at Washington.

"This Train Is Bound for Glory"[e]

---

3: "The Tom Thumb"
At the inner harbor of Baltimore City in the spring of 1830. Alderman Peter Cooper, of New York, has devised a curious gadget for the new railroad through the Ohio. An interested spectator is Charles Carroll, of Carrollton.

"Nancy Lee" "Old Grey Mare" "Casey Jones" "Old Bill"

4: "The Tom Thumb"
At the inner harbor of Baltimore City in the spring of 1830. Alderman Peter Cooper, of New York, has devised a curious gadget for the new railroad through the Ohio. An interested spectator is Charles Carroll, of Carrollton.

"Oh California"

II

1: "The Overland Trail"
The scene is on the road to the West—in 1849. Gold has been discovered in California and there is a steady trek of wagons and coaches and men and women afoot and on horseback.

"Oh California"

2: "The Gold Rush"
Sacramento, California, in the late fifties at the K Street Wharf . . . in the center of the rear stage the steamboat New World lies at the wharf ready to start for San Francisco. . . . In the foreground an early railroad train of the Sacramento Valley Railroad, the first railroad to be built in California, comes in and discharges five important passengers, Collis B. Huntington, Leland Stanford, Charles Crocker, Mark Hopkins, and Theodore D. Judah.

"Snagthoothed Sal" / "Oh California"[d] "My Darling Clementine"

3: "Lincoln Rides the Railroad"
The scene is at a station on the Hudson River Railroad in February 1861. President-elect Abraham Lincoln is on his way to his inauguration at Washington. He boards the train that is to carry him to his inauguration, his triumph, and his death.

"Battle Hymn of the Republic"

(continued)

Table 3.2 Continued

| 1939 Version | | | 1940 Version | | |
|---|---|---|---|---|---|
| Act | Scene and description of the action from the program | Music | Act | Scene and description of the action from the program | Music |
| | | | | 4: "Mr. Lincoln Returns" In the opposite the direction from the outgoing Lincoln train enters the historic funeral train; its locomotive and cars are draped in heavy black. There is a slow tolling of bells. Great sorrow everywhere. | "This Train Is Bound for Glory" |
| | 3: "The Golden Spike" The scene is at Promontory Point, Utah, 10 May 1869, upon the completion of the first transcontinental railroad. A distinguished company is present. | "I've Been Working on the Railroad" "Auld Lang Syne" | III | 1: "The Wedding of the Rails" The scene is at Promontory Point, Utah, 10 May 1869, upon the completion of the first transcontinental railroad. A distinguished company is present. | "I've Been Working on the Railroad" "Auld Lang Syne" |
| IV | 1: "Yesterdays" The scene is the depot in almost any small American town in the seventies. The arrival of the morning train is an occasion of importance. | (no quotations) | | 2: "Yesterdays" The scene is the depot in almost any small American town in the seventies. The arrival of the morning train is an occasion of importance. | (no quotations) |
| | 2: "The Day Coach of Yesteryear" Also sometime in the seventies. The old day coach and its passengers are typical of the time. The words for this scene are those of John Godfrey Saxe's stirring and oft-repeated poem Riding on the Cars. | "Riding on the Cars" (original) | | 3: "The Oldtime Day Coach" Also sometime in the seventies. The old day coach and its passengers are typical of the time. The words for this scene are those of John Godfrey Saxe's stirring and oft-repeated poem Riding on the Cars. | "Riding on the Cars" (original) |
| | | | | 4: "Twenty Years Afterward" Twenty years have elapsed since we first saw the country station in the seventies. There has been little change in the old place save in the character of the vehicles and the coming of the bicycles and the earliest automobiles. | "Two Little Girls in Blue" |

| IV | | "Stars and Stripes Forever" (trio only) |
|---|---|---|
| 1: "The Modern Terminal of Today" The concourse of a large railroad station in the city of New York today. | | |
| 2: "Riding on the Cars—Today" This scene takes place in the highly modern Pullman car—part sleeper and part lounge car. | | "Mile after Mile" (original) |
| Epilogue: There gradually ensues the choruses of railroad workers who assemble themselves in the foreground. The picture is that of the modern railroad and the tremendous role it plays in the world today. | | (no quotations) |

| | | |
|---|---|---|
| 3: "They Ride upon the Cars" The concourse of a large railroad station in the metropolitan city of New York at the present day. | | (no quotations) |
| 4: "Riding Pullman" The scene is the interior of the highly modern Pullman lounge car, *Luxuryland*, which is standing in the trainshed of the railroad station in the preceding scene. | | "Mile after Mile" (original) |
| V 1: "In the Little Red Caboose" At the rear of a manifest freight. | | (no music) |
| 2: "The Railroad under Test" A composite scene which typifies the modern railroad operation and shows a signal tower and the headquarters office that controls it. Both are brought upon the upper stage, although supposedly many miles apart. | | (no music) |
| Epilogue: The Railroad Triumphant | | (no quotations) |

---

[a] These are sung simultaneously, in the manner of a combination number.

[b] It is possible that "This Train Is Bound for Glory" also appeared after "Old Bill" in the 1940 version. The sources cue an insert containing "Old Bill," but do not indicate if these new pages were meant to replace what followed or to lengthen the scene. Because "This Train" does not appear on the recording in this position (although it does appear later in the Lincoln sequence) and because there does not appear to be additional stage business that would require more music, the most likely explanation is that "Old Bill" replaced "This Train."

[c] This song is a contrafact of Stephen Foster's "Oh Susanna."

[d] Sung as a combination number.

[e] This is not in the full score, but it is in both piano-vocal scores, as well as the recording. Its absence in the full score can be explained by the fact that it is *a cappella*, and the full score does not include vocal parts.

of "Mile after Mile" (sometimes called "Wheels through the Night" in the sources), which accompanied the Pullman scene.[68] The full score of the 1939 version is largely complete, and serves as the best indicator of what was presented onstage in that year.[69] Although Weill wrote out this score, it includes numerous emendations in several other hands, including performance annotations indicating that this was probably what van Grove used to conduct. Between 1939 and 1940, Weill filled a spiral notebook with sketches for the revisions, and made partial piano-vocal scores for the new numbers.[70] The full revisions survive as appendices to the full score. There is also a partial recording of about two-thirds of the piece that was made for radio broadcast.[71]

Throughout the compositional process, Weill consulted a variety of sources of American folk music. His primary reference was likely John A. and Alan Lomax's *American Folksongs and Ballads* (1934); the quotations of "John Henry," "Old Bill," "Snagtoothed Sal," and "This Train Is Bound for Glory" all appear in *Railroads on Parade* with the nearly the same tune, rhythms, and words transmitted in this collection.[72] Weill also probably consulted Dorothy Scarborough's *On the Trail of Negro Folksongs* (1925), given that his version of "Casey Jones" matches the tune in that volume, as does a rare second verse of "I've Been Working on the Railroad" as it appears in *Railroads on Parade*:

Sing me a song of the city
(Roll them cotton bales!)
Darky ain't half so happy
As when he's out of jail.

Mobile for its oyster shells,
Boston for its beans,
Charleston for its cotton bales,
But for yaller gals New Orleans.[73]

---

[68] WLA, Box 29 Folder 408.

[69] WLA, Box 28 Folders 405–6.

[70] The notebook is in WLA, Box 29 Folder 410. The piano-vocal scores are in WLA, Box 29 Folder 408.

[71] mcclung, "Liner Notes."

[72] John A. Lomax and Alan Lomax, *American Folk Songs and Ballads* (New York: Macmillan, 1934), 5, 100, 405, 593.

[73] Dorothy Scarborough, *On the Trail of Negro Folk Songs* (Cambridge: Harvard University Press, 1925), 248–9. "Yaller" is a dialect pronunciation of "yellow," and refers to individuals of primarily European ancestry who were legally considered black under the "one drop" rule.

Example 3.2 *Railroads on Parade*, "Prologue."

Weill probably used several tunes from Carl Sandburg's *American Songbag*, including "Old Grey Mare," "Low Bridge," and "She'll Be Coming 'round the Mountain."[74] "Heave Away" and "Whiskey Johnny" appear in identical versions in the Lomax and Sandberg collections (and the Lomaxes acknowledged that they took "Whiskey Johnny" from Sandburg).[75] I have not been able to identify the precise source of the other quotations, but they are well-known songs.

There are also several original tunes in *Railroads on Parade*, some based on folk idioms and some not. In the former category are two themes that recur throughout: the fanfare theme that opens the show, parts of which bear a strong resemblance to "Battle Hymn of the Republic" and "Old Grey Mare" (as well as "Democracy Advancing" from *Johnny Johnson*) (Example 3.2).[76] There is also a tune associated with the first sung words of the show that has the wide leaps and expansive melody of a cowboy song, which I will call the "I sing of the sea" theme based on the first lyrics that are set to that tune (Example 3.3). There is a hymn to Lincoln, a waltz for the 1870 scene, a cakewalk tune, and an original setting of John Godfrey Saxe's "Riding on the Cars," set in harmony reminiscent of a barbershop quartet.[77]

[74] Carl Sandburg, *The American Songbag* (New York: Harcourt, Brace, 1927), 102–3, 171–73, 372–73.

[75] Lomax and Lomax, *American Folk Songs and Ballads*, 485–6; Sandburg, *The American Songbag*, 403, 407. Interestingly, these two songs are adjacent in Lomax and are sung as a combination number in *Railroads on Parade*.

[76] Examples from *Railroads on Parade* are from WLA, Box 29 Folder 408.

[77] Weill reused the cakewalk tune in *Ulysses Africanus*.

**Example 3.3** *Railroads on Parade,* "Prologue."

There are several moments that show Weill becoming more comfortable with U.S. musical idioms. His setting of Saxe's "Riding on the Cars" is far less formulaic and musically awkward than similar historical pastiches from *One Man from Tennessee,* possibly because he was familiar with the barbershop quartet style from *Die sieben Todsünden,* and from a discarded song for *You and Me.* Other scenes show a growing aptitude for the nuances of genre and characterization. The contemporary platform scene (Act IV, Scene 3, in 1939, Act IV, Scene 1, in 1940) is a particularly good example: a variety of different individuals ask station workers for advice, each with their own unique melody and style. The impression is of busy, bustling station. Creating unity out of variety was something Weill continually tried to achieve throughout his career, with varying degrees of success, but the coherent variety in *Railroads on Parade* represents an important step toward Weill's postwar operatic works.

## "A Pageant Drama of Transport"

Both versions of the pageant, like the Fair itself, balanced "education and enlightenment" with "commercial interests who regarded their participation as a simple money-making proposition," as Warren Susman put it, combining

Popular Front aesthetics, narratives of American ingenuity, and populist-capitalist notions of luxury for all.[78] The way Weill employs folk song in *Railroads on Parade* embodies these disparate and often contradictory elements. With its use of live trains, its folk music–based score, and its poetic voice-over narration, the work resembles both progressive-era pageantry and many short documentary films of the 1930s. In *Railroads on Parade*, the genres of the pageant and the documentary are put to similar purposes: to situate the American railroad in the mythologized past of the rugged frontier and the luxurious gilded age, inscribing it into a nostalgic-nationalist version of U.S. history that dominated the Fair, especially in 1940.

Hungerford and Weill used several different terms to describe the genre of *Railroads on Parade*. Hungerford expressed his desire to draw on operatic techniques,[79] an idea echoed in Weill's biographical note in the program, which declared, "His intention was to write what he calls a 'circus opera,' a score full of light movement and popular melody and yet worked out as a complete musical form using all elements of theatre music from opera to circus."[80] But ultimately, the form and genre that defined how audiences interpreted *Railroads on Parade* was the pageant. The pageant craze swept through the United States around the turn of the century, as progressive reformers created large-scale community productions to both educate and provide wholesome entertainment to the citizens of the United States.[81] These pageants often employed casts of two hundred to five thousand, comprised mostly of amateur locals, depicting the "unfolding from the forest primeval to the 'City Beautiful'" through a series of scenes showing "past generations' successive adaptions to inevitable technological and material process."[82] By the late 1920s, the enthusiasm for town pageants diminished as the turn-of-the-century optimism faded in the wake of World War I, and the movement was all but gone by the Great Depression.[83] Instead, a new professionalized pageantry emerged. Large, historically minded productions were staples of the Century of Progress Exhibition in Chicago (1933–34), including Hungerford's transportation-themed *Wings of a Century* and Meyer

---

[78] Susman, "The People's Fair."

[79] Hungerford, *Setting History to Music*, 11–12.

[80] This idea may owe something to Billy Rose's *Jumbo* (1935).

[81] David Glassberg, *American Historical Pageantry: The Uses of Tradition in the Early Twentieth Century* (Chapel Hill: University of North Carolina Press, 1990), 71.

[82] Glassberg, *American Historical Pageantry*, 139–40.

[83] Naima Prevots, *American Pageantry: A Movement for Art & Democracy* (Ann Arbor: UMI, 1990), 9.

Weisgal's *The Romance of a People*, the precursor to *The Eternal Road*.[84] One of the most successful productions of the decade was Paul Green's outdoor drama *The Lost Colony* (1937), which concerned the failed Roanoke settlement in North Carolina. Frederick Koch declared that *The Lost Colony* had "lifted the popular pageant form, for the most part superficial and shallow today, to the plane of imagination and high poetry."[85]

Weill had been interested in large-scale theatre for several years when he started working with Hungerford. He first encountered the idea through *The Eternal Road* in 1934, and pursued similar projects throughout the second half of the decade. *The Common Glory* would have been a similarly large-scale production covering a grand historical sweep, moving from early colonial times to the early nineteenth century. At one point, Weill offered to write the music for *The Lost Colony*, but eventually decided against it. He also expressed interest in composing music for a version of Hugo von Hofmannsthal's *Der Salzburger große Welttheater* for Reinhardt's production at the Hollywood Bowl in 1937.[86]

Aspects of pageantry and large-scale theatre likely appealed to Weill on several levels. The notion of a revival of Greek theatre, one of Weill's interests, often appeared in connection with the genre. Green related *The Lost Colony* to that idea, writing that "The Greeks and the people of medieval and Elizabethan England produced outdoor plays like this."[87] Hungerford also made gestures toward ideas of reviving Greek theatre, noting that for *Railroads on Parade*, "I designed the great stage (or stages) as a Greek theater."[88] Pageants were meant not just to show democratic ideals, but to instill them in both the performers and the audience, transforming society in the process.[89] As progressive-era pageant master Percy MacKaye put it, effective pageants were "one of the very arteries of our future democracy."[90] This same

[84] Although the principals of *The Romance of a People* were professionals, most of the chorus were amateurs, situating the show in the transitional period from the amateur pageant to its more professional successor. Lauren Love, "Performing Jewish Nationhood: *The Romance of a People* at the 1933 Chicago World's Fair," *Drama Review* 55, no. 3 (2011): 62.

[85] Frederick H. Koch, "The Drama of Roanoke Island" (1938) excerpted in *History Into Drama: A Source Book on Symphonic Drama Including the Complete Text of Paul Green's* The Lost Colony," ed. William J. Free and Charles B. Lower (New York: Odyssey, 1963), 136.

[86] On Weill's interest in other pageant-like projects, see Carter, "Celebrating the Nation," 303–5.

[87] Paul Green, "Dialogue at Evening" (1946) in Paul Green, *The Lost Colony: A Symphonic Drama of American History* (1937), ed. Lawrence G. Avery (Chapel Hill: University of North Carolina at Chapel Hill Press, 2001), 143.

[88] Hungerford, *Setting History to Music*, 14.

[89] Glassberg, *American Historical Pageantry*, 4, 54.

[90] Percy MacKaye, *Community Drama: Its Motive and Method of Neighborliness* (Boston: Houghton Mifflin, 1917), 10.

didactic impulse is apparent in Weill's ideas for *The Common Glory*, which he hoped would give a "a picture of early America, completely different from the one we are used to read[ing] in school books and chronicles," a picture with a distinctly democratic bent, showing the United States as a melting pot of races, "black, white, yellow men and women, carried by the same idea: to find a new world of freedom and equality."[91] These impulses resemble Weill's idea of *gemeinschaftsbildenden* ("community-engendering") theatre, an idea he had pursued in the 1920s.[92]

But the point of all the pomp and ceremony for *Railroads on Parade* was to elevate the U.S. railroad to the status of American mythology rather than fortify the democratic impulse of the citizenry. Facing competition from modern modes of transportation, the Eastern Railroads Presidents Conference emphasized the railroad's historical importance, and presented a pageant that "recreates the railroad history of the United States and the epic conquest of the wilderness with historic engines [. . .] to the stream-lined luxury of rail-travel today."[93] The larger-than-life, antique quality of the pageant as a genre helped support this vision of the U.S. railroad. To ride the rails according to *Railroads on Parade* was to participate in a grand, all-American tradition that connected the traveler to hardy pioneers, brilliant engineers, and great statesmen. Trains are portrayed as a living link to America's frontier, the place where America became America. Reviewer Lucius Beebe wrote that "it is as natural that an American pageant should be evolved around the pattern of overland transport as that a parallel British theme should concern itself with England's supremacy of the seas."[94] The second part, with its parlor songs, emphasized gilded age opulence and genteel sensibilities, referencing another mythological era of American dominance. The railroad was not only part of the American history of conquest and ingenuity, but of elegance and refinement as well.

The folk music in *Railroads on Parade* serves the same functions as the historical and replica engines, emphasizing the all-American authenticity of the production. The live trains running on their own power on the stage enhanced the nonfictional, educational bent of the pageant. The folk tunes, brightly orchestrated and expertly performed, accompany antique engines

---

[91] Quoted in Carter, "Celebrating the Nation," 314–15.
[92] Kurt Weill, "Shifts in Musical Composition" (1927), trans. in *KWiE*, 480.
[93] *Official Guide Book, 1940*, 101–2.
[94] Lucius Beebe, "This New York," *Washington Post*, 4 August 1940, A4.

rolling across the stage under their own power. Both appear "good as new," so to speak, presented as artifacts of a living national history to be cherished.

*Railroads on Parade* also drew on the contemporary techniques of documentary filmmaking, which, like pageantry, employed voice-over narration and episodic construction. *Railroads on Parade's* closest aesthetic (if not ideological) cousins are films made by the circle associated with Frontier Films and its successor, American Documentary Films. Many members of these companies first became interested in documentary working with Pare Lorentz on films such as *The Plow That Broke the Plains* (1936) and *The River* (1937), both scored by Virgil Thomson with hymn tunes, minstrel numbers, cowboy songs, and other folk idioms. These films proved seminal for Depression-era documentary, inspiring a wave of similar projects combining social messages with hortatory rhetoric and patriotic sentimentality, many of which (including *The Plow That Broke the Plains*) played at the Fair.[95] Other similar films include Ralph Steiner and Willard Van Dykes's *The City* (1939, with music by Aaron Copland, which also played at the Fair),[96] Joris Ivens's *The Spanish Earth* (1937, music by Marc Blitzstein), and *Native Land* (1942, music by Marc Blitzstein).

In many of these documentaries, folk music highlights natural beauty; in *The River* and *The Plow That Broke the Plains*, Thomson used it to emphasize the magnificence of the American frontier.[97] The opening of *Railroads on Parade* is similar to the beginning of *The Plow That Broke the Plains*: both begin with a somber, minor-mode fanfare that quickly gives way to a pastoral tune. In *The Plow That Broke the Plains*, Thomson's arrangements of "I Ride Old Paint," "The Cowboy's Lament," and "Git Along Little Dogies" plays as cowboys shepherd their herds across the placid grasslands of the plains, as the narrator describes "a cattleman's paradise" of "unfenced range a thousand miles long, an uncharted ocean of grass. As in *The Plow That Broke the Plains*, in *Railroads on Parade* a minor-mode fanfare gives way to some early narration before the female narrator sings the "I'll sing of the sea" theme (Example 3.2). Like "Old Paint," the "I'll sing of the sea" tune consists of wide leaps, often fourths or fifths, accompanied by winds, guitar, and strings in

---

[95] Neil Lerner, "The Classical Documentary Score in American Films of Persuasion: Contexts and Case Studies, 1936–1945" (PhD diss., Duke University, 1997); David Davidson, "Depression America and the Rise of the Social Documentary Film," *Chicago Review* 34, no. 1 (1983): 82–85; "The Fair Today," *NYT*, 24 October 1939, 16.

[96] "The Fair Today," 16.

[97] Annegret Fauser, *Sounds of War: Music in the United States during World War II* (Oxford and New York, 2013), 157.

Example 3.4  *Railroads on Parade*, "Mile after Mile."

**Molto tranquillo** (calmly and slowly)

open spacing. Amateur film footage taken by Fairgoers in 1939 reveals a large but mostly bare stage at this point, save for a line of women in diaphanous costumes moving gracefully in imitation of the waves of the ocean, or like the waving grass in *The Plow That Broke the Plains*. This sequence of gestures quickly and effectively conveys a great deal of information.[98] The somber opening lends these moments an air of gravitas. The pastoral gesture that follows then gives the sense that we are traveling back in time to a pre-lapsarian paradise: America before she is tamed by the railroad, or the plains before they became the dustbowl. Folk music is pre-technological, signifying unspoiled nature.

But after this opening, *Railroads on Parade* diverges from its filmic cousins. While both use folk music to represent the natural world, in *The River*, *The Plow That Broke the Plains*, and *The City*, human intervention destroys that natural beauty. Musically and visually, *Railroads on Parade* evolves more gradually from the natural world to the technological one.[99] The pastoral first part of *Railroads on Parade* gives way to the folk songs set against the early stages of railroad building, then to the more generally nostalgic mode of the late-nineteenth-century scenes. This is followed by "Mile after Mile," which continues this nostalgic bent; while the music is typical of 1930s popular song, the lyrics describe the singer's longing for a lost love (see Example 3.4).[100] There is a continuous evolution from folk music, to parlor

---

[98] On the semiotics of the opening of *The Plow That Broke the Plains*, see Lerner, "The Classical Documentary Score," 85, 106.

[99] In this, resembles Aaron Copland's *The City*. See Crist, *Music for the Common Man*, 95–97.

[100] Example 3.4 is taken from the published sheet music for "Mile after Mile." Based on the full score, the version that appeared in the production probably had a slightly different melody and lyric, although the general sentiment of the song is the same.

songs, to modern pop, and no conflict is present between the natural and the technological world.

This gradual evolution is brought into sharp focus by the fact that "pre-technological" folk music accompanies huge pieces of machinery as they stream across the stage. The folk music creates the link between nature and industry. Hungerford's program notes make this idea clear. The railroad, he wrote,

> is the backbone of the country, no, even more, it is its veritable lifeblood. In its 250,000 miles of steel veins it flows to every far corner of a far-flung land, it binds in its living, throbbing embrace city and town and village, the open country, the forest, the mine, the forge, the factory, and the sea.

As the score evolves organically from past to present, the railroad industry follows a similarly unbroken path, becoming inextricably, even organically embedded into the nation and culture.

In uniting the pageant with the documentary, Hungerford and Weill drew on the artistic innovations of two generations of progressives to glorify one of the main drivers of capitalism in the United States. The choruses of happy workers singing folk songs as they work the rails or the docks obscure the labor troubles of the first half of the twentieth century, including the fight between the World's Fair Corporation and Equity that threatened to shut down not only *Railroads on Parade*, but also *American Jubilee* and *Aquacade* for the 1940 season.[101] Still, the pageant was effective at presenting a "people's" railroad rather than an enormous monopoly run by capitalist robber-barons. This appears to be intentional; Hungerford's original libretto includes a scene called "Builders of Empire (1870–1910)" that depicted a magnanimous Cornelius Vanderbilt of the New York Central Railroad, John Elgar Thomson of the Pennsylvania Railroad, and John W. Garrett of the Baltimore and Ohio Railroad all agreeing, "We are here always to serve America, and to serve it to the best of our ability."[102] But the scene was dropped, possibly because it strained credulity; the corruption of the nineteenth century railroad barons was still a part of public memory in the late 1930s.

The political, if not aesthetic, neutrality of *Railroads on Parade* marks the beginning of Weill's shift toward the political center, where he stayed until

---

[101] "Show at Fair Signs with Equity," *NYT*, 1 May 1940, 31.
[102] Hungerford, *Railroads on Parade*, 3-4-3.

the end of World War II. Weill never explicitly gave a reason for this shift, but rising anti-German, anti-immigrant, and anti-Semitic sentiment in the United States may have played a role. The other reason may have been simply economical. After *Johnny Johnson*, Weill had failed to get a Popular Front effort off the ground in the second half of the 1930s: *The Common Glory, One Man from Tennessee, The River is Blue* (a planned film with Clifford Odets and members of the Group Theatre in 1937), and *Ulysses Africanus* (1939) all stalled at various stages of production. Even the two major projects that eventually came to fruition—*You and Me* (1938) and *Knickerbocker Holiday* (1938)—turned out very differently in their politics than Weill's original conception. The Popular Front also faced serious difficulties. The FTP was suspended in 1939 partly due to accusations of putting on Leftist propaganda, and many other Popular Front organizations such as the Group Theatre were falling apart due to internal strife, so there were fewer venues for the kinds of socially engaged theatre Weill wrote.[103]

Still, the Leftist aesthetics (if not politics) of *Railroads on Parade* played an important role in Weill's evolving conception of "American" music. It represents Weill's first successful encounter with the autochthonous folk music of the United States. These songs and styles left an indelible mark on Weill's musical style, and he revisited them again after the war in another project that brought him one step closer to "American opera": 1948's *Down in the Valley.*

## Democratic Opera

As the situation in Europe deteriorated and the United States eventually joined the fray, Weill split his attention between mainstream Broadway, efforts to support the war, and raising awareness about the Holocaust (see Chapters 4 and 5). These works mark a distinct shift in Weill's approach to the idea of America. Until 1939, Weill's works had been (to greater or lesser degrees) critical of his new country. But with the exception of the pageant *We Will Never Die* (1943), which tacitly chided the nation for not doing more to prevent the slaughter of Jews in Europe, Weill's wartime pieces were either overtly patriotic or nominally apolitical. The reasons for this shift will

---

[103] On the end of the Federal Theatre Project, see Pollack, *Marc Blitzstein*, 417. On internal strife in the Group Theatre, see Smith, *Real Life Drama*, 265ff.

be explored in the following chapter, but for current purposes, it is important to note that Weill's turn toward patriotism was accompanied by a turn away from the American folk materials that had occupied much of his attention during his first years in the United States.

Equally important is his quick return to folk music as the war wound down. By September 1945 the war in Europe was over, and Weill and former FTP playwright Arnold Sundgaard had written *Down in the Valley*, a twenty-five-minute piece based on the folk song of the same name. Weill and Sundgaard intended the piece as the first in a series of folk song-based operas for radio, a project instigated by Charles MacArthur and *New York Times* music critic Olin Downes.[104] But the program did not get picked up, and the piece went on the shelf until Hans Heinsheimer of Schirmer Publishing (formerly of Universal Edition, Weill's European publisher) contacted Weill in 1947 to request a "school opera," something akin to his *Der Jasager* ("The Yes-Sayer," 1930), a *Lehrstück* (didactic play) which Weill wrote with Brecht in Germany.[105] Weill obliged with an expanded version of *Down in the Valley*, which by 1950 was licensed to nearly three hundred schools. On 14 January 1950, NBC broadcast a television performance with Marion Bell, making it the most widely performed of Weill's works during his lifetime and perhaps even beyond.[106] The shift from radio opera to *Lehrstück* likely seemed appropriate to Weill; the *Lehrstück Der Lindberghflug* ("Lindbergh's Flight," 1929) was conceived for radio performance, and Weill considered radio an inherently democratic medium. In the United States, radio "helped to mold uniform national responses; it helped create or reinforce uniform national values and beliefs," as Susman notes, by combining mass cultural entertainment like Amos 'n' Andy with the intimacy of programs like Roosevelt's Fireside Chats.[107]

Both Downes and Weill (but particularly Downes) hoped that *Down in the Valley* would shape the national psyche to better serve the democratic ideals of the postwar United States. The story of a businessman and a small-town everyman's rivalry for a girl reflects the briefly resurgent Popular Front of the postwar era, when folk song again became a signifier of Leftwing populist politics. On 31 December 1945, former members of Pete Seeger's Almanac

[104]  Olin Downes to Charles McArthur, 27 September 1945, ODP, Box 38 Folder 9.

[105]  Hans Heinsheimer to Kurt Weill, 4 September 1947, WLRC, Series 40 Folder "Heinsheimer, H.W.".

[106]  John Graziano, "Musical Dialects in *Down in the Valley*," in *A New Orpheus: Essays on Kurt Weill*, ed. Kim H. Kowalke (New Haven, CT: Yale University Press, 1986), 297.

[107]  Warren I. Susman, *Culture as History: The Transformation of American Society in the Twentieth Century* (New York: Pantheon, 1984), Kindle Edition.

Singers and other Leftist figures gathered in a basement in Greenwich Village and formed People's Songs, an organization that collected, published, and performed folk music, and hoped to "spread these songs around, to bring as many people as possible, the true democratic message."[108] Between 1946 and 1949, People's Songs promoted Leftist causes, and vocally supported the Progressive Party's Henry Wallace's run for president in 1948.[109] Downes was an outspoken supporter of Wallace, and spoke at multiple rallies for the candidate, where he no doubt encountered members of People's Songs.[110] *Down in the Valley* also attempts to set an aesthetic agenda for American opera. The story is remarkably similar to Rodgers and Hammerstein's *Oklahoma!*, which premiered on Broadway in 1943, overshadowing the success of Weill's *Lady in the Dark* (1941) and *One Touch of Venus* (1943). Both Weill and Downes admired *Oklahoma!* but thought that it was too commercial to be considered the foundation of American opera. *Down in the Valley* presented their musical response.

The project began on 11 July 1945, when Downes wrote to MacArthur about an idea for a series of radio operas based on U.S. folk songs. He hoped this opera would encompass a wide variety of forms, leading to "a new form, particularly adaptive to the radio. This form has relation to opera [*sic*]." Downes hoped that these operas would

> attack the snobbery which so far has accorded respect only to what we can call classical music and the music of prestige that is purveyed in concert halls and opera houses. If it fully achieves its purpose, it may have gone as far toward creating a new popular American operatic form as, for example, *The Beggar's Opera* produced in London in 1728, with a score consisting entirely of folk songs and the composed overture.[111]

Downes's reference to *The Beggar's Opera* may have brought Weill to mind given that the composer had reworked the piece into *Die Dreigroschenoper* in 1928. The composer also had experience writing for radio, having worked on German projects including *Das Berliner Requiem* ("The Berlin Requiem") (1928) and *Der Lindberghflug*, U.S. pieces like *The Ballad of the Magna Carta*

---

[108] Quoted in David King Dunaway and Molly Beer, *Singing Out: An Oral History of America's Folk Revivals* (New York: Oxford University Press, 2010), 69.

[109] Cantwell, *When We Were Good*, 165–66; Reuss and Reuss, *American Folk Music and Left-Wing Politics*, Chapter 8.

[110] See ODP, Box 64 Folder 6.

[111] Olin Downes to Charles MacArthur, 11 July 1945, ODP, Box 38 Folder 9.

(1940), and wartime efforts like *Your Navy* and *Towards the Century of the Common Man* (1942). Weill also held similarly democratic ambitions for the radio music, writing in 1929 (when he was still in Germany) that radio compositions should be "capable of interesting a large number of people of all classes."[112] Both radio and educational theatre were part of Weill's conception of *gemeinschaftsbildenden* art, as they both spoke to a broad public of people, and could serve as a means of exploring contemporary issues. Weill hoped *Das Berliner Requiem* would "express what the urban man of our era has to say about the phenomenon of death" and that, through performing the didactic opera *Der Jasager* (1930), the performers would learn "that a community which one joins demands that one actually bear the consequences."[113]

By 30 July, either Downes or MacArthur had brought Weill and playwright Maxwell Anderson onto the project. However, Downes reported that Weill felt that "a younger man more adaptive might work out the thing better." Downes also worried the project might be too similar to the radio program *Cavalcade of America* (1935–1953; it later ran on television 1952–1957), which dramatized important events in U.S. history, often to the sounds of folk music.[114] In its place, Weill suggested dramatizing individual songs. Arnold Sundgaard came onto the project soon after, on the recommendation of Lehman Engel.[115] Sundgaard graduated from the Yale drama school in 1936 and then moved directly into the Chicago FTP, for which he wrote the libretto for the Living Newspaper *Spirochete* (1938). The playwright recalled several meetings between himself and Downes (and probably Weill) in the early days of the project, indicating that, even though Downes was not the official author of the libretto, he profoundly shaped the story.

On 27 September 1945, Downes wrote to MacArthur that Sundgaard and Weill had finished *Down in the Valley*. As the basis of their story, Weill and Sundgaard chose a version of the title song in B.A. Botkin's *A Treasury of American Folklore* from 1942.[116] The original song does not tell a story aside

---

[112] Kurt Weill, "A Note Concerning *Das Berliner Requiem*" (1929), trans. in *KWiE*, 504. On Kurt Weill and the radio in Germany, see Nils Grosch, *Die Musik der Neue Sachlichkeit* (Stuttgart: J.B. Metzler, 1999), 226–39.

[113] Weill, "A Note Concerning *Das Berliner Requiem*," 504, and Kurt Weill, "Topical Dialogue about *Schuloper* Between Kurt Weill and Dr. Hans Fischer" (1930), trans. in *KWiE*, 524.

[114] Olin Downes to Charles MacArthur, 30 July 1945, ODP, Box 38 Folder 9.

[115] This and the following summary of Sundgaard's career and involvement with *Down in the Valley* is drawn from "Arnold Sundgaard: An Oral History Interview with David Farneth," WLRC, Series 60.

[116] Olin Downes to Charles MacArthur, no date, ODP, Box 38 Folder 10. See B.A. Botkin, ed., *A Treasury of American Folklore: Stories, Ballads, and Traditions of the People* (New York: Crown, 1944), 902–3 for the version of "Down in the Valley" used in *Down in the Valley*.

from a fleeting reference to "Birmingham Jail" (possibly in Birmingham, Alabama), so Weill and Sundgaard wrote an original scenario based on the third, fourth, and sixth verses. Sundgaard's story begins with Brack Weaver in jail the evening before his execution. He is charged with killing local businessman Thomas Bouché, and awaits a reply to his to letter to Jennie Parsons confirming that she loves him. When the letter does not arrive, he breaks out of jail to find her. The lovers meet in secret and reminisce about the events leading to Bouché's death, which instigates a long flashback sequence. We learn that Brack wanted to take Jennie to the local barn dance, but her father insisted she accompany Bouché, who was assisting Mr. Parsons with his business. Jennie defies her father to go to the dance with Brack, but Bouché arrives and pulls a knife. There is a scuffle, and Bouché dies. The action returns to the present, and Brack, knowing that Jennie truly loves him, returns to jail and accepts his fate.

The tune "Down in the Valley" provides the framework for the musical structure. A "Leader" sings verses of the song to fill in the narrative gaps (occasionally accompanied by the chorus) in a manner similar to the interscenes in *One Man from Tennessee*, and fragments of the melody reappear in the accompaniment throughout. Weill and Sundgaard also wove several other folk tunes into the score. Jennie and Brack sing "Lonesome Dove" as a love duet. The flashback begins with the townsfolk singing "Little Black Train" in church. Brack courts Jennie to the tune of "Hop Up My Ladies," which is ironically echoed by Bouché in the following scene. The fateful dance is accompanied by the fiddle tune "Sourwood Mountain." Weill drew these tunes from several sources; the published score acknowledges that "Lonesome Dove" came from *The Singin' Gatherin'* (1939), but no other quotes are acknowledged. Weill most likely used the versions of "Hop Up My Ladies" and "Little Black Train" found in John A. and Alan Lomax's *Our Singing Country* (which he owned) and the version of "Sourwood Mountain" from Botkin.[117]

After Sundgaard and Weill finished, Downes arranged to record a demo of the program, now called "Your Songs, America."[118] The demo includes a lengthy conversation between Downes and folk singer Tom Scott discussing many of the aims of the project. Downes made clear his sentiments about the benefits of miscegenation, noting that "these songs met and mingled" on

---

[117] John A. Lomax and Alan Lomax, *Our Singing Country: Folk Songs and Ballads* (New York: Macmillan, 1941), 46, 58; Botkin, *A Treasury of American Folklore*, 897.

[118] A copy of the demo resides in the WLRC, Series W3/14–17.

U.S. soil "just as all the races of the world came here, combining together, and made new types of men and songs." This is a theme in Downes's writing of the era. In 1940, Downes collaborated with Elie Siegmeister to produce *A Treasury of American Song*, with a second edition in 1943. In the introduction, Downes compared a people's music to their ethnic heritage, writing that "no nation in the world can point to an unadulterated musical ancestry, any more than it can point to a bloodstream exclusively its own," and that "all national music is an amalgamation of racial strands and historical processes consequent upon wars, migrations, trade, and other forms of interpenetration. And the richer and more characteristic the folk strains of a people, the more varied and colorful the music is likely to be."[119] He felt that miscegenation was the root of the strength and vibrancy not only of American music, but also of American democracy. In contrast to Europe, whose folk music "was essentially the song of the peasant and the illiterate," the folk music of America crossed both class and racial boundaries:

> With every great social revolution, such as the French and American revolutions that ushered in the nineteenth century, and the Civil War, accompanied by the freeing of the slaves in America and followed by the freeing of the serfs in Russia, so-called "folk music" and so-called "art music" came nearer together. But it is not until the founding of the American nation, wherein classes, types, and races mingled in a great polyglot, that we perceive the genuine diffusion of democratic essence, not only in our society, but in the body of our national music.[120]

In this, *Down in the Valley* resembles Walter Kerr's and Elie Siegmiester's *Sing Out, Sweet Land!*, a wartime musical that emphasized the breadth and depth of the America's musical heritage, in which "the sounds of American folk music were celebrated as beacons of global freedom."[121] Many critics celebrated *Sing Out, Sweet Land!* as an authentic expression of American ideals, although Downes disliked the flimsy plot that was structured merely to accommodate the music. He may have seen *Down in the Valley* as a corrective. But in many ways, Downes fell short of their professed ideals. While Downes wrote favorably of the heterogeneous heritage of American folk music, the

---

[119] Olin Downes, Introduction to *A Treasury of American Song*, by Olin Downes and Elie Siegmeister, 2nd ed. (New York: Alfred A. Knopf, 1943), 12.

[120] Downes, Introduction to *A Treasury of American Song*, 13.

[121] Fauser, *Sounds of War*, 154.

songs he initially proposed for the project and the ones that Weill included in the score are overwhelmingly Anglo-Saxon. The only nod to the idea that the strength of American folk song grew from its mixed roots is "Little Black Train," which he characterized as a mix of African American and white spiritual practices on the initial radio demo.[122]

Downes also had one eye on audiences on the other side of the Atlantic. For Downes, U.S. folk music not only reflected democracy; it also had the potential to instill democratic ideals around the world. In the early days of the project, Downes wrote to MacArthur:

> If we want an antidote to pernicious and undemocratic doctrine, here it is. If our army officers who are trying to administer and re-educate Germany had any particular degree of sense or imagination they would know that Fritz would have a far clearer understanding [of] our conceptions of life and government through hearing our songs and reading our poems and dramas than by other means.[123]

Downes's statement echoes a widespread feeling in the United States that, as one of the few nations to come out of World War II with its infrastructure and political institutions intact, it was the nation's responsibility to shape the postwar world. As popular columnist Walter Lippman wrote, "What Rome was to the ancient world, what Great Britain has been to the modern world, America is to be to the world of tomorrow," reiterating the "city on a hill" notion that had driven in the World's Fair several years before.[124]

The piece's similarity to *One Man from Tennessee* also helps to bring the piece's Leftist politics into focus. Like Davy Crockett, Brack is a simple country boy, albeit without any apparent political goals or ulterior motives. Although more subtle, Bouché is portrayed as just as much of a corrupt businessman as Spindle in *One Man from Tennessee*. Brack warns Jennie, "My Pa had business with Mr. Bouché. That's how we lost our place." Like Spindle, Bouché is also incapable of properly singing folk music. He only sings once in the show, and he just repeats Brack's rendition of "Hop Up My Ladies." Brack's version is accompanied by a cheerful "boom-chunk" pattern with

---

[122] This reflects Lomax's categorization under songs of the Holiness people, which Lomax writes sang both white and black spirituals. Lomax and Lomax, *Our Singing Country*, 44.

[123] Olin Downes to Charles MacArthur, 12 October 1945, ODP, Box 38 Folder 10.

[124] Quoted in James T. Patterson, *Grand Expectations: The United States, 1945–1974* (New York and Oxford, UK: Oxford University Press, 1996), 7.

pizzicato strings and the occasional brass accent and largely diatonic harmony. In contrast, Bouché is accompanied by markers of jazz: prominent trombone glissandos, hi-hat and ride cymbal-heavy percussion, and bluesy harmony. Although the libretto is far less obvious about Bouché's nefarious nature, Weill makes it clear in the music that this man does not belong in the community. He is an interloper from the city who uses the good folks of the town for his own corrupt purposes, resembling the "bosses" who appear in the proletarian literature of the 1930s.

In any case, the project did not find a backer, and *Down in the Valley* went back on the shelf. Weill was disappointed, writing to MacArthur on 21 January 1946,

> I have become convinced for a long time that in a deeply democratic country like ours, art should belong to the people. It should come out of their thinking and their emotions, and it should become part of their lives. It should be "popular" in the highest sense of the word. Only by making this our aim can we create an American art, as opposed to the art of the old countries which belonged to a selected class of aristocrats or "connoisseurs."[125]

Weill was likely paraphrasing rhetoric he heard from Downes, but his ideas show that he was interested in the project's political aspects. It also echoes much of Weill's writing on *Gebrauchsmusik* from the late 1920s and early 1930s.

The project gained new life when Heinsheimer contacted Weill in 1947, at which point Weill expanded the piece by adding an aria during the opening sequence for Brack ("Oh Where Is the One") and an aria for Jenny just before the lovers meet ("Brack Weaver, My True Love"), as well as making other minor adjustments.[126] The new version premiered on 15 July 1948 by students at Indiana University. The first professional production appeared a year later at the Lemonade Opera, a small company based in Greenwich Village down the street from Peoples Songs. The company resembled some of the 1930s collectives like the Group Theatre in its communal structure (performers contributed $25 as an investment, then split the profits at the

---

[125] Kurt Weill to Charles MacArthur, 21 January 1946, WLA, Box 47 Folder 11.
[126] For a complete catalog of the differences between the 1945 and 1948 versions, see Graziano, "Musical Dialects in *Down in the Valley*," 317–19.

end of the season) and in its goals of bringing high art to a popular audience.[127] It was this mix of dedication to elite art and populist principles that attracted Weill to the company: he wrote to his parents, "They call themselves the 'Lemonade Opera' because they sell lemonade during intermission to emphasize the difference from the formality of grand opera."[128]

The politics of *Down in the Valley* are subtler than those of *One Man from Tennessee* or Weill's contemporaneous works like *Lost in the Stars* and *Love Life*. This may be because, in *Down in the Valley*, Weill and Downes were testing the new, postwar cultural waters. The wartime surge of patriotism put Weill, as a German immigrant, in an uncomfortable position (discussed further in the following chapter), but when Weill began the project in the summer of 1945, the war with Germany had ended, even if the war in the Pacific had not. He and Downes may have deliberately made the politics inconspicuous as a way to carefully wade back into the waters of criticizing the nation. Weill intended to write a sequel to *Down in the Valley* with clear agitprop leanings. In August 1949, he wrote to Sundgaard with the idea for a similar piece based on the song "Shenandoah" that concerned the difficult lives of miners in Appalachia. His proposed scenario reads very much like a Depression-era proletarian play: "The story of a young miner and his girl, longing to escape from the mining town, but every time they want to leave they find that they are tied down through 'circumstances'—marriage, children, mortgages, etc. until the end, after the catastrophe, the man escapes to 'Shenandoah' in death."[129] Sundgaard seemed amenable to the idea, but Weill died a few months later.

## Rewriting *Oklahoma!*

*Down in the Valley*'s populism is a response to the contemporary idea of the "folk opera," particularly as exemplified by *Oklahoma!*. Downes had long been interested in the idea of folk opera, and Weill consistently rankled at Rodgers's success, feeling that he had done all the aesthetic work toward creating an "integrated" musical while Rodgers received most of the credit.

---

[127] On the history and goals of the Lemonade Opera, see Victoria Etnier Villamil, *From Johnson's Kids to Lemonade Opera: The American Classical Singer Comes of Age* (Boston: Northeastern University Press, 2004), 147–49.

[128] Quoted in Stephen Hinton, *Weill's Musical Theater: Stages of Reform* (Berkeley: University of California Press, 2012), 361.

[129] Kurt Weill to Arnold Sundgaard, 8 August 1949, WLA, Box 47 Folder 14.

He wrote to Lenya after the opening of Rodgers and Hammerstein's *Carousel* (1945), "So Rodgers 'is defining a new directive for musical comedy.' I had always thought I've been doing that—but I must have been mistaken. Rodgers certainly has won the first round in that race between him and me. But I suppose there will be a second and a third round."[130] *Carousel* must have particularly irked Weill. He had been interested in the idea of a musical version of Ferenc Molnár's *Liliom* (the play that was the basis for *Carousel*), and he entered into negotiations with the Theatre Guild over the idea in 1937, long before the Guild turned to Rodgers and Hammerstein to set *Oklahoma!*[131] When *Carousel* appeared on Broadway in 1945, critics hailed the show as an "American opera," preempting Weill's "Broadway opera" *Street Scene* (1946), its own kind of "folk opera," which he was just starting to compose when *Carousel* opened.[132]

Downes had long called on composers to develop a unique American voice in the concert hall and opera house. Generally speaking, Downes advocated for a popular style modeled on the *singspiel* or *opera buffa*, and encouraged composers to draw on popular and folk idioms. As precedents, he recommended Jerome Kern's *Show Boat* (1927), and Marc Connelly's *The Green Pastures* (1931, whose strong choral presence likely influenced *Down in the Valley*).[133] He had ambivalent feelings about George Gershwin, Ira Gershwin, and Dubose Heyward's *Porgy and Bess* (1935), which he called "a very expert and diverting by-product of the musico-dramatic stage rather than a thing prophetic of American tendencies in the opera house."[134] He felt *Oklahoma!* was a more positive step toward American opera, albeit a flawed one, as the score was "not folk music, but that of a Broadway composer writing in the popular vein."[135]

*Down in the Valley* and *Oklahoma!* share many similarities. Both concern the question of who will take the girl to the dance. Brack, like *Oklahoma!*'s Curly, is an everyman figure, rough around the edges but a good match

---

[130] *WLL(e)*, 460.

[131] Tim Carter, *Oklahoma! The Making of an American Musical* (New Haven, CT: Yale University Press, 2007), 5–7.

[132] On *Oklahoma!* as "American opera," see Carter, *Oklahoma!*, 174; On *Carousel* as "American Opera" see Mark D'Andre, "The Theatre Guild, *Carousel*, and the Cultural Field of American Musical Theatre" (PhD diss., Yale University, 2000), 237–8.

[133] Olin Downes, "*Porgy and Bess* and the Future of American Opera," in *Olin Downes on Music: A Selection of His Writings during the Half-Century 1906–1955*, ed. Irene Downes (New York: Simon and Schuster, 1957), 211; Olin Downes, "The Philharmonic Scores with *Show Boat*" (1941), in *Olin Downes on Music*, ed. Downes, 298.

[134] Downes, "*Porgy and Bess*," 211.

[135] Olin Downes, "*Oklahoma!*," in *Olin Downes on Music*, ed. Downes, 317.

for the wholesome farm girl. Bouché is a combination of the rival suitor in the two love triangles in *Oklahoma!*: Jud, and the peddler Ali Hakim (Will Parker's rival for Ado Annie in *Oklahoma!*), two characters who are linked through their status as outsiders.[136] Like Jud, who lusts after Laurey, Bouché is depicted as a sinister presence in the community, threatening to upend the established order. As for Ali Hakim, both he and Bouché are vaguely foreign businessmen who peddle somewhat dubious goods, although Hakim is treated as harmless comic relief at worst, and Bouché is clearly a danger. Both shows have the rejected side of the love triangle attacking his rival and dying in that fight.

On a musical level, *Down in the Valley* also resembles *Oklahoma!* Both begin with a short orchestral introduction followed by an *a cappella* folk-like song. In *Oklahoma!* the orchestra plays a pastoral interlude, and a measure or two later, Curly enters in $\frac{3}{4}$, singing "Oh, What a Beautiful Mornin'." *Down in the Valley* opens with a brief fanfare (meant to introduce the radio series, but later incorporated into the score), followed by the Leader singing a ballad in triple time in this case, $\frac{6}{8}$ (Example 3.5).[137] But whereas the scalar and triadic opening of *Oklahoma!* is bright and cheerful, the opening of *Down in the Valley* is chromatic, dark, and ambiguous. Although the key signature is F major, the prominent D-flat in the tenor and the V–I motion in C in the bass muddy the tonal waters, and the result is a feeling of either F minor or a Phrygian-inflected C. The entrance of the melody clears up the tonal confusion, but introduces modal confusion; the Leader's unambiguous F major contradicts the D-flat in the accompaniment. The entire effect speaks to something not quite right lurking in this community, whereas *Oklahoma!* opens on an idyllic frontier.

The dance sequences of "The Farmer and the Cowman" from *Oklahoma!* and "Sourwood Mountain" from *Down in the Valley* also invite comparison. Both sequences form the backdrop for the development of the major themes of each show. In *Oklahoma!* Aunt Eller declares that farmers and ranchers must learn to live together, foreshadowing farm girl Laurey's marriage to cowman Curly, and signaling the readiness of the Indian territory to take its place as the titular state.[138] But just as the ominous setting of

---

[136] Andrea Most, *Making Americans: Jews and the Broadway Musical* (Cambridge, MA: Harvard University Press, 2004), 116.

[137] See Graziano, "Musical Dialects in *Down in the Valley*," 317. Example 3.5 is taken from Arnold Sundgaard and Kurt Weill, *Down in the Valley* (New York: G. Schirmer, 1948).

[138] Carter, *Oklahoma!*, 192.

**Example 3.5** *Down in the Valley,* "Down in the Valley."

"Down in the Valley" darkly mirrors "Oh, What a Beautiful Mornin," the dramatic function of "Sourwood Mountain" reverses that of "The Farmer and the Cowman." In *Oklahoma!* the dance scene shows the community overcoming their differences, not always willingly (Andrew sings his verse held at gunpoint by Aunt Eller), but nevertheless in service of the greater good. In "Sourwood Mountain," the different elements of the community, represented by "everyman" Brack and businessman Bouché, come to blows, eventually destroying one another. The farmer, the cowman, and the merchant (as Ike Skidmore of *Oklahoma!* reminds us) of the community of *Down in the Valley* cannot live in peace. If, in *Oklahoma!* the community that dances together can be a state together, in *Down in the Valley*, the community that cannot dance together is destined for tragedy.

What happens after the dance also speaks to the differing cultures and aims of *Oklahoma!* and *Down in the Valley*. In *Oklahoma!* Curly is declared innocent in Jud's death, but *Down in the Valley* is less clear. While the narrator states that Brack "killed Tom Bouché, who had brought her [Jennie]

great sorrow," the stage directions for the fateful moment read, "Brack lunges toward Bouché. The men struggle for a moment and then the dancers close in on them," indicating that the actual death is obscured. In the NBC television broadcast, Bouché charges Brack with a knife, Brack grabs his arm, and they both fall out of the frame, so the death occurs off-screen. It is plausible that Bouché, like Jud, falls on his own knife.[139] Even if that is not the case, Brack (like Curly) at worst kills a man in self-defense.

The question of Brack's guilt becomes important considering the show's relationship to *Oklahoma!*. Rodgers and Hammerstein's ending significantly revises its source, Lynn Riggs's *Green Grow the Lilacs*, in which Curly is permitted to spend his wedding night with Laurey, but must stand trial the next day. The altered ending, in which Curly is unambiguously acquitted, cements the "overall feel-good factor" of the show, with its emphasis on "nostalgia, idealism, community spirit, and patriotism," all appropriate for wartime America.[140] But in *Down in the Valley*, the possibility of Brack's innocence renders the ending even more tragic, and speaks to a more uncertain environment in the early postwar era, when issues of guilt and innocence dominated both national and international politics. In wartime, the difference between heroes and villains was clear. In the era of McCarthyism, de-Nazification, and the nascent Cold War, those lines were becoming blurrier by the day.

The trajectory from *One Man from Tennessee* to *Down in the Valley* shows Weill becoming proficient at adapting to differing political contexts. The folk music pastiches of *One Man from Tennessee* betray a composer ill at ease with both the language and the music of his new country; awkward text setting combines with repetitive melodies that show none of the rhythmic or melodic invention of Weill's later U.S. works. In this sense, *One Man from Tennessee* belongs with *Johnny Johnson* and *You and Me* in Weill's *oeuvre*; it is an interesting experiment in combining the "tell-not-show" political aesthetic of epic theatre with the U.S. taste for melodrama and sentimentality, but the result is uneven at best. *Railroads on Parade* gave Weill a chance to study U.S. folk song on a much deeper level. His notebooks are filled with tunes copied from Lomax and others, showing a prolonged study of U.S. folk song, which resulted in a score much more sophisticated than *One Man from Tennessee*. The pastiches sit comfortably with the quotations, sounding like

[139] Ronald Sanders, in his biography, subscribes to this scenario. See *The Days Grow Short: The Life and Music of Kurt Weill* (New York: Holt, Rinehart, and Winston, 1980), 368.

[140] Carter, *Oklahoma!*, 186.

half-remembered tunes that one cannot quite place. This familiar, nostalgic musical language supports the patriotic and commercial thrust of the pageant, and appealed to a nation fearful of being drawn into conflict on the other side of the globe. *Down in the Valley* is the opposite; Weill's complex harmonic language makes the folk songs sound strange, asking the audience to think more deeply about the apparently simple story.

*Down in the Valley* shows that, for Weill, the United States remained a wonderful but imperfect place. Weill understood that the "city on a hill" was fragile, and that constant vigilance was required to maintain that "light unto the nations." During the war, Weill worked to show how these forces must be overcome in every generation, demonstrating that victory in the battles between multicultural democracy on the one hand and ethnically pure fascism would lie at the very core of American identity.

# 4

# Living History

## American History and World War II

On 18 August 1937, Weill heard a broadcast of President Franklin Roosevelt's speech before a performance of Paul Green's historical pageant *The Lost Colony*. He wrote to Green the next day:

> I have the feeling that most people who ever came to this country, came for the same reasons which brought me here: fleeing from the hate, the oppression, and the restlessness and troubles of the Old World to find freedom and happiness in the New World. It is exactly this idea which the President expressed in his speech: "Most of them—the men, the women and the children, come hither seeking something very different—seeing an opportunity which they could not find in their homes of the old world."[1]

At the time, Green and Weill were working on a pageant commemorating the signing of Constitution for the Federal Theatre Project called *The Common Glory*, which was set in the early days of the nation, and which explored the ways that U.S. history still informed national life.[2] This theme pervades several of Weill's works from the period, both finished and unfinished, including *One Man from Tennessee* (1937) and *Railroads on Parade* (1939, rev. 1940).

Soon after, Weill began work on *Knickerbocker Holiday* (1938), which focuses on the nation's immigrant roots. Later, when the U.S. entered the war, he endeavored to remind U.S. audiences of their historical responsibility to keep democracy alive and to protect the innocent from tyranny in the pageants *Fun to Be Free* (1941) and *We Will Never Die* (1943). Finally, in 1944 he wrote the music for *Where Do We Go from Here?* (released in

---

[1] Kurt Weill to Paul Green, 19 August 1937, WLA, Box 47 Folder 6. Weill accurately quotes Roosevelt's speech.

[2] On *The Common Glory*, see Tim Carter, "Celebrating the Nation: Kurt Weill, Paul Green, and the Federal Theatre Project (1937)," *Journal of the Society for American Music* 5, no. 3 (2011): 297–334.

*Kurt Weill's America*. Naomi Graber, Oxford University Press (2021). © Oxford University Press.
DOI: 10.1093/oso/9780190906580.003.0005

1945), a big-budget Hollywood musical that similarly looked to America's immigrant past (in the form of Columbus's voyage) to define her course for the present.

The questions of national identity raised in these projects—especially *Knickerbocker Holiday* and *Where Do We Go from Here?*—were fundamental to the wider public. Broadway and Hollywood have long been staging grounds for promoting various versions of American identity, and depictions of history in these contexts could be powerful ways to help Americans understand "their own cultural moments," and maybe even produce societal change.[3] In the 1910s, Van Wyck Brooks chastised professors of American literature for "severing the warm artery that ought to lead from the present back to the past," calling on the academy to examine the cultural and social circumstances of great works of literature, all in an effort to give aspiring writers a "usable past" on which to build.[4] The movement gained momentum during the 1930s; as the Depression worsened, the nation searched its roots for a new foundation on which to build their culture and community.[5] When World War II began, the issue of the "usable past" became even more urgent, as musicians like Henry Cowell, Aaron Copland, Virgil Thomson, and Elie Siegmeister focused on developing a musical tradition untainted by fascist Europe.[6]

*The Common Glory, One Man from Tennessee,* and *Railroads on Parade* embody this impulse, as Weill and his collaborators reframed history in order to inspire audiences of the day. This impulse also inflects *Knickerbocker Holiday* and *Where Do We Go from Here?*, which mix fact and fiction to create a usable past for immigrants, thus validating their place in contemporary culture. Both musically differentiate "Old World" and "New World" sensibilities, and ultimately show the latter to be superior, not just musically, but

[3] Elissa Harbert, "Remembering the Revolution: Music in Stage and Screen Representations of Early America During the Bicentennial Years" (PhD diss., Northwestern University, 2013), 16. See also John Bush Jones, *Our Musicals, Ourselves: A Social History of the American Musical* (Waltham, MA: Brandeis University Press, 2004); Andrea Most, *Making Americans: Jews and the Broadway Musical* (Cambridge, MA: Harvard University Press, 2004); Raymond Knapp, *The American Musical and the Formation of National Identity* (Princeton, NJ: Princeton University Press, 2006); Elizabeth Titrington Craft, "Becoming American Onstage: Broadway Narratives of Immigrant Experiences in the United States" (PhD diss., Harvard University, 2014).

[4] Van Wyck Brooks, "On Creating a Usable Past" (1918), in *American Literature, American Culture,* ed. Gordon Hutner (Oxford, UK: Oxford University Press, 1999), 216.

[5] Victoria Grieve, *The Federal Art Project and the Creation of Middlebrow Culture* (Urbana: University of Illinois Press, 2009), 51; Alfred Haworth Jones, "The Search for a Usable American Past in the New Deal Era," *American Quarterly* 23 (1971): 710–24.

[6] Annegret Fauser, *Sounds of War: Music in the United States During World War II* (Oxford, UK: Oxford University Press, 2013), 138–51.

culturally and politically. They also show that immigrants—even currently undesirable ones—could be easily assimilated into, and even redeemed in, the crucible of America. The portrayal of history, immigrants, and foreigners in *Knickerbocker Holiday* did not bother critics or audiences, but librettist Maxwell Anderson's ambiguous satire of New Deal politics alarmed many, including Weill. In the wartime *Where Do We Go from Here?* the creative team clashed with the Office of War Information (OWI), the propaganda wing of the government, which disapproved of their comic depiction of both historical events and foreigners.

## Negotiating the Politics of *Knickerbocker Holiday*

On 5 June 1936, Lenya wrote to her sister-in-law Rita Weill, "Yesterday we were invited to the countryside by Maxwell Anderson," who "is crazy about Kurt, and wants him to write music for his plays."[7] Weill had already expressed admiration for Anderson, who won the New York Drama Critics' Circle Award two years in a row for *Winterset* (1935) and *High Tor* (1936), the latter beating runner-up *Johnny Johnson*.[8] On 19 October 1938, Weill and Anderson's first collaboration opened on Broadway: *Knickerbocker Holiday*, a musical comedy loosely inspired by Washington Irving's satirical novel *Diedrich Knickerbocker's A History of New York* (1809). A Gilbert-and-Sullivan-esque satire of the New Deal, the story concerns Dutch colonists in seventeenth-century New Amsterdam struggling against the powerful new governor Pietr Stuyvesant, a stand-in for President Roosevelt. The hero, Brom Broeck, eventually convinces the colonists to defy the tyrannical governor, leading to the foundation of a democratic government.

*Knickerbocker Holiday* was one of the first productions of the Playwrights' Producing Company (PPC), formed in July 1938, comprising playwrights Anderson, S.N. Behrman, Robert Sherwood, Elmer Rice, and Sidney Howard, plus their legal adviser John Wharton.[9] The goal of the venture was twofold: regular access to professional critique, and bypassing the

---

[7] *W-Fam*, 346.

[8] *High Tor* also includes characters inspired by Washington Irving's *Diedrich Knickerbocker* novel.

[9] Albert Claude Gordon, "A Critical Study of the History and Development of the Playwrights Producing Company" (PhD diss., Tulane University, 1965), 49. Elmar Juchem describes the genesis, production, and reception history of *Knickerbocker Holiday* in *Kurt Weill und Maxwell Anderson: Neue Wege zu einem amerikanischen Musiktheater, 1938–1950* (Stuttgart: J.B. Metzler 1999), Chapter 2.

interference of outside producers.[10] Each member would submit their work to the others for review, and the best would be produced, although the PPC remained open to mounting productions by others. The match between Weill and the PPC proved fruitful for all parties. After a disappointing sojourn in Hollywood, Weill looked to return to live theatre. Anderson was interested in political satire, and Weill's work with Brecht in Europe may have made him an appealing partner. Indeed, several early songs in *Knickerbocker Holiday* are labeled "Ballad," hearkening back to songs like "Die Moritat von Mackie Messer" ("The Ballad of Mack the Knife") and "Ballade vom angenehmen Leben" ("Ballad of the Pleasant Life") from *Die Dreigroschenoper* (1928). More broadly, the PPC competed with other theatrical organizations dedicated to reforming Broadway, many of whom had begun to consider musical theatre the way of the future. The Theatre Guild's production of the Gershwins' *Porgy and Bess* (1935) and Weill and the Group's *Johnny Johnson* (1936) had opened to critical (though not necessarily popular) acclaim.

In April 1938, Anderson suggested turning Irving's novel into a musical, and he and Weill resolved to write the romantic lead, Brom Broeck, for their mutual friend Burgess Meredith.[11] But the main attraction of the novel for Anderson was the character of Governor Pietr Stuyvesant, whom he used to satirize Roosevelt on the basis of the president's Dutch heritage. Anderson also included a character named Roosevelt, a corrupt member of the town council who is ostensibly the president's ancestor.[12] But during the summer, Meredith suffered an emotional breakdown and took refuge in Europe, and in a rambling letter to Anderson, confessed that he was not emotionally able to return.[13] Around the same time, the PPC hired director Joshua Logan, the twenty-nine-year-old rising star of musical comedy.[14] He suggested hiring a "great star" to play Stuyvesant, and someone (no one remembers who) suggested Walter Huston. The actor expressed interest, but thought the character too unlikable (even for a villain), and requested that "just for a moment the old son-of-a-bitch be charming."[15] In response, Weill composed

[10] John F. Wharton, *Life Among the Playwrights: Being Mostly the Story of the Playwrights Producing Company* (New York: Quadrangle/New York Times Book Co., 1974), 27.

[11] Meredith starred in three previous Anderson plays and worked with Weill on the unfinished *One Man from Tennessee*.

[12] Roosevelt's ancestry does include a seventeenth-century New Amsterdam alderman, but it is unclear if Anderson knew that.

[13] Burgess Meredith to Maxwell Anderson, 20 July 1938, MAC, Series "Misc." Folder "Meredith, Burgess ALS TLS 2 Telegrams to Anderson, Maxwell 1937–1941."

[14] "News of the Stage," *NYT*, 1 July 1938, 22.

[15] Joshua Logan, *Josh: My Up and Down, In and Out Life* (New York: Delacorte, 1976), 110.

what would become *Knickerbocker Holiday*'s biggest hit, "September Song," for the actor's unique, gravelly voice, adapting material from *Der Kuhhandel* (1933) for the melody. Ray Middleton earned the role of author-narrator Washington Irving, and Broadway novices Richard Kollmar and Jeanne Madden were cast as young lovers Brom Broeck and Tina Tienhoven. Rehearsals began in August, and the show continued to develop during the out-of-town tryouts in Hartford, Boston, and Washington, DC, as well as the New York previews.

Having never written a musical, Anderson turned to Gilbert and Sullivan's *The Mikado* for inspiration.[16] Echoing *The Mikado*, the play begins with the council of New Amsterdam choosing someone to hang in honor of Governor Stuyvesant's arrival. They settle on Brom, a young man who is constitutionally unable to take orders, and who is in love with Tina Tienhoven, the daughter of the president of the council. Stuyvesant is impressed by Brom's cleverness, and grants him a reprieve, which is rescinded when Stuyvesant demands Tina's hand in marriage. Brom is subsequently thrown in jail. In Act II, Stuyvesant runs a series of military drills to expunge any sense of individuality. But when Native Americans attack, Brom saves the community, albeit in defiance of Stuyvesant's orders. Stuyvesant sentences Brom to death for disobedience, but the council refuses to carry out the execution. Stuyvesant relents when the narrator, Washington Irving, grants him the status of "American," and all ends happily.

The details of Anderson's libretto went through numerous revisions during rehearsals and tryouts.[17] In the "Preface to the Politics of *Knickerbocker Holiday*," which was published in the *New York Times* and with the libretto, Anderson wrote that government was in "continual danger of lapsing into pure gangsterism, pure terrorism and plundering," and that "the continent of Europe has been captured by such governments within the last few years, and our own government is rapidly assuming economic and social responsibilities which take us in the same direction."[18] But Weill, like many immigrants, considered the president an ally, and pushed back against Anderson's

---

[16] Logan, *Josh*, 109.

[17] See Juchem, *Kurt Weill und Maxwell Anderson*, 76–77, for a table that compares the various stages of the libretto. Since Juchem's study, one more libretto for *Knickerbocker Holiday* has been found, but it adds little of interest.

[18] Maxwell Anderson, "Preface to the Politics to *Knickerbocker Holiday*," in Maxwell Anderson and Kurt Weill, *Knickerbocker Holiday: A Musical Comedy in Two Acts* (Washington, DC, 1938), vi. It appeared in *NYT* as "On Government," on 13 November 1938, 177.

anti-Roosevelt stance.[19] The composer initially conceived of Stuyvesant as representing the corrupt leaders of the Weimar Republic, or "the father of all ambitious governments who try to help the country but cannot get along without the help of the crooks," as he wrote to Anderson. He continues, "Here may be your chance to draw a parallel between Stuyvesant and Roosevelt: the rich man is the one who wants to surrender the town" because "he expects better profits" that way. In the end, Stuyvesant "finally turns to the people in the street, but it is too late."[20] In Weill's version of the story, the problem with Roosevelt/Stuyvesant is not that he is too dictatorial, rather, he is too slow to act because he is overly concerned with his profit margin. Stuyvesant's failure to act echoes the inaction of the corrupt Weimar Republic, with the government's connections to "crooks" blinding them to the danger of the Nazi party. This reflects the trend of immigrants who, after overcoming the initial trials and tribulations of navigating a new language and culture, begin to think about the events that led up to their initial flight from Germany, and considering what went wrong.[21] Weill's version of the story might have been a warning to U.S. audiences that the situation in Europe posed a threat, and that they should act before it was too late.

Anderson did not adopt Weill's suggestion, but he did make some concessions. One was to soften the character of Councilman Roosevelt. In an early version of the opening scene, Councilman Roosevelt suggests using the impending execution as an excuse to levy an unnecessary tax, a line that was eventually deleted.[22] By the final libretto, Anderson made the Councilman the first to rebel against Stuyvesant's order to hang Brom. But as the fictional Roosevelt became more humane, Stuyvesant became more authoritarian, and in the process became more like Hitler than FDR. For example, the lyrics of the first draft of "All Hail the Political Honeymoon," in which Stuyvesant lays out his vision for New Amsterdam, read "Then hail the political honeymoon / And the honeymoon of time / To each individual man his boon / In a plenitude

[19] Anthony Heilbut, *Exiled in Paradise: German Refugee Artists and Intellectuals in America from the 1930's to the Present* (New York: Viking, 1983), 196. Logan and other members of the PPC also took issue with Anderson's characterization of Roosevelt. Juchem, *Kurt Weill und Maxwell Anderson*, 78–83.

[20] Kurt Weill to Maxwell Anderson, 17 April 1938, MAC, Series "Misc." Folder "Weill, Kurt 4 ALS 3 TLS 1 telegram to Anderson, Maxwell 1 – nd 7 – 1937–1947."

[21] Claus-Dieter Krohn, *Intellectuals in Exile: Refugee Scholars and the New School for Social Research*, trans. Rita and Robert Kimber (Amherst: University of Massachusetts Press, 1993), 129–39.

[22] Maxwell Anderson, *Knickerbocker Holiday*, draft deposited in the Library of Congress, 16 July 1938, Copy in WLRC, Series 20 Box K7 Folder 1938b, 1–22.

sublime."[23] By the final libretto, the line is "Then hail the political honeymoon / Sing the news to the hoi polloi / Of each individual man his boon / In an age of strength through joy!" The line is an allusion to the Nazi leisure organization "Kraft durch Freude." U.S. audiences could easily make the connection: on 3 July 1938 (about a month before the phrase appears in the libretto), the *New York Times* announced the imminent production of a new German car (the Volkswagen "Beetle") called the "Strength through Joy," which the paper named "Baby Hitlers."[24] By having the character quote a Nazi slogan, Anderson left little doubt as to who Stuyvesant represented. But Anderson still retained some of his most trenchant criticisms of the New Deal, including the scene in which Stuyvesant explains how his strategy of doubling prices, profits, and wages will save New Amsterdam: according to Stuyvesant, it will cause the total collapse of the economy, forcing a government takeover, which is undoubtedly what Anderson feared was Roosevelt's endgame. The result was a somewhat muddled satire.

Weill, Logan, and the PPC also convinced Anderson to cut many long-winded asides on the nature of democracy. Early drafts have Brom introducing himself with the song "Brom's Complaint" (Example 4.1), a patter song that details his inability to take orders.[25] But the collaborators may have felt it odd to introduce the "first American"—as Brom christens himself—to music that was so tied to British musical theatre, so "Brom's Complaint" was quickly replaced with "Why Should We Want a Democracy," which were the lyrics Weill originally set when composing the tune that eventually became "How Can You Tell an American?" "Why Should We Want a Democracy" described the birth of democratic governments from the corrupt ashes of tyranny (the indented lines indicate what Anderson hoped to express, but he never completed the lyrics):

> Before there were governments at all,
> There were robbers to circumvent,
> And so they very cleverly proceeded to install
> A gang as the government.
>
> Now on this robber gang devolved the duty and the pleasure
> Of keeping all competitors, and nothing at its leisure,
> And since it has experience at taxing mine and yours,

---

[23] Maxwell Anderson, *Knickerbocker Holiday*, Handwritten Draft, Copy in WLRC, Series 20 Box K7 Folder 1938c, 38.

[24] "German Car for Masses," *NYT*, 3 July 1938, 112.

[25] "Brom's Complaint" resides in WLA, Box 14 Folder 239.

**Example 4.1** *Knickerbocker Holiday*, "Brom's Complaint."

**Example 4.1** *Continued*

It's robbed us to the limit of what moral man endures.

For government by nature's a monopoly in crime

Has been, and will be till the end of time

    Throwing out the robbers periodically

    Replacing the professionals with amateurs

And that's a democracy![26]

[26] Maxwell Anderson, "Why Should We Want a Democracy?," MAC, Series "Works" Folder "[Knickerbocker Holiday]: 'Why Should We Want a Democracy?,' Ams with A revisions (2pp) n.d."

The change to "How Can You Tell an American?" was likely made because the song that served as the finale of the show at the time, "The Ballad of Democracy," expressed the same sentiment. "The Ballad of Democracy" was meant as a counterpart to "The Ballad of the Robbers," with Brom describing the overthrow of a tyrannical government:

> And so the common man rose up,
> Who much and long endures,
> And put a robber-gang in power
> Composed of amateurs.
>
> [. . .]
>
> But when these amateurs have learned
> To rob efficiently,
> We turn them out, and put in fresh,
> And that's democracy.[27]

Both "How Can You Tell an American?" and "Ballad of Democracy" appear in the first rehearsal script, but the latter's repetitive nature (eight stanzas in all) would have drastically slowed down the pace of the show, so Anderson replaced "The Ballad of Democracy" with a reprise of "How Can You Tell an American?"

With all these changes, *Knickerbocker Holiday* now told the story of how to become an American, even if you were not born on American soil. Other small shifts in the libretto accompanied the addition of "How Can You Tell an American?" that indicate that the creators of the show wanted to emphasize nationalist, rather than political, values. Brom's inability to take orders was originally "almost a congenital defect": "I left Holland thinking I could escape it in a new, free country, but it's worse here," as he tells Tina.[28] However, in the final libretto the condition only manifested itself in New Amsterdam. He explains, "I was never bothered this way in Holland. I used to take orders perfectly well. No, it started in this country that winter I was out in the woods living on wild turkey and Indian corn." In the earlier version, Brom's issues make him an American even before he arrives; his condition cannot be learned. However, in the later version, becoming an American is a choice that immigrants can make by participating in local culture.

---

[27] Anderson, *Knickerbocker Holiday*, Handwritten Draft, 77–78.
[28] Maxwell Anderson, *Knickerbocker Holiday*, copy from the estate of Henry Lea, WLRC, Series 20 Box k7 Folder 1938f, 1–14.

But these changes were not enough to save the show from accusations of pedantry when it opened at the Ethel Barrymore Theatre on 19 October 1938. The reviewer J.D.K. for the *Wall Street Journal* wrote that the operetta-like structure "seems to lend a heaviness rather than anything else to numbers." However, he wrote that Weill "has written a tuneful score," and that Huston "brings a zest and reality to the part which raises the tempo of the entire play."[29] Charles Angoff of the *North American Review* said that "such ponderous lyrics and so dull a tale have almost never before reached Broadway. Not even the able Mr. Walter Huston, who plays the part of Peter Stuyvesant, and Mr. Kurt Weill, an accomplished composer, can save *Knickerbocker Holiday* from embarrassing its author."[30] Roosevelt himself saw the show in Washington, DC, and reportedly laughed heartily throughout.[31]

After moving to the 46th Street Theatre on 13 February, *Knickerbocker Holiday* had its last Broadway performance on 11 March without turning a profit, so the PPC arranged for a tour, which played in Pittsburgh and St. Louis.[32] Weill and Anderson returned to the show once more in 1944 when they made the movie version with Nelson Eddy. Weill did not have much involvement in it, and only four songs from his original score made the final cut: "September Song," "Nowhere to Go but Up," "It Never Was You," and "One Indispensable Man."

## Good and Bad Germans

Most commentators look back on *Knickerbocker Holiday* as Anderson's show with Weill's music, and assume that the composer's newly found interest in folk culture rather than the playwright's politics was the reason he was attracted to the project, and that he had very little say in the overall tenor of the libretto.[33] But the project benefited from a variety of voices, including Weill's and Anderson's, but also Huston's, Logan's, and other members of the PPC, who also urged Anderson to rethink his politics.[34]

---

[29] J.D.K. "The Theatre: Knickerbocker New Deal," *Wall Street Journal*, 21 October 1938, 11.

[30] Charles Angoff, "Drama," *North American Review* 246, no. 2 (Winter 1938–39): 375.

[31] Stephen Hinton, *Weill's Musical Theatre: Stages of Reform* (Berkeley: University of California Press, 2012), 280.

[32] Juchem, *Kurt Weill und Maxwell Anderson*, 99, 120.

[33] See Ronald Taylor, *Kurt Weill: Composer in a Divided World* (Boston: Northeastern University Press, 1992), 240, and Ronald Sanders, *The Days Grow Short: The Life and Music of Kurt Weill* (New York: Holt, Rinehart and Winston, 1980), 271.

[34] On the rest of the PPC's critiques, see Juchem, *Kurt Weill und Maxwell Anderson*, 80–95.

Furthermore, reducing *Knickerbocker Holiday* to a simple New Deal satire ignores the show's refashioning of the American origin story to highlight the contributions of Germanic immigrants, and particularly in New York City. Although the characters are ostensibly from the Netherlands, in the early twentieth century, many German-American performers made their name on vaudeville stages in "Dutch" acts, in which "Dutch" was a mispronunciation of "Deutsch," producing a relationship between the two nationalities in the minds of U.S. audiences.[35] At a time when Germans faced increasing suspicion in the United States, *Knickerbocker Holiday* reminds audiences that some Germans were and had always been loyal Americans, and others had the potential to become loyal Americans. In the end, *Knickerbocker Holiday* is as much the story of historical assimilation—an issue of great concern to Weill during this period—as it is political satire.

In 1938, audiences in the United States still considered Weill a German in exile, which left him vulnerable to criticisms of being humorless or militaristic, not to mention unpatriotic. In a feature on *Knickerbocker Holiday* for the *New York Times*, Jack Gould wrote that "for all the imagination apparent in the score Mr. Weill's Teutonic preciseness constantly expressed itself."[36] However, even if the composer's public saw him as an over-regimented foreigner, he was portrayed as a friendly alien. In the words of Andy Hamilton of the *Los Angeles Times*, Weill was one of a group who was exiled for the crime of political beliefs that "do not dovetail with those of the dictators" and who contributed to "cultural windfall" that hit the United States in the late 1930s.[37] Some in the United States decried the arrival of so many of Germany's cultural and intellectual elite, fearing that the injection of Teutonic influence would stifle native-born artistic efforts.[38] While the United States recognized the human rights catastrophe that was Nazi Germany, the struggling economy engendered hostile feelings toward refugees. Congress refused to alter the quota system set in place by the Immigration Act of 1924 (also known as the Johnson-Reed Act), whose provisions only allotted 25,957 spaces per year for German immigrants. Between 1933 and 1940, authorities only filled the

---

[35] John Koegel, *Music in German Immigrant Theater: New York City, 1840–1940* (Rochester, NY: University of Rochester Press, 2009), 180–81.

[36] Jack Gould, "Dutch in the Forties: Nieuw Amsterdam in the Higher Forties," *NYT*, 15 September 1938, 155.

[37] Andy Hamilton, "Thanks to the Dictators," *Los Angeles Times*, 13 November 1938, 7.

[38] Alan Lessem, "The Émigré Experience: Schoenberg in America," in *Constructive Dissonance: Arnold Schoenberg and the Transformation of Twentieth Century Culture*, ed. Juliane Brand and Christopher Hailey (Berkeley: University of California Press, 1997), 61.

quota in 1939.[39] Although around 30,000 more immigrants received emergency visas above the quotas, the United States still denied entry to thousands of German refugees.[40] Although technically protected under the Fourteenth Amendment's provision that no state shall "deprive any person of life, liberty, or property, without due process of law; nor deny to any person within its jurisdiction the equal protection of the laws," states still passed laws banning immigrants from using national resources, and professional organizations sought to bar immigrants from obtaining licenses to work.[41]

As the situation in Europe grew worse, Weill became increasingly nervous. On 17 June 1940, Weill sent largely identical letters to Bruno Frank and Erika Mann (daughter of author Thomas Mann), in which he proposed forming an "Alliance of Loyal Alien Americans" which would reassure the public that "they can count on us in every effort to save American democracy and that they can consider us in every way as faithful American citizens." He hoped the organization could assist

the authorities in the investigations of the Fifth Column activities of all our members. We also could provide the press with material about the contributions of our friends to the economical, cultural and educational life in the U.S.A. The organization could protect possible victims of unjust accusations which might come up in the next months. We also could be helpful to those unfortunate friends who remained in the countries now conquered by Germany. (You know that the new immigration regulations provide exemptions for those "who could be helpful to the United States" and our knowledge of 'good and bad elements' might be used by the immigration officers.)[42]

Although nothing came of Weill's idea, the thoughts he expressed in this letter echo issues within *Knickerbocker Holiday*, particularly the idea that one must sort through the "good and bad elements" in German communities. Thomas Mann was especially concerned with the issue, which perhaps

[39] Roger Daniels, "American Refugee Policy in Historical Perspective," in *The Muses Flee Hitler: Cultural Transfer and Adaptation 1930–1945*, ed. Jarrell C. Jackman and Carla M. Borden (Washington, DC: Smithsonian Institution Press, 1983), 66.

[40] Jean-Michel Palmier, *Weimar in Exile: The Antifascist Emigration in Europe and America*, trans. David Fernbach (London: Verso, 2006), 466.

[41] Arnold Krammer, *Undue Process: The Untold Story of America's German Alien Internees* (London: Rowman and Littlefield, 1997), 3–4.

[42] Kurt Weill to Erika Mann, 17 June 1940, WLA, Box 47 Folder 11. The letter to Frank resides in WLA, Box 47 Folder 4. Mann responded on 2 July 1940 (WLA, Box 48 Folder 31).

inspired Weill to write to his daughter.[43] Anderson also admired Mann, and had in his files a copy of Mann's November 1938 manifesto "To the Civilized World," in which Mann decried the perversion of language by dictators and the cowardice of those democratic countries who refused to take action (ideas which also reflect Weill's proposal for Stuyvesant).[44] Weill and Anderson likely drew on Mann's example, as well as stories from other immigrants, who purported to take on an entirely new identity when they crossed the Atlantic. Around the same time, a number of prominent immigrants, including Mann, were publicly acknowledging a change of heart in regard to Germany. In February 1939, the Jewish-Italian anti-fascist Max Ascoli, a professor at the University in Exile at the New School for Social Research, proudly published his story of becoming a U.S. citizen in the *Atlantic Monthly*. He wrote "I could not become a Fascist. I became an American. Therefore Italy is my former country. The Italian culture is my former culture. These are the facts. . . . One cannot change his country as he changes his shirt. It is a great privilege to become an American."[45] Historian Anthony Heilbut quotes an unnamed immigrant professor as saying, "How wonderful it was [after emigrating] to simplify things. We Germans have this horrible trait of making green appear gold. This damnable love of paradox. It's just intellectual trickery, and you Americans cured us of it."[46]

The question of who was and was not an American was particularly important given that in early 1938, authorities uncovered a Nazi ring of spies in New York, which further inflamed American suspicion of Germans. The investigation and trial took place at the same time as the creation of *Knickerbocker Holiday*; the story broke in February 1938 and continued to make headlines throughout the year as the case became more serious. By June, eighteen people had been indicted in what the *Los Angeles Times* called "a gigantic plot against America."[47] Their trial began in early October, the

[43] After the war broke out, this became an important debate in immigrant communities, and persisted into the immediate postwar era. See Chapter 10 of Erhard Bahr, *Weimar on the Pacific: Exile Culture in Los Angeles and the Crisis of Modernism* (Berkeley: University of California Press, 2007).

[44] It resides in MAC, Series "Misc.," Folder "Mann, Thomas To the civilized world, a manifesto Tms/mimeo." Although written after *Knickerbocker Holiday* opened, the essay paints a picture of a dictator similar to Stuyvesant in that he promises freedom and prosperity but actually rules with an iron fist. Mann asks, "Shall we listen only to those who say 'peace,' when they mean war, 'order' when they mean 'anarchy,' 'resurrection,' when they think of bottomless abasement, 'freedom,' when slavery without hope is their goal, 'manliness,' when they mean bestiality, 'culture' when they speak in the name of the vengeful terrorism of stupidity?"

[45] Max Ascoli, "No. 38 Becomes an American," *Atlantic Monthly* (February 1939): 170.

[46] Heilbut, *Exiled in Paradise*, 76.

[47] "Hitler Aides Indicted in American Spy Plot," *Los Angeles Times*, 21 June 1938, 1–2.

month *Knickerbocker Holiday* opened.[48] Around the same time, the news-reel series *The March of Time* released a twenty-minute segment called "Inside Nazi Germany," which included a section warning its viewers that "propaganda extends far beyond Fascist frontiers, and today Hitler expects every German everywhere to help spread the Nazi creed," and warned citizens against the German-American Bund, calling it "the loudest mouthpiece of this Nazi propaganda drive."[49] That year, the Bund decided that the best way to recruit was to portray Nazism as the new Americanism, one specifically targeted at the nation's white populations. On 17 September 1938, the *New York Amsterdam News* reported that the Bund claimed to stand for "the Constitution, the American flag, and the lofty ideals of the founding fathers," and demanded "a socially just, white, gentile-ruled United States."[50] In this climate, anti-Nazi sentiment could have easily slipped into anti-German sentiment.

With so many bad Germans in the news, *Knickerbocker Holiday* offered a chance to address the issue of good and bad Germans in a way that demonstrated the viability of assimilation. If each German has the potential for good, then America might be able to persuade even "bad" individuals to adopt their way of life. Once on America's shores, the immigrants of *Knickerbocker Holiday* are faced with a choice: embrace fascism and the bad side of their national character, or listen to their better angels and embrace American democracy. Stuyvesant represents the bad, seeking to bring tyrannical German order to the chaotic New Amsterdam. At first, he seems almost reasonable—he praises Brom's ingenuity, and promises relief from the council's buffoonery. But he turns out to be a wolf in sheep's clothing with his demands for complete obedience. On the other hand, Tina, Brom, and Brom's friend Tenpin represent the German potential for good. They are immigrants, yet are comfortably assimilated. They do not speak in accents and embrace the American values of freedom (to choose a romantic partner) and independent thinking. Brom especially displays the stubborn individualism and ingenuity that characterizes conventional American identity. He constantly talks his way out of tricky situations, as in the beginning when he

[48] For a summary of these events and their effect on popular culture, see Eric J. Sanjeen, "Anti-Nazi Sentiment in Film: *Confessions of a Nazi Spy* and the German-American Bund," *American Studies* 20, no. 2 (1979): 69–81.

[49] "Inside Nazi Germany," *March of Time* 4, no. 6 (1938), the production is available online at https://www.youtube.com/watch?v=uUsB_jRtk9E. On the German-American Bund, see Palmier, *Weimar in Exile*, 469–72.

[50] "Stop the Bums," *New York Amsterdam News*, 17 September 1938, 10.

Example 4.2 *Knickerbocker Holiday,* "I Do Business in My Hat."

convinces the council to hang him by the waist instead of the neck, claiming it is more painful. Moreover, while the councilmen fawn over Stuyvesant, both Tina and Brom are immediately skeptical.

These differences are clear in the music. Just before opening night, the creative team replaced Brom's first number, "I Do Business in My Hat" (Example 4.2) a Gilbert-and-Sullivan style patter song that resembled the discarded "Brom's Complaint," with "Nowhere to Go but Up," which he based on a discarded tune from *One Man from Tennessee,* a breezy soft-shoe and a paean

to American optimism.[51] With this switch, the only operetta-like numbers in the show are sung by either Stuyvesant or the corrupt Dutch council.[52] The council's introductory song "Hush Hush" is based on a fast polka rhythm, even though Weill cast the song in common time and polkas are generally in $\frac{2}{4}$. Although he does not speak with an accent, much of Stuyvesant's music also identifies him with the Old World. He is introduced with "One Touch of Alchemy / All Hail the Political Honeymoon," which the souvenir program makes clear is based on German styles: "Since Stuyvesant was coming to New Amsterdam from Europe and since that time (1647) Europe was becoming strongly Prussianized, the music that Weill provided to herald the stage entrance of Walter Huston as the turbulent Dutchman is a take-off on an old Prussian military march."[53] By the final version of the show, the younger generation—though still immigrants— sing in the easy, comfortable style of American popular music. The older generation are musically stiff and unattractive (with the exception of "September Song," which was added late in the process), demonstrating the superiority of American culture over that of Europe.

Thus in *Knickerbocker Holiday*, "How Can You Tell an American?" becomes a very important question, alongside its implied corollary: "How can you become an American?" The show's suggestion that attitude rather than blood determines nationality runs counter to Nazi ideology. It also implies that nationality can be fluid, at least on the American side. Indeed, by the end of the show, the councilmen defy Stuyvesant's order to hang Brom, showing that the potential for good lurks in every immigrant. The narrator Washington Irving even bestows the status of American on Stuyvesant when the latter reveals that, like Brom, he was never able to take orders. The show's answer to both questions—the sign of being an American is rebelliousness, and anyone can become one—resonates with the concern Weill expressed to Mann and Frank that he and other faithful new Americans help make visible the loyalty of other, less prominent immigrants. If anyone can become an American, the show seems to be saying, then even Germans can be rehabilitated. The show is a reminder that central Europeans formed the core of New York City's past, and that American citizenship has always been learned

---

[51] WLA, Box 14 Folder 238.
[52] Hinton, *Weill's Musical Theater*, 286.
[53] Souvenir Program, *Knickerbocker Holiday*, available at the WLRC.

rather than bred. *Knickerbocker Holiday* frames America as a system of beliefs and values that speak to the good in everyone, even Germans.

Still, there is a dark side to this fable of immigration. This America is clearly an extension of Europe, as the climax of the story involves Brom defying Stuyvesant in beating back a Native American attack (rendering the "Indian corn" line problematic). By highlighting the capacity of immigrants to assimilate and build a better world, *Knickerbocker Holiday* glosses over the cultures those immigrants erased, treating the attack as an opportunity for an exoticized dance number. Although no music survives for the sequence, the librettos cue the "Algonquins from Harlem" dance, implying that it resembled similar jazz-inflected Native American spectacles like the "Totem Tom-Tom" from *Rose-Marie* (1924, films in 1928 and 1936).[54] Early on, Weill suggested a more racially diverse story in which Brom settled down with "a simple indian [*sic*] girl," and the "Indian corn" line is probably a holdover from that version of the plot.[55] This would have legitimized the settlers by linking them with Native Americans, but the miscegenation would have turned off contemporary audiences (which Weill may not have known). Although stage productions had featured interracial couples, they either ended badly (Charles Wakefield Cadman's *Shanewis*, 1918) or with the revelation that one partner was actually white (*Whoopie*, 1928).[56] Weill may have been attracted to the idea of an Indian-European romance given that Indians were often stand-ins for Jews on Broadway stages of the 1930s, but he also may not have been aware of that connection.[57] In the end, the elision of black and Native cultures adds to the idea that America needs civilizing through democracy, and the foundations of America in *Knickerbocker Holiday* are firmly white.

The reception of the Native American sequence (or lack thereof) points to the fact that, by the late 1930s, the United States considered the question of Native America's claim to the land settled, especially after the Indian Citizenship Act of 1924. While the 1910s and 1920s saw a proliferation of "Indian"-flavored shows and songs taking place in contemporary times, by the 1930s, these characters had become exotic touches in an imagined past.[58] This speaks to differences in the cultural climate that surrounded *Knickerbocker Holiday* and Weill's later projects. By the 1940s, as the United

---

[54] On "Indian" production numbers, see Michael V. Pisani, *Imagining Native America in Music* (New Haven, CT: Yale University Press, 2005), 280–85.

[55] Quoted in Juchem, *Kurt Weill und Maxwell Anderson*, 71.

[56] Pisani, *Imagining Native America in Music*, 276–77, 282; Most, *Making Americans*, 43.

[57] Most, *Making Americans*, 58–64.

[58] Pisani, *Imagining Native America in Music*, 286.

States became more aware of the atrocities of Nazi Germany, similar sequences in Weill's later works began to raise some eyebrows.

## World War II

Although Weill applied for citizenship in 1937, he did not complete the process until August 1943. Once the United States entered the war in late 1941, Weill's position as a German immigrant became even more precarious. In Los Angeles he was subject to a curfew, which hindered his professional work.[59] Still, Weill supported the war effort in both official and unofficial capacities. He publicly embraced his Jewish heritage for the first time since *The Eternal Road*, and composed music for both German- and English-language propaganda issued by the Office of Facts and Figures (OFF), which became the Office of War Information (OWI) in late 1942. He also launched the *Lunchtime Follies*, a series of revues for factory workers on the home front, and composed several songs independently.

Between *The Eternal Road* (1937) and World War II, Weill almost never broached the subject of his Jewish heritage in his published interviews and writings. This may have been because of the spike in anti-Semitism in the United States that accompanied the Great Depression (see Chapter 6). He may have felt that "German" was a more marketable identity than "Jew" or "German-Jew." This also may explain why *Knickerbocker Holiday*'s Stuyvesant has no official program of racial animosity (despite the casual slaughter of Native Americans)—Jews were accused of warmongering throughout this period.[60] But as the situation in Europe grew worse, Weill, like many German immigrants, began to rethink his relationship with Jewishness. Weill may have realized that, during the war, one way to prove his loyalty to America was to emphasize his "Jewish" rather than "German" self.[61]

He first approached the subject in 1941 with *Fun to Be Free*, a pageant by Ben Hecht and Charles MacArthur meant to galvanize the United States into joining the war in Europe. The pageant played on 5 October 1941 as part of a larger evening of entertainment at Madison Square Garden, then embarked on a tour. The event opened with a speech by Wendell Willkie, followed by

---

[59] Leonard Lyons, "Leonard Lyons," *Washington Post*, 28 March 1943, L1.
[60] Leonard Dinnerstein, *Antisemitism in America* (Oxford, UK: Oxford University Press, 1994), 129.
[61] Fauser, *Sounds of War*, 59.

the pageant, which featured Burgess Meredith introducing a series of prominent historical U.S. citizens who had fought against tyranny, from John Paul Jones to President Roosevelt. More speeches followed, and the evening ended with a patriotic revue. Although *Fun to Be Free* is a relatively minor work in Weill's output (his music was only used to cover scene changes), it represents Weill's first public foray into the war effort, and a tentative engagement with Jewish identity: one of the historical figures in the pageant was Chaym Solomon, a Jewish hero of the Revolutionary War era, thus inscribing Jews into America's usable past.

By 1943, Weill was willing to participate in a project that confronted these issues unambiguously. He again collaborated with Hecht and MacArthur for the ninety-minute pageant *We Will Never Die*.[62] The project grew out of Hecht's increasing frustration with the United States' public indifference to the plight of European Jews. To combat this apathy, he reunited with some of the team of *Fun to Be Free*, including MacArthur, Weill, and producer Billy Rose (born William Samuel Rosenberg). On 9 March 1943, *We Will Never Die* played in front of 40,000 people in two showings at Madison Square Garden, starring actors Edward G. Robinson and Paul Muni, and sponsored by the Committee for a Jewish Army, an organization that hoped to raise a military force of Jews to combat oppression in Europe. The action begins with a roll call of famous historical Jews, followed by a section on Jews in war, and ends with a plea to remember the Jews in their hour of need. Weill's score consisted of original music as well as bits of *The Eternal Road* and folk and liturgical settings. The event was a great success, with Eleanor Roosevelt calling it "one of the most impressive and moving pageants I have ever seen."[63] *We Will Never Die* toured the United States for the next few months, ending in a triumphant production at the Hollywood Bowl.

Weill also worked with the OFF, and its successor, the OWI. In 1942, he composed two scores for radio broadcasts. The first was Maxwell Anderson's *Your Navy*, a salute to the titular branch of the armed forces, the second in the thirteen-episode series "This Is War!" which ran between 14 February and

---

[62] On *We Will Never Die*, see Jürgen Schebera, "'Awakening America to the European Jewish Tragedy . . .' Sechs Jahre nach *The Eternal Road*: Ben Hecht / Kurt Weills Massenspiel *We Will Never Die* von 1943—Vorgeschichte und Wirkung," in *Kurt Weill: Auf dem Weg zum* Weg der Verheißung, ed. Helmut Loos and Guy Stern (Freiburg im Breisgau: Rombach, 2000), 255–64, and Christian Kuhnt, "Drei 'pageants'—ein Komponist: Anmerkungen yu *The Eternal Road, We Will Never Die* und *A Flag Is Born*," in *Auf dem Weg*, ed. Loos and Stern, 219–36, especially 227–30.

[63] Eleanor Roosevelt, "My Day," 14 April 1943, available online at *The Eleanor Roosevelt Papers Digital Edition* (2017), https://www2.gwu.edu/~erpapers/myday/displaydoc.cfm?_y=1943&_f=md056470.

9 May 1942 (with a break between the first and second episodes). At least in the New York City area, the program played on fifteen different stations.[64] Supervisor H.L. McClinton outlined the goals of the series in the *New York Times*: to inform domestic and international audiences of "the wartime resources and policies of America and her Allies," and to "dissipate complacency and overconfidence" while still "maintaining faith in the ability of America" to win the war.[65] The OFF recruited writers like Elmer Rice, Stephen Vincent Benet, and Clifford Odets, and stars like James Stewart, James Cagney, and Robert Montgomery for these broadcasts. Each program followed its own format; some were framed as radio documentaries, with narrators reading scripts and conducting "interviews" with servicemen, factory workers, and so on. Others were cast as dramas. Anderson wrote *Your Navy* as an informal conversation between Fredric March and Douglas Fairbanks Jr. (who was serving in the navy at the time), periodically interrupted by dramatizations of the situations they describe. Weill's score mostly eases the transitions between the conversation and the reenactments, helping the listener navigate the nonlinear narrative.

Also in 1942, Weill wrote the music for Archibald MacLeish's "Song of the Free" (also called the "Song of the Freemen") for an OFF radio program broadcast on 14 June (Flag Day) celebrating the Allied "Declaration of United Nations."[66] Given that Flag Day fell on a Sunday in 1942, the celebration was broadcast as *Towards a Century of the Common Man: A Dramatic Sermon for Sabbath Flag Day*, with a script by George Faulkner. The title also gestures toward the program's populist Leftist aspirations with the idea of the "Century of the Common Man," a phrase coined by Vice President Henry Wallace in a speech the previous May.[67] The broadcast began with a narrator recounting the roots of Democracy and "Christian morality" in the West before the dark turn of the 1920s.[68] Following this, the narrator introduces a series of speakers from members of the United Nations, each accompanied by "national" music: Russia, the United Kingdom, China, and France, as well as resistance fighters from Germany and other Eastern European countries. Throughout, fragments of "The Song of the Free" are woven into the soundtrack, with a rousing rendition emerging toward the

---

[64] See for example, "Radio Today," *NYT*, 2 May 1942, 27.
[65] H.L. McClinton, "'This Is War,'" *NYT*, 15 February 1942, X10.
[66] See material in WLRC, Series 30 Box 23 Folder 8.
[67] Fauser, *Sounds of War*, 266.
[68] A copy of the script is available in in WLRC, Series 30 Box 23 Folder 8.

end, a technique borrowed from *The Eternal Road*, *Johnny Johnson*, and *Lady in the Dark*.

Finally, Weill worked on a thirty-five-minute propaganda film for the OWI in 1944 called *Salute to France*.[69] In a narrative framework that resembles *Where Do We Go from Here?* and *Lady in the Dark* (and that foreshadows *Love Life*), the film follows three characters, an American named Joe (Burgess Meredith), a Brit named Tommy (Philip Bourneuf), and a Frenchman named Jacques (Claude Dauphin) who reappear in different guises throughout the film. First, they are fellow soldiers in a unit. Then, they are professionals teaching the importance of international cooperation in their home countries. The final third of the film features Joe and Tommy as downed air force pilots rescued by Jacques, a French priest. An undated memo reports that the film was shown in London and that authorities "were extremely pleased with the picture and felt it should be shown to every Frenchman in France."[70]

Weill's score for *Salute to France* highlights themes of cross-cultural cooperation and solidarity, juxtaposing the Nazi "Horst Wessel-Lied" against the Marseillaise and other French nationalist songs, including "The Time of the Cherries," with new lyrics by Maxwell Anderson.[71] The score also reuses large sections of *Johnny Johnson*, which may have been an effort on Weill's part to repurpose the music for an anti-war project—a somewhat regretful idea in hindsight—toward a cause more appropriate for 1944. Although the notes do not change drastically, the meaning of the music is altered by context; for example, the quotation of the Marseillaise in *Johnny Johnson's* "The Allied High Command," loses its irony and appears sincere in *Salute to France*.

Weill also independently composed individual songs motivated by the war. By early 1942, he had set three texts by Walt Whitman: "Beat! Beat! Drums," "O Captain! My Captain!" and "Dirge for Two Veterans" (he later set "Come Up from the Fields, Father" in 1947). However, only one was recorded during the war: Helen Hayes included "Dirge" among Weill's arrangements of "The

[69] The film is available on YouTube as "A Salute to France," filmed 1944, posted by Nora G. Gardner on 10 June 2017, https://www.youtube.com/watch?v=LdhHJM5hDL4. Although Jean Renoir directed the film, he all but disavowed it; see Jürgen Schebera, "Der 'alien American' Kurt Weill und seine Aktivitäten für den *War Effort* der USA 1940–1945," in *A Stranger Here Myself: Kurt Weill Studien*, ed. Kim H. Kowalke and Horst Edler (Hildesheim: Georg Olms, 1993), 281. OWI correspondence indicates that Burgess Meredith and a Lt. Col. Fairlis wrote the screenplay. See C.D. Jackson to Gen. R.A. Mclure, 1 May 1944, copy in WLRC, Series 30 Box 23 Folder 10.

[70] Unsigned memo, n.d., copy in WLRC, Series 30 Box 23 Folder 10.

[71] Lawrence G. Avery, ed., *Dramatist in America: Letters of Maxwell Anderson, 1912–1958* (Chapel Hill: University of North Carolina Press, 1977), 207. Weill also liberally drew from previous scores to fill out the music, including *Der Kuhhandel*, *Johnny Johnson*, *The River Is Blue*, and *Railroads on Parade*, indicating that the film came about very rapidly. *KWH*, 343.

Battle Hymn of the Republic," "The Star-Spangled Banner," and "America" on the album "Mine Eyes Have Seen the Glory," released that August. These Whitman settings combine the Schubertian impulse for atmospheric detail (the wind blowing through the fields in "Come Up from the Fields, Father" resembles the rustling leaves of "Der Lindenbaum") with Broadway tropes and sounds, like the loping rhythm in "O Captain! My Captain!"[72] These songs foreshadow Weill's postwar projects, which more freely mix operatic and Broadway idioms. Indeed, the bugles of "Beat! Beat! Drums!" re-emerge note-for-note in *Down in the Valley*. The soaring melodies and pentatonic harmonies look forward to *Down in the Valley* and *Street Scene* (which has its own Whitman setting in "When Lilacs Last in the Dooryard Bloom'd"), and the sophisticated bluesy harmony of "Captain" and "Dirge" foreshadows *Lost in the Stars*.[73]

Weill also wrote popular songs as propaganda. In the middle of 1942, he joined Moss Hart, actor Aline MacMahon, and the American Theatre Wing to put on the *Lunchtime Follies*, a series of patriotic revues meant to maintain morale on the home front, mounted in factories and shipyards starring Broadway and Hollywood A-listers.[74] Weill served as production coordinator, which required that he get special dispensation to enter the plants (as a German, he was initially barred). Each show lasted the length of the workers' lunch break, anywhere from fifteen minutes to a full hour. *New York Times* theatre critic Lewis Nichols described a performance at the Cramp Shipyard in Philadelphia.[75] This show featured comic Milton Berle, followed by Betty Garrett singing the Henry Nemo–Bob Musel song "Jeremiah" accompanied by dancing girls. The production also featured Gordon Gifford singing Weill's "Song of the Inventory," with lyrics by Lewis Allen (the author of "Strange Fruit"). Weill wrote two more songs for the *Follies*: "Buddy on the Night Shift," with lyrics by Oscar Hammerstein II, and "Schickelgruber" with lyrics by Howard Dietz. "Buddy," like "Inventory," salutes factory workers. "Schickelgruber" is an Anglicized spelling of Schicklgruber, the birth name of Hitler's father, and the source of the rumor that Hitler had a

---

[72] Kim H. Kowalke, "'I'm an American!' Whitman, Weill, and Cultural Identity," in *Walt Whitman and Modern Music: War, Desire, and the Trials of Nationhood*, ed. Lawrence Kramer (New York and London: Garland, 2000), 118–21.

[73] On the Whitman-esque qualities of *Street Scene*, see Kowalke, "I'm an American!"117–18.

[74] On the details of the *Lunchtime Follies*, see Fauser, *Sounds of War*, 59–62, and Robert C. Roarty, "Lunchtime Follies: Food, Fun and Propaganda in America's Wartime Workplace," *Journal of American Drama and Theatre* 11, no. 1 (1999): 29–48.

[75] Lewis Nichols, "Lunchtime Follies: The American Theatre Wing Sends out Entertainment to War Workers," *NYT*, 13 June 1943, X1.

**Example 4.3** "Schickelgruber."

[Allegro non troppo ♩ = 184]

In a ham-let in the Ty-rol an old la-dy is not
vi-rile, she is lan-gui-shing and hea-vy in her heart.

Jewish grandparent. The song tells of Hitler's troubled youth and his mother's shame. Musically, the song implies that the Fuhrer might be Jewish; it has many of the characteristics of Jewish novelty songs like Irving Berlin's "Sadie Salome" or "Yiddle on Your Fiddle." It falls into two parts, a minor-mode section followed by a major-mode one, and in the minor mode the stepwise melody emphasizes the minor third, with frequent chromatic inflections in the accompaniment (Example 4.3).[76] The lyrics even have Hitler's mother wondering what would have happened if she named her son "Abie."

Weill also wrote German-language songs: two with texts by Brecht, "Und was bekam des Soldetens Weib?" ("And What Did the Soldier's Wife Receive?") and "Lied einer Deutschen Mutter" ("Song of a German Mother"), and one more with a text by Walter Mehring, "Wie lange noch?" ("Yet How Long?"). These were broadcast in Germany to disrupt morale. Although "Lied einer Deutschen Mutter" is lost, the title and the two extant songs indicate that Weill was targeting civilian women. "Wie lange noch?" whose tune

[76] "Schickelgruber" is published in Lys Symonette, ed., *The Unknown Kurt Weill: As Sung by Teresa Stratas* (New York: European American Music Corporation, 1982), 50–55.

derives from the music for *Marie Galante,* is sung in the mournful voice of a woman whose sweetheart has promised her beauty and freedom but has not delivered—a thinly veiled metaphor for the people under Nazi rule. "Und was bekam," describes the gifts received by the soldier's wife as her husband marauds around Europe, all to a plodding, funereal tune. But Weill switches to the relative major for the final verse, in which the woman receives her gift from Russia: a widow's veil.

Weill's wartime efforts reveal that he remained as committed to his ideas of *Gebrauchsmusik* ("music for use") in the United States as he was in Germany.[77] For Weill, *Gebrauchsmusik* is (among other things) "not conceivable without the vast background of an ethical or social nature on which it is based," even if it superficially resembles "light" or popular music.[78] These songs and productions illustrate that Weill retained his belief that music could produce a more thoughtful, cohesive body politic, embodying Weill's idea of music as a *gemeinschaftsbildenden* ("community engendering") art.[79] Indeed, Weill held out hope that the *Lunchtime Follies* "might become the birthplace of a real people's theatre."[80] Throughout the war, Weill consistently framed the United States as a leader of an international and multicultural community standing against fascism. The blend of European and American, modernist and traditional that characterizes these works speaks to Weill's belief that by taking on U.S. citizenship he was not renouncing the international community, and that his personal sense of patriotism did not preclude criticizing the United States when he felt it necessary.

## Representing America

Along with Maxwell Anderson, Weill worked with only one other librettist on multiple U.S. projects: lyricist Ira Gershwin. After Ira's brother, composer George, died in 1937, Ira went into semi-retirement until 1940, when he was coaxed out by *Lady in the Dark.*[81] Weill and Gershwin struck up a friendship, and when Weill went to Hollywood to work on the film versions of *Lady in the Dark* and *Knickerbocker Holiday* in June of 1943, he stayed with the

---

[77] Schebera, "Der 'alien American,'" 267, and "Awakening America," 263.

[78] Kurt Weill, "Opera—Where To?" (1930), trans. in *KWiE,* 507.

[79] Kurt Weill, "Shifts in Musical Composition" (1927), trans. in *KWiE,* 480.

[80] Quoted in Fauser, *Sounds of War,* 62.

[81] bruce d. mcclung, *Lady in the Dark: Biography of a Musical* (Oxford, UK: Oxford University Press, 2007), 39.

Gershwins. They cast about for another project, eventually finding *Where Do We Go from Here?*, a time-traveling fantasy that places an American everyman at important junctures in U.S. history.

While both *Where Do We Go from Here?* and *Knickerbocker Holiday* focus on America's historical immigrants, the differences between the two works show Weill ability to adapt to cultural exigencies. In *Knickerbocker Holiday*, "America" is defined politically, reflecting the debates surrounding the role of government in the Great Depression. In *Where Do We Go from Here?* "America" is defined culturally, in accordance with the renewed patriotic spirit of World War II and the burgeoning consumer culture that would not have been possible during the Depression. Weill was also aware that the international markets were opening again, and the film clearly has one eye overseas. *Knickerbocker Holiday* is aimed at a domestic audience, and levels critiques against America's vices. *Where Do We Go from Here?* is aimed at both international and domestic audiences, and celebrates American virtues. But as a film, rather than a Broadway musical, *Where Do We Go from Here?* was subject to additional pressures, particularly from the Overseas Branch (later Overseas Bureau) of the OWI, which reviewed scripts and advised filmmakers with the aim of spreading the idea that America was a land of democratic principles and economic wealth.[82] In March 1944, the head of the OWI, Elmer Davis, tried to dissuade Hollywood from making films that portrayed crime, corruption, imperialism, racism, oppression, or injustice on American soil, and discouraged films ridiculing the United States or its Allies. To make sure Hollywood complied, he asked studios to send screenplays to their office for review.[83] While Hollywood's cooperation with these standards was allegedly voluntary, in practice, about seventy percent of films complied with the OWI's requests.

The differing visions of U.S. history put forward by the OWI and the creative team of the film speak to the problems facing the United States' powerful international status in the waning months of the war. The OWI was acutely aware of the strength of the usable past in defining a national identity, and felt that a comic portrayal of U.S. history demeaned the nation. They objected even more strenuously to the comic portrayal of minority cultures

---

[82] Fauser, *Sounds of War*, 85.

[83] On the relationship between Hollywood and the OWI, see Robert Lee Bishop, "The Overseas Branch of the Office of War Information" (PhD diss., University of Wisconsin, 1966), 87–94; Thomas Doherty, *Projections of War: Hollywood, American Culture, and World War II* (New York: Columbia University Press, 1993), 42–51.

on the grounds that the United States needed to project an image of inclusivity to counter Nazi ideologies. These ideals clashed with screenwriter Morrie Ryskind, whose roots were in the Broadway world of satire and ethnic comedy. Weill's contributions helped mitigate some of the tensions between the two sides; some of the musical sequences (particularly the Columbus number) take a much less comedic view of U.S. history. But ultimately the film did not answer the OWI's objections, and its late release and limited audience meant that it passed relatively unnoticed in Weill's career.

*Where Do We Go from Here?* was the brainchild of Ryskind—the author of the book for the Gershwins' *Of Thee I Sing* (1931)—and Sid Herzig. In June of 1943, they sold to Twentieth Century–Fox a story that followed the trend of singing-and-dancing soldier movies like *For Me and My Gal* (1942) and *Thousands Cheer* (1943).[84] Their idea was a man traveling through time experiencing important moments in U.S. military and naval history. Soon after, Herzig dropped the project, and Ryskind completed the first version of the screenplay in January 1944, sending it to the OWI later that month. This version of the script is missing, although the OWI's reader's report gives a good summary of the plot: Bill Morgan is infatuated with Lucilla, who only has eyes for men in uniform, but Bill has been designated 4-F (medically prohibited from serving in the armed forces).[85] Bill encounters a slightly muddled genie who takes him a fantastic journey through United States history, including Valley Forge, Columbus's voyage, Native American times, Dutch New York (shades of *Knickerbocker Holiday*), and Commodore Matthew Perry's negotiations with Japan in 1853. Along the way, he encounters beer-swilling Germans, operetta-like sailors, and vaudevillian Native Americans. In each period, Bill also meets different versions of Lucilla and his less glamorous friend Sally. Eventually, Bill realizes that Lucilla is too shallow for him, and that he is actually in love with Sally.

The OWI objected to the comic presentation of important milestones in the history of American Democracy, "particularly at this time when it is important to interpret these traditions to people overseas in the light of their vital significance to the world today." They also did not like that the war was played for comedy in the scene with the Nazi-like Hessian soldiers (German mercenaries who fought for Great Britain during the Revolutionary War) in

---

[84] "Screen News Here and in Hollywood," *NYT*, 15 June 1943, 17. On these kinds of films, see Allen L. Woll, *The Hollywood Musical Goes to War* (Chicago: Nelson-Hall, 1983), 86–93.

[85] Sandy Roth "Feature Script Review: Where Do We Go from Here," 12 January 1944, copy in WLRC, Series 30 Box 23 Folder 11.

a tavern in 1777, fearing that the frivolity would offend cultures subjugated by the Axis. The portrayal of Germany, Italy, and Japan as historical enemies of the United States also posed a problem, and the script was deemed "contrary to the aims agreed upon by the United Nations to establish a peaceful world order in which 'all States, great or small, victor or vanquished' will participate."[86] Furthermore, they found the comic treatment of other cultures, particularly Native Americans and Pacific Islanders distasteful: "It gives rise to serious doubts regarding our willingness to accept overseas minorities as equals." In the case of the Islanders, the OWI pointed out that burlesquing an important ally in the war against Japan was problematic.[87] They recommended removing the Valley Forge sequence entirely, and revising the 1853 and Native American scenes.

Meanwhile, Weill and Gershwin began working on the music and lyrics in November 1943, and likely finished the piano score for the principle numbers by the end of the following February.[88] The next draft of the screenplay, dated 9 May 1944, includes Gershwin's lyrics, indicating that his and Weill's work was complete by that stage.[89] In this version, Ryskind made some concessions to the OWI, such as removing the 1853 sequence. The screenplay opens in Bill's salvage yard with the number "That's How It Is," as he asks passers-by to donate to the war effort (both the scene and the song were eventually dropped). The script also includes two numbers for Sally that were later removed: "It Could Have Happened to Anyone," in which she laments the fact Bill ignores her, and "Woo Woo Woo Woo Manhattan," a Native American dance number. All of the songs that did make the final cut ("Morale," "All at Once," "If Love Remains," "Song of the Rhineland," and "Columbus") are present in this version.[90]

Fox sent the script to the OWI for another round of revisions, receiving a reply on 15 May.[91] The fact that the Columbus (Italian) sequence was now a

---

[86] The OWI report quotes the Atlantic Charter of 1941, which laid out the ultimate goals of the Allies.

[87] This is consistent with the broader OWI policy of encouraging more positive portrayals of foreign cultures. See Doherty, *Projections of War*, 46–47.

[88] Kurt Weill to Cheryl Crawford, 27 November 1943, Copy in WLRC, Series 40 Folder "Crawford, Cheryl."

[89] "Where Do We Go from Here?" 9 May 1944, LOC/GT, Box "Where Do We Go–Ziegfeld Follies" Folder "Where Do We Go from Here 1944 May 9."

[90] Weill's scores for all these songs survive in WLA, Box 33 Folder 453, along with "Theme for Cuban music in Columbus Sequence" that was later replaced by conga drums and "Theme for Church Scene in Dutch Sequence" that is a reprise of "It Could Have Happened to Anyone," which was later replaced by a reprise of "All at Once."

[91] Sandy Roth, "Feature Script Review: Where Do We Go from Here," 15 May 1944, copy in WLRC, Series 30 Box 23 Folder 11.

musical number allayed the OWI's fears over presenting the Axis nations as traditional enemies of the United States. But Ryskind kept the Valley Forge scenes, including a note in the script that "In spite of the obvious fact that Washington's army was barefoot and ragged and that the whole story of Valley Forge is a somber one, we now take a full set of dramatic licenses here and go in for charm and beauty."[92] This seems to be the crux of the disagreement: the OWI hoped for something more didactic and informative, while Ryskind conceived the project as light-hearted fun.[93] Accordingly, he kept the Hessians as well, which raised the same objections as the previous script. Furthermore little was done to assuage the OWI's fears about the portrayal of Native Americans, and the inclusion of the new song "Woo Woo Woo Woo Manhattan" likely did not help matters. Other objections related to the comic portrayal of U.S. government figures and the draft.

Ryskind completed another version of the script on 5 September 1944, which Fox again sent to the OWI for comments. This version eventually became the shooting script. Around this time, the cast and crew were assembled: Fred MacMurray as Bill, June Haver as Lucilla, and Joan Leslie as Sally, under the direction of Gregory Ratoff. David Raksin was hired to write "incidental music" for the film, although he was assisted by the Fox music department. Most cues contain tunes written by multiple composers. For example, the music that plays under Bill's journey from Columbus's ship to Manhattan begins with a version of Weill's "Columbus" song, which was then "developed" by David Buttolph (that is, composed out into a longer cue) and orchestrated by Leo Shuken. This gives way to the "Big Chief" tune (the jazzy strain that plays as the camera shows a signpost giving directions to various Manhattan locations), which has Buttolph and Alfred Newman credited as composers, still orchestrated by Shuken. Neither Raksin nor Weill had much to do with the Dutch New York sequence (except for the reprise of "All at Once"), which was mostly composed, developed, and orchestrated by Cyril J. Mockridge and Sidney Cutner. Others who worked on the film include Maurice De Pakh (the only credited orchestrator), Charles Henderson, Arthur Morton, Emil Newman, Wallace Wheeler, and Jack Virgil.

Weill remained in Los Angeles throughout the summer of 1944, but he had little involvement with these musical decisions as he was focused on *The*

---

[92] Ryskind, "Where Do We Go from Here?" 9 May 1944, 22.
[93] On the didactic potential of Hollywood films, see Doherty, *Projections of War*, 34–35.

*Firebrand of Florence.* In August he returned to *Where Do We Go from Here?* to supervise the recording and dubbing sessions, particularly the Columbus sequence.[94] Principal photography began soon after the 5 September script was approved, and continued (including reshoots) through December, at which point the film went into editing.

At least one major sequence was shot but cut in editing: "Woo Woo Woo Woo Manhattan," in which a "Princess White Feather" (Sally) leads the "Woo Woo Woo Woo" dance. The number was supposed to be a showstopper; publicity advertisements and posters feature Joan Leslie striking a provocative pose in "Native American" garb to the left of Fred MacMurray's face, with a sultry close-up of June Haver to his right. In later materials, the women are switched (see Figures 4.1a and 4.1b). Even though the OWI objected to the sequence on other grounds, it was cut for aesthetic reasons; Gershwin told Weill that the sequence was "really very bad."[95]

The delays that resulted from efforts to please the OWI likely interfered with the success of the film. In January 1944, when Ryskind wrote the first script, the tide of the war had only begun to turn toward the Allies, but when the film went into production in September 1944, the Germans had already surrendered Paris.[96] By the time the film was released on 23 May 1945, the Allies had declared victory in Europe. Even so, reviews were mostly positive. Critics praised the film's imagination, with Alton Cook of the *New York World Telegram* calling the picture "a gem of a fantasy," and "T.M.P." of the *New York Times* observing that the film was "as far removed from any semblance to reality as the most ardent escapist could wish, and a bit of an innovation as screen musicals go."[97] They also praised the close connection between music and drama.[98] Still, despite the reviews, the film came and went without much comment in the wider world, probably because it was no longer relevant by May 1945.

---

[94] *WIl(e)*, 415, 418, 420–21.

[95] Ira Gershwin to Kurt Weill, 9 December 1944, WLA, Box 48 Folder 33. My thanks to Michael Owens for assistance in dating this letter.

[96] The OWI acknowledged this. A letter from William S. Cunningham to Col. Jason Joy notes that "the progress of the war may be such that the reaction to certain sequences will depend to a great extent on conditions existing at the time the picture is seen by foreign audiences." WLRC, Series 30 Box 23 Folder 11.

[97] Alton Cook, "Movies: Gem of Fantasy Keeps Mirth Aglow at Roxy," *New York World-Telegram*, 6 June 1945; T.M.P., "At the Roxy," *NYT*, 7 June 1945. These and the rest of the reviews cited are available as clippings in the Scrapbooks in LOC/Gershwin, Box 78 Book 7 Microfilm 93/20013<Mus>.

[98] See Florabel Muir, "Weill-Gershwin Blazing New Trail," 11 June 1945, and Anonymous, "Where Do We Go from Here?" *Variety*, 23 May 1945.

**Figure 4.1a** Early advertisement for *Where Do We Go from Here?*. Margaret Herrick Library, Core Collection, *Where Do We Go from Here?*

**Figure 4.1b** Advertisement for *Where Do We Go from Here?*. Academy of Motion Picture Arts and Sciences.

## Selling America

Unlike most of Weill's projects, in which he worked closely with librettists and lyricists, he was not involved in most of the development of the story of *Where Do We Go from Here?*. Consequently, little can be said regarding his thoughts on the project outside of the songs themselves. He bucked the OWI with "Woo Woo Woo Woo" and "Song of the Rhineland." However, the "Columbus" sequence—the centerpiece of the film—does conform to many of the OWI's objectives. That sequence was important to the composer. *Where Do We Go from Here?* was Weill's third attempt at revolutionizing musical film. Although Weill's early experiences with the film industry with *The River Is Blue* and *You and Me* had soured him on Hollywood, he held on to dreams of developing "film-opera," or an opera composed for film (rather than a film version of a work composed for the stage), well into the late 1940s.[99] Contemporary trends in Hollywood seemed favorable to the idea. During World War II, studios used opera to paint the United States as a bastion of culture in a barbaric world, while at the same time, "democratizing" opera by having classically trained singers like Deanna Durbin and Kathryn Grayson playing "girl-next-door" roles.[100] In general, opera became associated with the United States' attempt to promote itself as the new leader of the free world.[101] Weill worked toward a similar democratization of opera on the stage, and had nurtured a desire to bring opera to film since his time in Germany. In *Where Do We Go from Here?* Weill saw the chance to further explore these ideas with collaborators he trusted (at least more than Fritz Lang and the rest of the *You and Me* team). In particular, the sequence on Christopher Columbus's ship—which Weill called "a regular little comic opera"—blends numerous styles (opera, operetta, Broadway pop) into a long-form experiment in musical film.[102]

Like *Knickerbocker Holiday*, the film also demonstrates the process by which foreigners become American, although the terms that define that identity changed between 1938 and 1945. In *Where Do We Go from Here?* American identity is defined in terms of shared culture and consumer goods. This is first made explicit in the 1777 sequence. When Bill sings "If Love

---

[99] Hinton, *Weill's Musical Theater*, 322–28.

[100] Gina Bombola, " 'Can't Help Singing': The 'Modern' Opera Diva in Hollywood Film, 1930–1950" (PhD diss., University of North Carolina at Chapel Hill, 2017), 232–39.

[101] Fauser, *Sounds of War*, 161–66.

[102] Kurt Weill, "Music in the Movies," *Harper's Bazaar* 80, no. 9 (September 1946): available at https://www.kwf.org/pages/wt-music-in-the-movies.html.

Remains," he celebrates the technological marvels of the future: "Electric Light by Edison / Marconi's wireless wave / The sulpha drugs in medicine / The Safety Razor shave." The breezy foxtrot is then contrasted with "Song of the Rhineland," a stiff waltz in the Hessian tavern, which lists increasingly silly virtues of Germany: "Life is milk and honier / Where the sun is sunnier / And the rain is rainier / And the brain is brainier." Compared with the American virtues enumerated in "If Love Remains," these ring hollow; Germans cannot take credit for "rainier rain" the same way Americans can credit their own ingenuity for electricity. (This important contrast may explain why the song remained in the film despite the OWI's objections.) The song also fits within the broader trend of Hollywood films parodying German propaganda.[103]

These themes are continued in "Columbus." Musically, the sequence draws on Rossinian operatic conventions. It begins with a short *scena* in which a sailor named "Benito" (Carlos Ramirez) declares mutiny against Columbus (Fortunio Bonanova). (Benito's name is clearly a reference to Mussolini, but the name is never spoken aloud in the film.) This is followed by Benito's forceful arioso in which he and the sailors "offer for your scrutiny / the reasons for the mutiny." It begins like a typical AABA song of the time, but the bridge is extended and gives way to the *cantabile* of Benito's "Every Night We are in Tears," in which the sailors declare that they miss the trappings of Italy: macaroni, minestrone, wine, and Donizetti's operas (among other things). The crew applauds Benito's vocal prowess, but Columbus interrupts with his *tempo di mezzo*, invoking "loyalty to royalty," eliding Italian and Spanish identity by demanding that the crew respect the name of Queen Isabella of Spain, who financed the voyage. A heated exchange between Columbus and Benito ensues, but Bill interrupts to introduce his peppy *cabaletta* section "The Nina, the Pinta, the Santa Maria." To convince the crew to keep sailing toward the New World, he yet again enumerates the virtues of America. But instead of just technology as in "If Love Remains," this time he gives a broader description of what America has to offer: bustling cities, beautiful landscape, attractive women, Hollywood, democracy, Abbott and Costello, Heinz pickles, and Radio City. These signifiers of American culture convince the crew, but Benito attempts one more time to sway them to his side. However, he is interrupted by the sight of land, and the sequence abruptly ends.

Along with adapting operatic forms to the American screen, the sequence also traced the evolution of American identity in music. The scene begins

---

[103] Doherty, *Projections of War*, 29–30. The song is also a parody of the "Drinking Song" from Sigmund Romberg's *The Student Prince* (1924).

with Benito and Columbus singing in typical operatic fashion, marked "very Puccini" in a draft of the lyrics.[104] The addition of the mandolin during the "Every Night We Are in Tears" *cantabile* further establishes Benito's overdetermined Italian—and therefore fascist—identity.[105] Columbus's arguments for respecting the monarchy are similarly musically Italianate, and are unsuccessful in bringing the crew around to his way of thinking. Bill's music, however, heralds a distinct change in style. Weill marks the beginning of "The Nina, the Pinta, the Santa Maria," as "à la tarantella," referencing the popular Italian dance form. But U.S. audiences would likely associate the combination of tarantella rhythm and clever lyrics not just with Italians, but also the British Gilbert and Sullivan, whose operettas are rife with tarantellas, for example, the nightmare song from *Iolanthe* or "We're Called Gondolieri" from *The Gondoliers*. With the tarantella, Weill instigates musical movement from the Axis (Italy) to the Allies (England). The style shifts again at the line "The girls are breathtaking," although here Weill's copy of the music diverges from the final score. For one, censors objected to Gershwin's original line, "The girls are delightful / Their sweaters are quite full," but Weill's scores (and the published copies) retained the original. More importantly, Weill's copy moves into common time and is marked "slow foxtrot," (Example. 4.4) but in the dubbing materials, this section is marked "valse" and is in $\frac{3}{4}$ (Example 4.5), which is how it sounds in the final cut.[106] Both shifts signal a move away from the Gilbert-and-Sullivan-esque tarantella into a more typical American style, although Weill's foxtrot rhythm is a stronger gesture than the waltz.[107] Even in waltz-time, orchestrator Maurice De Packh drastically changed the accompaniment for this section from a clipped, clear tarantella rhythm to long, lyrical notes in the strings—a typical American waltz arrangement, with an easy lilt and swing.

The sequence subtly implies that the American music in this sequence is superior. The entire scene hinges on who controls the loyalty of the crew

[104] Ira Gershwin, "Columbus," LOC/Gershwin, Box 47 Folder 6.

[105] A copy of the score in Weill's hand is marked "mandolin" in the section, indicating that including the instrument was his idea rather than orchestrator Maurice De Packh's. The copy is in LOC/Gershwin, Box 47 Folder 6.

[106] Example 4.4 is taken from "The Nina, the Pinta, the Santa Maria," which was published as sheet music in 1946, and is reprinted in *Kurt Weill Songs: A Centennial Anthology Volume 2*, compiled by Edward Harsh and Dave Stein (Los Angeles: Alfred Publishing, 1999), 10–20. The music matches Weill's holograph piano-vocal score in WLA, Box 33 Folder 453. Example 4.5 is drawn from the conductor's dubbing score in WLRC, Series 10 Box W6 Folder 1.

[107] A copy of the full score is in three volumes in the WLRC, Series 10 Box W6. A copy of the conductor's score is in WLRC, Series 10 Box 26 Folder 1. I have omitted a line in Example 4.5 that largely doubles the accompaniment.

**Example 4.4** *Where Do We Go from Here?* "Columbus," Weill's score.

**Example 4.5** *Where Do We Go from Here?* "Columbus," film version.

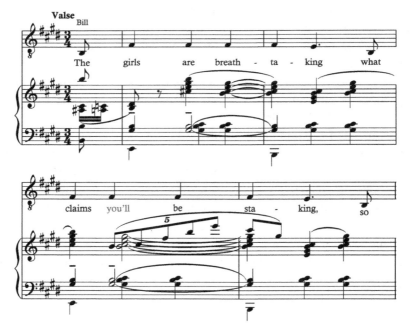

who, at various junctures, echo each of the three soloists (Benito, Columbus, Bill). Columbus briefly captures their attention, but his Italianate music is insufficient to keep them in line. Bill's tarantella and waltz, however, are more convincing. Indeed, the sailors declare, "Let's not argue with him / We like the waltz rhythm," demonstrating that it is America's music as much as

her culture that entices them. By having the Italian sailors easily move from Puccini to Broadway, the song also reassures international audiences that this culture is easily adopted, and that they will be welcomed into this new democratic and consumer paradise called "America." Within every Italian lurks a potential American—only music is needed to bring him or her out. As in *Knickerbocker Holiday*, immigrants have the potential to be "good" or "bad," but America always brings out the best in them. Thus, the long operatically inspired form shows a nation with sophisticated tastes and appreciation for "good music," while also demonstrating that American popular styles can hold their own against European art music.

The following scene reinforced the message that America and Europe had strong ties, albeit in ways that proved troubling to the OWI. The scene depicts Bill swindled by the Native American Chief Badger and his wife (another incarnation of Lucilla), leaving Bill with the deed to New York, which he bought from the Badgers for twenty-four dollars, referencing the famous legend of Dutchman Peter Minuit and leading to the Knickerbocker sequence. As is the case with numerous stage Indians of the time, they speak in pidgin English, and are portrayed as corrupt, yet ultimately stupid, trading twenty-four dollars for what would ultimately become one of the most profitable pieces of land in the nation.[108] The "nation of immigrants" account of history put forward by the "Columbus" number rewrites the history of land theft (indeed, Bill is the victim rather than the perpetrator of the crime) that forms an inconvenient alternative narrative to the origin of American identity. Weill and Gershwin's "Woo Woo Woo Woo Manhattan" number would have contributed to this cover-up, as it emphasizes the supposed savagery of the Native Americans, who declare "More fun than tomahawking / It is to go a-squawking," and dance to music that includes upward-rising whooping melodies, pounding "tom-tom" rhythms, and pentatonic parallel fifths, invoking what Michael Pisani calls the "war-dance trope" (Example 4.6).[109] In *Where Do We Go from Here?* history cuts both ways, damaging the reputation of one vulnerable group, even as it was used to support another.

*Where Do We Go from Here?* was Weill's final wartime project, and the last of his overtly patriotic works. When the film came out in the spring of 1945, the composer had already begun adjusting his composition for peacetime: he

---

[108] On stage Indians of the early twentieth century, see Pisani, *Imagining Native America in Music*, 280–81.

[109] Ibid., 252–53. The music example comes from *Where Do We Go from Here?* Holograph piano-vocal score.

**Example 4.6**  *Where Do We Go from Here?* "Woo Woo Woo Woo Manhattan."

was in the process of writing *Down in the Valley*, which—though a love letter to American folksong—is more contemplative, and at times narratively disturbing, particularly in comparison to his wartime works. But Weill's love affair with American history would continue after the war, re-emerging especially in *Love Life* (1948). Like both *Knickerbocker Holiday* and *Where Do We Go from Here?* and the historical pageants of the war years, *Love Life* looks to history for answers to contemporary dilemmas. Weill also remained concerned with the fate of immigrants in America, addressing their plight in his first large-scale postwar work: *Street Scene* (1947). But the optimism that characterizes *Knickerbocker Holiday* and *Where Do We Go from Here?* also left Weill's work after the war ended. Although he remained a patriotic American until the day he died, after the war Weill set his sights on improving the nation, rather than celebrating it.

## Postlude: *The Firebrand of Florence*

As *Where Do We Go from Here?* was shooting, Weill remained in Los Angeles to work on *The Firebrand of Florence*, which became the only true flop in his post–*Lady in the Dark* career. Weill worked with lyricist Ira Gershwin

and playwright Edwin Justus Mayer to make a musical out of Mayer's 1924 play *The Firebrand*, a fictional retelling of the Renaissance Florentine artist Benvenuto Cellini based on Cellini's autobiography. *The Firebrand of Florence* (called *Much Ado About Love* on the road) opened on 22 March 1945 to lackluster reviews, and closed after only forty-three performances. Casting problems, a troubled book, and some miscalculations on Weill's part likely doomed the piece.

The project has some similarities to *Where Do We Go from Here?* as well as other pieces of the period, particularly its lavish period costumes and setting. Weill also initially conceived of *Firebrand* as an operetta, similar to the "Columbus" sequence. Both *Where Do We Go from Here?* and *Firebrand* may have been inspired by recently successful musical comedy costume pieces like Cole Porter's *Du Barry Was a Lady* (Broadway 1939, film 1943), which includes a long dream sequence in eighteenth-century France. There had also been a number of successful revivals of earlier operettas, both U.S. and European, on Broadway in 1944, including a new version of Offenbach's *La Belle Hélène* (1864) called *Helen Goes to Troy* and Sigmund Romberg and Oscar Hammerstein II's *The New Moon* (1928, previously revived 1942), along with the newly arranged *Song of Norway*, which featured the music of Edvard Grieg.[110]

Weill was originally sanguine about the project, and even held out the hope that the project "might very well become an Opera for Broadway [*sic*]."[111] The notion that *Firebrand* could be an opera for Broadway speaks to Weill's continued enmity toward Richard Rodgers, whose *Oklahoma!* (1943) had started a widespread discourse about the possibilities for uniting musical comedy with more "art music" theatre, a goal Weill had long cherished. Still, there were clear contrasts in the composer's mind. Weill hoped to write an "intimate romantic-satirical operetta for the international market."[112] In 1945, "operetta" usually referred to genre featuring long passages of music for trained classical singers consisting mostly of recitatives, arias, and other older dance forms. Indeed, most of the songs in *Firebrand* have little of the jazzy syncopation and bluesy harmony of typical Broadway songs. Weill

---

[110] Charles Hamm, "The Firebrand of New York: Kurt Weill and His Broadway Operetta," *Music and Letters* 85, no. 2 (2004): 239–40.

[111] *WII(e)*, 391.

[112] Kurt Weill to Ira Gershwin, 3 April 1944, LOC/GT, Box "Warner-Wodehouse" Folder "Weill, Kurt 1940–1948."

instead opts for pseudo-madrigals like "The Little Naked Boy," dances like the tarantella "When the Duchess Is Away," and large choruses.[113]

Weill's "international" aspirations might also be a jab at *Oklahoma!*'s self-conscious Americana, which Weill may have seen as provincial. By 1944, as he was writing *Firebrand*, Weill had begun to think about producing shows across the Atlantic again. Somewhat naively, he held out hopes for European productions of *One Touch of Venus* (which he initially conceived as an operetta), writing to his agent Leah Salisbury in November 1943 that "*Venus* can become an international operetta. It can be played in London, Paris, Berlin and Moscow."[114] By 1944, because of his work on propaganda and on *Where Do We Go from Here?* Weill knew that markets overseas were beginning to reopen to U.S. culture. Indeed, *Firebrand* seems calculated for an international audience; Charles Hamm notes that it is "the most 'European' of Weill's pieces written in the United States."[115] This "European" quality might have partially accounted for its domestic failure. Weill lobbied hard to cast Lotte Lenya as the Duchess against the objection of Gershwin and others, arguing that he was sure her presence would "add a very special and interesting and classy touch to the show of a highly accomplished actress of the continental type," perhaps with European audiences in mind.[116] But Billy Rose remembered that Lenya's performance "was gay and expert—but she wasn't the sexy Duchess," and Lewis Nichols of the *New York Times* bluntly observed that Lenya was "miscast."[117] The contributions of producer Max Gordon also likely did not help. While Weill envisioned an "intimate" piece, Gordon was known for his sumptuous costume pieces like the Johann Strauss Sr. and Jr. pastiche *The Great Waltz* (1934) and Cole Porter's *Jubilee* (1935). But his most recent musical *Sunny River* (1941)—another period piece—had flopped. Gordon's luxurious sets and costumes may have been meant to dazzle the audiences of a war-ravaged Europe, but overwhelmed the singers and the slight story. More broadly, U.S. audiences of 1945 were in no mood to be international, and the idea of operetta was tarnished by the end of World War II, given the genre's unsavory associations with Europe,

---

[113] Introduction to Edwin Justus Mayer, Ira Gershwin, and Kurt Weill, *The Firebrand of Florence: Broadway Operetta in Two Acts*, ed. Joel Galand, *KWE*, Series I, Volume 18 (New York: Kurt Weill Foundation for Music/European American Music, 2002), 15.

[114] Kurt Weill to Leah Salisbury, 27 November 1943, WLRC, Series 40 Folder "Leah Salisbury (1 of 2)." Salisbury attempted to negotiate a London production, but it came to nothing.

[115] Hamm, "The Firebrand of New York," 243.

[116] Quoted in Galand, Introduction to *The Firebrand of Florence*, 29.

[117] Billy Rose, "Reveals His 'Other Name,'" *Atlanta Constitution*, 24 January 1947, 10; Lewis Nichols, "The Play," *NYT*, 23 March 1945, 13.

and particularly Italy, where *Firebrand* is set.[118] In early 1945, on the cusp of victory in Europe, U.S. audiences saw themselves as the new cultural arbiters of world taste, and were firmly convinced that their autochthonous forms of musical theatre were superior.

Perhaps a better book or more conscientious casting could have turned the show into a modest success, but with the United States a newly emergent political and cultural power, audiences were eager to consume stories and music that drew on Americana. Less than a month after its opening, *Firebrand* was eclipsed by Rodgers and Hammerstein's *Carousel*, which critics also spoke about in semi-operatic terms.[119] Once again, Weill found himself upstaged by Rodgers and Hammerstein, who had laid claim to the next phase of "Broadway opera" while Weill's extravagant production floundered. But Weill was a quick learner, and even as *Firebrand* withered, he began making plans with New York Times music critic Olin Downes on the project that would become the folk opera *Down in the Valley*, with its *Oklahoma!*-inspired plot. Furthermore, Weill spent most of 1946 working on *Street Scene*, which was eventually hailed as a "folk opera" in its own right.

Perhaps the most important thing that Rodgers and Hammerstein did for Weill was to prove that opera—or at least something vaguely operatic— could be viable on Broadway. After *Carousel* opened, Weill began to use a more operatic style in his shows, as well as operatic forms. Tessituras got higher, forms more elaborate, and melodies more complex. This, combined with his newly established U.S. citizenship (acquired in August 1943), inspired some of Weill's most musically and politically adventurous shows in the postwar era.

---

[118] Galand, Introduction to *The Firebrand of Florence*, 15; Hamm, "The Firebrand of New York," 242.
[119] Tim Carter, *Rodgers and Hammerstein's* Carousel (Oxford, UK: Oxford University Press, 2017), 20, 47.

# 5

# Alienation and Integration

## Gender and Sexuality

Kurt Weill got his first chance to work in mainstream commercial theatre in early 1940, when playwright Moss Hart proposed writing a show about psychoanalysis, with the dreams of the patient set to music.[1] The result, *Lady in the Dark* (1941), with lyrics by Ira Gershwin, was Weill's first Broadway smash hit, and hailed for its innovative integration of music and drama. The show played 777 performances over the course of two Broadway runs and a national tour, becoming one of the most popular productions of the time.

But when Rodgers and Hammerstein's *Oklahoma!* opened in March 1943, Weill found himself struggling to catch up, particularly considering that he was already deep into his next project: *One Touch of Venus*, with a book by musical comedy veteran S.J. Perelman and lyrics by Broadway newcomer Ogden Nash. *Venus* was too far into development for substantial changes (although they had hired *Oklahoma!*'s choreographer Agnes de Mille before Rodgers and Hammerstein's show opened). Still, when *Venus* opened on 7 October 1943, it received good notices, ultimately playing 567 performances, and relaunching the career of Mary Martin, who took the title role.

Weill continued to resent *Oklahoma!* and later, Rodgers and Hammerstein's *Carousel* (1945). Most of Weill's post-*Oklahoma!* Broadway projects to a greater or lesser extent engage with the ideas and innovations that critics credited to Rodgers. This is most obvious in *Love Life* (1948), which traces the history of American marriage, commenting on it through vaudeville. The show opened a season after Rodgers and Hammerstein's *Allegro* (1947), and the two shows share structures and themes. *Allegro* received tepid reviews, which Weill may have seen as an opportunity to outperform Rodgers. But *Love Life* ran only a respectable but disappointing 252 performances, sixty-three shy of *Allegro*'s 315.

---

[1] bruce d. mcclung, *Lady in the Dark: Biography of a Musical* (Oxford, UK: Oxford University Press, 2007), 44.

*Kurt Weill's America*. Naomi Graber, Oxford University Press (2021). © Oxford University Press.
DOI: 10.1093/oso/9780190906580.003.0006

While Weill never felt he got the better of Rodgers and Hammerstein, these three shows reveal that the composer could be acutely perceptive of U.S. culture. They trace the ways perceptions of gender, working women, and female sexuality changed as the Great Depression gave way to World War II and its aftermath. In *Lady in the Dark*, Liza is a highly successful but sexually repressed career woman who discovers that she would be happier ceding her professional responsibilities to her male colleagues. Venus, on the other hand, represents an untamed sexuality that cannot abide the restraints of "normal" femininity, evoking World War II–era fears of unruly women on the prowl for servicemen. In the case of *Venus*, however, choreographer Agnes de Mille added nuance to the show's politics, challenging the dominant narrative through the dance sequences. *Love Life* blends a Leftist anticapitalist stance with conservative gender politics, as the traditional gender roles of a fantastical agrarian past are portrayed as the antidote to the ills of modern life.

## Sophisticated *Lady*

*Lady in the Dark* proved difficult for contemporaries to classify; John Anderson in the *New York Journal* simply labeled it "Broadway's most spectacular whatyoumaycallit."[2] Blurring genres on Broadway was common during the late 1930s and early 1940s, as writers and composers sought to imbue musical comedy with the prestige of opera or the gravitas of straight drama. The desire to elevate the Broadway musical speaks to the complex cultural position that musical comedy occupied in the late 1930s and early 1940s. Although it was ostensibly popular theatre, composers, lyricists, playwrights, and theatrical organizations saw in it the potential to provide the foundations of a more prestigious form. This impulse sprang from several sources. With its jazz-inflected musical language, musical comedy became one of the battlegrounds for composers to prove that jazz constituted a legitimate contribution to transnational highbrow culture, a debate that crystalized in the reception of composers like George Gershwin.[3] The issue

---

[2] John Anderson, "Gertie Saves the Evening," *New York Journal*, 2 February 1941. Unless otherwise noted, all clippings regarding *Lady in the Dark* are preserved in the Gershwins' scrapbooks, LOC/Gershwin, Box 78 Book 7 Microfilm 93/20012 <Mus>.

[3] David Savran, *Highbrow/Low Down: Theater, Jazz, and the Making of the New Middle Class* (Ann Arbor: University of Michigan Press, 2009), 66–72.

of "integration," that is, the idea that music, dancing, settings, and so on, are all in service of the plot, was at the forefront of these debates. Bruce Kirle speculates that the idea of an "integrated" musical held more cultural capital because it represented "an American appropriation of the *Gesamtkunstwerk*," even before the premier of *Oklahoma!*.[4] The darkening situation in Europe exacerbated these anxieties; composers and lyricists wondered if a democratic culture could produce art that rivaled that of Wagner, Puccini, and other composers who hailed from Axis nations.

Weill, Hart, and Gershwin continued that effort, or at least said so in their publicity. The souvenir program reported that Hart told Weill that he wanted to "inject a fresh note into the rigid musical comedy formula."[5] Weill had been searching for a similar opportunity since his arrival in the United States; in 1937 he wrote "There are already many starting points for a new kind of musical comedy here."[6] As his composer brother George's primary partner, lyricist Ira Gershwin had already experimented with the boundaries between musical comedy, opera, and operetta. The brothers' *Of Thee I Sing* (1931) presented a Gilbert-and-Sullivan-esque satire, and their *Porgy and Bess* (1935) drew on black vernacular traditions, vaudeville, and European opera. But since George's sudden death in 1937, Ira had virtually retired. The idea of *Lady in the Dark* was enough to coax him back into show business.

The story follows Liza Elliot, the editor-in-chief of a fashion magazine, who begins psychoanalysis because she is unhappy, despite her professional accomplishments. At issue seems to be her romantic life. She is the longtime mistress of Kendall Nesbitt, a wealthy but married older man. She is also pursued by Randy Curtis, a handsome movie star. When Kendall's wife grants him a divorce, he asks for Liza's hand, sending her into a panic. With the help of her analyst Dr. Brooks, Liza discovers that she loves Charley Johnson, her advertising manager and rival for the editor's chair. Throughout, Dr. Brooks analyzes three of Liza's dreams: in the first, she is a glamorous socialite ("Glamour Dream"), in the second, a bride ("Wedding Dream"), and in the third, a circus performer ("Circus Dream"). A fourth dream sequence called the "Hollywood Dream" was cut before rehearsals. Throughout the show, a simple tune signifies some lost part of Liza's psyche. It appears in all three

---

[4] Bruce Kirle, *Unfinished Business: Broadway Musicals as Works-in-Progress* (Carbondale: Southern Illinois University Press, 2005), 18.

[5] Souvenir Program for *Lady in the Dark*, available in the WLRC.

[6] Kurt Weill, "The Future of Opera in America," *Modern Music* 14, no. 4 (1937), available at https://www.kwf.org/pages/wt-the-future-of-opera-in-america.html.

dreams but is only heard in full as "My Ship" when Liza realizes she associates it with the trauma of her father telling her she will never be beautiful.[7]

Hart first considered writing a show about psychoanalysis in 1937, when he and his playwriting partner George S. Kaufmann drafted the first act of a musical comedy for Marlene Dietrich based on the idea of free association.[8] But despite convincing Rodgers and Hart to write the music, they dropped the project soon after. Moss Hart returned to the idea in late 1939 when director Hassard Short introduced Hart and Weill, hoping the playwright and composer might collaborate on an unrelated script called "The Funnies." Both Hart and Weill found the psychoanalysis idea more appealing, and Hart brought the idea to Gershwin on New Year's Day 1940. Hart originally hoped to write for Katharine Cornell, an idea he had cherished since witnessing her performance in George Bernard Shaw's *Candida* (1894) in 1924.

Cornell's reputation as a serious tragedienne would have been in line with the idea of combining the prestige of straight theatre with the entertainment value of Broadway. However, after beginning to write in March 1940, Hart began to have doubts about the non-singing Cornell, as Weill's music became a larger part of the concept. Around the same time, Hart saw Gertrude Lawrence performing in an armed services benefit, and offered her the lead. Lawrence expressed interest, but replied that her astrologer told her not to make decisions until 7 April, and asked Hart to have a more complete script, at this stage called *I Am Listening*, by the late spring.[9] After finishing the first act in May and several months of back-and-forth, Lawrence signed the contract in late July, and suggested changing the title to *Lady in the Dark*. Hart finished the complete first draft of the script in August. Weill and Gershwin worked concurrently; whenever Hart finished a scene, he passed along the material to composer and lyricist, who were responsible for working out the placement and content of the dream sequences.

Lawrence proved a better fit than Cornell. Not only had Lawrence worked in highbrow straight theatre, starring in Noël Coward's sophisticated

[7] The flashback of events leading up to the full statement of "My Ship" is sometimes called the "Childhood Dream." The use of "My Ship" owes much to "Johnny's Song" in *Johnny Johnson*, the march in *The Eternal Road* (1937), and the "motto motive" in the unfinished *One Man from Tennessee* (1937).

[8] This account of the early genesis of *Lady in the Dark* is drawn from the Introduction to Moss Hart, Kurt Weill, and Ira Gershwin, *Lady in the Dark: A Musical Play in Two Acts*, ed. bruce d. mcclung and Elmar Juchem, KWE, Series I, Volume 16 (New York: Kurt Weill Foundation for Music/European American Music Corporation, 2017), 14–20.

[9] Moss Hart, "The Saga of Gertie: The Author of *Lady in the Dark* Tells How He Found a Star," *NYT*, 2 March 1942, X1, cont. on X3.

comedies, she also had musical comedy experience with the Gershwins' *Oh, Kay!* (1926). She was also known for her eccentric personal life, having divorced her first husband, then quickly becoming engaged again, only to call it off. In summer 1940, she married theatre owner Richard Aldritch, but carried on numerous affairs with both men and women throughout her life.[10] Her reputation formed a striking intertext for Liza, who appears repressed in her "real life," yet sexually liberated in the dream sequences. They also cast the borscht-belt comic Danny Kaye as Russell Paxton, *Allure*'s flamboyant photographer. Later, Bert Lytell was cast as Kendall, matinee idol Victor Mature took the role of Randy, and the unknown MacDonald Carey was cast as Charley. With the cast and crew complete, rehearsals began in mid-November. Directorial duties split between Hassard Short (musical sequences) and Hart (everything else).

In the publicity, the creative team characterized their project as more sophisticated than the typical show. Producer Sam Harris's office's official release described the show as "neither a musical comedy, a revue, a play with incidental music or just a straight play," and called it "a happy amalgam of all of these, and quite different from anything ever done in this country."[11] They also highlighted Weill's German heritage. According to the souvenir program, Weill told Hart "I started my career in music by writing chamber music, symphonies, sonatas, and so forth," before discovering opera. But he found contemporary operas too "formalized" until he met Georg Kaiser, who "occupied the same cultural position in Germany in those days as Eugene O'Neill does in America." (He also mentions Brecht.) By emphasizing Weill's experience with instrumental music, the program lends him the prestige of the concert hall that Broadway theatres lacked. By equating Kaiser with O'Neill, the program further established his highbrow credentials, and emphasizes Weill's ability to write American shows.

The publicity also highlighted Lawrence's sophistication, painting her as classy and elegant, yet also occasionally difficult—a typical diva. Hart wrote an article in the *New York Times* describing the trials and tribulations of securing Lawrence, emphasizing in her eccentricities, particularly her reliance on her astrologer.[12] Still, he made sure to portray her as devastatingly charming throughout the process, and to emphasize her dedication to her

---

[10] Tim Carter, Review of *Lady in the Dark: Biography of a Musical*, by bruce mcclung, *Kurt Weill Newsletter* 25, no. 1 (2007): 14.

[11] "News of the Stage," *NYT*, 23 January 1941, 18.

[12] Hart, "The Saga of Gertie."

craft; he wrote that as soon as rehearsals started, "Gertie was the very antithesis of her contract-signing self. A brilliant and intelligent actress I knew her to be, but what I did not know was that she was also a perfect angel once past a stage door." Overall, Hart paints a portrait of a high-maintenance yet sophisticated artist who was worth the trouble.

During the next few months of production meetings and rehearsals, *Lady in the Dark* underwent further changes. The long "Song of the Zodiac" sequence (inspired by Lawrence's indecision and reliance on her astrologer) was cut, then replaced by two numbers: "Tchaikowsky," which was specially written for Kaye, and "The Saga of Jenny" for Lawrence. These "specialty" numbers fell into the realm of traditional musical comedy, giving stars an opportunity to show off their talents rather than express emotion or move the story forward, a fact which made the collaborators nervous given their aspirations of breaking the traditional musical comedy formula. Still, they remained in the show for the sake of their stars. Other new numbers and dance sequences were added for Lawrence and Kaye, but most were cut for time during rehearsals or previews, along with other changes to account for the practicalities of performance, such as timing the music to the scene changes.[13] Previews began at Boston's Colonial Theatre on 30 December 1940 with the official Broadway opening on 23 January 1941.

Reviews were mostly positive, and Lawrence's versatility dazzled critics. In Boston, Elinor Hughes raved that "Gertrude Lawrence is given the opportunity to play a perfect Hamlet of a part and play it with the utmost brilliance and many-faceted charm."[14] The *Times*' Brooks Atkinson simply wrote "She is a goddess: that's all."[15] However, reviewers were mixed on *Lady in the Dark*'s aspirations to revolutionize musical theatre. The mainstream press (large city papers with daily distribution) generally proclaimed that this goal had been fulfilled. This achievement was predicated on successfully integrating the various styles and genres at work in the production. In the *Times*, Atkinson noted the subtitle "musical play" (rather than a "musical comedy") indicated that "the music and the splendors of production rise spontaneously out of the heart of the drama, evoking rather than embellishing the main theme." For

[13] These include a dance sequence after "One Life to Live," "Bats About You," and "It's Never Too Late to Mendelssohn."

[14] Elinor Hughes, "The Theatre: Gertrude Lawrence in Hart-Weill-Gershwin Musical," *Boston Herald*, 31 December 1940.

[15] Brooks Atkinson, "The Play in Review: Gertrude Lawrence Appears in Moss Hart's Musical Drama *Lady in the Dark*, with a Score by Kurt Weill and Lyrics by Ira Gershwin," *NYT*, 24 January 1941.

these critics and their middle- and upper-middle-class readership, *Lady in the Dark* had the potential to bring Broadway into the conversation about the stature of American art in the international artistic community. The *Boston Globe* even wrote that "the highbrows will no doubt murmur of Proust and Pirandello."[16] Weill's European career often came up in this context. Peggy Doyle of the *Boston American* declared that "Europe's Jacques Deval, Bert Brecht and George [*sic*] Kaiser have at one time or another collaborated on Weill on what they called musical plays, but last night's pace-setter was the first of its kind ever offered on the American stage."[17] Atkinson went the furthest in his patriotic defense of the show, writing in his second review that *Lady in the Dark* drew on "the ideal of Wagner's music drama" in the way the score was integral to the story, concluding that "the American musical stage is a sound basis for a new, centrifugal dramatic form, and *Lady in the Dark* takes a long step forward in that direction."[18] The fact that so many critics used this kind of language in their reviews of *Lady in the Dark* speaks to the looming cultural crisis in the United States of 1941. As the nations responsible for the West's artistic heritage (Germany, Italy, and to a lesser extent France) fell into fascism, the United States felt increasing pressure to prove that democracy could produce "great" works of art, not just entertainment, especially on the musical stage.[19]

But specialists were more suspicious of *Lady in the Dark*'s aspirations. U.S. modern music circles took Weill to task for failing to write in the contemporary "American" style. In the *New York Herald Tribune*, Virgil Thomson wrote that "all is monotonous heavy, ponderously German," with the exception of "The Saga of Jenny." Weill, he noted, was best when "parodying cheap sentiment." But since abandoning Brecht, Weill had "avoided all contact with what our Leftist friends used to call 'social significance,'" and his music lost its satirical edge: "It is just as banal as before, but its banality expresses nothing."[20] In *Modern Music*, Samuel Barlow bemoaned the United States' effect on formerly great German composers. He described *Mahagonny* and *The Threepenny Opera* as "authentic, devastatingly personal, alive," but then mourned the fact that "since no producer wants his best stuff here, Weill has

---

[16] "Two New Plays: Colonial Theatre *Lady in the Dark*," *Boston Globe*, 31 December 1940.

[17] Peggy Doyle, "*Lady in the Dark*," *Boston American*, 31 December 1940.

[18] Brooks Atkinson, "*Lady in the Dark*," *NYT*, 2 February 1941.

[19] Annegret Fauser, *Sounds of War: Music in the United States during World War II* (Oxford, UK: Oxford University Press, 2013), 161–66.

[20] Virgil Thomson, "Plays with Music," *New York Herald Tribune*, 23 February 1941. Weill called this review a "vicious attack."

attempted to attune himself to our ears. The results have been tragic. His musical sentences persist in having the verb at the end." He concluded that "In *Lady in the Dark* the catastrophe is upon us."[21] Herb Sterne in the Leftist *Script* was particularly disdainful, writing that audiences "were wheedled by the revolving stage, the legerdemain of Hassard Short's staging, and the chorean histrionics of Miss Lawrence into believing they were witnessing a substantial exploratory of psychoanalysis."[22]

This split in the reviews of *Lady in the Dark* speaks to the Weill's complex cultural position. In the mainstream press, his German heritage was an asset, as it spoke to Broadway's sophistication. But for critics like Thomson, hoping to establish a uniquely autochthonous American sound, his German identity proved a hindrance, as it prevented him from writing something uniquely and genuinely American no matter how hard he tried. The lack of political bite also seems to have troubled modernist Leftist reviewers like Barlow and Sterne, who lamented Weill's shift toward the commercial. Thus with *Lady in the Dark*, Weill lost what little respect he had from modern music communities in ways from which he never recovered in his lifetime.

## "No Queer Twists"

In *Lady in the Dark*, Weill, Hart, and Gershwin's keen sense of the gender dynamics of the Great Depression and its aftermath reveals numerous tensions and anxieties that permeated American culture of the era. As a working woman in 1941, Liza was not a sympathetic protagonist, so the show sets about making her more likable as it goes on. During the 1930s, men were often uncomfortable with working women. Psychiatrist Nathan Ackerman told oral historian Studs Terkel that wives were "belittling and emasculating" their out-of-work husbands. As a result, Ackerman said, "These men suffered from depression. They felt despised, they were ashamed of themselves."[23] In *Lady in the Dark*, Charley represents this type. Although he is employed, in his first appearance he is rumpled and hung over, indicating a lack of self-respect, springing from his position under his demanding female boss. Liza

---

[21] Samuel I.M. Barlow, "In the Theatre," *Modern Music* 18, no. 3 (1941): 192.

[22] Herb Sterne, "Screen," *Script*, 5 February 1944.

[23] Studs Terkel, *Hard Times: An Oral History of the Great Depression* (1970) (repr. New York: The New Press, 2005), 196.

appears as the negative stereotype of the modern woman: alienated from her own sexuality, she dominates the men around her, and yet cannot find happiness. Her affair with Kendall Nesbitt is problematic on several fronts. First, she is convincing another woman's husband to spend money on her even though she has money of her own, and second, as Dr. Brooks observes, he is more of a father figure to Liza than a lover. Because of this, audiences would likely have been skeptical of Liza's claim to Dr. Brooks that she has "no queer twists" and that her romantic life is "completely normal, happy, and satisfying." Just her appearance would raise doubt; she is "plain to the point of austerity" and wears "a severely tailored business suit, with her hat pulled low over her eyes [. . .] no single piece of jewelry graces her person." In an era when gender performance was believed to be inextricably tied to sexual orientation, Liza's masculine appearance at the beginning of the show speaks to some defect in her sexual life.

In this context, Liza's use of the term "queer" is telling; the word was in use throughout the 1920s and 1930s as a term for gay men who maintained a masculine carriage and appearance, in contrast to the effeminate "fairies" (like Russell).[24] The term was also associated with lesbian or bisexual women, as in the phrase "queer bird" or the lesbian pulp novel *Queer Patterns* (1935).[25] Often the simple fact that a single woman maintained a career rendered her a coded lesbian based on the conflation of sexuality and gender.[26] In popular culture, such career women often sported a similar look, inspired by Marlene Dietrich's short bleach-blonde bob, cigarettes, and penchant for men's clothing. Liza, with her similarly severe blonde hair, pencil thin eyebrows, masculine dress, and constant smoking recalls Dietrich on several levels, and possibly relates to Hart's interest in a similar musical for Dietrich. Liza's brusque yet nervous manner might also remind audiences of other contemporary queer women on stage, particularly Martha Dobie in Lillian Hellman's *The Children's Hour* (1934). The fact that Liza spends her days looking at beautiful women yet seems indifferent to the dashing Randy further calls her sexuality into question. Throughout most of the story, the only person Liza connects to emotionally is her

[24] George Chauncey, *Gay New York: Gender, Urban Culture, and the Making of the Gay Male World 1890–1940* (New York: BasicBooks, 1994), 14–15, 24–27.

[25] Lillian Faderman, *Odd Girls and Twilight Lovers: A History of Lesbian Life in 20th Century America* (New York: Columbia University Press, 1991), Kindle Edition.

[26] David M. Lugowski, "Queering the (New) Deal: Lesbian and Gay Representation and the Depression-Era Cultural Politics of Hollywood's Production Code," *Cinema Journal* 38, no. 2 (1999): 7.

wisecracking employee Maggie Grant, whom John Clum calls a "not-so-straight woman."[27]

For a woman in 1941, such a defect might best be addressed with psychoanalysis. At the turn of the century, U.S. Freudians took an optimistic view of Freud's theories, believing that acknowledging repression was the first step toward liberating people from the Victorian disdain of sex. Female and male reformers alike argued that, within marriage, middle-class, white women should fully realize their sexuality.[28] But if a healthy woman found a sexual outlet in marriage, an unhealthy one rejected or repressed her sexuality, causing debilitating neuroses.[29] Lesbianism or bisexuality constituted one possible manifestation of such repression. For Freud, female homosexuality developed when a woman failed to resolve her penis envy correctly, and thus adopted masculine traits as compensation, much like Liza's severe dress and executive manner.[30] Such women (and homosexual men) were diagnosed with "sexual inversion," that is, behaving as if they were the "wrong" gender.

In 1941, homosexuality was a taboo subject on the stage. During the 1920s, "pansy acts" that frankly acknowledged the existence of homosexuality became popular in mainstream nightclubs in Times Square.[31] But the padlock bill of 1927 forbad theatres from "depicting or dealing with, the subject of sex degeneracy or sex perversion," and the "pansy" trend peaked soon after.[32] Nevertheless, Broadway and Hollywood built a number of stereotypes that coded characters as homosexual or queer, even if they were never explicitly labeled as such, and the middle-class still enjoyed gawking at such "homosexual exotica" in their theatrical tastes.[33] Homosexuality, then, became "present in public discourse as an unthinkable alternative."[34] These circumstances explain the popularity of the Russell Paxton role, originally played by Danny Kaye, who clearly echoed the pansy acts of the 1920s.[35] Hart describes Russell as "mildly effeminate in a rather charming fashion," and has

[27] John Clum, *Something for the Boys: Musical Theater and Gay Culture* (New York: St. Martins, 1999), 106.

[28] See Chapter 3 of Christina Simmons, *Making Marriage Modern: Women's Sexuality from the Progressive Era to World War II* (Oxford, UK: Oxford University Press, 2009).

[29] Simmons, *Making Marriage Modern*, Chapter 4.

[30] Mari Jo Buhle, *Feminism and Its Discontents: A Century of Struggle with Psychoanalysis* (Cambridge, MA: Harvard University Press, 1998), 67–69.

[31] Chauncey, *Gay New York*, 308–11.

[32] Chauncey, *Gay New York*, 352.

[33] Chauncey, *Gay New York*, 314.

[34] Philip Brett, "Britten's Dream," in *Musicology and Difference: Gender and Sexuality in Music Scholarship*, ed. Ruth A. Solie (Berkeley and Los Angeles: University of California Press, 1993), 261.

[35] Clum, *Something for the Boys*, 104; mcclung, *Lady in the Dark*, 149–51.

him flounce around in women's clothing and fawn over Randy. Critics often referred to him as "swishy" and a "pansy," clear euphemisms for homosexual. His presence throws Liza's queer tendencies into sharp relief.

Along with these onstage elements, offstage components of the show disposed the audience to experience *Lady in the Dark* as a narrative of Liza overcoming her bisexual tendencies. As Bruce Kirle observes, performers' offstage personas and onstage styles have profound impacts on the way audiences interpret shows.[36] Gertrude Lawrence was known as sexually adventurous, and had affairs with both men and woman throughout her life, although because of the taboo nature of the subject, the extent of her same-sex relationships is unknown. More importantly, she was close friends with Noël Coward, whose own homosexuality was an open secret, and whose social circle included a number of other well-known closeted figures. Prior to *Lady in the Dark*, she had played androgynous roles in Coward's *Private Lives* (1930) and *Tonight at 8:30* (1936). There are also elements of Liza's character that Hart obviously modeled on Lawrence, particularly her final number; Liza's trial for the crime of indecision was likely inspired by Hart's ordeal in getting her to sign the contract. Blurring the lines between Liza and Lawrence would help the audience map any queerness associated with the latter onto the former.

Hart's reputation also might have predisposed audiences to read Liza as queer. Many critics noted that the show was based on Hart's experiences with psychoanalysis, which began in 1936.[37] Hart's biographer speculates that one of the reasons the playwright entered therapy was to rid himself of his homosexual leanings, and his doctor since 1937, Lawrence S. Kubie, was known for treating men who struggled with their sexual identity.[38] Hart made no effort to conceal his association with Kubie, dedicating *Lady in the Dark* to "L.S.K," and engaging him to write the preface to the published libretto (under the pseudonym "Dr. Brooks"). Kubie referenced Liza's queerness in his public analysis of the show, drawing on his own theories of infantile bisexuality, and what he called "the drive to become both sexes."[39] In what was undoubtedly a marketing stunt, Sidney Whipple of the *New York World Telegram* purported to have attended the show with his psychiatrist friend "Dr. K." Whipple reports Dr. K's analysis of the show to his readers:

[36] Kirle, *Unfinished Business,* 50.
[37] mcclung and Juchem, Introduction to *Lady in the Dark,* 14.
[38] Steven Bach, *Dazzler: The Life and Times of Moss Hart* (Cambridge, MA: Da Capo), 214–16.
[39] See mcclung, *Lady in the Dark,* 151–53.

It appears Liza's Oedipus complex was aggravated by unconscious jealousy of her mother's beauty, which, she was cruelly told, she completely lacked; narcissism played its part and there was a bi-sexual predisposition that worked itself out, so to speak, in editing a magazine devoted to feminine beauty, while she herself remained in a plain, unadorned state.[40]

Here, Dr. K makes explicit what the show implies: that Liza is in danger of succumbing to her bisexual tendencies. But for Liza, there was hope: "The proper prescription," according to Dr. K, "was a good healthy husband," which she acquires at the end of the show.

Weill and Gershwin's dream sequences reinforce the idea of a homosexual-to-heterosexual conversion narrative. The music tracks Liza's coming to terms with her gender in several ways. The first is the emergence of "My Ship," which signifies Liza's repressed trauma. When Liza remembers the tune, she comes to terms with the reality of her gender identity. But the score also tracks the emergence of her sexuality through musical style and other operatic tropes beyond the use of "My Ship." As Liza descends into the depths of her psyche, her music becomes progressively more "primitive" and "exotic." She starts in the idealized "white" world of operetta, passes through "brown" in the second dream, and finally finds herself in "black" musical context, each time coming closer and closer to her submerged sexuality.

Liza's journey begins in the relatively chaste world of operetta.[41] The transition from the spoken world to the musical one begins with Liza's haunting, wordless intonation of "My Ship," but quickly gives way to tinkling bells, breezy strings, and muted trumpets. At the start of the dream, she is bathed in glitter and elegance, but like Hannah in *The Merry Widow*, keeps her distance from her male admirers. The witty lyrics, airy waltzes, and lightly dotted foxtrots of "Oh, Fabulous One," "Huxley," and "One Life to Live," with occasional interruptions of the sweeping "Oh, how thrilled she ought to be"[42] theme create an atmosphere of sexless sophistication. However, a "marine" (actually Charley) sees through her glamorous persona and paints a severe portrait of her as she appears in "real life." At this moment, when the marine metaphorically penetrates her mask, the song "Girl of the Moment" becomes

---

[40] Sidney B. Whipple, "Diagnosis of Liza Authentic," *New York World Telegram*, 22 February 1941.

[41] mcclung, *Lady in the Dark*, 74.

[42] The melody first appears before Sutton sends Liza's admirers away, but first receives lyrics just before Liza has her portrait painted.

a "wild rhumba,"[43] injecting a Latin tinge into the proceedings. The dream becomes a nightmare as the first inkling of repression emerges.

The score continues to link Liza's repression and Latin styles in the "Wedding Dream," which is permeated by an insistent bolero rhythm. The Spanish and Middle Eastern tropes (the chromatic thirds in the winds overlaying the bolero rhythm) recall long-standing associations in opera between the exotic/primitive and the sexual. The association with Latin styles and Liza's repressed sexuality becomes explicit, as the rhythm signifies her dread at her upcoming nuptials. The rhythm vanishes only twice: when she distracts herself with Randy in the smooth, elegant foxtrot "This Is New," and then in the memory of her childhood play "The Princess of Pure Delight." In both cases, the absence of the rhythm indicates a return to the comfortable world of asexuality. In "This Is New," it suggests a lack of sexual connection with Randy, and in the "The Princess of Pure Delight," a return to childhood. This latter song also recalls opera, as its riddle-telling princess recalls another exotic operatic woman who refuses to commit to a man: Turandot.

Everything comes to a head in the "Circus Dream," in which Liza is put on trial for failure to make up her mind. Originally, Gershwin and Weill planned this sequence as a minstrel show, and even when they settled on a circus, elements of minstrelsy remained; for example, the ringmaster (Russell) and two "lawyers" (Randy and Charley) function as the interlocutor and the endmen. Liza finally unleashes herself in "The Saga of Jenny," a blues-inspired number that Lawrence turned into a bump-and-grind performance, which Hart remembered as almost a "strip tease."[44] While not a classic "blues," the number conforms to contemporary Broadway ideas of the blues ballad, with its swung rhythms, flat thirds, and sharp fourths/flat fifths recalling other Gershwin numbers "The Half of It Dearie Blues," from *Lady Be Good* (1924) or "Sam and Delilah" from *Girl Crazy* (1930). Vaudeville, burlesque, and minstrelsy had long been a site for play with gender and sexual identity, with some gay nightclubs and cabarets even staging "circuses" for their patrons.[45] It is within such setting that Liza sings "Saga of Jenny" and comes to terms with her status as a sexual being, drawing on contemporaneous associations between the blues and sexuality. But problematically, she seems fixated on a woman—the fictional Jenny—rather than a

---

[43] The 1941 published copy of the script calls it a bolero, but the rehearsal scripts are correct.
[44] Bach, *Dazzler*, 226.
[45] Chauncey, *Gay New York*, 37; Lugowski, "Queering the (New) Deal," 5.

man. In this, the blues also plays a role. During the interwar era, Harlem became one of the New York City's two gay enclaves (the other was Greenwich Village), and one of the few cultural spaces where same-sex relationships could even be celebrated, particularly in the realm of the blues.[46] Indeed, singers like Bessie Smith, Ma Rainey, Gladys Bentley, and Ethel Waters made no secret of their female lovers, and even sang numbers that blatantly celebrated same-sex relationships.[47] For audiences in 1941, Liza might be seen to channel these singers. In this context, her blues number about a woman of dubious sexual morals underscores the possibility that Liza's newly awakened sexuality will take a queer turn. She lavishes more attention on Jenny than either of her two putative suitors (Randy or Kendall), illustrating that Liza is indeed about to make up her mind, although her decision might be worse (in 1941) than not choosing at all—after all, the moral of the song is "Don't make up your mind." Indeed, her defense seems convincing until "My Ship" interrupts, reminding both her and the audience that she has still not achieved a "healthy" sexual identity.

In the end, the audience finds out that Liza's repressed sexuality results from the failure to resolve her Oedipus complex. She finds happiness in submission to Charley, represented by the child-like song "My Ship." The gentle, passive image of a woman waiting for her prince to the tune of a simple lullaby replaces the sexually aggressive, possibly bisexual woman who sings "The Saga of Jenny." After all, Jenny's efforts to seek out pleasure and her inability to make up her mind resulted in misery, while the gentle patience of the unnamed protagonist of "My Ship" is rewarded with true love.

In *Lady in the Dark*, bisexuality, represented by the blues, becomes an obstacle Liza must confront and overcome on her way to a healthy sexual identity. But with the entrance of the United States into World War II, women were encouraged to join the work force, and as the war went on, sexual repression became less of a concern than the possibilities of overly sexual women spreading venereal diseases in their efforts to show soldiers a good time. Weill, attuned to these cultural trends, featured the reverse Liza in his next project: a woman whose uncontrolled sexuality must be tamed lest she destroy the community around her.

---

[46] Chauncey, *Gay New York*, 244–57.

[47] Chauncey, *Gay New York*, 251–53; St. Sukie de la Croix, *Chicago Whispers: A History of LGBT Chicago before Stonewall* (Madison: University of Wisconsin Press, 2012), 98–101, 108.

## Integrating *Venus*

When *One Touch of Venus* opened on 7 October 1943 at Broadway's Imperial Theatre, *New York Times* critic Lewis Nichols wrote that the show was "not another *Oklahoma!* although it well may be the best new musical show to have opened since that time."[48] Comparisons to Rodgers and Hammerstein's juggernaut were inevitable. When *Oklahoma!* opened the previous March, it changed the critical standards for Broadway musicals. Like *Lady in the Dark* (whose second Broadway run closed about six weeks after *Oklahoma!* opened), Rodgers and Hammerstein's show was billed as a new kind of serious musical theatre in which story, song, and dance were integrated into a coherent dramatic whole. But the folksy characters and simple story were a stark contrast to *Lady in the Dark*'s neurotic women and emasculated men, and proved more attractive to war-weary audiences. If *Lady in the Dark* delved into the national psyche and found it steeped in trauma, the wartime *Oklahoma!* examined the origins of the national character, and found it full of simple, wholesome goodness.

Weill initially thought that *Oklahoma!* was well-done, if unremarkable. He saw a New Haven preview, and attended the Broadway version again in 1944, when he told Ira Gershwin that the show was "beautifully produced, staged and directed," with songs that "are just perfect for this kind of show" even though "the show is designed for a very low audience I.Q., and that, in my opinion, explains the terrific success."[49] Beyond Weill's personal evaluation, *Oklahoma!* posed a problem for the composer and his collaborators: book writer S.J. Perelman, lyricist Ogden Nash, and producer Cheryl Crawford. The documents surrounding *One Touch of Venus* reveal the turmoil produced by the sudden success of *Oklahoma!*, particularly in terms of the publicity. Yet for all that *Oklahoma!* informs the backstage drama of *Venus*, outside of the ballets (choreographed by *Oklahoma!*'s Agnes de Mille), the show owes almost nothing to Rodgers and Hammerstein, likely because its genesis predates the opening of *Oklahoma!* by nearly a year. Structurally, *Venus* is Weill's most conventional show; it rarely strays outside of musical comedy formulas, and the score is relatively typical Broadway fare.

---

[48] Lewis Nichols, "*One Touch of Venus*, Which Makes the Whole World Kin, Opens at Imperial," *NYT*, 8 October 1943, 14.

[49] Kurt Weill to Ira Gershwin, 3 April 1944, LOC/GT, Box "Warner–Wodehouse" Folder "Weill, Kurt 1940–1948."

In late 1941, *Lady in the Dark*'s costume designer Irene Sharaff introduced Weill to F. Anstey's novel *The Tinted Venus* (1898), the story of a barber who places a ring on a statue of Venus, accidentally bringing her to life.[50] Weill initially hoped to work with Ira Gershwin again, writing to him that Anstey's novel could be "a very entertaining and yet original kind of 'opéra comique' on the Offenbach line," but Gershwin was not interested.[51] In early 1942, Weill brought the project to producer Cheryl Crawford, whom he had known since his work with the Group Theatre. In July, they contacted the veteran Broadway book writer Bella Spewack.[52] Ogden Nash agreed to write the lyrics and Weill and Crawford approached Marlene Dietrich for the title role, which she accepted.[53] Spewack delivered the script in January, but she and Crawford differed on the direction of the story, so Spewack was replaced with veteran Hollywood screenwriter S.J. Perelman in January on the suggestion of Nash, even though Spewack had completed at least three drafts of her version of the story, which included some of the songs that made the final show.[54] Perelman finished a new script by early spring, but when they showed it to Dietrich, she left the project, deeming it "too sexy and profane."[55] Around the same time, Crawford and Weill approached Agnes de Mille in early March (just before the Broadway premiere of *Oklahoma!* but after the previews had begun), and de Mille brought on Japanese-American Sono Osato as the principle dancer.[56] Elia Kazan, another Group Theatre alum (he played a soldier in *Johnny Johnson* in 1936), came on board as director around the same time. In July, Crawford contracted Mary Martin to replace Dietrich.[57]

A number of scripts for *One Touch of Venus* survive (all with lyrics by Nash), falling into three broad stages: Spewack's original version, *One Man's Venus*;[58] the first Perelman version, completed in mid-March 1943 (when he deposited it for copyright in the Library of Congress), which went through

---

[50] Kurt Weill to Irene Sharaff, 15 October 1942, WLA, Box 47 Folder 14.

[51] Kurt Weill to Ira Gershwin, 13 November 1941, LOC/Gershwin, Box 66 Folder 23.

[52] Weill had already tried to work with Spewack and her husband Sam in the late 1930s. They got as far as outlining "The Opera from Mannheim," but nothing ever came of it. See *KWH*, 286–89.

[53] Kurt Weill to Marlene Dietrich, 24 July 1942, WLA, Box 47 Folder 3; Cheryl Crawford, *One Naked Individual: My Fifty Years in the Theatre* (Indianapolis, IN: Bobbs-Merrill, 1977), 121.

[54] Crawford, *One Naked Individual*, 121–23; Michael Baumgartner, *Exilierte Göttinnen: Frauenstatuen im Bühnenwerk von Kurt Weill, Thea Musgrave, und Othmar Schoeck* (Hildesheim: Georg Olms, 2012), 274–75.

[55] Crawford, *One Naked Individual*, 124.

[56] Baumgartner, *Exilierte Göttinnen*, 277, n60.

[57] "Miss Martin to Act in Crawford Play," *NYT*, 30 July 1943, 18.

[58] Three versions of this script survive in the WLRC, Series 20 Box O6 Folder 1942, Folder 1942a, and Folder 1942b. The libretto in folder 1942a is probably the latest of the three (the WLRC classifies the librettos in the order in which they are acquired).

several titles but which I will call *Love in a Mist* for simplicity's sake (its third title);[59] and Perelman's second (and final) version, written after Agnes de Mille began to work on the project in earnest, called *One Touch of Venus* (see Table 5.1).[60]

Spewack took Weill's idea of an " 'opéra comique' in the Offenbach line" as her starting point. Her version depicts the mundane marital problems of gods and goddesses, likely inspired by Offenbach's *Orphée aux Enfers* (1858). Her story begins with a banker named Bolton who owns and worships a statue of Venus. Ernie Bliss, an unsuspecting barber, inadvertently brings the statue to life by placing a ring (originally meant for his fiancée Agnes) on her finger. When Ernie is arrested for stealing the statue, Venus goes back to Olympus, where it is revealed that Bolton is the human incarnation of the god Vulcan, her estranged husband. Venus begs Zeus to make her human so that she can have a real relationship with Ernie. Zeus obliges, but gives her a twenty-four-hour time limit, ending Act I. Ernie's trial opens Act II, where Venus appears, providing an alibi. Ernie and Venus celebrate the verdict, winning a dance contest in the process, and retire to Ernie's apartment for a tender moment. But Venus's time is up, and Zeus calls her back to Olympus. The statue reappears in Bolton's garden, joined by a sculpture of Adonis that resembles Ernie.

Along with many songs that made it to the final show that were planned for this version, there are also several numbers that were cut. Spewack opened the show with "Who Dealt?" an ensemble for gossiping ladies playing bridge. Early in Act I, Ernie sings "If I Could Find a Rhyme for Love" to his absent fiancée Agnes, and the ensemble sings "Same Time, Same Place" in the middle of Act I. Starting in the middle of Act I, the Three Fates appear to comment on the action. They sing "Venus Was a Modest Goddess" (which eventually received a new lyric and became "One Touch of Venus"). "Who Am I?" saw Vulcan describing the difficulties of living between the human and divine worlds (later given to Savory in the first Perelman version, then cut) and "Vive la Différence" had Zeus and Venus discussing human love.[61]

---

[59] The WLRC holds three versions of this libretto. Series 20 Box O6 Folder 1943a is the earliest, and is still called *One Man's Venus*, as is the one in Folder 1943b. The WLRC also holds an uncatalogued version of the libretto called *Love in a Mist* which was deposited for copyright purposes in the Library of Congress in April, after the March draft (which does not reside at the WLRC), even though the March draft bears the title *One Touch of Venus* according to the Library of Congress's catalog.

[60] They reside in WLRC, Series 20 Box O6 Folders 1943, 1943c, 1943d, and 1943e. The version in 1943d is likely the earliest of these librettos, and 1943e is the promptbook used in rehearsals.

[61] This song only appears in Spewack's final draft.

**Table 5.1** Development of *One Touch of Venus*

| One Man's Venus (Spewack) | Love in a Mist (Perelman) | One Touch of Venus (Perelman) |
|---|---|---|
| I.1: Terrace garden of V. Crandell Bolton<br>Songs:<br>"Who Dealt?" (female ensemble)<br>"West Wind" (Bolton) (sung in combination with "Who Dealt?")<br>"If I Could Find a Rhyme for Love" (Ernie) | I.1: Main gallery of the Whitelaw Savory Foundation of Modern Art<br>Songs:<br>"Opening Chorus" (ensemble, cued but not yet written)<br>"Venus Was a Modest Goddess" (Molly) | I.1: Main gallery of the Whitelaw Savory Foundation of Modern Art<br>Songs:<br>"Opening Chorus" (Savory and ensemble)<br>"One Touch of Venus" (Molly and Girls) |
| I.2: The terrace, later that evening | I.2: Rodney's room<br>Song:<br>"How Much I Love You" (Rodney, here called "More Than a Catbird") | I.2: Rodney's Room<br>Song:<br>"How Much I Love You" (Rodney) |
| I.3: The top of the Chrysler Building<br>Song:<br>"I'm a Stranger Here Myself" (Venus) | I.3: Radio City Plaza<br>Song:<br>"I'm a Stranger Here Myself" (Venus) | I.3: Radio City Plaza<br>Song:<br>"I'm a Stranger Here Myself" (Venus) |
| I.6: Subway platform<br>Song:<br>"Same Time, Same Place" (ensemble) | I.6: Arcade of the NBC Building<br>Songs:<br>"Realist Ballet" (ensemble)<br>"West Wind" (Savory and ensemble) | I.6: Arcade of the NBC Building<br>Songs:<br>"Ballet: Forty Minutes for Lunch" (ensemble)<br>"West Wind" (Savory) |
| I.6a: A series of flashes | I.5: Waiting room of a mid-city bus terminal<br>Song:<br>"New Jersey" (Mrs. Kramer, Gloria, Rodney, cued but not yet written) | I.5: Waiting room of a mid-city bus terminal<br>Song:<br>"Way Out West in Jersey" (Rodney, Gloria, Mrs. Kramer) |
| I.5: Barbershop interior | I.6: The patio adjoining the museum<br>Song:<br>[Untitled production number] (Savory and students) | I.6: The roof garden of the Foundation<br>Song:<br>"Foolish Heart" (Venus) |
| I.6: [Unspecified]<br>Song:<br>"Venus Was a Modest Goddess" (Three Fates) | I.7: Rodney's barbershop<br>Song:<br>"The Trouble with Women" (Rodney, Savory, Taxi, Smitty) | I.7: Rodney's barbershop<br>Songs:<br>"The Trouble with Women" (Rodney, Savory, Taxi, Stanley)<br>"Speak Low" (Venus) |

*(continued)*

Table 5.1  Continued

| One Man's Venus (Spewack) | Love in a Mist (Perelman) | One Touch of Venus (Perelman) |
|---|---|---|
| I.7: On Mount Olympus<br>Songs:<br>[Untitled recitative] (residents of Olympus)<br>"Who Am I?" (Bolton/Vulcan)<br>"Vive la Différence" (Zeus and Venus)<br>"Down to Earth" (unclear, presumably ensemble) | I.8: The patio of the museum<br>Songs:<br>"Surrealist" production number (ensemble)<br>"Dr. Crippen" (Venus) | I.8: The roof garden of the Foundation<br>Songs:<br>"Cancan" (ensemble)<br>"Dr. Crippen" (Savory) |
| II.1: High noon—court room<br>Songs:<br>"That's How Much I Love You" (Ernie, note moving it to following scene)<br>"Dr. Crippen" (Bolton)<br>"That's Him" (Venus)<br>[Untitled song] (Three Fates) | II.1: Savory's bedroom<br>Song:<br>"Who Am I?" (Savory) | II.1: Savory's bedroom<br>Song:<br>"Very, Very, Very" (Molly) |
| II.2: High Time, Madison Square Garden<br>Song:<br>[Untitled song] (Reprise) (Three Fates) | II.2: Two cells in the Tombs [prison]<br>Songs:<br>"Too Soon" and "Production Number" (Venus, Rodney, ensemble, probably an early version of "Speak Low," cued but not yet written) | II.2: The Tombs [prison]<br>Songs:<br>"Speak Low (Reprise)" (Venus and Rodney)<br>"Catch Hatch" (Savory, Molly, Taxi, Stanley, Mrs. Kramer, Sam, Zuvetli, the Anatolians) |
| II.3: [Harvest Moon Ball]<br>Song:<br>[Untitled jitterbug] (ensemble) | II.3: The sitting room of a deluxe hotel suite.<br>Songs:<br>"That's Him" (Venus)<br>Reprise of "Too Soon" (Venus) | II.3: The sitting room of a deluxe suite<br>Songs:<br>"That's Him" (Venus)<br>"Wooden Wedding" (Rodney)<br>"Ballet: Venus in Ozone Heights" (includes "Bacchanale") (ensemble) |
| II.4: High tide, bedroom<br>Song:<br>[Untitled song] (Reprise) (Three Fates) | II.4: A wharf on the waterfront, lower Manhattan<br>Songs:<br>"Savage Ritualistic Dance" (ensemble)<br>"Love in a Mist" (Venus, cued but not yet written) | II.4: The main gallery of the Foundation<br>Song:<br>"Speak Low (Reprise)" (Rodney) |
| II.5: Park scene | II.5: Main gallery of the museum | |
| II.6: Penthouse terrace | | |

Spewack notes that much of the Olympus scene takes place in recitative, and the Fates' "Down to Earth" served as the Act I finale.[62] The Fates also sing an untitled number after Scenes 1, 2, and 3 of Act II to warn Venus that her time on earth is almost up.

Perelman's first script, *Love in a Mist*, is a more traditional Broadway musical comedy. In this version, the statue of Venus resides in Whitelaw Savory's art gallery, and the barber who awakens the goddess is named Rodney Hatch. As in previous versions of the story, Rodney is engaged to another woman, here named Gloria. Venus "dissolves" Gloria, leading to the authorities to arrest Rodney and Venus for murder. Act II opens with Rodney and Venus in jail, where they confess their love for one another. After Venus engineers their escape, they retreat to a hotel room, where Venus brings back Gloria to exonerate Rodney. But cultists kidnap Rodney and threaten to kill him unless Venus returns to being a statue. She agrees, but at the last moment, pulls Rodney into a passionate embrace, and both are transformed into a sculpture resembling Rodin's "The Kiss."

In this version, Perelman pokes fun at the modern art world. One scene in Savory's gallery opens with an art class drawing two nude models, but the students' canvases "depict cubes, triangles, guitars, watches, disembodied eyes and other abstract symbols."[63] A party at the end of Act I opens with a "surrealist production number" making fun of Salvador Dali, with a set including "colored lanterns of grotesque design," "enormous limp watches," and "a dead tree, sprayed pink" which "bears a variety of strange fruits" including "a corset, a horseshoe crab, an artificial leg."[64] *Love in a Mist* also sees the introduction of typical musical comedy figures: Molly, Savory's assistant and a comic belter; Gloria's overbearing mother; and two comic gangsters who work for Savory.

Perhaps the most important change between *One Man's Venus* and *Love in a Mist* is a new emphasis on dance. The latter script includes brief scenarios for several ballets along with the "surrealist production number" for a party at the gallery. The first is a sequence in which Venus encounters modern life for the first time just after "I'm a Stranger Here Myself," which

---

[62] Weill's preliminary drafts for this version are in WLA, Box 38 Folder 390. At this stage, Weill had completed the music for all the songs that made the final show, along with "Who Dealt?" "Vive la Différence," "Who Am I?" and "Jersey Plunk," an early version of "Way Out West in Jersey." Several other unused sets of lyrics and songs survive in Weill's papers, but when they were written and where they would have fit remains unclear.

[63] Perelman, *Love in a Mist*, 1-6-38.

[64] Perelman, *Love in a Mist*, 1-8-54.

Perelman describes as "a realistic ballet" with a variety of New Yorkers going about their business.[65] A scene in the jail at the beginning Act II featured a ballet to "Speak Low" (called "Too Soon" in this script) depicting "a series of vignettes, drawn from the past, to illustrate the fact that lovers must seize the present moment. In each of these Venus symbolizes the beauty of the era, such as Elaine, the Lilly Maid, Louise de La Valliere, Langtry, etc."[66] Finally, a cult kidnaps Rodney and puts on a ritual at the waterfront with the cultists worshiping Venus. It would feature "a score of figures, men and women, are engaged in a savage ritualistic dance—Oriental in character, yet suggesting Hellenic fertility rites."[67] No music was ever composed for these sequences.

Perelman's second and final version of the script (the third overall) hews closely to Love in a Mist, although the dance sequences are very different, speaking to the importance that de Mille assumed in shaping the project, as all of these sequences made the final production. Rather than a "realistic ballet" after "I'm a Stranger Here Myself," de Mille invented "Forty Minutes for Lunch," in which Venus arranges a romantic encounter between a sailor and a young woman. The "surrealist production number" was replaced by a more typical party sequence. The ballet in the jail was dropped altogether, and a new dance number was added to "Foolish Heart" to cover a scene change.[68] A dance was also inserted after "Way Out West in Jersey" to showcase de Mille's choreography. Perhaps de Mille's most important contribution was to change the ending. Rather than being extorted into transforming back into a statue, Venus makes the decision independently in the "Venus in Ozone Heights" ballet. The scene may have been inspired by the "Laurey Makes Up Her Mind" ballet that closes Act I of Oklahoma!, which also depicted a woman working through a romantic decision in dance. The sequence shows Venus as a typical suburban housewife who eventually becomes restless with her humdrum existence and is tempted back to Olympus by a flock of nymphs and satyrs. To preserve the happy ending, de Mille suggested that Martin re-emerge as a girl from Ozone Heights, the perfect match for Rodney.[69]

---

[65] Perelman, Love in a Mist, 1-4-16. Perelman indicates that this ballet includes dialogue as well as dance.

[66] Perelman, Love in a Mist, 2-2-12.

[67] Perelman, Love in a Mist, 2-4-19.

[68] Kara Ann Gardner, Agnes de Mille: Telling Stories in Broadway Dance (Oxford, UK: Oxford University Press, 2016), 64.

[69] Ronald Sanders, The Days Grow Short: The Life and Music of Kurt Weill (New York: Holt, Rinehart, and Winston, 1980), 327.

Even though *Venus* only loosely follows the principles of integration (i.e., that the music, settings, dance, costumes, etc. all serve the narrative rather than spectacle), everyone involved with the production saw *Oklahoma!* as their primary competition. Kazan believed that Rodgers and Hammerstein's success contributed to his hiring, despite his never having directed a musical. In his autobiography, he recalled that he was brought on because they wanted the show "directed as if it was a drama, not in the old-fashioned, out-front staging tradition of our musical theatre. That style was dated now; *Oklahoma!* had changed everything."[70] A few months after *Venus* opened, Nash proudly wrote to Weill that the "theatre contained our usual quota of standees," while "there have been empty seats at *Oklahoma!*"[71] Weill spent months trying to convince Crawford to model the publicity for the show on Rodgers and Hammerstein's hit, writing, "the entire publicity for *Oklahoma!* was built around the show itself. They gave such a build-up to the show, the book, the dances and the music that the pure mentioning of the show name of the show is good advertising," while complaining that *Venus* had been advertised as "just another musical, or, at best, a good vehicle for Mary Martin," whereas one of the advertised charms of *Oklahoma!* was its true ensemble character with no big-name stars.[72] Similarly, he urged his publisher not to treat *Venus* as a "one-number-score" based on the success of "Speak Low," noting that *Oklahoma!* "proved that it is quite possible to work several songs from a show."[73]

Still, *Venus's* relatively conventional format proved successful. Despite difficulty during the Boston previews, when the show opened, *New York Times* critic Lewis Nichols praised it for straying just far enough from the formula to remain interesting, writing, "Since music and girls are the soul of musical comedy, *One Touch of Venus* has thought of them also. There is not a Rockette chorus kicking from left to right; rather Miss de Mille has gone to work with her sense of humor so that the dancing all seems new and cheerful."[74] Similarly, John Chapman wrote that "the plot is boy-girl stuff, with a lot of magical interludes."[75] Critics also praised Weill's music, with "Speak Low" singled out by Nichols as a "sure hit," and L.A. Sloper described the score

[70] Elia Kazan, *Elia Kazan: A Life* (New York: Alfred A. Knopf, 1988), 234.
[71] Ogden Nash to Kurt Weill, 22 December 1943, WLA, Box 49 Folder 50.
[72] Kurt Weill to Cheryl Crawford, 20 January 1944, WLRC, Series 40 Folder "Cheryl Crawford."
[73] Kurt Weill to Max Dreyfus, 31 December 1943, WLA, Box 47 Folder 3.
[74] Lewis Nichols, "The Play," *NYT*, 8 October 1943, 14.
[75] John Chapman, "Good Show Finally Comes to Broadway Stage," *Chicago Tribune*, 17 October 1943, 4.

as full of "rhythmic vitality" and "real musical interest in texture and instrumentation" in the *Christian Science Monitor*.[76] They also nearly unanimously loved Mary Martin in the title role. But inevitably, critics compared *Venus* to *Oklahoma!* and found it inferior, even if they did like the show. Arthur Pollock wrote that the show "isn't quite so good as *Oklahoma!*" even though it was still "sure of full houses and long lines at box office."[77]

Weill's efforts to influence the publicity of *Venus* reveals one of the limits of his grasp of U.S. theatrical trends and audiences. The appeal of *Oklahoma!* was more than integration: it was also the homespun story, which tapped into deep-seated myths of rugged American individualists forming the heart of the nation. While Weill correctly surmised that the Broadway musical of the late 1930s was approaching a closer relationship between music, text, and dance, he missed the public's desire for a more "Arcadian" national origin story. Ironically, it may have simply been poor timing; Weill had been interested in using folk music and drama as the basis for his new form of musical theatre in *One Man from Tennessee* (1937) and to a lesser extent *Railroads on Parade* (1939, rev. 1940), only to find better success writing about urban communities, at least until *Down in the Valley* (1948). Indeed, Weill's three mainstream Broadway musicals to that point (*Knickerbocker Holiday* [1938], *Lady in the Dark*, and *One Touch of Venus*) mostly follow the principle that music and dance work to either move the drama forward or to express emotion, but all three shows are rooted in urban sensibilities. Still, Weill would continue to use *Oklahoma!* and Rodgers and Hammerstein's shows as benchmarks for the rest of his career.

## Love and War

While Hollywood, encouraged by the Office of War Information, turned out World War II–inflected film musicals, Broadway shows—free from government oversight, and popular escapist entertainment for soldiers on leave—rarely addressed the war directly.[78] Still, the cultural shifts instigated by the conflict had profound effects on the productions of the early 1940s. While

---

[76] L.A. Sloper, "*One Touch of Venus* Premiere at Shubert," *Christian Science Monitor*, 18 September 1943, 4.

[77] Arthur Pollock, "The Theater," *Brooklyn Daily Eagle*, 8 October 1943, 15.

[78] John Bush Jones, *Our Musicals, Ourselves: A Social History of the American Musical* (Waltham, MA: Waltham University Press, 2003), Kindle Edition.

the early scripts of *One Touch of Venus* ignore World War II, Agnes de Mille directly addressed the conflict in the ballets, perhaps because her new husband was stationed in New Mexico during the show's genesis. The decision was smart—the presence of Weill and the Japanese-American Osato forced the creative team to address the war in publicity materials.[79] While the *Lady in the Dark* program pronounces Weill an "eminent German composer," in the *Venus* program, he is described as a proud American (having obtained citizenship the previous August) who "used his great gift for music in fighting fascism right under the noses of the rising Nazi power in Germany."[80] The program glosses over Osato's foreign name and striking appearance, emphasizing that she was "an American product" who "hails from Omaha, Nebraska," without mentioning her Japanese father.[81] But even though *Venus* only addresses the war in passing, it informs much of the show's politics, particularly in issues of gender and sexuality. While the show traces Venus's domestication, de Mille's ballets reveal alternative points of view, challenging prevailing gender narratives of both the show and the broader culture.

Throughout the war, women's bodies and lives were subject to competing ideals. Soon after Pearl Harbor, government entities like the Office of Civilian Defense and the Office of Strategic Services (the precursor to the CIA) made clear that civilians needed to rally around the cause.[82] For women, this meant taking up formerly male-dominated jobs while preserving traditional standards of femininity.[83] Both the government and corporate world reminded women that servicemen needed to know that their way of life was worth protecting. Maintaining a slim body and pretty face became a sign of patriotism, as it contributed to morale.[84] A striking series of advertisements in the *One Touch of Venus* playbill for the "DuBarry Success School" exemplified these trends. The first featured "before and after" photos of Peggy

[79] Although the final script includes a few war-related gags, those were added only after de Mille joined the production.

[80] Souvenir Program, *One Touch of Venus*, author's private collection.

[81] On the ways Osato's Japanese heritage informed *One Touch of Venus*, see Carol Oja, *Bernstein Meets Broadway: Collaborate Art in the Time of War* (Oxford, UK: Oxford University Press, 2014), 135–38.

[82] See Chapter 5 of Holly Allen, *Forgotten Men and Fallen Women: The Cultural Politics of New Deal Narratives* (Ithaca, NY: Cornell University Press, 2015).

[83] On the various pressures on wartime women, see Melissa A. McEuen, *Making War, Making Women: Femininity and Duty on the American Home Front, 1941–1945* (Athens: University of Georgia Press, 2010); Marilyn E. Hegarty, *Victory Girls, Khaki-Wackies, and Patriotutes: The Regulation of Female Sexuality during World War II* (New York: New York University Press, 2008); Allan M. Winkler, *Home Front, U.S.A.: America during World War II*, 3rd ed. (Wheeling, IL: Harlan Davidson, 2012), 57–65.

[84] McEuen, *Making War, Making Women*, 161–66.

Frank of the Women's Voluntary Service. The "before" photo depicts a stern, overweight woman, while the "after" shows her new trim figure and smiling, made-up face. The advertisement tells the reader that "the program of diet, exercises, posture correction, DuBarry skin care and make-up, personalized hair-do, manicure and pedicure, and other exciting activities make her as fit and fair as she wants—and *ought*, in these times—to be."[85] Still, in their relationships with servicemen, women were carefully watched. The film *Stage Door Canteen* (1943) illustrates the narrow path between respectable and inappropriate behavior. Eileen, the protagonist, is a hostess at a USO canteen. At first she is chastised for treating a soldier with indifference, but when she falls for him and makes a date with him after hours, she loses her job for bad behavior.[86] Like Eileen, women were supposed to be friendly and cheerful with servicemen, but any hint of a sexual relationship risked their reputation.

Rodney's fiancée, Gloria Kramer, and her mother illustrate the wrong way to be a woman in wartime. Gloria is "young, aggressive, attractive in a tasteless

**Figure 5.1**  *One Touch of Venus* program, advertisement for DuBarry's Success School. WLRC.

---

[85]  *One Touch of Venus* playbill, week of 12 December 1943, 13, emphasis in the original, WLRC, *One Touch of Venus* Production files.
[86]  Allen L. Woll, *The Hollywood Musical Goes to War* (Chicago: Nelson-Hall, 1983), 136–38.

way. Her clothes just miss being chic. Her skirt is too short, her hat too extravagant." Her aggression and lack of fashion sense mark her as disturbingly unfeminine. Her short skirt speaks to her promiscuity (confirmed by her flirtation with "Sam," a traveling companion), and her ostentatious hat reveals her profligate spending, a cardinal sin during the rationing of wartime. She is unpleasant and bossy, and unreceptive to Rodney's polite affection. Worse is the "large, noisy, vindictive" Mrs. Kramer, who represents contemporary stereotype of the overbearing mother, a figure often blamed for the evils in American society in wartime.[87] In his 1942 bestseller *Generation of Vipers*, Philip Wylie coined the term "momism" to describe America's misguided worship of this "thundering third sex" who were responsible for sapping the virility of American men, leaving the door open for fascism. "Like Hitler," Wylie wrote, "she betrays the people who would give her a battle before she brings up her troops," and continued, "the good-looking men and boys are rounded up and beaten or sucked into pliability."[88] Rodney's deference to his future mother-in-law shows that he is in danger of becoming weak-willed and subservient, and he only learns how to "be a man" after he gets involved with Venus, who (at least initially) only wants "to choose his neckties for him," and to be an otherwise perfect wife.

As Venus, Mary Martin was the antithesis of Gloria: optimistic, beautiful, amiable, and devoted to Rodney. With the help of Osato, Martin learned to "think tall" so that she would make the most of her slight five-foot-four frame.[89] This regal bearing gave her an aura of power, yet designer Mainbacher's costumes for her consisted mostly of pale pinks and purples, making sure she never lost her feminine charm.[90] The fact that Venus is devoted to Rodney also spoke to expectations that women remain alluring, yet only for the sake of a single (often absent) partner. Where Gloria is coarse and unpleasant, Venus is lively and genuine. Where Gloria constantly badgers Rodney for help, Venus is powerful and self-sufficient. Most importantly, Gloria is promiscuous yet sexually unavailable to her fiancée (Venus notes that they are "still vertical" after five years of engagement), and Venus only has eyes for Rodney.

But when Agnes de Mille came onto the project, she complicated the story's gender politics. Newly married herself, de Mille chafed at the conservative gender expectations of the era, and used dance to explore that

[87] See chapter 4 of Buhle, *Feminism and Its Discontents*.
[88] Philip Wylie, *Generation of Vipers* (New York: Ferris, 1942), 192, 193.
[89] Mary Martin, *My Heart Belongs* (New York: Morrow, 1976), 114.
[90] Martin, *My Heart Belongs*, 110.

discomfort.[91] Venus's character arc traces the character's increasingly tamed sexuality, from the exuberant "I'm a Stranger Here Myself," to the melancholy "Foolish Heart," to the sensual "Speak Low," and finally to the romantic but chaste "That's Him." But de Mille's dance sequences tell the opposite story through the arc of "premier danseuse" Osato, who takes on multiple personas that move from sexual repression to fulfillment.[92] In "Forty Minutes for Lunch" Venus arranges a romantic liaison between Osato and a sailor. In "Foolish Heart," Osato reappears to seduce another sailor. Finally, in "Venus in Ozone Heights," Osato comes into her own as the leader of the nymphs and satyrs that disrupt Venus's humdrum suburban life with their sexual escapades, eventually tempting her back to Olympus.

Weill composed the music for the dance sequences with de Mille's choreography in mind.[93] In the 1990s, the De Mille Project Workshop produced a reconstruction of the choreography of "Forty Minutes for Lunch" and the "Bacchanal" that forms the second part of "Venus in Ozone Heights" with the help of some of the original dancers, which illustrates the close connection between score and dance.[94] For "Forty Minutes," Weill rewrote "I'm a Stranger Here Myself" as a chaconne, with several intermingled episodes in which the bass line is absent. Immediately after Venus sings "I'm a Stranger Here Myself," midday strikes, and New Yorkers pour into the streets with rigid, mechanical movements and hunched postures, barely interacting with one another. This is accompanied by a rigid, chromatic, and melodically narrow bass line (Example 5.1a).[95] Weill injects tension by introducing a hemiola, adding an accent to every other beat, which causes friction with the established $\frac{6}{8}$, representing underlying erotic desire (Example 5.1b). When the "Stranger" melody enters, the chaconne vanishes, but the melody it has becomes a jerky waltz, as the dancers break their static formation and rush about the stage, their movements still sudden and angular, like marionettes.

Venus spots Osato and brings her out of the crowd, as the metrical tension comes to the forefront. The underlying wood block and pizzicato strings (represented in the left hand of the piano score) are still in $\frac{6}{8}$, but the winds play the "Stranger" melody in an elongated $\frac{3}{4}$, signifying the girl's emerging

[91] Gardner, *Agnes de Mille*, 48–49.
[92] Gardner, *Agnes de Mille*, 64–65.
[93] Gardner, *Agnes de Mille*, 55–58.
[94] A VHS of the reproductions is available at the WLRC. All observations regarding choreography come from that tape.
[95] All examples come from Weill's fair copy of the *One Touch of Venus* piano-vocal score, David Drew Collection, WLRC.

**Example 5.1a** *One Touch of Venus*, "Forty Minutes for Lunch."

**Example 5.1b** *One Touch of Venus*, "Forty Minutes for Lunch."

**Example 5.1c** *One Touch of Venus*, "Forty Minutes for Lunch."

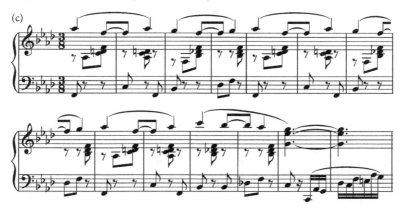

femininity (Example 5.1c). Venus teaches her how to walk, flirt, and carry herself like a woman. Once her pupil has mastered the art of femininity, Venus introduces her to a passing sailor (Peter Birch). The duple time, first introduced as a signal of underlying sexual tension, almost entirely takes over as the girl and the sailor begin a romantic *pas de deux* to the B section of "Stranger" (the music that first accompanies the lyrics "I dream of a day, of a gay warm day . . ."), restored to its original meter. Although the underlying $\frac{6}{8}$ remains, it is only in the violas and keyboard, and the range has widened considerably, sweeping across multiple octaves, lending the moment a sense of freedom that

all the previous music lacks. As Osato and the sailor dance, the crowd begins to mimic their graceful, balletic movements, indicating that the romance is contagious. But the chaconne breaks in again as Osato and the sailor begin to despair, and the crowd reverts to their earlier movement profile. The company forms a semi-circle around the couple, literally breathing down their necks. The lovers must part, and the ballet ends as it began, with the bare bass line ticking mechanically away, but both the sailor and Osato thank Venus for the moment of happiness before they exit to opposite sides of the stage.

De Mille's choreography and Weill's music work together to illustrate some of the dilemmas women faced during the early 1940s. As a working woman, the girl in the ballet has lost her femininity, which Venus restores. She promptly uses her newfound skills to please a serviceman, but the ephemeral nature of their relationship raises objections from the crowd. The boundary between good behavior and bad for women was ambiguous and blurry, reflecting cultural issues of the era. Instances of premarital sex rose sharply during the war years, and women consented to intercourse with servicemen in the name of fulfilling their patriotic duty, often with the tacit permission of some parts of the armed forces, who felt that men needed sexual release to remain healthy.[96] At the same time, such encounters fed fears of venereal disease, and both the government and the military worked hard to discourage such liaisons. Posters warning soldiers to stay away from young girls "even if she looks clean" were prominently displayed in camps across the country. These fears are manifested in the reaction of the crowd. Initially, the company seems enchanted by the couples' infectious romance, but that becomes public disapproval as the dance goes on, and eventually forces them to part. Yet the ballet depicts the encounter as necessary to the happiness of both participants. It breaks both out of their humdrum lives, giving them a fleeting moment of joy.

Depicting a sailor in such a fashion was not novel, but to portray the girl in so positive a light was rare in the war era. Popular media insisted that women who had intimate encounters with servicemen should marry them (see *Stage Door Canteen, On the Town* [1944], *Anchors Aweigh* [1945]). But the sequence celebrates the ephemeral nature of the romance. To drive the point home, de Mille told a similar story in the second Osato ballet, a short dance after "Foolish Heart." After Venus exits, Osato appears and flirts with another sailor. De Mille told her "bolt straight up, slap your skirts, hitch your bosom,"

---

[96] John D'Emilio and Estelle B. Freedman, *Intimate Matters: A History of Sexuality in America* (Chicago and London: University of Chicago Press, 2012), 260; Robert L. McLaughlin and Sally E. Parry, *We'll Always Have the Movies: American Cinema during World War II* (Lexington: University of Kentucky Press, 2006), 261–66. See also Hegarty, *Victory Girls*.

and catch his eye. After a brief dance, they both do "one quick take at the audience and strut off."[97] Osato's character has internalized Venus's lessons from the previous ballet. As with "Forty Minutes," the "Foolish Heart" music traces a path from sexual inhibition to expression. It begins with a reprise of "Foolish Heart," but gives way to the sea shanty "What Do You Do with a Drunken Sailor?" (de Mille's suggestion), which becomes more raucous as Osato gets her man. However, that sequence was not included in the reconstruction, so a close reading is not possible.

There was not enough information to reconstruct the beginning of "Venus in Ozone Heights," but dancers' recollections and de Mille's letters to Weill provide some clues as to what appeared on stage. In July of 1943, de Mille sent Weill a detailed scenario of her thoughts for the final ballet.[98] As Rodney begins to describe his vision of a perfect life in "Wooden Wedding," Venus begins to get nervous. She imagines herself in the suburbs, inhabiting one of three identical houses, cooking and cleaning for a "very appreciative but matter-of-fact" Rodney. Outside, a series of nymphs and satyrs led by Osato manipulate girls and boys (including an air force pilot) into falling in and out of love, all the while calling to Venus. When "Venus can bear no more," she "stands up with an ancient and terrible cry," and runs out to join them. At this point a drum begins to pound softly and an orgiastic ritual begins, accompanied by music that resembles "the rhythm and pace of Glazunov's Bacchanal." Ozone Heights drops away, and Rodney is left alone with Gloria. At that moment, "Venus appears, naked, translucent, Olympian, awful." She walks into a star-filled sky, back to Olympus once more.

The ballet underwent numerous changes over the course of rehearsals and previews (de Mille describes at least five versions).[99] Weill's music does bear some resemblance to Glazunov's "Autumn" bacchanal from his ballet The Seasons (1900) in its dynamic orchestration and the rush of melodic fragments, but the "pounding drum beat" does not last for much of the music.[100] In the end, there was no "unearthly cry"; instead, Venus was "triumphantly carried away be her people amid great rejoicing," alongside Osato, who appeared as the ringleader of the nymphs and satyrs. But the overall trajectory remained the same, as did some of the details, including the aviator, who walks off into the distance with his sweetheart just before the apotheosis of Venus and Osato.

[97] Sono Osato, Distant Dances (New York: Knopf, 1980), 218–19.
[98] Agnes de Mille to Kurt Weill, 14 July 1943, WLA, Box 48 Folder 28.
[99] Agnes de Mille, And Promenade Home (Boston: Little, Brown, 1958), 110–14.
[100] De Mille may have been inspired by "That Bacchanale Rag," a number in The Passing Show of 1912 that put lyrics to Glazunov's "Autumn."

Like de Mille's scenario, Weill's score for the ballet falls into two parts, "Venus in Ozone Heights" and the "Bacchanal," and the choreography survives for the second. The first opens with a segue from "Wooden Wedding," repeating that melody in delicate pizzicato strings, followed by a simple new melody in the piccolo.[101] These light strings and winds set up the idyllic suburban life, which is then interrupted by a bluesy piano rendition of "I'm a Stranger Here Myself," which likely would have accompanied the first entrance of the nymphs and satyrs. This is followed by a sensual reprise of "Speak Low." Two new melodies follow in quick succession, a fandango and a charleston. The first part ends with series of vocal sighs. In the second part, the "Bacchanal," the vocal sighs continue throughout, climbing in register, as the music presents a whirlwind of old and new melodies, including snatches of "Speak Low" and the pastoral piccolo melody from the opening. The fandango rhythm, accompanied by castanets, returns in a possible reference to Saints-Saëns' bacchanal from *Samson et Dalila* (1877). The whole sequence culminates in a triumphant vocal cry from the chorus, as both Osato and Venus strike poses and are lifted into the air by the male dancers and carried triumphantly offstage.

The joyful release at the end of the "Bacchanal" is a damning commentary on the pleasant but boring life of the suburbs, and speaks to the tragedy at the heart of the ballet: that female fulfillment is not possible within the confines of contemporary earthly society. The exuberance casts the humdrum neighborhood in a dim light, and reveals the restricted lives of its residents, particularly the women. Venus is trapped inside, frustrated with her repetitive and limited life, while husbands can escape the gilded cage. Osato, who earlier had been Venus's pupil, now becomes her teacher. Having been exposed to Venus's penchant for flouting the restrictions of normative female sexuality, Osato now reminds Venus of that lesson, thus bringing both character arcs to their conclusion. But both women, having experienced the world outside of their prescribed gender roles, can no longer be happy (as much as Venus might try) on earth, and must ascend to Olympus. Ultimately, de Mille reveals that the perfect woman is, like Venus herself, a myth.

## Balancing Acts

After the war, Weill returned to issues of gender and marriage in *Love Life* (1948). The show traces the history of marriage through Sam and Susan

---

[101] Weill borrowed the tune from the unused title music for *The River Is Blue*.

Cooper, a generic American couple who appear, without aging, in 1791, 1822, 1857, the 1890s, the 1920s, and 1948. The show has a revue-like format, consisting of a series different kinds of vaudeville "acts" and, according to an article in the *New York Times* by Weill and librettist Alan Jay Lerner, the narrative is told in a series of vaudevillian "sketches" in different theatrical styles: "musical play" (probably 1791), "American ballad" (probably 1822), "straight comedy" (1857), "satire" (1890s), "musical comedy" (1920s), "dramatic" (1948), and ballet (the divorce).[102] These narrative scenes alternate interscene musical numbers (also based on vaudeville) that elucidate the reasons for Sam and Susan's crumbling relationship. The show ends with a minstrel sequence in which the pair confront their flaws, and agree to face reality together. Weill and Lerner emphasized the inherent Americanness of this structure, writing that vaudeville and minstrelsy were "the most typical form of American theatre," and therefore the best way to tell "an American story."[103]

*Love Life* was somewhat autobiographical for Lerner (as *Lady in the Dark* was for Hart), who had just entered his second marriage, which would last only a few years, and be followed by six more. The original draft also included an incident from his own parents' failed marriage (the scene "A Ticket to the Fight," discussed later). But *Love Life*'s innovative framework also owes much to Weill's previous output, both European and American. The separation of plot and commentary resembles *Die Dreigroschenoper* and *Aufstieg und Fall der Stadt Mahagonny*, and having characters appear in different guises is reminiscent of *Where Do We Go from Here?* (1945) and *Lady in the Dark*, whose circus dream (originally a minstrel show) foreshadows *Love Life*'s vaudevillian turns. Perhaps *Love Life*'s closest cousin is *You and Me* (1938), which includes non-narrative commentary sequences not justified by a plot device.[104]

Beyond Weill's own output, Rodgers and Hammerstein's *Allegro*, which opened the previous October and closed the following July, also likely influenced *Love Life*. Like *Love Life*, *Allegro* examines societal pressures, particularly materialism and professionalization, on American marriage over the course of a long period of time—about thirty years. Also like *Love Life*, *Allegro* is interspersed with choral commentary numbers, and the Agnes de Mille–directed production used elements that are reminiscent of Weill's European

[102] Kurt Weill and Alan Jay Lerner, "Two on the Street: Collaborators Stage a Scene Aimed at Explaining Their Musical Play," *NYT*, 3 October 1948, available at https://www.kwf.org/pages/wt-two-on-the-street.html.

[103] Weill and Lerner, "Two on the Street."

[104] See Stephen Hinton, *Weill's Musical Theater: Stages of Reform* (Berkeley: University of California Press, 2012) 407–8, for a detailed summary of precedents for *Love Life*'s innovations in Weill's work.

works, particularly the spare settings and projections. Furthermore, the "cavalcade of Americana" in *Love Life*—to use *Variety*'s description—might be an
answer to the folksy qualities of *Allegro*, a show Brooks Atkinson wrote was
"lovingly presented like an American legend."[105] Indeed, according to the
souvenir program, *Love Life* "describes the life of an average American small
family, who could be any family." Given *Allegro*'s relative failure and Weill's resentment of *Oklahoma!* and *Carousel*, he may have seen a chance to compete
with Rodgers on the more familiar ground of the experimental musical.

Love Life begins where *Oklahoma!* ends, with a happily married couple
settling down in a small town at the dawn of the nation. This is made more
explicit by framing the 1791 and 1822 scenes as a "musical play" (also the
designation of *Oklahoma!*) and an "American ballad." The latter designation is likely a reference to Weill's own *Down in the Valley*, a project which
clearly responds to *Oklahoma!*, and which had premiered the previous July.
Like *Down in the Valley*, the 1822 scene includes a long folk-dance sequence
to "Green-Up Time," which resembles the "Sourwood Mountain" sequence
in *Down in the Valley*, along with "The Farmer and the Cowman Should Be
Friends" from *Oklahoma!* and "June is Busting Out All Over" from *Carousel*.
If *Oklahoma!* and *Carousel* end with excising, redeeming, or reforming the
"bad" elements of the community, allowing it to move forward, *Love Life* asks
the question, "Forward into what?"

But balancing so many different styles and ideas proved difficult for Lerner
and Weill, who hoped to use *Love Life* to level a serious critique of American
life. As in *Lady in the Dark*, Lerner and Weill tried to inject the musical, with
its entertainment value, with some of the serious themes of straight plays.
But Lerner's cynicism regarding marriage made audiences uncomfortable,
demonstrating the difference between the expectations for a musical and
straight play, where such cynicism was more accepted. The development of
the project shows them struggling to make characters likable enough for a
musical, yet flawed enough to carry out this critique.

The relationship between sexuality, domesticity, and the nation remained
fraught after the war. As the economy demobilized, fears of another crash developed. To compensate, such Right-wing groups as the National Association
of Manufacturers and Left-wing groups as the Congress of Industrial
Organizations both advocated for increasing private consumption to replace
government support of wartime manufacturing—consumption which often

---

[105] Abel, "*Love Life*," *Variety*, 13 October 1948; Brooks Atkinson, "*Allegro* a Fragment of the
American Legend," *NYT*, 2 November 1947, X1.

took the form of household appliances, and was thus inherently gendered.[106] Women were encouraged to focus on childrearing and homemaking in new suburban neighborhoods, and to let men support them financially. Both the public and private sectors instituted policies that pushed married women out of the well-paying jobs they held during the war.[107] Most women were legally prohibited from opening lines of credit without male approval, and medical, business, and law schools maintained very low quotas for female applicants, if they admitted women at all.[108] This new family, living in a technologically advanced household, signaled capitalism's superiority over communism, which, in contrast, allegedly overworked and desexualized women.[109]

Many families struggled with the weight of these expectations. Although it took until 1963's *The Feminine Mystique* for Betty Friedan to label women's discomfort and malaise "the problem that has no name," it was apparent in the late 1940s that the new gender politics were not making people happy.[110] The ideals of femininity proved so unattainable that many women sought psychiatric help, only to be told to more deeply embrace their role as wives and mothers, much like Liza in *Lady in the Dark*.[111] Despite widespread disapproval of divorce, rates spiked immediately after the war. Although they began to fall again in the late 1940s, the divorce rate never returned to 1930 levels.[112] Indeed, in the case of *Love Life*, Susan's sexual frustration and desire for a career are an early acknowledgment that the postwar family left women unsatisfied, just as Venus's fear of isolation was troubling in 1943. Men struggled as well. In 1950, David Riesman's bestselling *The Lonely Crowd* acknowledged that men's professional life had moved away from "craft skill"—that is, manufacturing—to "manipulative skill," or working with people, resulting in adverse psychological effects: "The machine-tool man began in the shop; as V.P. for sales and advertising he has become an uneasy manipulator of people and of himself."[113] Those who could not adjust became "anomics," consumed

---

[106] Philip M. Gentry, *What Will I Be: American Music and Cold War Identity* (Oxford, UK: Oxford University Press, 2017), 47.

[107] Stephanie Coontz, *The Way We Never Were: American Families and the Nostalgia Trap*, rev. ed. (Philadelphia: Perseus, 2016), 53.

[108] Gentry, *What Will I Be*, 46–47; James T. Patterson, *Grand Expectations: The United States: 1945–1974* (Oxford, UK: Oxford University Press, 1996), 34–35.

[109] Elaine Tyler May, *Homeward Bound: American Families in the Cold War Era*, rev. ed. (New York: Basic Books, 2008), 153–55.

[110] Betty Friedan, *The Feminine Mystique*, 50th anniversary ed. (New York: W.W. Norton, 2013), 10.

[111] Buhle, *Feminism and Its Discontents*, 165–94.

[112] U.S. Department of Health, Education, and Welfare, "100 Years of Marriage and Divorce Statistics United States, 1867–1967," December 1983, 8, available at https://www.cdc.gov/nchs/data/series/sr_21/sr21_024.pdf.

[113] David Riesman, with Nathan Glazer and Reuel Denny, *The Lonely Crowd: A Study of the Changing American Character* (1950, repr. New Haven: Yale University Press, 2001), 129.

with "hysteria or outlawry," and "who lack even the spark for living." Riesman estimated that such people "constitute a sizable number in America."[114] In *Love Life*, Sam's uncomfortable transition from furniture maker in 1791 to glad-handing businessman by the 1920s certainly would have spoken to such members of the audience anxious about national masculinity, whether or not they had experienced a similar career shift.

Despite the undercurrent of unrest, most musicals of the era reinforced the conservative fantasy, often by emphasizing the forces of history. Stories in which "a rough tomboy is transformed, not without difficulty, into a married woman," flourished, often set in a fantastical, nostalgic past.[115] In Irving Berlin's *Annie Get Your Gun* (1946, produced by Rodgers and Hammerstein), the rambunctious tomboy Annie Oakley deliberately loses a shooting match, but gains a husband. Even musicals set in the present were pervaded with a wistful longing for "tradition." In Lerner and Loewe's *Brigadoon* (1946), the sophisticated Jane Ashton cannot compete with the simple Fiona MacLaren and the eighteenth-century Scottish Highlands. In Cole Porter's *Kiss Me, Kate* (1948), the aggressive Lily Vanessi is tamed into marriage, as is her Elizabethan counterpart.

If musicals presented the postwar fantasy, plays often focused on the trials and tribulations of reality. Two plays, along with *Allegro*, are often noted in reviews of *Love Life*: Thornton Wilder's *The Skin of Our Teeth* (1942, and like *Love Life*, directed by Elia Kazan) and Moss Hart's *Christopher Blake* (1946).[116] Wilder's time-traveling family moves through history, reconfiguring themselves to match the norms of the era, often causing friction, similar to Sam, Susan, and their children. *Christopher Blake* tells the story of a divorce from the standpoint of a twelve-year-old boy (the title character). Realistic scenes in the court room alternate with Christopher's elaborate fantasies of his parents' reconciliation (possibly inspired by *Lady in the Dark*).

This was the theatrical landscape in 1947 when Lerner first approached Cheryl Crawford, the producer of his successful *Brigadoon*, with the idea that became *Love Life*. Lerner's partnership with composer Fritz Loewe was always contentious, and even after the success of *Brigadoon*, Lerner was eager to look for new collaborators, so Crawford suggested Weill.[117] The match likely seemed

---

[114] Riesman et al., *The Lonely Crowd*, 245.

[115] Gentry, *What Will I Be*, 75–77.

[116] Reviews in the *Boston Traveler*, *Cue*, and *Star* all mention *The Skin of Our Teeth*, while reviews in the *Boston Globe* and another unknown Boston paper mention *Christopher Blake*. See *Love Life* Production Files at the WLRC. When no page number is given, review may be found in the *Love Life* production files at the WLRC. Stephen Hinton summarizes the ways Wilder influenced *Love Life* in *Weill's Musical Theatre*, 411–15. Weill also hoped to collaborate with Wilder, it never materialized. See correspondence in WLA, Box 50 Folder 71.

[117] Milly S. Barranger, *A Gambler's Instinct: The Story of Broadway Producer Cheryl Crawford* (Carbondale: Southern Illinois University Press, 2010), 109–10.

obvious as Weill shared a background similar to Loewe, Lerner's erstwhile partner; both Weill and Loewe were German immigrants (though Loewe's parents were Austrian, and he arrived in the United States in the 1920s) who sometimes traded on putative continental success to maintain an air of sophistication. Loewe even claimed to have studied with Weill's teacher Ferruccio Busoni.[118] Crawford announced their project to the press in July 1947, and by September Weill and Lerner had completed eleven songs and several scenes.[119]

Originally, *Love Life* was billed as "the history of a woman," a female-driven star vehicle like *Lady* and *Venus*.[120] Crawford and Lerner considered both Gertrude Lawrence and Mary Martin, along with Ginger Rogers (who played Liza in the 1944 film of *Lady in the Dark*), for the lead. By May 1948, they settled on Nanette Fabray.[121] At same time, the *New York Times* reported that the musical had been reconceived so that "the husband has assumed increased importance."[122] Ray Middleton, of *Knickerbocker Holiday* and recently of *Annie Get Your Gun*, was cast as Sam. Crawford then brought in Kazan to direct. Although Kazan's only experience directing musicals remained *One Touch of Venus*, he had served as an uncredited play doctor on *Sing Out, Sweet Land!* (1944), which had a similar time-traveling concept.[123] Furthermore, his work on Wilder's *The Skin of Our Teeth* showed him capable of directing complex, nonlinear plots, and his staging of Tennessee Williams's *A Streetcar Named Desire* (1947) demonstrated his ability to handle stories about complex marital problems. Michael Kidd, fresh off the success of *Finian's Rainbow* (1947), came on as choreographer.

The show went into rehearsals in summer 1948 as "A Dish for the Gods," and began previews as *Love Life* in New Haven in September, undergoing drastic changes in between (see Table 5.2).[124] The most noticeable change

[118] Geoffrey Block, *Enchanted Evenings: The Broadway Musical from* Show Boat *to Sondheim and Lloyd Webber*, 2nd ed. (Oxford, UK: Oxford University Press, 2009), 262.

[119] Barranger, *A Gambler's Instinct*, 110; Sam Zolotow, "New Team May Do Song, Dance Show," *NYT*, 30 July 1947, 27.

[120] Sam Zolotow, "Another Musical Draws Top Notice," *NYT*, 17 September 1947, 30.

[121] Dominic McHugh, ed., *Alan Jay Lerner: A Lyricist's Letters* (Oxford, UK: Oxford University Press, 2014), 14–16.

[122] Lewis Funke, "News and Gossip of the Rialto," *NYT*, 2 May 1948, 81.

[123] Richard Shickel, *Elia Kazan: A Biography* (New York: HarperCollins, 2005), 125.

[124] Three copies of the earliest version survive in the WLRC, Series 20 Box L8 Folders 1948, 1948a, and 1948e, all with slightly different annotations. The New Haven version survives in WLA, Box 20 Folder 337 (though this version lacks the "fight scene") with a partial copy in Folder 339, and in WLRC, Series 20 Box L8 Folders 1948b and 1948c. The final version survives WLA, Box 20 Folder 338. One more libretto, WLRC, Series 20 Box L8 Folder 1948d, represents an intermediate stage between the first version and the New Haven version. In the later librettos, Lerner uses "scene" rather than "act," although the programs use "act," which I have adopted for the Table 5.2.

**Table 5.2** Development of *Love Life*

| | "A Dish for the Gods" | Love Life (New Haven version)[a] | Love Life (Broadway version)[b] |
|---|---|---|---|
| Part I | Act I: The Magician | Act I: The Magician | Act I: The Magician |
| | Act II: Eight Men<br>Songs: "Progress" | Act II: The Cooper Family (1791)<br>Songs:<br>"Who Is Samuel Cooper?/My Name Is Samuel Cooper"<br>"Here I'll Stay" | Act II: The Cooper Family<br>Songs: "Who Is Samuel Cooper?/My Name Is Samuel Cooper"<br>"Here I'll Stay" |
| | Act III: The Cooper Family (1816, flashback to 1790s)<br>Songs:<br>"I Remember It Well"<br>"Green-Up Time"<br>"Here I'll Stay" | Act III: Eight Men<br>Song: "Progress" | Act III: Eight Men<br>Song: "Progress" |
| | Act IV: A Quartette<br>Songs:<br>"Economics"<br>"Susan's Dream" | Act IV: The Farewell (1821)<br>Songs:<br>"I Remember It Well"<br>"Green-Up Time"<br>Dance:<br>"Green-Up Time" | Act IV: The Farewell (1821)<br>Songs:<br>"I Remember It Well" "Green-Up Time"<br>Dance:<br>"Green-Up Time" |
| | Act V: The Return (1876) | Act V: Quartette<br>Songs:<br>"Economics"<br>"Susan's Dream" | Act V: Quartette<br>Song:<br>"Economics" |
| | Act VI: The Three Tots and a Woman<br>Song:<br>"Mother's Getting Nervous" | Act VI: The New Baby (1857) | Act VI: Bedroom (1857) |
| | Act VI: Murder in the Museum (1896)<br>Songs:<br>[unnamed duet for Kate and Joe]<br>[unnamed song for Susan and Suffragettes] | Act VII: The Three Tots and a Woman<br>Song:<br>"Mother's Getting Nervous" | Act VII: The Three Tots and a Woman<br>Song:<br>"Mother's Getting Nervous" |
| | | Act VIII: "My Kind of Night" (1890s)<br>Songs:<br>"My Kind of Night"<br>"Women's Club Blues" | Act VIII: "My Kind of Night" (1890s)<br>Songs:<br>"My Kind of Night"<br>"Women's Club Blues" |

| | | | |
|---|---|---|---|
| | Act VIII: A Ventriloquist<br>Song:<br>"Economics (Reprise)" | Act IX: [no name]<br>Song:<br>"Progress (Reprise)"<br>Dance: [unnamed] | Act IX: A Love Song<br>Song:<br>"Love Song" |
| | Act IX: The Cruise (1920s)<br>Songs:<br>"Nothing Left for Daddy but the Rhumba"<br>"You Understand Me So" | Act X: The Cruise (1920s)<br>Songs:<br>"I'm Your Man"<br>"You Understand Me So" | Act X: The Cruise (1920s)<br>Songs:<br>"I'm Your Man"<br>"You Understand Me So" |
| Part II | | | Act I: Radio Night (the present) |
| | Act I: Madrigal Singers<br>Song:<br>"Ho Billy O" | Act I: [unnamed]<br>Song:<br>"Ho Billy O" | Act II: Madrigal Singers<br>Song:<br>"Ho Billy O" |
| | Act II: "A Ticket to the Fight" (the present)<br>Song:<br>"Is It Him or Is It Me?" | Act II: A Ticket to the Fight" (the present)<br>Song:<br>"Is It Him or Is It Me?" | Act III "Farewell Again" (the present)<br>Song:<br>"I Remember It Well (Reprise)"<br>"Is It Him or Is It Me? |
| | Act III: The Locker Room Boys (the present)<br>Song:<br>"Locker Room" | Act III: The Locker Room Boys (the present)<br>Song:<br>"Locker Room" | |
| | Act IV: The All-American Ballet | Act IV: The Divorce (the present)<br>Dance:<br>"Puppet Show"<br>Song:<br>"This Is the Life" | Act IV: Punch and Judy Get a Divorce<br>Dance: [ballet] |

*(continued)*

Table 5.2 Continued

| "A Dish for the Gods" | Love Life (New Haven version)[a] | Love Life (Broadway version)[b] |
|---|---|---|
| | | Act V: A Hotel Room (the present) Song: "This Is the Life" |
| Act V: The Minstrels Songs: "Minstrel Parade" "Madam Zuzu" "Takin' No Chances" "Mr. Right" | Act V: The Minstrels Songs: "Minstrel Parade" "Madam Zuzu" "Takin' No Chances" "Mr. Right" | Act VI: The Minstrel Show Songs: "Here I'll Stay (Reprise)" "Minstrel Parade" "Madam Zuzu" "Taking No Changes" "Mr. Right" |
| Act VI: Afterpiece and Finale Song: Finale | Finale | |

[a] Titles are taken from the program, which largely matches the librettos from this stage, although there are some minor differences. There are two major discrepancies, however, between libretto and program. None of the librettos include "I Remember It Well," although the song appears on the program, suggesting the presence of another intermediate stage. Furthermore, the librettos still have the ventriloquist performing this act, but Rex Weber's departure necessitated an abrupt revision.

[b] Titles are taken from the opening night program. The libretto has slightly different numbering.

follows the report in the *New York Times* that the male lead's role grew considerably. "A Dish for the Gods" begins with Susan interrupting a magician in the middle of his act, demanding that he explain the failure of her marriage; Sam is nowhere to be found. The revised New Haven version has a silent magician sawing Susan in half—a metaphor for her being "half homemaker, half breadwinner" as she tells the audience—and levitating Sam, who describes his being "stuck up here in the currents, without strength, without purpose, without direction."[125] (The final version uses a combination of these, with a speaking magician, and slightly different dialogue, but similar tricks.) The first narrative sequences also initially focused on Susan; the show originally opened 1822 with Sam entering in the middle of the scene; 1791 is only depicted in a flashback and lacks any musical numbers. The revised version opens in 1791 sequence and shifts the focus to Sam, who introduces his family with "Who Is Samuel Cooper?/My Name Is Samuel Cooper."

Weill and Lerner also rewrote the suffragette scene to include Sam. "A Dish for the Gods" includes a scene called "Murder in the Museum" (a comic operetta) which begins with "Joe," an "ingenuous and helplessly stupid" cop flirting with Kate, the daughter of the curator.[126] Susan and a crowd of suffragettes interrupt, plotting the "murder" of a statue of Venus. The dirty deed accomplished, Kate declares "You men are nothing but clumsy, good-for-nothing, no-brain bullies" and marches off with the suffragettes.[127] In New Haven, the scene opened with Sam relaxing on the porch ("My Kind of Night") while Susan hosts a political meeting in the house, where participants grow increasingly militant ("Women's Club Blues"). Sam also takes an expanded role in the "Locker Room" scene in the New Haven version, in which he speaks with a divorce lawyer who encourages Sam to take Susan for everything she is worth—an exchange that does not appear in "A Dish for the Gods." In the subsequent scene, he gets another solo: "This Is the Life."

Despite the changes, the New Haven try-out proved troublesome, largely due its long running time and inconsistent use of the vaudeville theme in Part II, which takes place entirely in 1948, and so abandons the time-traveling device. John Wharton, the business manager of the Playwrights Producing

---

[125] Lerner, *Love Life*, WLA, Box 20 Folder 337, 1-2.
[126] Lerner, *Love Life*, WLRC, Series 20 Box L8 Folder 1948, 1-7-40.
[127] Lerner, *Love Life*, WLRC, Series 20 Box L8 Folder 1948, 1-7-51.

Company, of which Weill was now a member, offered advice in a letter from 10 September.[128] He felt the show "ran beautifully up to the New Year's Eve scene," a booze-cruise in the 1920s, which at this stage of the libretto included Susan having an affair with a man named Clifford Taylor. But after that, "the fight ticket scene seems to repeat the theme of the New Year's Eve scene in a different form," with a "pretty weak" result. Wharton felt the fight reduced *Love Life* "from a story about all men and all women, to a somewhat petty story of particularly quarrelsome, suspicious people." After that, the locker room sequence "fails to come off," since it had no obvious relationship to the theme of societal pressures on marriage; he suggested removing it entirely. He also wrote that, after the second-act madrigal, "you abandon the technique of using vaudeville acts to explain the coming scene," and that the result was confusing.

Wharton's letter reveals that Lerner's cynicism was still too sharp for audiences used to the gentle nostalgia of *Brigadoon* or the redemptive apotheosis of *Carousel*. Indeed, the "fight ticket scene" (called "A Ticket to the Fight" in the program)—based on a real incident from Lerner's childhood— was particularly unpleasant.[129] An exhausted Susan comes home from work and confronts Sam, whom she suspects is having an affair. She also accuses him of being profligate, which causes Sam to accuse her of being a "martyr" and reminding her, "You don't have to work and you know it." She replies angrily: "A couple of years ago they told me it was patriotic!" Eventually, the fight turns to their sex life:

SAM: How do you know I'm out with a dame, as you call it?

SUSAN: Because you're a man and you've got to sleep with somebody and you sure don't with me. (*Sam looks as if he were going to answer, then doesn't.*) You don't have an answer to that one, have you? I should say not. (*She pauses.*) I don't even want you. Did you ever think of that? (*Very proud*) You don't satisfy me.

SAM: Nobody could.

SUSAN: What do you mean?

SAM: You can't get wine from a rock. (*Susan reacts as if she had been shot thru the heart.*)[130]

---

[128] John Wharton to Kurt Weill, 10 September 1948, WLA, Box 50 Folder 71.

[129] See Alan Jay Lerner, *The Street Where I Live: A Memoir* (1978, repr. New York: Norton, 2018), 28.

[130] Lerner, *Love Life*, WLRC Series 20 Box L8 Folder 1948, 2-2-13–2-2-14. The dialogue is slightly different in the New Haven version.

Susan's job has made her cold, causing her husband to stray. Yet Sam does not appear in a good light either. He all but admits to the affair, and it is he who eventually asks for the divorce. The idea that a husband and wife would speak to each other so cruelly was likely too shocking for musical theatre audiences (though not for straight plays). The "Locker Room" scene suffered similar problems. In the New Haven version, Sam becomes a little more sympathetic, as he is appalled when a lawyer suggests bankrupting Susan, but Lerner still depicts men in general as weak and hypocritical. The scene opens with a man receiving phone call from his wife, to whom he speaks with obsequious deference. However, when other men asked what he said, he replies, "I told her to go to hell," to which the men cheer, "Atta boy!"[131]

Weill and Lerner adopted most of Wharton's suggestions over the course of the Boston previews.[132] They replaced "A Ticket to the Fight" with a scene in which Sam wants to listen to a political round table on the radio, but is pre-empted by his son's desire to hear a boxing match, then Susan's reminder that "you know how depressed I get when I miss the Cinema Star Theatre" after she comes home from work. But the radio breaks, and the family finds they have nothing to say, and each bids the other a tense goodnight.[133] They put the actual divorce—now mutual, and much less acrimonious—into the following scene, replacing the ineffective "Locker Room" sequence. They also moved the madrigal from the beginning of Part II to between Acts I and II in order to maintain the alternating of narrative and interscene acts. Meanwhile, Rex Weber, who would have played the magician, ventriloquist, and interlocutor, dropped out, necessitating some revisions of the first and last moments; the ventriloquist vanished altogether.[134]

When *Love Life* opened on 7 October 1948 at Broadway's 46th Street theatre, it received mixed reviews. Walter Winchell enthused that it was "packed with whiz and zing," and was "Show Business at Its Big-Time Best,"

---

[131] Lerner, *Love Life*, WLA, Box 20 Folder 337, 3-2.

[132] See David Kilroy, "Kurt Weill on Broadway: The Postwar Years (1945–1950)" (PhD diss., Harvard University, 1992), 242–4, for a detailed timeline of the Boston previews.

[133] Quotes from the show are taken from the libretto in the WLA, Box 20 Folder 338, which matches the program in terms of act and song order.

[134] Kilroy, "Kurt Weill on Broadway," 239–40.

but Brooks Atkinson called it "joyless, a general gripe masquerading as entertainment."[135] Many critics informed audiences that the experimental form did not hinder comprehensibility, such as Leo Gaffney, who reassured readers, "Don't be disturbed; it is still a musical play, with all the old joyous, familiar things."[136] Still, most critics found the message banal. Richard Watts Jr. of the *New York Post* wrote that he could not "take the editorial viewpoint of the show as seriously as was apparently the plan," even though he enjoyed the production.[137] As for those who liked the show, they mostly admired just its entertainment value.

An AFM-ASCAP strike in 1948 prevented the original cast from making a recording, and the official libretto has never been published. After the show closed on 14 May 1949, Weill blamed Crawford for putting together a "mismatched" team, singling out Kazan, who the composer felt did not have an ear for musicals (even though Weill later briefly considered him for *Lost in the Stars*). Crawford blamed the short run on Lerner's cynicism, and Lerner rarely mentioned the project again. It would take almost twenty years, with shows like *Cabaret* (1967) and *Company* (1970), for Crawford and others to recognize the innovations of *Love Life*.[138]

## Marriage in Black and White

Although *Love Life* purports to tell an all-American story, its version of America was of, by, and for white people. *Love Life*'s innovative form cannot be dissociated from race, as black and blackface styles are crucial to the constructions of the characters' sexuality and psychology. The culminating minstrel show, although not performed in blackface, still drew connections between contemporaneous ideas of blackness and sexual knowledge. Blackface minstrelsy was increasingly unacceptable in the 1940s (although it did still occur, as in 1944's *Minstrel Man*), but many writers, composers, and actors still drew on its structures in an effort to promote a uniquely

---

[135] Walter Winchell, "In New York," *New York Mirror*, 10 October 1948; Brooks Atkinson, "At the Theatre," *NYT*, 8 October 1948.

[136] Leo Gaffney, "*Love Life* Just Grand," *Boston Daily*, 15 September 1948.

[137] Richard Watts Jr., "Two in the Aisle: Expressing Frank Admiration for the New Show *Love Life*," *New York Post*, 17 October 1948.

[138] Barranger, *Gambler's Instinct*, 110–11.

American form of theatre, and its tropes were remembered fondly well into the following decade (as demonstrated by the non-blackface minstrel sequence in 1954's *White Christmas*).[139] Weill understood minstrelsy as kind of ur-form of American musical theatre rather than something degrading to African Americans, telling Margaret Arlen that "in this country, musical comedy developed from the revue, which came out of the minstrel show."[140] A version of this narrative plays out in the unfinished show *Ulysses Africanus* (1939), in which Weill depicts a black man taking over a minstrel troupe, de-racializing it, and founding the modern—and de-racialized—Broadway show. *Love Life* thus represents a particularly postwar take on the tradition of using blackness to speak that which is inappropriate or unspeakable, to perform an "exorcism," to use Toni Morrison's word, on the issues plaguing the white community.[141] This is apparent not just in the minstrel show finale, but in the way African American bodies appear onstage and also in musical style.

Race proved another crack in the façade of postwar American domestic bliss. Although much of U.S. media claimed a "postwar color-blind pluralism," this idea prevented discussion of the fact that the "traditional" family in their suburban home was clearly a white construction.[142] The Federal Housing Administration explicitly favored giving loans to white families.[143] After the victories desegregating the armed services and some manufacturing facilities during the war, blackness was once again forced to the margins. Broadway reinforced these boundaries. In many of the most popular shows of the era, African Americans and other characters of color, if they are present at all, exist only to support the white couple. For example, the mulatto Julie in the 1951 film of *Show Boat* directly pushes Ravenal to reunite with Magnolia, unlike any other version of the story. The racial politics of these musicals also helped audiences understand the

---

[139] Jeffrey Magee, *Irving Berlin's American Musical Theater* (Oxford, UK: Oxford University Press, 2012), 25–26; Krin Gabbard, *Black Magic: White Hollywood and African American Culture* (New Brunswick, NJ: Rutgers University Press, 2004), 42–47.

[140] "WCBS Presents Margaret Arlen," broadcast 7 January 1950, transcript available at https://www.kwf.org/pages/wt-wcbs-presents-margaret-arlen.html.

[141] Toni Morrison, *Playing in the Dark: Whiteness and the Literary Imagination* (New York: Vintage, 1993), 39.

[142] Judith E. Smith, *Visions of Belonging: Family Stories, Popular Culture, and Postwar Democracy* (New York: Columbia University Press, 2004), 174, 243.

[143] Patterson, *Grand Expectations*, 27.

ways blackness functions in *Love Life*, where African American performers are not even characters; they are vaudeville acts who do not exist in the show's "real" America. Yet, like Julie, they have special insight into Sam and Susan's world, and a temporary "descent" into "primitive" theatre, in the form of the minstrel show, and black musical style, ultimately fixes the marriage.

In *Love Life*, the interscene numbers alternate between turn-of-the-century or "Victorian" styles reminiscent of early Tin Pan Alley or operetta, and "black" styles like ragtime, blues, and minstrelsy. The Victorian styles are associated with sexual repression, while the black styles represent revelation and sexual knowledge, hearkening back to *Lady in the Dark*.[144] The first interscene number inaugurates this pattern. After establishing the idyllic world of the United States in 1791, an eight-man chorus labeled "The Go-Getters" in the program enters in formal costumes, a stark contrast to the homespun atmosphere of the previous scene, to sing "Progress." The number begins in an airy 𝄴 describing the Edenic state of the world, when men and women were content to love each other. But the music turns dark as they describe how technological innovation inspired ambition and greed, causing the economy to crash. Nevertheless, the octet ironically uses a peppy, syncopated tune to remind us that economic progress is "the greatest thing we'll ever see" and a "heavenly thing." True to the message of the song, in the following scene (set in 1822), a cloud hangs over the family, as Sam is leaving to take a factory job the next day.

The subsequent appearance of an African American quartet singing the next interscene number, "Economics," is striking. The number is a bluesy reminder that what is good for the pocketbook is often bad for the bedroom (Example 5.2).[145] The appearance of black bodies onstage—the only time in the show—establishes the association of blackness and sexuality. If the white octet ironically celebrates progress, the black quartet reveals its drawbacks, particularly when it comes to sex. Blackness and black musical style reveal the truth about eroticism that can only be approached ironically in white

---

[144] This recalls Weill's strategy in *Lady in the Dark*, which similarly equates Victorian operetta with sexual repression ("Glamour Dream") and blues and jazz with sexual revelation ("Circus Dream").

[145] Holograph piano-vocal score for *Love Life*, WLA, Boxes 22–24 Folders 346–55.

**Example 5.2** *Love Life,* "Economics."

**Example 5.2** *Continued*

paradigms.[146] Yet these black figures are positioned outside the white world of the main narrative; the four performers who sang "Economics" appear nowhere else in the program (although they may have appeared in ensembles), even as most of the white actors appeared in multiple roles, both within and outside of the narrative.

A scene in 1857 follows "Economics," which opens with Sam and Susan in bed. After some unsubtle hinting, Susan tells Sam that she wants another child. Sam is initially enthusiastic, but demurs when he realizes that another child will interfere with his job. The scene ends with him leaving for a business trip. Subsequently, a trapeze act consisting of a woman and three "tots" take the stage to perform "Mother's Getting Nervous." The song is another waltz which, combined with the onstage acrobats, likely evoked 1867's "The

---

[146] Gabbard points out that this is a prominent function of black music in Hollywood in *Black Magic*, 4–7.

Man on the Flying Trapeze," and the spelling out of "Mother" ("M is for the maximum of grieving" and so forth) directly references Howard Johnson and Theodore Morse's 1915 song "M-O-T-H-E-R."[147] If "Economics" associated black masculinity with sexual wisdom, "Mother's Getting Nervous" emphasizes white feminine sexual repression. Its evocation of Victorian styles creates a winking naiveté, made more incongruous by racy lyrics like "She feels like a violin nobody fiddles / like tiddle-de-winks [sic] that nobody tiddles." The disingenuous cheerfulness highlights the façade that papers over the cracks "Economics" reveals. Its frank sexual nature also spoke to the fact that many psychiatrists and psychologists, following Freud, assumed that women's neuroses came from sexual repression and dysfunction.[148] In "Mother's Getting Nervous," white femininity is cast high-strung (literally), fragile, and bordering on hysterical, presenting a stark contrast to the cool, confident, and sexually knowledgeable black men who sing "Economics."

Love Life's equation of the blues and blackness with sexuality and revelation and Victorian styles with repression and neurosis continues throughout the show. In "Women's Club Blues," Susan and the suffragettes reveal that their political ambitions are sublimating their sexual energies, singing "I toss and turn in bed alone at night / My body aching for the right / To vote." Again, blackness is portrayed as something disruptive. In the following act, a white "hobo" sings "Love Song," a number linked to "Economics" through its bluesy harmony (Example 5.3) and its lament for the ways industry interferes with relationships.[149] Although the performer was white, giving the song to a hobo casts this as a point of view from the margins of society, of one who can observe, but not participate. Conversely, the Gilbert-and-Sullivan-esque madrigal "Ho Billy O!" describes several affairs, including one between a man who sings "The world is idiotic / Oh, faith is gone and faith is dead; / And worse, I am neurotic" and a woman who replies "I'm overly aggressive, / And doctors ev'rywhere agree / I'm manic and depressive."

---

[147]  Kilroy, "Kurt Weill on Broadway," 263.

[148]  Friedan, *The Feminine Mystique*, 112.

[149]  Because this song was added later, it is not in Weill's piano-vocal score, but a photocopy in a copyist's hand resides in the Alan Jay Lerner Papers, LOC, Box 31 Folder 10.

**Example 5.3** *Love Life*, "Love Song."

These racial associations come to a head in the final minstrel sequence. The figures in set designer Boris Aronson's color sketches for the number have the chorus with peach-toned skin, indicating it was not performed in blackface.[150] Still, the association of blackness with sexuality and revelation lurks in the subtext, as Sam and Susan adopt the black personas, if not black faces, of endmen in order to speak the secrets that have been preventing them from facing the truth of their marriage. Minstrelsy becomes a safe space to explore these troubles and inappropriate thoughts precisely because it lies outside the boundaries of polite (that is, white) society. Once all is out in the open, the white family can once again prosper, and blackness fades to the margins.

---

[150] The sketch is available in *WPD(e)*, plate 21. A photograph of "Madam Zuzu" in the souvenir program confirms that at least some of the performers in the sequence did not wear blackface. *WPD(e)*, 259.

In an era in which the stability of the white, patriarchal family was equated with the strength of the nation, Weill and Lerner set out to reveal the system's inherent contradictions. *Love Life* aimed to show that economic success requires sacrificing the comfortable marriage it was supposed to produce. But even though *Love Life* critiques many of the sexist politics of the postwar era, its nostalgia for traditional gender roles (as depicted in the idyllic 1791 scene) betrays its conservative mindset. Furthermore, African American voices (both explicit and implicit) are reduced to injecting their wisdom into the story, and providing magical spaces in which unspeakable truths can be spoken. As with many of Weill's depictions of American life, *Love Life* unwittingly reproduces the failings as well as ideals of the nation.

The fact that the gender and racial politics of *Lady in the Dark*, *One Touch of Venus*, and *Love Life* are so deeply rooted in their time helped them achieve contemporary success (at least in the case of *Lady in the Dark* and *One Touch of Venus*), but has likely hindered possibilities for a Broadway revival until this point. All seem hopelessly sexist in today's climate. *Love Life* in particular, with its racialized politics of sexuality and nostalgia for a time when patriarchal gender structures were uncomplicated by the careers of either husband or wife, would make modern audiences cringe.

But perhaps creative decisions from these productions might help put them in perspective. After all, as Bruce Kirle observes, all Broadway shows must adapt to survive for posterity.[151] One recent production of *Lady in the Dark* cast Dr. Brooks as a woman, helping to alleviate some of the more uncomfortable aspects of the story.[152] In that vein, Broadway has recently seen a number of "revisals" of Golden Age musicals that attempt to reckon with the uncomfortable gender or racial politics of the original.[153] Barlett Scher's 2018 revival of *My Fair Lady* (1956) was hailed for taking a show that represented "a failure of feminism" and making Eliza the hero who "sculpts herself, with Higgins as her tool."[154] For other shows, the gender politics have not hindered

---

[151] Kirle, *Unfinished Business*, 9.

[152] Seth Colter Walls, "Review: *Lady in the Dark* is Kurt Weill on the Couch," *NYT*, 26 April 2019, available at https://www.nytimes.com/2019/04/26/arts/music/weill-lady-in-the-dark-mastervoices-review.html.

[153] See chapter 4 of Elizabeth Titrington Craft, "Becoming American Onstage: Broadway Narratives of Immigrant Experience in the United States" (PhD diss., Harvard University, 2014) for an in-depth analysis of the 2002 revival of *The Flower Drum Song* (1958).

[154] Jesse Green, "Review: Whose *Fair Lady*? This Time, Eliza's in Charge," *NYT*, 19 April 2018, available at https://www.nytimes.com/2018/04/19/theater/my-fair-lady-review-lincoln-center-lauren-ambrose.html.

successful revival, as in the case of the 2018 *Carousel*, which Ben Brantley called "sexy," "vibrant," and "erotic" despite feeling a certain "queasiness" at the story's inherent violence.[155] Presented as a "period piece," *Carousel* becomes another *Don Giovanni*—acknowledged as a "classic" despite its uncomfortable aspects. Most likely, simple name recognition has prevented revivals of Weill's shows, which could benefit from similar revisalist treatment or from being presented as historical revivals with frank acknowledgment of their problematic politics.

---

[155] Ben Brantley, "Review: A *Carousal* That Spins on a Romantically Charged Axis," *NYT*, 12 April 2018, available at https://www.nytimes.com/2018/04/12/theater/carousel-review-broadway.html.

# 6

# Israel in Egypt

## Race and Ethnicity

In the second half of the 1940s, many U.S. Jewish communities focused on establishing a Jewish State in Palestine.[1] Weill was no exception. Having already contributed to several efforts in support of Jewish causes during the war, in 1946 he turned his attention to Palestine with another Ben Hecht pageant, *A Flag Is Born*. The piece opened on 5 September and played fifteen performances before embarking on a successful tour. As with *We Will Never Die* (1943), Weill liberally borrowed music from *The Eternal Road* (1937), another grand Jewish pageant he had written with German poet Franz Werfel.[2] *A Flag Is Born* heralded a distinctly post-Holocaust vision of Jewish life. It exemplified the new image of a "muscular Judaism," which reframed Jews as healthy and virile rather than helpless victims.[3] The casting of Marlon Brando as the young hero David, and the bare-chested figures on the show's poster (Figure 6.1), reinforced this message.[4] A trip to Europe and Palestine (where his parents were living) the following spring confirmed Weill's commitment to the Jewish state. He wrote to Maxwell Anderson that London was "grim" and Paris was "corrupt," but

> Palestine is like fresh air after Europe—one sees happy faces everywhere, youth, hope, and the general theme is construction. The most fascinating aspect for us here is the mixture of civilizations. It is all basically oriental and very colorful, but overimposed by Christian civilization of the last 2,000 years and now a new Jewish civilization which is very impressive."[5]

---

[1] Edna Nahshon, "From Geopathology to Redemption: *A Flag Is Born* on the Broadway Stage," *Jewish Quarterly* 47, no. 2 (2000): 55–56.

[2] Christian Kuhnt, "Approaching the Music for *A Flag Is Born*" *Kurt Weill Newsletter* 20, no. 1 (2002): 8 ; see also Garrett Eisler, "'This Theatre Is a Battlefield': Political Performance and Jewish-American Identity, 1933–1948" (PhD diss., City University of New York, 2012), 167–68.

[3] Karen Brodkin, *How Jews Became White Folks and What That Says About Race in America* (New Brunswick, NJ: Rutgers University Press, 2002), 107.

[4] Eisler, "'This Theatre Is a Battlefield,'" 181–83.

[5] Kurt Weill to Maxwell Anderson, 30 May 1947, MAC, Series "Misc." Folder "Weill, Kurt."

*Kurt Weill's America*. Naomi Graber, Oxford University Press (2021). © Oxford University Press.
DOI: 10.1093/oso/9780190906580.003.0007

Figure 6.1   Billy Rose Theatre Division, the New York Public Library. "American League for a Free Palestine presents *A Flag Is Born* <u>by Ben Hecht</u>." New York Public Library Digital Collections. http://digitalcollections.nypl.org/items/ 99f64a30-fbbe-0130-465a-58d385a7bbd0

*A Flag Is Born* represents a continuation of an important trend in Weill's career. After the financial failure of *The Eternal Road*, Weill preferred to frame himself as a German political refugee, avoiding references to his Jewishness. During the war, he began publicly to acknowledge his Jewish

heritage, but only in connection to Hecht's explicitly Jewish pageants, effectively cordoning off his Jewish identity from the rest of his Broadway career. However, after the war, Weill cautiously began to explore the ways his German, Jewish, and American identities intersected in the context of the post-Holocaust world.[6]

Weill's postwar work also represents the composer's return to themes that had preoccupied him in the 1930s. As a German Jew, Weill's concept of self was profoundly shaped by Richard Wagner's "Judaism in Music." Even if he never read it, Wagner's ideas permeated German and German-Jewish musical thought in the early twentieth century.[7] Wagner claimed that "only he who has unconsciously grown up within the bond" of the European community "takes also any share in its creations. But the Jew has stood outside the pale of any such community."[8] Thus, in music, Jews could imitate genius "just as parrots reel off human words and phrases," but their compositions always present a "marked peculiarity" that betrays their outsider status.[9] Despite Wagner's attacks, many German Jews held Wagner in high regard, and fiercely debated his conclusions. Weill admired *Tristan und Isolde*, *Die Meistersinger*, and *Tannhäuser*, even as he argued that young composers should "withdraw as much as possible from the sphere of influence of Richard Wagner."[10] The question of whether or not Jews could be part of a broader national and international community (and write music that fully represented that community) seems to haunt Weill's career. *The Eternal Road* combines Jewish liturgical music with Baroque structures to show that Jewishness and German-ness could coexist without tension. *Street Scene* (1947) explores how Jews interact with broader culturally pluralist communities. The piece also adapts the folkloric atmosphere of *Down in the Valley* (which Olin Downes called

---

[6] Kim H. Kowalke, Jürgen Schebera, Christian Kuhnt, and Alexander Ringer, "*The Eternal Road* and Kurt Weill's German, Jewish, and American Identity," *Theater* 30, no. 3 (2000): 92.

[7] For a summary of these debates, see James Loeffler, "Richard Wagner's 'Jewish Music': Antisemitism and Aesthetics in Modern Jewish Culture," *Jewish Social Studies* 15, no. 2 (2009): 2–36; Leon Botstein, "German Jews and Wagner," in *Richard Wagner and His World*, ed. Thomas Grey (Princeton, NJ: Princeton University Press, 2009), 151–200; and Part II of Klára Moricz, *Jewish Identities: Nationalism, Racism, and Utopianism in Twentieth-Century Music* (Berkeley: University of California Press, 2008).

[8] Richard Wagner, "Judaism in Music," in *Richard Wagner's Prose Works Volume III: The Theatre*, trans. William Ashton Ellis (London: Kegan Paul, Trench, Trübner, 1907), 84.

[9] Wagner, "Judaism in Music," 89.

[10] Kurt Weill, "New Opera" (1926), trans. in *KWiE*, 464. On Weill's fraught relationship with Wagner, see Stephen Hinton, "Weill Contra Wagner: Aspects of Ambivalence," in '... *Das alles auch hätte anders kommen können': Beiträge zur Musik des 20. Jahrhunderts*, ed. Susanne Schaal-Gotthardt, Luitgard Schader, and Heinz-Jürgen Winkler (Berlin: Schott, 2009), 155–74.

a "pendant" to *Street Scene*)[11] to the urban milieu of the 1940s, creating space in American folklore for Jews. While *Lost in the Stars* (1949) does not feature Jewish characters, its structure and music resemble *The Eternal Road*. *Lost in the Stars* also borrows from *Ulysses Africanus*, an unfinished musical Weill started with Maxwell Anderson in 1939. These links to Weill's previous work emphasize connections between black and Jewish concerns, which was an important theme of Jewish discourse of the era.

## An "Answer to Hitler"

Weill's sense of his Jewish heritage was constantly in flux.[12] He grew up playing organ in the synagogue where his father was the cantor, and he remained active in Jewish life at university in Berlin. He worked at the Jewish Community Center in Berlin-Friedenau, and even considered writing a thesis on synagogue music in 1921.[13] Weill set a number of Jewish texts for his earliest compositions, including "Mi Addir" (1913), poems by the medieval poet Jehuda Halevi known as *Ofrahs Lieder* (1916), and a Latin setting of Lamentations called *Recordare* in 1923.[14] Still, he felt his Jewish heritage restricted his compositional abilities, writing to his brother in 1919 that "We Jews are just not productive, and if we are, then we have a subversive, not a constructive impact."[15] By 1924, he wrote to his mother that he felt alienated by the Jewish community, and that Jews "are impossible in every way." Still, he continued: "We must find our way back to our childhood faith."[16]

Weill returned to Jewish themes in 1934, a year after he left Germany, when he began work on *The Eternal Road*. Weill's score grapples with how Jews fit into larger national and international communities, an urgent question given recent Nazi political victories; producer Meyer Weisgal even hoped

---

[11] Stephen Hinton, *Weill's Musical Theater: Stages of Reform* (Berkeley: University of California Press, 2012), 360.

[12] On Weill's Jewish identity in his younger years, Kowalke et al., "*The Eternal Road* and Weill's German, Jewish, and American Identity," 86–92.

[13] Christian Kuhnt, *Kurt Weill und das Judentum* (Saarbrücken: Pfau, 2002), 10.

[14] For a full account of Weill's early Jewish compositions, see Kuhnt, *Kurt Weill und das Judentum*, 11.

[15] Trans. in Hinton, *Weill's Musical Theater*, 4. This foreshadows Adorno's critique of Weill's legacy discussed in the Introduction.

[16] Kowalke et al., "*The Eternal Road* and Kurt Weill's German, Jewish, and American Identity," 89.

that the project would be "our answer to Hitler."[17] If Nazis believed (following Wagner) that Jewish music could never speak to non-Jews, Weill's efforts to promote the work emphasized the idea that Jewish themes were universal. The *New York Times* reported that "it is Mr. Weill's conviction that the Old Testament, of which [*The Eternal Road*] is a résumé, is primarily a great human document belonging in its appeal, not to any particular era, but to all time."[18] In terms of the music, Weill's score combines Jewish liturgical themes along with other styles within a structural model similar to Bach's *St. Matthew Passion* and Handel's oratorios.[19] This blend problematizes the distinction between German and racialized identities that his Nazi contemporaries tried to establish, but that many German Jews were eager to erase.

*The Eternal Road* was the brainchild of Meyer H. Weisgal, a Polish-American Zionist who specialized in producing large-scale pageants, most famously *The Romance of a People*, which ran successfully at the 1933 Chicago World's Fair. That same year, Weisgal began gathering Jewish artists who had fled Germany to raise awareness about the Nazi regime.[20] In November, he approached German director Max Reinhardt, at the time residing in Paris, who was known for his large-scale productions of the classics in Berlin and Salzburg. Reinhardt suggested poet Franz Werfel for the librettist and Weill for the composer. By February of 1934, the premiere was planned for London's Royal Albert Hall, but the plan changed because the venue could not accommodate Reinhardt's grandiose vision.[21] By summer 1934, Werfel had finished the libretto, which Weill (then in France) began to set, likely finishing around the end of the year.[22] Eventually, the

---

[17] Meyer Weisgal, *Meyer Weisgal . . . So Far: An Autobiography* (New York: Random House, 1971), 117.

[18] N.S., "Kurt Weill's New Score: Music for *Road of Promise* Written in Modern Contemporary Style," *NYT*, 27 October 1935, available at https://www.kwf.org/pages/wt-kurt-weills-new-score.html.

[19] On Jewish liturgical music in *The Eternal Road*, see Kuhnt, *Kurt Weill und das Judentum*, 114–18. On the influence of the *St. Matthew Passion*, see Helmut Loos, "Kurt Weill: *Der Weg der Verheissung*—Geistliche Oper und Oratorium," in *Kurt Weill: Auf der Weg zum* Der Weg der Verheissung, ed. Helmut Loos and Guy Stern (Freiburg im Breisgau: Rombach, 2000), 199; Stephen Hinton, *Weill's Musical Theater*, 241, 244.

[20] Weisgal, *Meyer Weisgal*, 117.

[21] Karin Kowalke, "*Ein Fremder ward ich im fremden Land . . .*" Max Reinhardts Inszenierung von Franz Werfels und Kurt Weills The Eternal Road (Der Weg der Verheissung) 1937 in New York, Volume I (Munich: Hieronymus, 2004), 58 n37.

[22] The full score of *The Eternal Road* is lost, but a photocopy survives in the WLRC, Series 10 Box E8 Folder 1. Two piano-vocal scores survive: a German copy in Weill's hand (WLA, Box 4 Folder 63) and one in a copyist's hand with Weill's annotations that was used in U.S. rehearsals in the WLRC, Series 10 Box E8. All musical examples are taken from the latter.

premiere was set for New York's Manhattan Opera House (a Broadway theatre) in winter 1934 or early 1935. The pageant depicts a Jewish congregation waiting out a pogrom in their synagogue. A young boy expresses curiosity about his heritage, so the Rabbi tells stories from the *Tanakh* (Hebrew Bible) to illustrate various moral lessons, acted out on raised platforms upstage of the congregation. These stories fall into four parts: "The Patriarchs," "Moses," "The Kings (Saul, David, Solomon)," and "The Prophets (Isaiah, Jeremiah, the Angel of the End Days)." A character designated "the adversary" tries to refute the lessons, but the boy is entranced. In the end, the Angel of the End Days appears, foretells the coming of the Messiah, and leads the congregation and biblical characters in a song of redemption, a march-like setting of Psalm 126.

For the music, Weill claimed that he found his memory inadequate, telling the *New York Times* that he "put down all the Hebraic melodies I had learned from childhood on," then traced their sources at the Bibliothèque Nationale, only to discover that many "had been written in the eighteenth and nineteenth centuries." He continued, "Those I dismissed, retaining only the traditional music."[23] There are several liturgical melodies scattered throughout *The Eternal Road*, most likely adapted from Abraham Baer's *Baal Tefillah* ("Master of Prayer," 1877). Sometimes Weill set melodies in their entirety; he used a version of "L'cha Dodi," part of the Friday night Shabbat liturgy (Example 6.1a) as the basis for David's song in Part III (Example 6.1b).[24] More often he adapted melodic formulas into original melodies. Sometimes these formulas had specific liturgical connections. For example, readings from the books of Jeremiah, Isaiah, and *Eicha* (Lamentations) form the core liturgy of *Tisha B'Av* (the Ninth of Av, the fifth month of the Jewish ecclesiastical calendar), which commemorates the fall of the First and Second Temples. The cantillation for *Eicha* 1:1 found in *Baal Tefillah* includes a striking seven-note natural-minor descent, ending with a half-step (Example 6.2a), which Weill adapted for the character Isaiah, and which repeats (in variation) throughout the opening of the "Prophets" sequence (Example 6.2b).[25]

---

[23] "Score for *The Eternal Road*," *NYT*, 27 December 1936, available at https://www.kwf.org/pages/wt-score-for-the-eternal-road.html.

[24] Abraham Baer, ed., *Baal Tefillah: Oder der practische Vorbeter*, 2nd ed. (Frankfurt am Main: J. Kauffmann, 1883), 90.

[25] Baer, *Baal Tefillah*, 37–39. I have omitted an ossia in example 6.1a for clarity.

**Example 6.1a** *Baal Tefillah,* "L'cha Dodi."

**Example 6.1b** *The Eternal Road,* "David's Song."

**Example 6.2a** *Baal Tefillah*, "*Eicha*, 1:1."

**Example 6.2b** *The Eternal Road*, "Isaiah."

But while some melodies in *The Eternal Road* have Jewish origins, the framework of the piece is rooted in German traditions. In his notes, Reinhardt wrote that *The Eternal Road* was "an oratorio like Bach's *St. Matthew Passion*."[26] The resemblance between *The Eternal Road* and the *St. Matthew Passion* is clear. The *St. Matthew Passion* operates on two different levels of time: biblical time in the recitatives and choruses, and contemporary time in the chorales and arias, with the Evangelist serving as the mediator.[27] Similarly, *The Eternal Road* alternates between the scenes in the present-day synagogue and biblical

[26] Max Reinhardt, "Layout for *The Eternal Road*," WLA, Box 49 Folder 58.
[27] Ruth HaCohen, *The Music Libel against the Jews: Vocal Fictions of Noise and Harmony* (New Haven, CT: Yale University Press, 2011), 88.

stories, with the Rabbi's recitatives linking the two. There is also some resemblance to Handel's biblical oratorios, particularly in the use of the chorus. Weill has the chorus act as both the crowd and the commentators, often meditating on the action in counterpoint throughout the work.

Weill's use of these models refutes contemporary trends in German musicology. In the early 1930s, German historians and theorists began to frame Bach as the founder of the "Nordic" style. In particular, they cited Bach's contrapuntal skill as a uniquely Nordic ability, and contrasted that with allegedly inferior Jewish composition. Richard Eichenauer's 1932 book *Musik und Rasse* ("Music and Race") argued that Bach's facility in polyphony affirmed his pure racial heritage, while the atonality of Jewish composers like Arnold Schoenberg revealed that the modernists "are obeying the law of their race when they seek to destroy harmonic polyphony, which is totally foreign to them."[28] But Weill saw Bach's music as a potential model for universal appeal; in 1925, he wrote that the recitative in the *St. Matthew Passion* was a masterful example of "the heightened experience—the refined expression of an emotion—the human condition."[29] This idea of Bach as universal had been common in German-Jewish communities since the nineteenth century, a phenomenon crystallized in Mendelssohn's revival of the *St. Matthew Passion*.[30] The neo-Baroque aspects of *The Eternal Road* sought to prove not only that a Jew could write "German" music, but that Jewish and German culture were inseparable. In that light, *The Eternal Road* is a Mendelssohnian project, reminding German audiences of the debt owed to Jews for reviving Bach. The entire project stands as a monument to the interconnectedness of German and Jewish music-making. Handel's operas and oratorios had seen a revival in the 1920s, a phenomenon that turned nationalist in the early 1930s; Alfred Rosenberg cited Handel as a precursor to Wagner, and dubbed him "the Viking of music."[31] The year 1935, the year of the planned premiere of *The Eternal Road*, was also the 250th anniversary of Bach's and Handel's birth, and saw numerous celebrations of his music throughout Germany.[32]

---

[28] Quoted in Pamela M. Potter, *Most German of the Arts: Musicology and Society from the Weimar Republic to the End of Hitler's Reich* (New Haven, CT: Yale University Press, 1998), 180. On the Nazis and Bach, see Christa Brüstle, "Bach-Rezeption im Nationalsozialismus: Aspect Und Stationen," in *Bach und die Nachwelt III: 1900–1950*, ed. Michael Heinemann and Hans-Joachim Hinrichsen (Laaber: Laaber, 2002), 115–53, especially 115–36.

[29] Kurt Weill, "Commitment to Opera" (1925), trans. in *KWiE*, 459.

[30] See Ruth HaCohen, *The Music Libel against the Jews*, 84–85, 90–98.

[31] Pamela Potter, "The Politicization of Handel and His Oratorios in the Weimar Republic, the Third Reich, and the Early Years of the German Democratic Republic," *Musical Quarterly* 85, no. 2 (2001): 319–20.

[32] Brüstle, "Bach-Rezeption im Nationalsozialismus," 134–36.

But *The Eternal Road* faced practical complications. Its grandiose conception required extensive renovations to the dilapidated Manhattan Opera House, including ripping out several rows of the orchestra section, the most expensive seats in the house, which later hurt the revenues. A water pipe burst in the process, flooding the theatre and further slowing things down.[33] The overhaul required more money than Weisgal had budgeted for the project, so by 29 January 1936, all support had dried up, and Equity ordered rehearsals stopped because the chorus and actors had not been paid. Later that month, after Weisgal failed to raise the necessary $200,000 within the ten-day grace period, the project went dark for year, and Weill looked for other opportunities.[34]

When the project finally opened in January 1937, critics generally praised the piece, particularly Weill's music, with Brooks Atkinson writing in the *New York Times* that "when the portals to heaven open, disclosing a sacred choir of angels, the glory that floods the theatre is the voice of an inspired composer."[35] Other critics similarly spoke of the piece's universalizing intentions.[36] However, Weill's neo-Bachian writing went unreported. Rather, most critics approached the work as a comment on Jewish-American identity, so the work's German roots were not legible to U.S. critics.

Weill may have shied away from publicly emphasizing his Jewish heritage after *The Eternal Road* for several reasons. For one, the piece did not pay. Weill wrote several letters demanding his share of the royalties, but Louis Nizer (the lawyer in charge of the finances) constantly deferred, explaining that "the large Christian masses," were "frightened by the words 'religious' and 'biblical.' The fact that the spectacle is Jewish does not help either."[37] In reality, the show did not have a problem selling tickets, but operating expenses exceeded income, and the finances never got straightened out. Nizer was likely trying to appease Weill, but the composer had no way of knowing that. Furthermore, *The Eternal Road* also opened amid a sharp increase in U.S. anti-Semitism. The high unemployment rate of the Great Depression combined with stereotypes of corrupt Jewish businessmen made many in the United States wary

[33] Ronald Sanders, *The Days Grow Short: The Life and Music of Kurt Weill* (New York: Holt, Rinehart, and Winston, 1980), 223. On the troubles facing *The Eternal Road*, see Guy Stern, "The Road to *The Eternal Road*," in *A New Orpheus: Essays on Kurt Weill*, ed. Kim H. Kowalke (New Haven, CT: Yale University Press, 1986), 273–76.

[34] "Equity Edict Ends Show Rehearsals," *NYT*, 29 January 1936, 14. The *Times* reported that Weisgal had already spent an unprecedented $259,519 before Equity got involved.

[35] Brooks Atkinson, "The Play," *NYT*, 8 January 1937, 14.

[36] Tamara Levitz, "Either a German or a Jew: The German Reception of Kurt Weill's *Der Weg der Verheißung*," *Theater* 30, no. 3 (2000): 98.

[37] Louis Nizer to Kurt Weill, 10 February 1937, WLA, Box 49 Folder 56.

of—if not outright hostile toward—the Jewish community. Figures like radio personality "Father" Charles Coughlin and avowed fascists like William Dudley Pelley and his "silver shirts" kept anti-Semitism in the mainstream discourse.[38] Weill rarely mentioned his Jewish heritage again for the rest of the decade.

Still, Weill pursued smaller Jewish projects, contributing two songs to a collection of Israeli folk music in 1938, and considering a series of radio plays on biblical subjects.[39] Some of his unfinished works also reflect themes that were relevant to his experience as a German-Jewish refugee. These include the "Opera from Mannheim," a project he discussed with E.Y. "Yip" Harburg and Sam and Bella Spewack from March through June 1937. The story concerned a traveling group of Jewish players who escape Germany and come to America, only to discover they have left their performance materials behind. They attempt to reconstruct their memories, represented by a waltz tune that recurs in fragments throughout the show, and in full at the end in the manner of the march in *The Eternal Road*, "Johnny's Song" in *Johnny Johnson*, and "My Ship" in *Lady in the Dark*.[40]

When the war began in Europe, Weill's willingness to work on Jewish projects increased, exemplified by the Hecht pageants, even though Coughlin, Pelley, and others accused Jews of warmongering in order to fulfill a private vendetta against the Nazis.[41] After the war, Weill continued to take down the wall he had put up around his Jewish heritage. The year 1946 saw Weill writing music for the synagogue for the first time in his setting of the "Kiddush," which was commissioned by the Park Avenue Synagogue for its seventy-fifth anniversary.[42] That same year, Weill began composing his first overtly Jewish Broadway characters: the Kaplans in *Street Scene*.

## Revising *Street Scene*

Weill emerged from the war years an established Broadway success, with ties to many prestigious organizations and individuals. One particularly

---

[38] Jonathan D. Sarna, *American Judaism: A History* (New Haven, CT: Yale University Press, 2004), 214–15.

[39] Kuhnt, *Kurt Weill und das Judentum*, 128–39.

[40] "Telephone Interview with E.Y. "Yip" Harburg Conducted by Ronald Sanders," 10 April 1978, Ronald Sanders Papers, NYPL, Box 20 Folder 6.

[41] Sarna, *American Judaism*, 265–66.

[42] *KWH*, 355. Other composers commissioned included Darius Milhaud, Ernest Bloch, and David Diamond.

important group was the Playwrights Producing Company (PPC), a collective of writers formed in 1938 who pooled their resources to produce each other's works. Weill and PPC member Maxwell Anderson became close friends in the late 1930s, writing one full-length show together (*Knickerbocker Holiday*, 1938) and working several shorter projects in the early 1940s. In September 1946, Weill officially became a member of the PPC, replacing founding member S.N. Behrman, who had resigned over differences in artistic priorities. Behrman's departure left only three writers (another founding member, Sidney Howard, had died in 1939), which they felt was insufficient to sustain their level of activities.[43]

Weill's first mainstream postwar work was a version of PPC member Elmer Rice's Pulitzer-winning play *Street Scene* (1929), with a new libretto by Rice and lyricist Langston Hughes, which they called a "dramatic musical." As Weill and Rice began the process of adaptation, the broad outlines of the original story remained the same. The play depicts a day in the life of one city block. The central characters are the Irish Maurrants: Anna, her husband Frank, and their children Rose and Willie. Mr. Maurrant is prone to violent outbursts, so Mrs. Maurrant seeks comfort in the arms of Mr. Sankey. When Mr. Maurrant finds out, he kills them both. Consequently, Rose decides to leave New York with Willie to start a fresh life, which devastates her Jewish sweetheart, Sam Kaplan. Meanwhile, a family faces eviction, an expectant father frets about his child's birth, and the residents gossip about the Maurrants. The show's mix of high tragedy, musical comedy, and melodrama resembled other experiments like *Porgy and Bess* (1935) and *Carousel* (1945), but was still relatively rare on Broadway in 1947.

Mixed-ethnic neighborhoods were commonplace in 1929, but in 1947, urban demographics had begun to shift, and this kind of neighborhood began to seem anachronistic. These developments produced changing conceptions of race which, in turn, produced new ideas of what it meant to be "American." In the nineteenth century, Irish, Italians, Jews, Finns, Greeks, Poles, other Eastern Europeans, and so on, were considered "races," and judged inferior to Anglo-Saxon or Nordic stock. However, beginning in the middle 1920s, individual races, including Jews, began to redefine themselves as "ethnics," and a single, monolithic white race began to develop, a transition

---

[43] "Minutes of the PPC, 4 September 1946," ERP, Box 68 Folder 1. See also Albert Claude Gordon, "A Critical Study of the History and Developments of the Playwrights' Production Company" (PhD diss., Tulane University, 1965), 160–70, 182.

that was not complete until 1950s.[44] The early twentieth-century idea of the "melting pot"—popularized by Israel Zangwill in his 1908 play *The Melting Pot*—posits a vision of assimilation in which the best parts of each immigrant culture would blend together to form a new whole, exemplified by the other overarching metaphor of the play: the symphony.[45] Before the war, Jewish clowns like Willie Howard and Eddie Kantor subscribed to this version of American assimilation, highlighting their Jewishness (or at least their status as outsiders) in order to maintain a separate identity, yet become part of the American body politic through show business.[46]

The shift in ideas of assimilation owed much to governmental policy. After the war, many working-class ethnic families received favorable loans from the Federal Housing Administration or the Veterans Authority, and were able to move into the suburbs. Such programs had previously excluded Jews, Catholics, and African Americans, but in the postwar era, the first two groups gained access, which left working-class African Americans in the city.[47] Now separated geographically by race rather than class, these communities now chose to define themselves religiously rather than ethnically; in 1955, professor of Judaic studies Will Herberg described America as a "triple melting pot," blending together Protestants, Catholics, and Jews in a bulwark against the atheist communism and fascism.[48] This formulation allowed Jews and Catholics to sincerely adopt middle-class standards in the eyes of their Protestant neighbors. While prewar notions of assimilation valued difference, postwar assimilation required the adoption of an idealized middle-class lifestyle, building on the ideas of figures like Henry Ford and Woodrow Wilson from the 1920s.[49] Jews, striving for acceptance in white suburban neighborhoods, adopted markers of American culture, up to and including cosmetic surgery to erase their "Jewish noses," and the celebration

---

[44] Matthew Frye Jacobson, *Whiteness of a Different Color: European Immigrants and the Alchemy of Race* (Cambridge, MA: Harvard University Press, 1998); Brodkin, *How Jews Became White Folks*.

[45] Michael Rogin, *Blackface, White Noise: Jewish Immigrants in the Hollywood Melting Pot* (Berkeley: University of California Press, 1998), 65–66. See also chapter 2 of Jeffrey Melnick, *A Right to Sing the Blues: African Americans, Jews, and American Popular Song* (Cambridge, MA: Harvard University Press, 1999); Bruce Kirle, *Unfinished Business: Broadway Musicals as Works in Progress* (Carbondale: Southern Illinois University Press, 2005), 44–45; Elizabeth Titrington Craft, "Becoming American Onstage: Broadway Narratives of Immigrant Experiences in the United States" (PhD diss., Harvard University, 2014), 4–6.

[46] See chapter 2 of Andrea Most, *Making Americans: Jews and the Broadway Musical* (Cambridge, MA: Harvard University Press, 2004), and Kirle, *Unfinished Business*, 47–49.

[47] Brodkin, *How Jews Became White Folks*, 45–48.

[48] Mark Silk, "Notes on the Judeo-Christian Tradition in America," *American Quarterly* 36, no. 1 (1984): 75; K. Healan Gaston, *Imagining Judeo-Christian America: Religion, Secularism, and the Redefinition of Democracy* (Chicago: University of Chicago Press, 2019), 10.

[49] Kirle, *Unfinished Business*, 45–46.

of a secular Christmas.[50] As Elizabeth Titrington Craft observes, this "tension between the aims of universality and cultural specificity" is a defining feature of Broadway productions that concern the immigrant experience.[51] Often, these tensions play out as a battle between nativism, that is, the idea that citizenship is predicated on a single race, ethnicity, or religion, and "cultural pluralism," that is, the idea that America, unlike other nations, has the strength the encompass a variety of ethnicities and races, and is thus stronger for it.[52] In terms of *Street Scene*, these tensions played out against the backdrop of early postwar U.S. culture.

Other changes to Rice's original play directly related to the war. The revelations of the extent of the Holocaust shocked the world, and the casual anti-Semitism of the 1920s and 1930s was no longer tolerated by the middle of the 1940s.[53] This necessitated a change in the way Jews were portrayed on Broadway. Before the war, typical Jewish characters often spent time being chased by law enforcement or mobs; this was no longer tenable after the revelations of the suffering of European Jews at the hands of official law enforcement. Still, anti-Semites continued to flourish in public life. Ellen Posner wrote in the 1946 edition of the *American Jewish Yearbook* that "While responsible polls have intimated that the rise of anti-Semitic feeling in the United States [...] has halted in the last two years, the professional purveyors of hate have brought a strong revival of overt anti-Semitism. Largely of American stock and financed by Americans, as compared with the foreign agents and Nazi propagandists before Pearl Harbor, these 'nationalists,' have been busily promoting bigotry, distrust, dissention, and discord throughout the nation."[54] She had reason to be worried. After the war, Gerald L.K. Smith took the movement into the realm of electoral politics by re-founding "America First" Party, which under Smith's leadership it became virulently anti-Semitic, with platforms against "internationalists" in the government. Smith ran for president in 1944 and lost handily, but nevertheless remained in the public eye. Furthermore, fears of a renewed link between communists and Jews arose in the late 1940s; the *American Jewish Year Book* reported that as religiously fueled anti-Semitism waned, anti-Semites changed tactics and began to make "propaganda based on the false identification of Jews with

---

[50] Brodkin, *How Jews Became White Folks*, 142–3, 165; Leonard Dinnerstein, *Antisemitism in America* (Oxford, UK: Oxford University Press, 1994), 167.

[51] Craft, "Becoming American Onstage," 16.

[52] Craft, "Becoming American Onstage," 36–41.

[53] Brodkin, *How Jews Became White Folks*, 36; Sarna, *American Judaism*, 276.

[54] Ellen H. Posner, "Anti-Jewish Agitation," *American Jewish Year Book* (1946–1947): 172.

Communism," and that several new journals "came into existence with the 'Jew-Communist' line as their principle commodity."[55]

These pressures all informed the process of adaptation. Weill had been interested in *Street Scene* since he saw a German production in 1930, but it took until the summer of 1945 before he and Rice felt ready to take on the project.[56] Initially, Maxwell Anderson was to write the lyrics, but by September, African American poet Langston Hughes was given the job, although he was on a lecture tour for most of the writing.[57] Weill and Rice decided where to insert songs, and then informed Hughes, who delivered lyrics by mail. Thus, Hughes had very little input on the overall shape of the show, even though he had a profound effect on individual moments. The assembling of the production team reveals much about the goals of the creative team. The successes of Rodgers and Hammerstein loomed large over the production. Initially, PPC hoped Rodgers and Hammerstein would produce the show, but eventually convinced Dwight Deere Wiman—who had worked extensively with Rodgers and Hart—to join the project. For director, they first approached Rouben Mamoulian, who had staged *Porgy and Bess*, *Oklahoma!*, and *Carousel*, but he turned them down. They then turned to Charles Friedman, who had directed Hammerstein's *Carmen Jones* (1943), another work that straddled the line between Broadway and opera. Friedman had Leftist connections as well, having directed and written parts of the International Ladies' Garment Workers' Union's *Pins and Needles* (1937). For the set, they hired the original designer of *Street Scene*, Jo Mielziner, one of the most well-respected figures of the era, and with whom they had worked on several previous shows, including *Knickerbocker Holiday* and *Firebrand of Florence*. He was also responsible for *Carousel*'s sets. Maurice Abravanel conducted. Weill did most of his own orchestrations, but he also turned to Ted Royal for help on passages that required a jazzier touch, such as the dance break after "Moon-Faced, Starry-Eyed." For many of the roles, they turned to opera singers. Polyna Stoska—whose Metropolitan Opera debut followed her time in *Street Scene*—played Mrs. Maurrant. Norman Cordon and Sydney Rayner, whose operatic careers had largely been in the previous decade, played Mr. Maurrant, and Mr. Fiorentino. Hollywood starlet Anne Jeffreys earned the roll of Rose, and Brian Sullivan was cast as Sam.

---

[55] Isaiah Minkoff, "Inter-Group Relations," *American Jewish Year Book* 49 (1947–1948): 189. See also Dinnerstein, *Antisemitism in America*, 164.

[56] Minutes of the PPC, ERP, Box 68 Folder 1.

[57] Elmar Juchem, *Kurt Weill und Maxwell Anderson: Neue Weg zum amerikanischen Musiktheater, 1938–1950* (Stuttgart: J.B. Metzler, 2000), 157–58.

Before rehearsals, the creative team conceived of *Street Scene* as a celebration of a culturally pluralist America: Weill wrote in the *New York Times*
that "the play lent itself to a great variety of music, just as the streets of
New York embrace the music of many lands and many people."[58] In order
to broaden the cultural make-up of the block, the first major change they
made to the play was the addition African American characters: the janitor
Henry and his family. Rice and Weill also planned several songs to highlight this theme, although not all made it to the final production.[59] Henry
initially had a bigger role, opening the second act with "Great Big Sky," in
which he declares "It's a great big sky / And there's room enough for all /
Underneath that Great Big Sky / Where earth's a little ball," but that was cut
before rehearsals.[60] Two other numbers in Act II highlighted the theme of a
culturally pluralist America: "Bon Giorno, Signore," an exchange in Italian
between Mr. Fiorentino and "Mike," a character who later disappeared, and
"Italy in Technicolor" for Rose and Mr. Fiorentino, which has Rose longing
to visit Italy and Mr. Fiorentino singing the praises of the United States.
Both were cut after the Philadelphia try-out.[61] Weill sketched another
number called "It's the Irish," but there is no indication where it would have
fit in the show.[62]

Another number that was dropped was called "Nation of Nations," which
was suggested by a moment in the original play: a brief argument about
who discovered America in which Mr. Fiorentino (an Italian immigrant)
says it was Columbus, but Mr. Olsen (a Swede) insists it was Leif Eriksson.
In the final version, the entrance of Mary Hildebrand and the graduating
school children interrupts this argument, leading to "Wrapped in a Ribbon

---

[58] Kurt Weill, "Score for a Play," *NYT*, 5 January 1947, available at https://www.kwf.org/pages/wt-score-for-a-play.html.

[59] The earliest version of the libretto is in ERP, Box 28 Folder 5, along with Rice's initial outline. The next draft resides in ERP, Box 28 Folder 7. Two versions of the rehearsal script survive. The ear-liest is labeled "Final Pre-Rehearsal Version" but has Stoska's blocking annotations, and survives with her annotations in WLRC, Series 20 Box S6 Folder 1946a. The second rehearsal version (also labeled "Final Pre-Rehearsal Version" but substantially different from Stoska's script) resides in ERP, Box 28 Folder 8. The promptbook for the final production survives in WLRC, Series 20 Box S6 Folder 1946, and another unannotated copy of the same script is in WLRC, Series 20 Box S6 Folder 1946b. The WLRC classifies librettos in order of acquisition, accounting for the discrepancy in numbering.

[60] The lyrics are crossed out in the ERP, Box 28 Folder 5 libretto, and never appear after. Weill did set them to music; he called the song a "peach." Kurt Weill to Langston Hughes, 22 January 1946, WLRC, Series 40 Folder "Hughes, Langston."

[61] The program for this performance is in the WLRC *Street Scene* Production files.

[62] The sketch, along with those for "Great Big Sky," "Italy in Technicolor," and "Buon Giorno, Signore," is in WLA, Box 31 Folder 434.

and Tied with a Bow."[63] But according to Rice's notes, this moment would have led into

> an important ensemble musical number, with a kind of melting pot theme, half serious, half humorous, Maurrant and perhaps Mrs. Jones representing the America-for-Americans point of view, while each of the other characters speaks for the contributions made by his particular race or nationality to the general projects and culture of America. Olsen speaks for the Swedes, Lippo for the Italians, Mrs. Fiorentino for the Germans, Jones for the Irish, and in the course of it, the Negro Janitor, and eventually even Kaplan to speak for the Jews.[64]

(Rice apparently did not notice that Mrs. Jones plays both sides of the argument.) Several drafts of lyrics survive, but in terms of music, only sketches for the Fiorentinos and Henry the janitor exist.[65] These show each member of the community singing in the style of his or her national origin: Mr. Fiorentino sings a rollicking aria (Example 6.3a), Mrs. Fiorentino (a German) sings a Viennese waltz (Example 6.3b), Henry sings a boogie-woogie (Example 6.3c).

But on 20 September, just before rehearsals began, Weill wrote to Hughes that they had yet "to find a brilliant idea for the Melting Pot."[66] The problem was likely exacerbated by the presence of "Ice Cream," which served a purpose; both are Act I ensembles that celebrate American identity. "Ice Cream"

**Example 6.3a** *Street Scene*, "Nation of Nations," Mr. Fiorentino.

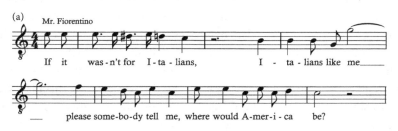

If it was-n't for I-ta-lians, I-ta-lians like me___

___ please some-bo-dy tell me, where would A-mer-i-ca be?

---

[63] In the early rehearsal scripts, "Wrapped in a Ribbon" is formatted differently than the rest of the text, indicating it was inserted later.

[64] Elmer Rice, "Outline of a Musical Version of *Street Scene*," ERP, Box 28 Folder 5.

[65] See WLA, Box 31 Folder 434.

[66] Kurt Weill to Langston Hughes, 20 September 1946, WLRC, Series 40 Folder "Hughes, Langston."

**Example 6.3b** *Street Scene,* "Nation of Nations," Mrs. Fiorentino.

**Example 6.3c** *Street Scene,* "Nation of Nations," Henry.

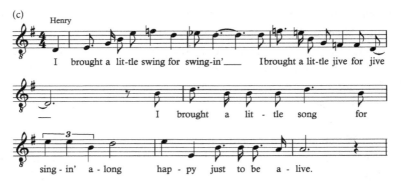

won out, likely because it resonated with a more contemporary view of assimilation. Weill's reference to the "Melting Pot" links "Nation of Nations" to the Zangwill play, and indeed, the song has each immigrant celebrating their culture's unique contribution to the United States, emphasizing their difference. "Ice Cream," on the other hand, has a group of immigrants all celebrating one thing: a simple American pleasure. Rather than each contributing their own national melody, they all sing in harmony in a mock-Puccinian ensemble with some jazzy touches, blending the American vernacular with the classical art music tradition. "Ice Cream" became the most memorable ensemble of the act, showing that, no matter where someone comes from, everyone loves America. Differences melt away (pun intended) into one, homogenous ensemble.

Weill and Rice differed on how to treat the Jewish characters. In January 1946, Weill wrote to Mamoulian assuring him that "The political element in the original play will be considerably toned down" and that "Sam,

instead of being always the beaten jew [sic] will be the young poet trying to adjust himself to the world and to the hateful surroundings he is living in."[67] But Rice hoped to emphasize the politics, particularly in the character of Mr. Maurrant, who represented nativist ideas. Rice wrote in his notes that in Mr. Maurrant's aria, "it might be well to consider giving it an overtone of political significance by suggesting the old America First psychology of narrowness and bigotry, the kind of incipient fascism that is typical of the America Firsters of the Christian Front, of whom Maurrant might very well be a member."[68] The Christian Front was an anti-Semitic political movement organized by Coughlin in the 1930s that was responsible for a number of crimes against Jews. The various stages of the libretto show the careful deliberations between Weill and Rice over this disagreement. Mr. Maurrant's (and Mrs. Jones's) racism is significantly attenuated from the original play (although some lines denigrating "foreigners" remained), as is Mr. Kaplan's hardline Marxism. Given that the Democrats had been badly beaten in the 1946 congressional elections due to Truman's unpopularity, Weill's instincts to "tone down" the politics were likely better than Rice's. Indeed, both Joseph McCarthy and Richard Nixon entered Congress in 1946, signaling a new stage of domestic anti-communist politics.[69]

Weill's new vision for Sam is mostly borne out, as the character is more substantial than his 1929 antecedent. Unlike previous Jewish or Jewish-like characters in musicals—comics who must be assimilated into the community (sometimes forcibly, as in the case of Ali Hakim in *Oklahoma!*)—Sam is already assimilated.[70] He presents a stark contrast to his father Mr. Kaplan, whose heavy Yiddish accent and radical political views mark him as an outsider. The juxtaposition proves that, even if the older generation proves unassimilable, younger Jews like Sam can integrate into American life. Moreover, Sam's youth and innocence enable him to chastise the gossips and advocate for kindness without the dramatic irony that mars Mrs. Maurrant's articulation of the same ideas, given that she is compromised by her extramarital affair. Weill and Rice also gave Sam the most important number: "Lonely House," a moment that does not have an analog in the 1929 play. Weill called

[67] Kurt Weill to Rouben Mamoulian, 22 January 1946, WLA, Box 47 Folder 11.

[68] Elmer Rice, "Outline of a Musical Version of *Street Scene.*"

[69] James T. Patterson, *Grand Expectations: The United States, 1945–1974* (Oxford, UK: Oxford University Press, 1996) 146–48.

[70] On Ali Hakim, see Most, *Making Americans*, 107–18.

it "a theme song for the show," and here Sam articulates the contradiction at the heart of the story: "Funny, you can be so lonely / With all these folks around."[71]

Sam's importance is evident in the struggles the creative team had regarding his entrance (see Table 6.1 for an outline of the changes to Act I). They knew they needed to introduce Sam earlier than he appears in the original play, which is deep in the middle of Act I. Weill's initial conception had Sam entering during "Nation of Nations"; he told Hughes that Sam should introduce "the Melting Pot idea," which "has the great advantage that Sam has a very strong entrance," and which would further have established Sam's moral authority.[72] Their next idea was to have Sam's entrance coincide with his scolding the gossips just before "Lonely House." But while that establishes his moral position, it also makes him seem petulant, and is still very late. By the time rehearsals started, his entrance had been moved to just after "Ice Cream." By the final version, Sam enters just after the opening sequence and has a conversation with Mrs. Maurrant about how much he loves books. This solves several dramatic problems: it introduces Sam in the first moments of the story, and it establishes him as a sensitive poet and intellectual.

Moving Sam's entrance earlier also helped the audience connect him with Mrs. Maurrant. This is another change from the play, in which these two characters rarely interact. Yet in 1929, Mrs. Maurrant is clearly a sympathetic character despite her affair, stating one of the morals of the show: "I think the trouble is people don't make allowances. They don't realize that everybody wants a kind word, now and then." To transfer some of her moral authority to Sam in 1947, they are linked musically. Even before the story begins, the overture connects them, beginning with a dissonant harmonization of "Lonely House," followed by the joyful middle section of Mrs. Maurrant's aria "Somehow I Never Could Believe" (the music that accompanies the lyrics "Hoping I'd discover / Some wonderful lover"). Then, in the introduction to "Lonely House," that "joy" motive sounds again in the flutes. The dissonant version of "Lonely House" returns as Mrs. Maurrant invites Sankey up to her room just before her murder, revealing the deadly consequences of the loneliness Sam described. After she dies, Sam sings the opening music of "Somehow I Never Could Believe" in "The Woman Who Lives Upstairs," to

---

[71] Weill to Hughes, 22 January 1946.
[72] Weill to Hughes, 22 January 1946.

**Table 6.1** Evolution of the Act I of *Street Scene*

| *Street Scene* (1929) | Pre-Rehearsal 1 | Pre-Rehearsal 2 | Rehearsal 1 | Rehearsal 2 | *Street Scene* (1947) |
|---|---|---|---|---|---|
| Mrs. Jones, Mrs. Fiorentino, and Mrs. Olsen complain about the heat. | Mrs. Jones, Mrs. Fiorentino, and Mrs. Olsen complain about the heat ("Ain't It Awful the Heat"). | Mrs. Jones, Mrs. Fiorentino, and Mrs. Olsen complain about the heat ("Ain't It Awful the Heat"). | Mrs. Jones, Mrs. Fiorentino, and Mrs. Olsen complain about the heat ("Ain't It Awful the Heat"). | Mrs. Jones, Mrs. Fiorentino, and Mrs. Olsen complain about the heat ("Ain't It Awful the Heat"). | Mrs. Jones, Mrs. Fiorentino, and Mrs. Olsen complain about the heat ("Ain't It Awful the Heat"). |
| | Shirley gives Mr. Kaplan (her father) the paper ("Oi de Skendels"). | Shirley gives Mr. Kaplan (her father) the paper ("Oi de Skendels"). | Shirley gives Mr. Kaplan (her father) the paper ("Oi de Skendels"). | Shirley gives Mr. Kaplan (her father) the paper ("Oi de Skendels"). | Shirley gives Mr. Kaplan (her father) the paper ("Oi de Skendels"). |
| | | | | | Henry Davis, the janitor, enters ("I Got a Marble and a Star"). |
| Mrs. Maurrant gives Willie money for ice cream. Mrs. Jones, Mrs. Fiorentino, and Mrs. Olsen gossip about Mrs. Maurrant. Mrs. Maurrant interrupts. | Mrs. Maurrant gives Willie money for ice cream. Mrs. Jones, Mrs. Fiorentino, and Mrs. Olsen gossip about Mrs. Maurrant ("Get a Load of That"). Mrs. Maurrant interrupts. | Mrs. Maurrant gives Willie money for ice cream. Mrs. Jones, Mrs. Fiorentino, and Mrs. Olsen gossip about Mrs. Maurrant ("Get a Load of That"). Mrs. Maurrant interrupts. | Mrs. Maurrant gives Willie money for ice cream. Mrs. Jones, Mrs. Fiorentino, and Mrs. Olsen gossip about Mrs. Maurrant ("Get a Load of That"). Mrs. Maurrant interrupts. | Mrs. Maurrant gives Willie money for ice cream. Mrs. Jones, Mrs. Fiorentino, and Mrs. Olsen gossip about Mrs. Maurrant ("Get a Load of That"). Mrs. Maurrant interrupts. | Mrs. Maurrant gives Willie money for ice cream. Mrs. Jones, Mrs. Fiorentino, and Mrs. Olsen gossip about Mrs. Maurrant ("Get a Load of That"). Mrs. Maurrant interrupts. |
| | | | | | Sam comes home and has a brief conversation with Mrs. Maurrant about books. |

*(continued)*

**Table 6.1** Continued

| Street Scene (1929) | Pre-Rehearsal 1 | Pre-Rehearsal 2 | Rehearsal 1 | Rehearsal 2 | Street Scene (1947) |
|---|---|---|---|---|---|
| Mr. Buchanan frets about the impending birth of his daughter. Mr. Maurrant enters, chastises Mrs. Maurrant for not knowing where the children are, and leaves. Mrs. Maurrant laments the fact that people don't get along better. Mr. Sankey enters and has an awkward conversation with the women on the block, then exits. | Mr. Buchanan frets about the impending birth of his daughter ("When a Woman Has a Baby"). Mr. Maurrant enters, chastises Mrs. Maurrant for not knowing where the children are, and leaves. Mrs. Maurrant laments the fact that people don't get along better and reminisces about her life ("Somehow I Never Could Believe"). Mr. Sankey enters and has an awkward conversation with the women on the block, then exits. | Mr. Buchanan frets about the impending birth of his daughter ("When a Woman Has a Baby"). Mr. Maurrant enters, chastises Mrs. Maurrant for not knowing where the children are, and leaves. Mrs. Maurrant laments the fact that people don't get along better and reminisces about her life ("Somehow I Never Could Believe"). Mr. Sankey enters and has an awkward conversation with the women on the block, then exits. | Mr. Buchanan frets about the impending birth of his daughter ("When a Woman Has a Baby"). Mr. Maurrant enters, chastises Mrs. Maurrant for not knowing where the children are, and leaves. Mrs. Maurrant laments the fact that people don't get along better and reminisces about her life ("Somehow I Never Could Believe"). Mr. Sankey enters and has an awkward conversation with the women on the block, then exits. | Mr. Buchanan frets about the impending birth of his daughter ("When a Woman Has a Baby"). Mr. Maurrant enters, chastises Mrs. Maurrant for not knowing where the children are, and leaves. Mrs. Maurrant laments the fact that people don't get along better and reminisces about her life ("Somehow I Never Could Believe"). Mr. Sankey enters and has an awkward conversation with the women on the block, then exits. | Mr. Buchanan frets about the impending birth of his daughter ("When a Woman Has a Baby"). Mr. Maurrant enters, chastises Mrs. Maurrant for not knowing where the children are, and leaves. Mrs. Maurrant laments the fact that people don't get along better and reminisces about her life ("Somehow I Never Could Believe"). Mr. Sankey enters and has an awkward conversation with the women on the block, then exits. |
| Miss Cushing discusses her dying mother with the women. | | | | | |
| Mrs. Maurrant exits, and the women continue to gossip. Mr. Maurrant enters and asks about his wife. | Mrs. Maurrant exits and the women continue to gossip ("Get a Load of That [Reprise]"). Mr. Maurrant enters and asks about his wife. | Mrs. Maurrant exits and the women continue to gossip ("Get a Load of That [Reprise]"). Mr. Maurrant enters and asks about his wife. | Mrs. Maurrant exits and the women continue to gossip ("Get a Load of That [Reprise]"). Mr. Maurrant enters and asks about his wife. | Mrs. Maurrant exits and the women continue to gossip ("Get a Load of That [Reprise]"). Mr. Maurrant enters and asks about his wife. | Mrs. Maurrant exits and the women continue to gossip ("Get a Load of That [Reprise]"). Mr. Maurrant enters and asks about his wife. |

| | | | | | |
|---|---|---|---|---|---|
| Shirley gives Mr. Kaplan (her father) the paper. | Henry Davis, the janitor, enters ("I Got a Marble and a Star") while the women continue to gossip ("Get a Load of That" cont.) | Henry Davis, the janitor, enters ("I Got a Marble and a Star"). | Henry Davis, the janitor, enters ("I Got a Marble and a Star"). | Henry Davis, the janitor, enters ("I Got a Marble and a Star"). | Mr. Fiorentino enters with ice cream ("Ice Cream"). |
| Mr. Fiorentino enters with ice cream. | Mr. Fiorentino enters with ice cream ("Ice Cream"). | Mr. Fiorentino enters with ice cream ("Ice Cream"). | Mr. Fiorentino enters with ice cream ("Ice Cream"). | Mr. Fiorentino enters with ice cream ("Ice Cream"). | |
| A woman from a charity organization asks about the Hildebrands, who are about to be evicted. Mr. Kaplan complains about the capitalist system. | | | | | |
| Mrs. Maurrant returns and she and Mr. Maurrant get into an argument. | Mrs. Maurrant returns and she and Mr. Maurrant get into an argument ("Let Things Be Like They Always Was"). | Mrs. Maurrant returns and she and Mr. Maurrant get into an argument ("Let Things Be Like They Always Was"). | Sam enters and has a brief conversation about books with Mr. Fiorentino. | Sam enters and has a brief conversation about books with Mr. Fiorentino. | Mrs. Maurrant returns and she and Mr. Maurrant get into an argument. |
| The charity worker and Mr. Kaplan continue to argue. The charity worker leaves in frustration. | | | Mrs. Maurrant returns and she and Mr. Maurrant get into an argument ("Let Things Be Like They Always Was"). | Mrs. Maurrant returns and she and Mr. Maurrant get into an argument. | |

(continued)

**Table 6.1** Continued

| Street Scene (1929) | Pre-Rehearsal 1 | Pre-Rehearsal 2 | Rehearsal 1 | Rehearsal 2 | Street Scene (1947) |
|---|---|---|---|---|---|
| Mr. Maurrant and Mr. Kaplan get into an argument. The block generally agrees with Mr. Maurrant until he lashes out at "foreigners." Mr. Maurrant and Mr. Kaplan almost come to blows. | Mr. Maurrant and Mr. Kaplan get into an argument. The block generally agrees with Mr. Maurrant until he lashes out at "foreigners." Mr. Maurrant and Mr. Kaplan almost come to blows. | Mr. Maurrant and Mr. Kaplan get into an argument. The block generally agrees with Mr. Maurrant until he lashes out at "foreigners." Mr. Maurrant and Mr. Kaplan almost come to blows. | Mr. Maurrant and Mr. Kaplan get into an argument. The block generally agrees with Mr. Maurrant until he lashes out at "foreigners." Mr. Maurrant and Mr. Kaplan almost come to blows. | Mr. Maurrant and Mr. Kaplan get into an argument. The block generally agrees with Mr. Maurrant until he lashes out at "foreigners." Mr. Maurrant and Mr. Kaplan almost come to blows ("Let Things Be Like They Always Was"). | Mr. Maurrant and Mr. Kaplan get into an argument. The block generally agrees with Mr. Maurrant until he lashes out at "foreigners." Mr. Maurrant and Mr. Kaplan almost come to blows ("Let Things Be Like They Always Was"). |
| Mr. Fiorentino and Mrs. Olsen argue about the origins of America. | Mr. Fiorentino and Mrs. Olsen argue about the origins of America ("A Nation of Nations" is cued, but largely removed from this version). | Mr. Fiorentino and Mrs. Olsen argue about the origins of America. | Mr. Fiorentino and Mrs. Olsen argue about the origins of America. | Mr. Fiorentino and Mrs. Olsen argue about the origins of America. | Mr. Fiorentino and Mrs. Olsen argue about the origins of America. |
|  |  | The Hildebrand children come home from school graduation, dancing in the streets ("Wrapped in a Ribbon and Tied with a Bow"). | The Hildebrand children come home from school graduation, dancing in the streets ("Wrapped in a Ribbon and Tied with a Bow"). | The Hildebrand children come home from school graduation, dancing in the streets ("Wrapped in a Ribbon and Tied with a Bow"). | The Hildebrand children come home from school graduation, dancing in the streets ("Wrapped in a Ribbon and Tied with a Bow"). |
| Sam comes home and talks with Mr. Fiorentino, Mrs. Jones, and Mrs. Maurrant about books and music. |  |  |  |  |  |

| | | | | | |
|---|---|---|---|---|---|
| Mr. Sankey interrupts and Mr. Maurrant returns, acting suspicious of Mr. Sankey. Willie enters, sobbing. Mrs. Maurrant calms him down, but Mr. Maurrant frightens him. The Maurrants go upstairs. | Mr. Sankey interrupts and Mr. Maurrant returns, acting suspicious of Mr. Sankey. Willie enters, sobbing. Mrs. Maurrant calms him down, but Mr. Maurrant frightens him. The Maurrants go upstairs. | Mr. Sankey interrupts and Mr. Maurrant returns, acting suspicious of Mr. Sankey. Willie enters, sobbing. Mrs. Maurrant calms him down, but Mr. Maurrant frightens him. The Maurrants go upstairs. | Mr. Sankey interrupts and Mr. Maurrant returns, acting suspicious of Mr. Sankey. Willie enters, sobbing. Mrs. Maurrant calms him down, but Mr. Maurrant frightens him. The Maurrants go upstairs. | Mr. Sankey interrupts and Mr. Maurrant returns, acting suspicious of Mr. Sankey. Willie enters, sobbing. Mrs. Maurrant calms him down, but Mr. Maurrant frightens him. The Maurrants go upstairs. | Mr. Sankey and Mr. Maurrant returns, acting suspicious of Sankey. Willie enters, sobbing. Mrs. Maurrant calms him down, but Mr. Maurrant frightens him. The Maurrants go upstairs. |
| The rest of the company gossip about the Maurrants, but Sam objects. Everyone goes inside. | The rest of the company gossip about the Maurrants, but Sam objects. Everyone goes inside. Sam laments his loneliness ("Lonely House"). | The rest of the company gossip about the Maurrants, but Sam objects. Everyone goes inside. Sam laments his loneliness ("Lonely House"). | The rest of the company gossip about the Maurrants, but Sam objects. Everyone goes inside. Sam laments his loneliness ("Lonely House"). | The rest of the company gossip about the Maurrants, but Sam objects. Everyone goes inside. Sam laments his loneliness ("Lonely House"). | The rest of the company gossip about the Maurrants, but Sam objects. Everyone goes inside. Sam laments his loneliness ("Lonely House"). |
| Easter and Rose arrive home. Easter flirts with Rose, but she rebuffs him. Mr. Maurrant comes down and chastises her for staying up late, then goes back into the house. | Easter and Rose arrive home. Easter flirts with Rose ("Wouldn't You Like to Be on Broadway?"), but rebuffs him ("What Good Would the Moon Be?"). Mr. Maurrant comes down and chastises her for staying up late, then goes back into the house. | Easter and Rose arrive home. Easter flirts with Rose ("Wouldn't You Like to Be on Broadway?"), but she rebuffs him ("What Good Would the Moon Be?"). Mr. Maurrant comes down and chastises her for staying up late, then goes back into the house ("What Good Would the Moon Be? [Reprise]"). | Easter and Rose arrive home. Easter flirts with Rose ("Wouldn't You Like to Be on Broadway?"), but she rebuffs him ("What Good Would the Moon Be?"). Mr. Maurrant comes down and chastises her for staying up late, then goes back into the house ("What Good Would the Moon Be? [Reprise]"). | Easter and Rose arrive home. Easter flirts with Rose ("Wouldn't You Like to Be on Broadway?"), but she rebuffs him ("What Good Would the Moon Be?"). Mr. Maurrant comes down and chastises her for staying up late, then goes back into the house ("What Good Would the Moon Be? [Reprise]"). | Easter and Rose arrive home. Easter flirts with Rose ("Wouldn't You Like to Be on Broadway?"), but she rebuffs him ("What Good Would the Moon Be?"). Mr. Maurrant comes down and chastises her for staying up late, then goes back into the house ("What Good Would the Moon Be? [Reprise]"). |

(continued)

**Table 6.1** Continued

| Street Scene (1929) | Pre-Rehearsal 1 | Pre-Rehearsal 2 | Rehearsal 1 | Rehearsal 2 | Street Scene (1947) |
|---|---|---|---|---|---|
| Mr. Buchanan rushes on, informing Rose that his wife in labor. Rose calls the doctor. Dick and Mae stroll home and go up to an abandoned apartment. | Mr. Buchanan rushes on, informing Rose that his wife in labor. Rose calls the doctor. Dick and Mae stroll home and go up to an abandoned apartment ("The Streetlight Is My Moonlight," replaced later with "Moon-Faced, Starry-Eyed"). | Mr. Buchanan rushes on, informing Rose that his wife in labor. Rose calls the doctor. Dick and Mae stroll home and go up to an abandoned apartment ("Moon-Faced, Starry-Eyed"). | Mr. Buchanan rushes on, informing Rose that his wife in labor. Rose calls the doctor. Dick and Mae stroll home and go up to an abandoned apartment ("Moon-Faced, Starry-Eyed"). | Mr. Buchanan rushes on, informing Rose that his wife in in labor. Rose calls the doctor. Dick and Mae stroll home and go up to an abandoned apartment ("Moon-Faced, Starry-Eyed"). | Mr. Buchanan rushes on, informing Rose that his wife in labor. Rose calls the doctor. Dick and Mae stroll home and go up to an abandoned apartment ("Moon-Faced, Starry-Eyed"). |
| Vincent manhandles Rose, but Sam intervenes. Vincent knocks down Sam and goes up to his room. | | | | | Vincent manhandles Rose, but Sam intervenes. Vincent knocks down Sam and goes up to his room. |
| Sam and Rose share a tender moment. The doctor finally arrives for the Buchanans. | Sam and Rose share a tender moment ("Remember That I Care"). The doctor finally arrives for the Buchanans as Henry returns ("I Got a Marble and a Star [Reprise]"). | Sam and Rose share a tender moment ("Remember That I Care"). The doctor finally arrives for the Buchanans as Henry returns ("I Got a Marble and a Star [Reprise]"). | Sam and Rose share a tender moment ("Remember That I Care"). The doctor finally arrives for the Buchanans as Henry returns ("I Got a Marble and a Star [Reprise]"). | Sam and Rose share a tender moment ("Remember That I Care"). The doctor finally arrives for the Buchanans as Henry returns ("I Got a Marble and a Star [Reprise]"). | Sam and Rose share a tender moment ("Remember That I Care"). The doctor finally arrives for the Buchanans as Henry returns ("I Got a Marble and a Star [Reprise]"). |

the words "Now love and death have linked their arms together," bringing the musical connection full circle.

Sam's father, Mr. Kaplan, proved even more of a challenge. In the 1929 play, he is a vocal communist, but the political circumstances of 1946–47 rendered that depiction problematic. Although in 1929 the public was somewhat suspicious of communism, in 1947 the emergent Cold War made such associations even more dangerous, particularly for Jews. Thus, Mr. Kaplan's presence in Act II—when some of his most pointed commentary occurs in the original play—was reduced to only a few lines, and his presence in Act I was significantly revised. During rehearsals, Rice rewrote the argument between Mr. Kaplan and Mr. Maurrant several times to make Mr. Kaplan more sympathetic (see Table 6.1). The sequence originally began with the Maurrants arguing about corporal punishment for children, leading to Mr. Maurrant's song "Let Things Be Like They Always Was." After the aria, Mr. Kaplan explains that "de verkers will be at de moicy of de property-owning klesses" until the revolution—dialogue drawn from the original play. This upsets Mr. Maurrant, and he and Kaplan almost come to blows. However, by the later rehearsal version of the libretto, Mr. Kaplan interrupts the Maurrants' argument by asking Mr. Maurrant if he thinks "by beatings you can make in a child improvements?" In the ensuing dialogue, Mr. Kaplan connects child-beating to "dis philosophy w'ich results in imperialism and war and de exploitation of de verkers by de kepitalist klesses." Then, after a brief skirmish, Mr. Maurrant sings his aria. Having Mr. Kaplan argue with Mr. Maurrant about child-beating makes him much more sympathetic, and moving the aria after the skirmish puts the focus on Mr. Maurrant rather than Mr. Kaplan, which helps to smooth over the potentially politically problematic moment.

Still, Rice received several letters complaining that Mr. Kaplan exemplified harmful stereotypes. Herbert Lizt of the Anti-Defamation League wrote "like it or not, one of the canards widely prevalent today is that all Jews are communists and all communists are Jews."[73] Lizt had a point; in a similar letter, Alfred Greenberg wrote to Rice that he had been upset by the audience's reaction to Mr. Maurrant: "During the scene when Mr. Maurrant said something like: 'That's the trouble with all you foreigners. They ought to send you back from where you came from!,' there was actually a burst of applause from parts of the audience."[74] But Rice stood by his characterization of

---

[73] Herbert Lizt to Elmer Rice, 11 February 1947, ERP, Box 74 Folder 7.
[74] Alfred Greenberg to Elmer Rice, 26 January 1947, ERP, Box 74 Folder 7.

Mr. Kaplan, writing that "I think the Jews come off very well in *Street Scene*" and that Mr. Kaplan was "a credit to his race."[75] In his response, Rice revealed his insensitivity to the cultural climate. With the increasing pressure of the Cold War, any hint of sympathy toward communism was becoming increasingly dangerous, particularly for Jews.

The revisions to the themes and characters of *Street Scene* reflect the ways Jews were redefining their place in American life in the wake of World War II. The creative team paid such careful attention to the ways race and ethnicity worked in *Street Scene* because of their larger ambitions for the work; they hoped it would be considered part of the post–Rodgers and Hammerstein Broadway revolution to bring serious, dramatic, and (most importantly) operatic works to Broadway stages. With *Street Scene*, the creators put explicitly Jewish characters in the center of the discussion, working them into the larger fabric of the American cultural landscape.

## Ghetto Pastoral

*Street Scene* opened on 9 January 1947 to mostly positive reviews. Despite the designation "dramatic musical," many critics placed *Street Scene* among other shows that exemplified a new trend toward American Opera. The *New York Times*' Brooks Atkinson noted that in *Street Scene*, Weill had "gone about about as far a theatre musician can in extending the song in the direction of opera," and that "not since *Oklahoma!* has a stage play yielded so fine a musical." He also counted *Street Scene* among "three excellent musical plays" that indicated an operatic trend: Duke Ellington and John La Touche's *Beggar's Holiday* (a 1946 update of John Gay's *The Beggar's Opera*), and E.Y. Harburg, and Fred Saidy's *Finian's Rainbow* (1947), and later compared it to Giancarlo Menotti's double bill *The Telephone* and *The Medium* (1947).[76] These works, along with *Oklahoma!*, were placed in the lineage of the genre's prototype: *Porgy and Bess* (1935). Richard Watts Jr. of the *New York Post* termed *Street Scene* a "folk opera" and assured readers that it was "a finer

---

[75] Elmer Rice to Nita Thurswel, 27 February 1947, ERP, Box 74 Folder 7. Rice was responding to Thurswel's initial letter, which voiced complaints similar to Greenberg's and Lizt's.

[76] Brooks Atkinson, "The New Play," *NYT*, 2 May 1947, 28; Brooks Atkinson, "Mr. Rice's *Street Scene* and Mr. Weill's score," *NYT*, 19 January 1947, X1. The *New York Herald-Tribune* also mentions *Finian's Rainbow* and the *Chicago Sunday Tribune* mentions both *Beggar's Holiday* and *Finian's Rainbow* alongside *Street Scene*. When no page numbers are included, reviews come from the *Street Scene* production file in the WLRC.

thing than *Porgy and Bess*" and "the most exciting event in the history of the American musical show since *Oklahoma!*" before going on to review both *Street Scene* and *Finian's Rainbow* in the same article.[77] In the *New York Herald-Tribune*, Howard Barnes wrote that *Street Scene* and *Finian's Rainbow* are "exciting examples of a languishing form" and that *Street Scene* in particular "has emerged as a genuine American folk opera," which "resembles the Gershwin classic."[78] But despite relatively good reviews, *Street Scene* did not attract an audience large enough to sustain it. Rice, Weill, and Hughes (the last somewhat reluctantly) all voluntarily reduced their shares of the royalties in order to keep it running, but it still closed the following May, after 148 performances.[79]

The idea of "folk" is as integral to *Street Scene* as "opera."[80] Although Weill often used "Broadway opera" to describe *Street Scene* (especially after critics started calling it an "opera"), the terms "Broadway opera" and "folk opera" were inextricably linked in the 1940s. The idea of folk opera rose to prominence in 1935 when George Gershwin used the term to describe *Porgy and Bess*. When *Oklahoma!* premiered critics also designated it folk opera, and used similar language for Rodgers and Hammerstein's *Carousel* (1945).[81] Weill framed *Street Scene* as part of this lineage. The designation "dramatic musical" served two purposes: it steered audiences away from the negative connotations of "opera," but reassured them that it was serious piece of musical theatre.[82] Weill explicitly claimed Gershwin in his compositional heritage while doing publicity for *Street Scene*, writing in the *New York Times* that one of his first actions on U.S. soil was attending a rehearsal of *Porgy and Bess*, where he "discovered that the American theatre was already on the way to the more integrated musical theatre that we had developed in Europe."[83]

---

[77] Richard Watts Jr., "Two on the Aisle," *New York Post*, 25 January 1947.

[78] Howard Barnes, "The Theatre: Broadway's Bull Market in Musicals," *New York Herald-Tribune*, 19 January 1947. Reviews in the *Chicago Daily News*, *Cue*, and *New York Post* also mention *Porgy and Bess*.

[79] On the issue of royalties, see Kurt Weill to Langston Hughes, 19 April 1947, WLRC, Series 40 Folder "Hughes, Langston" and Maxim Lieber (Hughes's attorney) to Kurt Weill, 22 April 1947, WLA, Box 48 Folder 44. According to Lieber, Hughes did not object on principle, but felt that since he was already making less, his cut should be less drastic.

[80] Many scholars have explored the ways *Street Scene* is an "opera." See especially Hinton, *Weill's Musical Theater*, 364–87, and Kim H. Kowalke, "Kurt Weill, Modernism, and Popular Culture: *Offentlichkeit als Stil*," *Modernism/Modernity* 2, no. 1 (1995): 36–53.

[81] Tim Carter, *Oklahoma! The Making of an American Musical* (New Haven, CT: Yale University Press, 2007), 174; Tim Carter, *Rodgers and Hammerstein's* Carousel (Oxford, UK: Oxford University Press, 2017), 47.

[82] Larry Stempel, "*Street Scene* and the Problem of Broadway Opera," in *A New Orpheus*, ed. Kowalke, 328.

[83] Weill, "Score for a Play."

Indeed, much of *Street Scene* is indebted to *Porgy and Bess* in its setting on a single city block, its quick transitions from humor to pathos and violence, and its mix of operatic and popular idioms.

Still, the urban setting of *Street Scene* sets it apart from *Porgy and Bess*, *Oklahoma!*, *Carousel*, and their descendants. In the 1930s and early 1940s, many of the "folk"-inspired pieces (Aaron Copland's ballets, Virgil Thomson's film scores, Roy Harris's symphonies) presumed that "folk" identity emerged from rural communities, evoking ideas of America's pioneer past.[84] Although *Porgy and Bess* takes place in a city (Charleston, South Carolina), the common stereotype of African Americans as "primitive" played into contemporary ideas "of African Americans as pastoral antidote to modern life."[85] Gershwin also based his claims of musical authenticity on his trip to Folly Island, further cementing the music as outside of an urban world.[86] But even though Weill had begun his U.S. career writing folk-inspired pieces (*One Man from Tennessee* in 1937, *Railroads on Parade* in 1939 and 1940), he found better success writing for more urban sensibilities (*Knickerbocker Holiday* in 1938, *Lady in the Dark* in 1941), only to see Rodgers and Hammerstein rise to success with the kind of folklore-inspired productions that he could not seem to get off the ground. In this light, the initial failure of *Down in the Valley* to find backing in 1945 must have been particularly frustrating.

However, American folklore underwent several shifts in the 1930s and into the 1940s, as tenement life developed its own mythology. Rice's original 1929 play was part of a genre of literature written by first-generation urbanites who examined life on the city streets in what Michael Denning calls the "ghetto pastoral."[87] These coming-of-age stories set in ethnic or black, urban, working-class neighborhoods painted the city as violent yet innocent, where the pleasures of food and family evoked a simpler time, if not a better one. They balanced depictions of the tragedy and violence of these neighborhoods with the humanity of their residents. In this context, the pastoral mode became a "space for the mutable," in which classes, genders, races, and ethnicities negotiated their places in society, as David Kilroy

---

[84] See Part III of Beth E. Levy, *Frontier Figures: American Music and the Mythology of the American West* (Berkeley: University of California Press, 2012).

[85] Ellen Noonan, *The Strange Career of* Porgy and Bess: *Race, Culture, and America's Most Famous Opera* (Chapel Hill: University of North Carolina Press, 2012), 154–55.

[86] Ray Allen, "An American Folk Opera? Triangulating Folkness, Blackness, and Americanness in Gershwin and Heyward's *Porgy and Bess,*" *Journal of American Folklore* 117, no. 465 (2004): 250–51.

[87] Michael Denning, *The Cultural Front: The Laboring of American Culture in the Twentieth Century* (London: Verso, 1997), 230–54.

observes.[88] This is particularly true of American pastorals, in which conflict is much more prominent than in their more idyllic European counterparts.[89] These stories interwove naturalism and allegory, lowbrow and highbrow, and balanced the depiction of the tragedy and violence of the ghetto with the humanity of its residents. Along with the original *Street Scene*, novels like Michael Gold's *Jews without Money* (1930) and Henry Roth's *Call It Sleep* (1934) established the tragicomic world of the tenement. Indeed, in *Jews without Money*—ostensibly an autobiography—Gold recalls an event that strikingly resembles the climax of *Street Scene*, even though Rice's play predates the novel:

> One summer night (I shall never forget it), a man burst from the tenement into the street, screaming like a madman. A revolver was in his hand. We were sitting on the stoop, calmly eating ice-cream cones. The spectacle of this wild, swarthy Italian in his undershirt, shrieking and waving a pistol, appalled us like a hallucination. He rushed by us, and dived into the cellar. A crowd gathered. A policeman ran up. He hadn't the nerve to follow the Italian into the cellar, but stood uncertainly on the sidewalk, growling: "Get up out of there before I shoot yuh." At last the Italian stumbled out, sobbing like a child. His bronzed, rocky face was grotesquely twisted with grief. He wrung his hands, beat his chest, and clawed at his cheeks until the blood spurted. I have never heard such dreadful animal howls. The ferocious and dangerous agony of a dying wolf. He had just killed his brother in a quarrel over a card came.[90]

The ice cream, the murderer running into the cellar, the hesitation of the police, and the tearful confession of family violence all resemble the events of *Street Scene*.

Although many elements of *Street Scene* do not conform to the traditional idea of the ghetto pastoral, the mode still serves as a useful interpretative frame for the work.[91] Ghetto pastorals became the basis of an American immigrant mythos, making "Ellis Island as sacred as Plymouth Rock" by the

---

[88] David Kilroy, "Kurt Weill on Broadway: The Postwar Years (1945–1950)" (PhD diss., Harvard University, 1992), 172.

[89] Levy, *Frontier Figures*, 156–58.

[90] Michael Gold, *Jews without Money* (1930) (New York: Carroll & Graf, 2004), Kindle edition.

[91] I use pastoral "mode" after Robert Hatten, who writes that the pastoral is not so much a "coherent genre," but rather a "mode of interpretation." Robert S. Hatten, *Interpreting Musical Gestures, Topics, and Tropes: Mozart, Beethoven, Schubert* (Bloomington: Indiana University Press, 2004), 67.

middle of the century.[92] The time between the 1929 *Street Scene* and the 1947 version contributed to this sense of the "mythical"; by 1947, the multi-ethnic working-class neighborhood was rapidly fading due to white flight, accruing a patina of nostalgia as it did so. When these families moved out to the suburbs, a new folklore emerged, as the lives of their parents and grandparents faded into myth.

Perhaps the most "folkloric" moment in *Street Scene* is "Catch Me if You Can," the child's game that opens Act II. Hughes revealed in 1955 that before writing "Catch Me if You Can," he and Weill conducted rudimentary field-work by observing "children at play in the New York streets," after which they "went to a session of the folklore society devoted to children's games." He continued that Weill wrote "a children's game so real that many people thought that it was real" and concluded that this made Weill a "universal folk artist."[93] The number had replaced Henry's "Great Big Sky," showing a multi-ethnic group of children making American pop culture references, again speaking to the idea that assimilation now meant conforming to white middle-class standards rather than celebrating difference, as do the lyrics of "Great Big Sky."

Because both landscape and "the folk" are crucial to the pastoral mode, pastoral topics often juxtapose evocations of the natural world with folk music. The soundscape of *Street Scene* is infused with urban equivalents. Asphalt and railroad tracks become urban rivers and brooks in the overture's evocation of the chugga-chugga rhythm of the subway, and a child's call of "Come in, come in wherever you are" serves as urban birdsong throughout the first act. Rice drew inspiration for the original *Street Scene* from his own tenement upbringing, which would have been infused with children's street games, ethnic folk music, and Tin Pan Alley popular song.[94] As such, the later *Street Scene*'s sound-scape evokes those genres: the child's call grows into "Catch Me if You Can," and Henry's "I Got a Marble and a Star" along with "Moon-Faced, Starry-Eyed," evoke the atmosphere of Rice's childhood. These songs and sounds established the city as its own pastoral space, where the simple folk live in harmony with their surroundings. Within this landscape, the juxtaposition of popular and operatic styles recalls the pastoral clash of

---

[92] Denning, *The Cultural Front*, 231.

[93] Langston Hughes, "Happy New Year Harbors Happy Happenings and Hopes," *Chicago Defender*, 31 December 1955, 7.

[94] David Kilroy also notes the influence of the pastoral paintings of Claude Lorraine in Kilroy, "Kurt Weill on Broadway," 174–75.

classes and genders. Dick and Mae frolic like a satyr and nymph, while Mr. Easter courts his employee Rose Maurrant to the dulcet tones of a Broadway soft-shoe, like a knight seducing a shepherdess with a *pastourelle*. But Sam, Rose, and Mrs. Maurrant dream of a better life in operatic tones, and Mr. Maurrant's stentorian baritone marks him as the villain.

The pastoral elements of *Street Scene* come to the forefront in "Lonely House." Sam sings the introduction ("At night when everything is quiet…") accompanied by a low drone and slow-moving ostinato, bleating taxi-horns, and a gentle variation of the B section of "Somehow I Never Could Believe" in the flutes, what David Kilroy calls the "pastoral 'sound-motif.'"[95] This introduction frames the aria proper as a moment of peaceful repose amid the hustle and bustle of the block. Weill calls the aria a "blues," a genre that, at least for Gershwin, embodied a particularly American kind of folk music, even if critics debated whether or not African American folk idioms could stand for all Americans.[96] Still, given *Street Scene*'s debt to *Porgy and Bess* and Weill's general understanding of African American genres as "universal" (he described jazz as "international folk music" in the 1920s), Weill likely saw the blues as an emblem of America rather than African Americans. The Jewish Sam's music marks him as quintessentially part of the "folk," showing how deeply rooted he is in the landscape of the mythological city, further cementing his status as an integral part of American life.

Weill, Rice, and Hughes took the pastoral topos of *Oklahoma!* and *Carousel* and transported it from an imagined rural past onto a modern city block. Thus, when critics called *Street Scene* a "folk opera," they did not mean just an opera based in folk music, but rather, an opera about "the folk." Moreover, this depiction of "the folk" prominently includes Jews in places of moral (if not actual) authority. Adding *Street Scene* to the historiography of American folk operas reveals the changing nature of the conception of the "folk." But it also reveals who has been left out of that body politic. In 1929, when Rose departs the neighborhood, her future is precarious. But in 1947, she could be in the audience, having moved to the suburbs to start a better life. Now, with her newfound prosperity, she would be able to enjoy a Broadway show mythologizing her childhood, invoking a privilege that would not have been available to Henry.

---

[95] Kilroy, "Kurt Weill on Broadway," 167.
[96] See Allen, "An American Opera?," and Craft, "Becoming American Onstage," 65–67.

## From *Ulysses Africanus* to *Lost in the Stars*

Although Weill and Anderson were close friends, until the late 1940s they had only collaborated on one major project. Their second large-scale collaboration came in 1949, when they reworked material they had written in 1939 for a project called *Ulysses Africanus* into *Lost in the Stars*, an adaptation of Alan Paton's novel *Cry, the Beloved Country* (1948). Anderson had drafted the libretto and Weill had drafted (but not orchestrated) most of the score of *Ulysses Africanus* before both moved on.[97] Given that the relationship between African Americans and Jews in the 1930s was characterized by a good deal of hope and good will, but also resentment and misunderstanding, the collapse of the project likely helped Weill in the long run, as it gave him time to develop a more nuanced understanding about U.S. race relations. *Ulysses Africanus* was one of several nascent or incomplete race-related projects Weill contemplated in the late 1930s and early 1940s. Among his lists of project ideas there are suggestions for plays with racial themes, including one on *Uncle Tom's Cabin*, and he was briefly interested in an all-African-American production of *The Threepenny Opera* in 1942, but ultimately killed the project because he would not have control of the score.[98] When *Lost in the Stars* opened on 30 October 1949, it represented a culmination of Weill's efforts to address racial discrimination.

The U.S. Jewish interest in racial justice blossomed in 1915, when Leo Frank, a Jew from Marietta, Georgia, was convicted of raping and murdering thirteen-year-old Mary Phagan. During the trial, a wave of anti-Semitism town swept over the state, and when governor John Slaton commuted Frank's sentence to life in prison, a mob kidnapped Frank and lynched him.[99] After that, the two most prominent Jewish populations in the United States—those with either Eastern European or German heritage—stepped up efforts to speak out against racial injustice, albeit in different ways. Eastern European Jews were a mostly Orthodox community whose firsthand experience with violent pogroms engendered a sense that African Americans in the United

---

[97] The piano-vocal score is in WLA, Box 32 Folder 442. Two librettos survive, a handwritten copy and a typescript. The former is in MAC, Series "Works" Folder "Ulysses Africanus; a musical play; Tms with A title page," and the latter is in MAC, Series "Works" Folder "Ulysses Africanus [play] Composite A and Tccms."

[98] KWH, 390. On the African American *Threepenny Opera*, see the correspondence between Weill and Clarence Muse in WLA, Box 47 Folder 11.

[99] For a detailed examination of the effects of the case, see Jeffrey Paul Melnick, *Black–Jewish Relations on Trial: Leo Frank and Jim Conley in the New South* (Jackson: University of Mississippi Press, 2000). Decades later, Frank was officially pardoned.

States held a position analogous to Jews in Europe.[100] Ben Hecht referred to efforts to illegally smuggle Jewish refugees into Palestine in the early 1940s as an "underground railway."[101] However, Frank, like many German Jews, was an assimilated, native-born U.S. citizen by several generations. After his death, German Jews sensed that their position in society was not so secure, and began to champion African American causes in order to work toward broader racial acceptance, even if they did not directly identify with African Americans. The 1931 case of the Scottsboro Boys, in which two white girls wrongfully accused nine African American teenagers of rape in Alabama, especially captured German-Jewish attention. The German-Jewish *Opinion* took pride in the fact that the lead attorney for the defense was Jewish, writing that "both as a member of such a group and as an inheritor of his own tradition, it is inevitable that the Jew should take active and leading parts in all such struggles."[102]

However, the Frank affair also revealed deep divisions between Jews and African Americans. Many African Americans were frustrated by the fact that the decades of lynching received little coverage, but the country exploded over the lynching of a Jew. "It seems that after all," opined the editor of the *Chicago Broad-Ax*, "it all depends upon whose ox is gored."[103] The prominence of Jewish blackface performers further complicated matters. The complex racial implications of blackface have been well explored in the literature, especially the idea that it "passed immigrants into Americans by differentiating them from the black Americans through whom they spoke," to quote Michael Rogin.[104] Even when they did not paint their faces, the prominence of Jewish songwriters writing in traditionally black genres led to charges of cultural theft. When *Porgy and Bess* premiered, choir director Hall Johnson accused the authors of "slumming in a very smudgy coat of burnt cork."[105]

Weill did not fit neatly into either U.S. Jewish community. Like the U.S. Jews with German ties, he had been raised in a middle-class conservative

---

[100] Hasia Diner, *In the Almost Promised Land: American Jews and Blacks, 1915–1935* (Westport, CT: Greenwood, 1977), 76–77.

[101] Eisler, " 'This Theatre Is a Battlefield,' " 161.

[102] Quoted in Diner, *In the Almost Promised Land*, 114.

[103] Quoted in Eugene Levy, " 'Is the Jew a White Man?' Press Reaction to the Leo Frank Case," in *Strangers & Neighbors: Relations Between Blacks & Jews in the United States*, ed. Maurianne Adams and John Bracey (Amherst, MA: University of Massachusetts Press, 1999), 264.

[104] Rogin, *Blackface, White Noise*, 47. See also chapter 2 of Most, *Making Americans*, and chapter 2 of Kirle, *Unfinished Business*.

[105] Quoted in Ray Allen and George P. Cunningham, "Cultural Uplift and Double-Consciousness: African American Responses to the 1935 Opera *Porgy and Bess*," *Musical Quarterly* 88 (2005): 358.

**Figure 6.2**  Advertisement for the "Entartete Musik" exhibition, Dusseldorf, 1938. Alamy.

household, but he had stopped practicing almost entirely.[106] Still, like communities with Eastern European roots, he had come to the United States to escape horrific violence. He also had reason to see a kinship between African Americans and Jews; the cover of the guide to the *Entartete Musik* ("Degenerate Music") exhibition in 1938 featured a black (or possibly blackface) man with a yellow Jewish star on his lapel (Figure 6.2). These

---

[106] Kowalke et al., "*The Eternal Road* and Kurt Weill's German, Jewish, and American Identity," 87–89.

ideas inflected Nazi reception of his music; an unnamed reviewer of the
*Nazionalsozialistische Monatshefte* wrote of *Mahagonny*:

> When Weill deliberately puts Negro rhythms into German art music—
> with serious intentions, no less—he only puts into practice what the Jew
> Bernhard Sekles, as the director of the Conservatory in Frankfurt am Main,
> more or less announced with the introduction of a class for Jazz music: that
> a transfusion of Negro blood could do us no harm. So, the people that pro-
> duced Bach, Mozart, Beethoven, and Wagner need to be freshened up with
> Negro blood. Negro blood, which just might be related to Sekles and his
> comrades of the Semitic race![107]

In the United States, Weill found similar rhetoric had been applied to
African Americans. While doing research for *Ulysses Africanus*, he came
across Newman I. White's *American Negro Folksongs* (1928), which stressed
that African American music-making "originated in an imitation frustrated
by imperfect comprehension and memory, and by a fundamentally different idea of music. One of the means by which new Negro folk-songs are
being created to-day [ . . . ] is by variational imitation of the popular songs
of the white man."[108] White's notion that African American culture was essentially derivative of white culture echoes Wagner's claims about Jewish
composition.

These pressures and ideals inform both *Ulysses Africanus* and *Lost in the
Stars*. *Ulysses Africanus* was adapted from Harry Stillwell Edwards' 1920
epistolary novela *Eneas Africanus*. The story begins with a plea from the
Southern planter Major Tommey for news of his former slave Eneas, to
whom he entrusted the family silver to keep it safe from the Union army.[109]
The rest consists of letters to Major Tommey relating Eneas's journey, and
ends with the latter's triumphant return home. The novel is full of contemporary stereotypes; Eneas is portrayed as a skilled gambler but otherwise
dimwitted, and while his white hosts are kind, they are also paternalistic.

---

[107] Quoted in Jürgen Schebera, "Zur Wirkungs Geschichte bis 1933," in *Brecht/Weill Mahagonny*,
ed. Fritz Hennenberg and Jan Knopf (Frankfurt am Main: Suhrkamp, 2006), 238. Translation assistance from Francesca Kuehlers.

[108] Newman I. White, *American Negro Folksongs* (Cambridge, MA: Harvard University Press,
1928), 25. Weill's notes on minstrelsy for *Ulysses Africanus* are in WLA, Box 68 Folder 18.

[109] For a detailed account of *Ulysses Africanus*, see Naomi Graber, "Colliding Diasporas: Kurt
Weill's *Ulysses Africanus* and Black–Jewish Relations During the Great Depression," *Musical
Quarterly* 99, no. 3–4 (2017): 321–55.

Anderson hoped to revise the story to show the high moral character of African Americans, and to enlist Paul Robeson as the star. As he wrote to Robeson, his version would follow the intellectual growth of a slave who "has never been obliged or encouraged to make an ethical decision for himself," who must decide whether to return the silver. At first, the former slave refuses, "justifying his conduct by reflection on the years of labor for which he was never paid." But he discovers the family in poverty and restores the silver, "having discovered that freedom brings with it responsibilities as a person which he never had to worry about before." He also promised romance and humor, and assured Robeson that "it won't include propaganda of one kind or another," but rather, "it is the story of a man in a chaotic world in search of his own manhood and his own rules of conduct."[110] Robeson's wife and manager Eslanda "Essie" Robeson turned down the part on her husband's behalf, writing, "The general public's idea of a Negro is an Uncle Tom, an Aunt Jemima, Ol' Mammy, and Jack Johnson" (the famous boxer) but that these stereotypes "don't exist any more except in the sentimental minds of credulous people" and that she did not want "to prolong their non-existent lives!!!"[111]

After that setback, Anderson and Weill retooled the show for tap-dancer Bill "Bojangles" Robinson. In this version, transmitted in the extant libretto and music, the protagonist (renamed Ulysses) is still entrusted with the silver and sent away from the family home. But Ulysses runs out of money and is forced to perform in a minstrel show. After he uses the silver to buy out the troupe, he turns the second-rate operation into a first-rate show. When he learns his former masters are in desperate straits, he reclaims the silver and returns home. However, Robinson's commitments to *Hot Mikado* prevented him from starting work on *Ulysses Africanus*, and both Weill and Anderson moved on in early 1940.

Eslanda Robeson's reference to *Uncle Tom's Cabin* reveals one of the ways Weill misjudged U.S. race relations. Weill may have been attracted to the story of *Ulysses Africanus* because of its resemblance to Harriet Beecher Stowe's *Uncle Tom's Cabin* (1852), which famously depicts the kind master/loyal slave relationship. The novel enjoyed widespread popularity in German translation, where it was received as "a universal tale of oppression and deliverance,"

---

[110] Lawrence G. Avery, ed., *Dramatist in America: Letters of Maxwell Anderson, 1912–1958* (Chapel Hill: University of North Carolina Press, 1977), 194.
[111] Eslanda Goode Robeson to Anderson, 29 March 1939, MAC, Series "Misc" Folder "Brandt and Brandt Dramatic Dept."

according to Heike Paul.[112] Predisposed to see *Uncle Tom's Cabin* as a story exemplifying universal suffering, Weill may have seen elements of his own life in *Ulysses Africanus*, which adds the element of a man forced to flee his home, encountering obstacles along the way. The story in the draft of *Ulysses Africanus* includes a number of elements that resemble Weill's experience of exile, including a flight from home with little warning, disbelief that the war was going to last very long, and series of trials and tribulations that end with the protagonist revolutionizing a popular form of musical theatre. But that same reliance on the framework of *Uncle Tom's Cabin* would likely have offended the African American community, who criticized Stowe's book for perpetrating stereotypes of the loyal, docile slave.

Weill and Anderson first tried use the material from *Ulysses Africanus* during Anderson's brief tenure with *Street Scene*—Henry would have sung "Lost in the Stars" to Sam.[113] In summer 1947, Weill considered a show about an interstellar journey to "a place which is really earth again, but a different kind of earth, different not in appearance or in more technical perfection, but in spirit and emotion."[114] Anderson hoped to add a racial element, "with a negro singing 'Lost in the Stars' at the opening as he's washing dishes—and a group of youngsters living there who don't know what do to with their lives. The space ship is just one of the fantastic projects that float through the room."[115] *Cry, The Beloved Country* came into the picture in 1948, when Hammerstein's wife lent Anderson her pre-publication copy of the novel.[116] Anderson reported that he "immediately called Kurt Weill and told him I thought I had found the story we'd been searching for during the last ten years."[117] Indeed, Anderson's adaptation of *Cry, the Beloved Country* highlights the theme of men in "in a chaotic world" searching for their own "rules of conduct," as he had written to Robeson nearly a decade before. According to Anderson, another key figure in the early days of the

[112] Heike Paul, "Cultural Mobility Between Boston and Berlin: How Germans Have Read and Reread Narratives of American Slavery," in *Cultural Mobility: A Manifesto*, ed. Stephen Greenblatt (Cambridge, UK: Cambridge University Press, 2010), 128.

[113] Unless otherwise noted, my account of the genesis of *Lost in the Stars* comes from Juchem, *Kurt Weill und Maxwell Anderson*, 157–215.

[114] Kurt Weill to Maxwell Anderson, 10 July 1947, MAC, Box "Misc." Folder "Weill, Kurt."

[115] Maxwell Anderson to Kurt Weill, n.d., WLA, Box 48 Folder 19.

[116] Harry Gilroy, "Written in the Stars: Composer Kurt Weill and Playwright Maxwell Anderson Air Views on Racial Harmony in Latest Collaboration," *NYT*, 30 October 1949, available at https://www.kwf.org/pages/wt-written-in-the-stars.html.

[117] Maxwell Anderson, "Assembling the Parts for a Musical Play," *New York Herald Tribune*, 30 October 1949, available in the *Lost in the Stars* production files, WLRC.

project was Dr. Everett Clinchy, a Presbyterian minister and president of the National Conference of Christians and Jews (NCCJ). Just before reading *Cry, the Beloved Country*, Anderson found himself on a cruise ship with the Hammersteins and the Clinchys discussing how theatre could improve race relations. When he accepted an award for *Lost in the Stars* from the NCCJ in 1950, Anderson said that "*Lost in the Stars* would probably not be on Broadway," without those conversations with Clinchy.[118] Although Anderson probably embellished Clinchy's influence for his audience, the recollection hints at the larger universalizing ambitions of the show, discussed in detail later.

After Weill finished work on *Love Life* (1948) and Anderson on *Anne of a Thousand Days* (1948), they began adapting *Cry, the Beloved Country*. By March of 1949, they had a complete draft of the libretto and music, which incorporated a number of songs from *Ulysses Africanus*, including "Lost in the Stars," "Trouble Man," and "Little Grey House."[119] They retitled the piece *Lost in the Stars*. The libretto follows the general outline of the novel, though many details are left out.[120] Stephen Kumalo, a black Anglican reverend in the village of Ndotsheni, goes to Johannesburg in search of his errant son Absalom, where he learns that Absalom killed a white man named Arthur Jarvis. Arthur's father James lives near Ndotsheni, and maintains racist attitudes, which had driven a wedge between him and his son. The other two individuals involved in the crime lie about their participation, but Absalom tells the truth, and receives the death penalty. A heartbroken Stephen agrees to perform a marriage ceremony for Absalom and his pregnant girlfriend Irina before returning to Ndotsheni. His faith shaken, Stephen tries to resign from his pastoral duties, but the congregation begs him to stay. As Stephen waits for his son's execution, the elder Mr. Jarvis offers to keep up the church if Stephen will stay on as pastor, and reveals that his son's ideals, Absalom's courage, and Stephen's decency has him reconsidering his racist beliefs. The curtain falls on the two men sitting together as the clock strikes the

---

[118] Avery, *Dramatist in America*, 446.

[119] Kurt Weill to Alan Paton, 17 March 1949, WLRC, Series 40 Folder "Paton, Alan." Weill and Anderson also hoped to incorporate two more songs from *Ulysses Africanus* into *Lost in the Stars*: "Little Tin God" and "Discernable Today." Both songs are present in Maxwell Anderson's handwritten version of the libretto, available in the WLRC, Series 20 Box L7 Folder 1948–1949.

[120] Five versions of the libretto survive. In order of creation, Anderson's handwritten draft is the earliest (see note 119), followed by the version in the WLA, Box 15 Folder 261 (copy in the WLRC, Series 20 Box L7 Folder 1949a), then the version in WLRC, Series 20 Box L7 Folder 1949b, then WLRC, Series 20 Box L7 Folder 1949c. The final draft is transmitted in WLA, Box 15 Folder 260, with a copy in WLRC, Series 20 Box L7 Folder 1949, although this copy was likely used on tour given that some of the names of the original cast are crossed out and replaced.

fateful hour, indicating that Absalom has been executed. This final scene is not in the original novel, which ends with Stephen alone, coming to terms with his own mortality.

The PPC searched for funding, but quickly ran into trouble. Rodgers and Hammerstein, hard at work on *South Pacific*, declined to finance the show. Weill also hoped to enlist financial help from producer Billy Rose, who had worked with him on the Jewish pageants and who had also produced *Carmen Jones*. Rose thought the project was "a distinguished job and a fine thing for the theatre," but nevertheless turned it down because "its commercial chances are only so-so."[121] In the end, the PPC produced the show without outside assistance, and Weill and Anderson even invested their own money.[122] In April, Weill sought out Rouben Mamoulian to direct the project, and he agreed.[123] The director played a large role in shaping the production, including casting, sets, business arrangements, and subsequent drafts of the script. For casting, the team looked to the group of African American actors and singers who had been part of other similar "crossovers" between the Broadway and operatic worlds. Mamoulian suggested Todd Duncan, the original Porgy, for the role of Kumalo. Inez Matthews, who had played Theresa I in Virgil Thomson's *Four Saints in Three Acts* and the lead in *Carmen Jones*, was cast as Irina, and Sheila Guyse of *Finian's Rainbow* earned the role of the nightclub singer Linda. Julliard-trained Frank Roane played the Leader of the choral ensemble, Julian Mayfield played Absalom, and Leslie Banks played James Jarvis.

Because of the shortage of funds, *Lost in the Stars* had no out-of-town try-outs, only previews in New York.[124] The production, billed as a "musical tragedy," opened on 30 October 1949 to mixed reviews from white critics, who almost universally agreed that Anderson's adaptation lacked the power of Paton's novel. *New York Times*' Brooks Atkinson wrote that the libretto was "too blunt and ponderous in treatment," although Weill's score elevated the show to "the high plane of spiritual existence."[125] Critics were mixed on whether the material worked on Broadway. In his review of the 1949–1950

[121] Billy Rose to Kurt Weill, 12 October 1949, WLA, Box 49 Folder 62.

[122] Foster Hirsch, *Kurt Weill on Stage: From Berlin to Broadway* (New York: Alfred A. Knopf, 2002), 314.

[123] Anderson, "Assembling the Parts for a Musical Play." Elia Kazan and Agnes de Mille were also considered.

[124] Hirsch, *Kurt Weill on Stage*, 315.

[125] Brooks Atkinson, "*Lost in the Stars*: Musical Tragedy Is Put Together from Paton Novel about South Africa," *NYT*, 6 November 1949. When no page number is given, clipping available in the *Lost in the Stars* production file at the WLRC.

season, the conservative George Jean Nathan wrote that the actors had been "Mamoulianed from Zulus to Oklahomans (with the Broadway exclamation point)," and leveled a racially tinged critique at Todd Duncan, calling his performance one of "smirking smugness and oily benignity," evoking images of "uppity" African Americans.[126] Other critics praised Weill and Anderson for putting a serious subject on a Broadway stage. Richard L. Coe of the liberal-leaning *Washington Post* commended *Lost in the Stars* for speaking "the language of our people" with a score of "immensely sophisticated simplicity to evoke the spirit of the compassionate story."[127]

Of the major African American periodicals, only the *Chicago Defender* paid much attention to *Lost in the Stars*. Three different reviews appeared in that paper: Lillian Scott reviewed the New York production, Robert Elliot reviewed the Chicago tour, and Walter White discussed the piece in the context of depictions of black life on stage and screen. Both Scott and Elliot agreed that Anderson's adaptation paled in comparison to Paton's novel; Scott wrote that "the book was a beautiful experience, but to this reporter, at least, the dramatic production was something else again," and Elliot wrote, "In Anderson's hands, Paton's simplicity often becomes dull clumsiness."[128] Both White and Elliot approved of the sensitive handling of racial issues; White called it "one of the most poignant dramas of modern times."[129] But Scott disagreed, writing, "By weaving in all the scenes devoted to the sordid life of natives in Johannesburg, no matter how true, and by distorting several events, *Lost in the Stars* can hardly help reinforcing the bitterness of whites toward Negros." Other African American periodicals only mentioned *Lost in the Stars* to tout the wealth of black talent in the cast.[130]

*Lost in the Stars* closed on 1 July 1950 after 281 performances, about three months after Weill died. The show then toured in late 1950, including a stop in Chicago, where racial tensions were particularly high. There, Duncan wrote an emotional letter to Anderson that is uncharacteristically riven with typos,

[126] George Jean Nathan, *The Theatre Book of the Year 1949–1950: A Record and Interpretation* (New York: Alfred A. Knopf, 1950), clip available in *Lost in the Stars* production files, WLRC.

[127] Richard Coe, "*Lost in the Stars* Talks the Language of the United States," *Washington Post*, 5 February 1950, L1.

[128] Lillian Scott, "*Lost in the Stars* Proves Novel Is a Novel, Critic Says," *Chicago Defender*, 12 November 1950, 26; Robert Elliot, "*Lost in the Stars* a Little Earthbound," *Chicago Defender*, 11 November 1950, 21.

[129] Walter White, "Columnist Walter White Sees Brighter Side of Negro Life," *Chicago Defender*, 7 January 1950, 7.

[130] For example, see "Duncan's Role Lauded in *Lost in the Stars*," *Baltimore Afro-American*, 11 May 1949, 21, and "*Lost in the Stars Is* Not Lost on Box Office in NY," *Pittsburgh Courier*, 7 January 1950, 18.

revealing how deeply he cared about the show. He believed that the "recent bombing of Negro homes in White neighborhoods" and "the race issues in the coming elections" contributed to the negative reviews: "I've concluded that your play is too powerful, too tmue [*sic*; probably "true"], too much at home here in Chicago *now* and it wont [*sic*] go over here anymore than it would in Johannesburg or Biloxi Mississippi."[131] When the tour closed in December, he wrote to Anderson, "Human beings haven't learned their lesson."[132]

## Cry, the Lost Tribe

Weill's grudge against Rodgers and Hammerstein may have contributed to his initial attraction to *Cry, the Beloved Country*. Rodgers and Hammerstein were turning James A. Michener's 1947 Pulitzer Prize–winning *Tales of the South Pacific* into a musical, and Weill may have seen *Lost in the Stars*, also based on recent book addressing issues of racial strife, as another chance to respond. He certainly saw a connection between the two shows. After spending an April 1949 evening playing the score of *Lost in the Stars* at Hammerstein's house in an effort to raise money for the show, Weill wrote to Alan Jay Lerner that Rodgers obviously "suffers from a terrible inferiority complex" and "I almost began feeling sorry for him, and that 3 days after the opening of *South Pacific!*"[133] But *Lost in the Stars* also reveals the evolution of Weill's conception of his place in the complex network of race in the United States. During and after the war, many Jewish communities strengthened their ties to other religious groups in the United States, and a new "Judeo-Christian" identity began to emerge. This newly emergent fellow-feeling provided Weill another opportunity to explore the ideals of universal brotherhood in his music.

During the late 1930s and into the 1940s, the increasingly desperate plight of the Jews in Europe and the revelations of the Holocaust inspired a religiously based anti-fascist movement rooted in highlighting similarities between Christian and Jewish faiths.[134] Thinkers like the Catholic Jacques Mauritain and the Jewish Louis Finkelstein began to use the term "Judeo-Christian" to describe this movement, and draw contrasts between themselves and the self-styled Christian of figures like Coughlin, who employed

---

[131] Todd Duncan to Maxwell Anderson, 2 November 1950, MAC, Series "Misc." Folder "DR–DV."
[132] Todd Duncan to Maxwell Anderson, 9 December 1950, MAC, Series "Misc." Folder "DR–DV."
[133] Quoted in Juchem, *Kurt Weill und Maxwell Anderson*, 181.
[134] Healan, *Imagining Judeo-Christian America*, 99–102, 120.

racist rhetoric.[135] As the 1940s went on, this formulation served a variety of causes, oftentimes at cross-purposes from one another; for some, Judeo-Christian identity signaled the superiority of Western religion and an alliance against secularism, while others used Judeo-Christian identity to represent a broader religious pluralism that could include all beliefs, as well as nonbelief (a formulation more popular among Jews).[136] It also inspired further determination in some corners of the Jewish community to fight against both racial and religious discrimination of all kinds, which they framed as related problems.[137] In terms of anti-racist pursuits, it added a religious component to the Jewish push for racial justice of the previous decade. Much of this was through the NCCJ, which was organized in 1928, but increased its activities as the situation in Europe got worse. In 1942, it organized a statement, signed by clergy of Catholic, Protestant, and Jewish congregations, that included the declaration:

> We reject theories of race which affirm the essential superiority of one racial strain over another. We acknowledge every man as our brother. We respect and champion his inalienable rights and are determined to do all in our power to promote man's temporal and spiritual welfare as necessary consequences of our duty to God.[138]

This emerging idea of a "Judeo-Christian" identity continued to inflect Jewish identity after the war, as Judaism joined Catholicism and Protestantism as one of the exemplars of healthy religious life in the United States.[139]

The desire for the kind of hybridity offered by a "Judeo-Christian" identity is clear in the publicity for *Lost in the Stars*. In an interview with Harry Gilroy in the *New York Times*, Weill highlighted the project's "biblical tone that we hope people will like."[140] In turn, many critics remarked on the "biblical" tone of *Cry, the Beloved Country*, and commented on whether Anderson's adaptation was successful. For example, the anonymous reviewer of the *New York Post* wrote that capturing the "biblical loveliness" of the original novel "was

---

[135] Silk, "Notes on the Judeo-Christian Tradition in America," 66–67, 69; Anita Norich, *Discovering Exile: Yiddish and Jewish American Culture during the Holocaust* (Stanford: Stanford University Press, 2007), 78–95.

[136] Healan, *Imagining Judeo-Christian America*, 7ff, 118–19.

[137] Sarna, *American Judaism*, 266–71.

[138] Quoted in Lillian Greenwald, "Inter-Group Relations," *American Jewish Year Book* 44 (1942–1943): 164.

[139] Sarna, *American Judaism*, 267.

[140] Gilroy, "Written in the Stars."

a task of heroic proportions," even if the adaptation sometimes fell flat.[141] Still, the creative team had different ideas regarding how this biblical tone functioned. For Anderson, the story was about transferring spiritual feelings from organized religion to a broader love of humanity. He envisioned an "extraordinarily moving tale of lost men clinging to odds and ends of faith in the darkness of our modern earth. For the breaking of the tribe is only a symbol of the breaking of all tribes and all the old ways and beliefs."[142] Mamoulian, for his part, used the biblical tone of the story to strengthen the sense of tragedy. He urged Anderson and Weill to bring out "the cry of a loving, bleeding heart, biblical in nature," in Stephen's soliloquy.[143] For Weill, the idea of biblical overtones helped to reinforce the idea of universal brotherhood, which included both African Americans and Jews. He framed the show not just as a tale of South Africa, but as a larger story about the dangers of racism, one that showed that "we're all here on this same little planet, floating along in the universe, and we're all lost in the stars. Do you see the perspective it gives on relations between races, between majority and minority groups, between one man and another all over the globe?"[144]

For a story with universal implications, Weill tried to write universal music. Even though Weill listened to some Zulu music (provided by Paton), he told the *Times*, "I wasn't trying to reproduce the native music of Africa," but rather, "get at the heart of the public, and my public wouldn't feel anything if I gave them African chimes." Indeed, the score is rife with pentatonicism and reed timbres, reminiscent of the scores for the emerging "biblical epic" genre of films, and possibly reflecting the "oriental" and "colorful" atmosphere that Weill perceived in Palestine. In addition, Weill returned to styles he had developed for *The Eternal Road*. Anderson wrote to Paton that he hoped to keep "as much as possible of the dialogue and the story structure" to preserve the "powerful and delicate effect" of the novel, which "would only be possible if a chorus—a sort of Greek chorus—were used to tie together the great number of scenes, and to comment on the action as you comment in the philosophic and descriptive passages."[145] The idea of a chorus likely came from Weill, who had employed such choruses in many of his works on both sides of the Atlantic, including *The Eternal Road*. The piece was on his

[141] "The Anderson Version of Alan Paton Novel," *New York Post*, n.d.
[142] Maxwell Anderson to Alan Paton, 15 March 1948, MAC, Series "Correspondence" Folder "P–Q."
[143] Rouben Mamoulian, "Notes on *Lost in the Stars*," WLRC, Series 20 Box L7 Folder 1949n.
[144] Gilroy, "Written in the Stars."
[145] Avery, *Dramatist in America*, 351.

**Example 6.4** *Lost in the Stars,* "The Wild Justice."

mind during the 1940s, as he had adapted large passages of it for the pageants *Fun to Be Free* (1941), *We Will Never Die,* and *A Flag Is Born.* Like *The Eternal Road, Lost in the Stars* is told as a set of short scenes, often connected by choral interludes that comment and reflect on the story. In many ways, the Leader in *Lost in the Stars* fulfills the same dramatic role as the Rabbi in *The Eternal Road,* who both sets the scene and elucidates the moral messages of the story.

Weill also directly adapted passages of *The Eternal Road* for *Lost in the Stars.* The motive that opens "The Prophets" (Example 6.2a)—likely inspired by Jewish cantillation of the book of *Eicha*/Lamentations—appears in two crucial places in *Lost in the Stars.* The opening of the second act, "The Wild Justice," poses questions about the nature of the law, then describes a cycle of murder and revenge, culminating in the death of a prince. A truncated instrumental version of the motive opens the piece, and then lurks in the accompaniment until the Leader sings of the final murder, which Weill set to a whole-tone version of the tune (Example 6.4), retaining the Phrygian inflection by raising the final pitch a half step. The motive reappears in the accompaniment of "O Tixo, Tixo Help Me," as Stephen describes the murder of Arthur Jarvis (Example 6.5).[146] The entire soliloquy is also permeated with long, descending scales in the accompaniment, linking it to "The Wild Justice."

These three moments—"The Prophets," "The Wild Justice," and "O Tixo, Tixo Help Me"—share the idea of lament for an unjust and untenable society. In terms of Western music, descending scales have long been signaled

---

[146] The phrase also appears briefly in *Love Life* in Sam's "This Is the Life," in which he laments the absence of his family. Examples are drawn from Kurt Weill and Maxwell Anderson, *Lost in the Stars* (New York: Chappell, 1950).

Example 6.5  *Lost in the Stars,* "O Tixo, Tixo Help Me."

lament, a connection Weill made in his motet *Recordare,* a Latin setting of the Lamentations from 1923, which is permeated by a Phrygian descent on the word "recordare." In *The Eternal Road,* Weill fuses Jewish and European traditions of lament, which he then transfers to *Lost in the Stars,* connecting all three through the book of *Eicha*/Lamentations. Although audiences would not likely register the specific connections, the modal melodies with their cantillation-like contours combine in *Lost in the Stars* to evoke a hazy sense of the religious, but that religion is rarely clearly defined for more than a moment. This speaks to the emerging idea of "Judeo-Christian" values. Weill's hope that the work would speak to a shared biblical heritage paid off in at least one instance; on 26 February, during National Brotherhood week, the NCCJ presented an abridged version of the piece on CBS radio stations.[147] The broadcast emphasized the tale's universal applicability, as the narrator reminded audiences, "The story of *Lost in the Stars* takes place in South Africa, but it could happen anywhere. . . . It could happen in your town."

The emphasis on the "universal" at the expense of specific racial politics cut both ways. With some notable exceptions (including Brooks Atkinson),

[147] Transcript in MAC, Folder "Lost in the Stars—Excerpts."

few reviewers directly mention the racial politics of the story, instead writing in terms of suffering and compassion. In the wake of the racial atrocities of World War II, the United States faced uncomfortable questions about domestic racial politics, including treatment of African Americans. But in the mainstream culture, these issues were often pushed aside in favor of notions of a "universal brotherhood" that, nevertheless, forced African Americans to the margins.[148] *Street Scene* is emblematic; although Rice and Weill added the African American janitor Henry, and he participates in the "Ice Cream" sextet, the character is marginal, and does not reflect the realities of the African American experience.

Indeed, the efforts to make the story "universal" often obscure the particularities of black experiences. Anderson focused on the events of *Cry, The Beloved Country* which emphasize that knowledge and wisdom come from suffering—a common theme in his plays—and less on issues of race relations. An episode in Scene 9, set in Arthur Jarvis's study, has his father James reading his late son's thoughts about equality, and responding to them with white supremacist remarks, but this was cut. *Cry, the Beloved Country* also contains long passages describing the injustice of the South African mining industry, which Weill and Anderson considered incorporating into *Lost in the Stars* in the form of the song "Gold," a dance number which Absalom and his friends sing just before the murder, elucidating their motives. In the end, this shift disturbed Paton, who particularly disapproved of the ways Anderson and Weill glossed over some of the issues of racism and their disregard for the strength of Stephen's Christian faith. Paton wrote that the show "didn't have a big black audience" because "blacks had so many problems that they didn't relate to Africa."[149]

Weill was not done with race relations after *Lost in the Stars*. Almost immediately, he began work with Anderson on a musical version of Mark Twain's *Adventures of Huckleberry Finn*, which at various points was called *Raft on the River*, *Huck and Jim*, and *River Shanty*. Anderson drafted one complete libretto and several scenes, and Weill completed a few songs before his death in April 1950.[150] As in *Lost in the Stars*, Anderson considered framing the story with a narrator (at one point, Huck himself), but the music hearkens back to the folksy sounds of *Down in the Valley*. Their version of the

[148] Judith E. Smith, *Visions of Belonging: Family Stories, Popular Culture, and Postwar Democracy, 1940–1960* (New York: Columbia University Press, 2004), Chapter 6.

[149] Quoted in Hirsch, *Kurt Weill on Stage*, 316.

[150] The materials are in MAC, Series "Works" under "Huck and Jim."

story included a romance between Huck and Mary Jane Wilks, which provided opportunities for romantic numbers that would be marketable as sheet music, but Weill died before setting the lyrics. The overall impression is of a much lighter show than *Lost in the Stars*, but one that still engages with the history of racism in America.

Both *Street Scene* and *Lost in the Stars* (along with *Love Life*) show a composer still willing to push boundaries, both theatrical and cultural. They also reveal Weill's abiding commitment to socially conscious musical theatre. Whether integrating Jews into the body politic, or attempting to inspire compassion between races, Weill's late works demonstrate that the *enfant terrible* of Weimar Germany never vanished entirely. Rather, the exigencies of World War II and his status as a foreigner encouraged him to speak to the more conservative ideals of the early 1940s. Once Weill attained citizenship, he returned to more controversial issues. Weill himself felt that was the common thread of his multifaceted career. During an intermission feature for a broadcast from the Metropolitan Opera in 1949, Boris Goldovksy asked the composer, "What brings out the Weill in Weill?" Weill responded: "Looking back on many of my compositions, I find that I seem to have a very strong reaction in the awareness of the suffering of underprivileged people—of the oppressed, the persecuted." He continued, "When the music involves human suffering, it is, for better or worse, pure Weill."[151]

---

[151] "Opera News on the Air," 10 December 1949, transcript available online at https://www.kwf.org/pages/wt-opera-news-on-the-air-1949.html.

# Conclusion

For Weill, "America" represented both possibilities and challenges. Artistically, it was a prism through which to refract European culture, the source of a potential transnational musical language, a technological marvel, an Arcadian frontier, a welcoming homeland, and a nation in danger of being torn apart by racial and ethnic strife. America also presented a set of more concrete difficulties. Translating his German style for U.S. audiences proved harder than he anticipated; learning how to write musicals that were dramatically coherent while still including songs that could be published as hits took until "September Song" in 1938, three years after his arrival. Success and recognition in Hollywood eluded the composer, even though as late as 1946 he still expressed hope of composing an original opera for film.[1] The shifting ground of U.S. theatre also caught Weill off-guard. Just after his first hit, *Lady in the Dark* (1941), Rodgers and Hammerstein's *Oklahoma!* redefined Broadway for years to come. Weill spent the rest of his career responding to Rodgers and Hammerstein's innovations.

By the end of the war, America had become something more to Weill. In the spring of 1947, he took his one and only trip outside of the United States after his initial arrival: a European tour and a stay in Palestine to visit his parents and brother. When he returned in June, he wrote to Maxwell Anderson, "With all its faults (and partly because of them), this is still the most decent place to live in," and "to me, Americanism is (or ought to be) the most advanced attempt to fill the gap between the individual and the technical progress."[2] In the context of Weill's earliest experiments with *Amerikanismus*, this letter is striking. The idea that "Americanism" was an attempt to balance "individual" and "technical" progress contradicts fears that haunted the Weimar Republic, when many feared that American capitalism, mass culture, and overmechanization of culture would obliterate the individual. Parts of Weill's

---

[1] Kurt Weill, "Music in the Movies," *Harper's Bazaar* 80, no. 9 (September 1946), available at https://www.kwf.org/pages/wt-music-in-the-movies.html.
[2] Kurt Weill to Maxwell Anderson, 22 June 1947, MAC, Series "Misc." Folder "Weill, Kurt."

*Kurt Weill's America*. Naomi Graber, Oxford University Press (2021). © Oxford University Press.
DOI: 10.1093/oso/9780190906580.003.0008

European output reflect these ideas, particularly *Aufstieg und Fall der Stadt Mahagonny* ("The Rise and Fall of the City of Mahagonny," 1930) and *Die sieben Todsünden* ("The Seven Deadly Sins," 1933). But while Brecht used America to depict an apocalyptic capitalist wasteland, Weill's views were less solidified in the 1920s, which allowed for more flexibility in the second part of his career. By the 1940s, his time in the United States and World War II—when a fully industrialized Germany turned monstrously collectivist—convinced Weill that America could be solution to, rather than an emblem of, the world's troubles.

Still, Weill understood that while America's attempt to bridge individual and technological development was "the most advanced," it was not ideal. Weill's three large-scale postwar works all wrestle with the challenges of American modernity. *Street Scene* (1947) shows the debilitating loneliness and dehumanization of modern urban life; *Love Life* (1948) demonstrates the detrimental effect of technological progress on human relationships; and *Lost in the Stars* (1949) reckons with the limited possibilities for justice in a world without moral absolutes. But for all his criticism of his adopted homeland, Weill remained hopeful, albeit sometimes overly so: in the same letter, he wrote "I have a suspicion that Russia could become, in this sense, 'Americanized'—if we want it," which must have seemed tragically optimistic only two years later, when the U.S.S.R. began testing its own nuclear arsenal.

That same optimism—sometimes well-founded, sometimes naive—characterizes much of Weill's career. Even in his most bitter Brechtian satires, the goal was not simply to condemn humanity, but to reflect humanity back on itself, to clarify the experience of modernity, and to spur audiences to consider possibilities for a better world. Weill believed that, as he wrote in 1925, "ultimately what moves us in the theater is the same as what affects us in all art: the heightened experience—the refined expression of an emotion—the human condition."[3] Fifteen years later and an ocean away, he echoed the same sentiments: "I write only to express human emotions. If music is really human, it doesn't make much difference how it is conveyed."[4] Whether in Europe or the United States, that desire to be expressive remained, and probably contributed in some part to the dissolution of his partnership with Brecht.

---

[3] Kurt Weill, "Commitment to Opera" (1925), trans. in *KWiE*, 459.
[4] William G. King, "Composer for the Theater: Kurt Weill Talks about 'Practical Music,'" 3 February 1940, *New York Sun*, available at https://www.kwf.org/pages/wt-composer-for-the-theater.html.

These goals—to reach audiences and to engage them more thoughtfully in the world—are also crucial to Weill's understanding of his own legacy. As he told the *New York Sun* in 1940:

> Schoenberg, for example, has said he is writing for a time fifty years after his death. But the great "classic" composers wrote for their contemporary audiences. They wanted those who heard their music to understand it, and they did. As for myself, I write for today. I don't give a damn about writing for posterity.[5]

Weill clearly positions himself outside the nineteenth-century ideal that values increasing complexity, abstraction, and autonomy.[6] But far from abnegating any responsibility to "posterity," Weill positions himself among a different set of "classic" composers. Weill likely used the idea of "classic" after his teacher Busoni, who advocated for a "New Classicality" in art, defining "classic" as "beautiful, masterful, of lasting value, simple, and forceful."[7] For Weill, this meant speaking to the present. In 1929, he wrote "I am convinced that great art of all periods was topical in the sense that it was intended not for eternity, but for the time in which it originated, or at least for the near future, to whose formation it was intended to contribute."[8] Thus "classic" art was not just beautiful, it helped to build a better future. For Weill, the best way to serve posterity was to help ensure it came about. In fact, he associated all good musical theatre with this attitude; in an interview in 1950, when Margaret Arlen remarked that composing "was not like the old days when a composer sat in a garret composing and never stirred out of there," Weill replied, "I don't believe those days ever existed. With symphonic composers, yes. But for theatrical composers, no," and continued that "Mozart, Verdi, and Puccini certainly never could cut themselves off from life."[9] For Weill, the music of Mozart, Verdi, and Puccini, along with many others, captured "the simplest, most moral, ancient and yet always new emotional stirrings,"

---

[5] King, "Composer for the Theater."

[6] See Janet Wolff, "Forward: The Ideology of Autonomous Art," in *Music and Society: The Politics of Composition, Performance, and Reception*, ed. Richard Leppert and Susan McClary (Cambridge, UK: Cambridge University Press, 1987), 1–4, and Susan McClary, "Terminal Prestige: The Case of Avant-Garde Music Composition," *Cultural Critique* 12 (1989): 57–81.

[7] Quoted in Tamara Levitz, "Teaching New Classicality: Busoni's Master Class in Composition, 1921–24" (PhD diss., University of Rochester, Eastman School of Music, 1994), 69.

[8] Kurt Weill, "Topical Theater" (1929), trans. in *KWiE*, 510.

[9] "WCBS Presents Margaret Arlen," broadcast 7 January 1950, transcript available at https://www.kwf.org/pages/wt-wcbs-presents-margaret-arlen.html.

thus achieving "classic" status.[10] Indeed, as Kim H. Kowalke and Stephen Hinton observe in the critical edition of Weill's "popular adaptations" (that is, versions of his songs arranged by others to be published as sheet music), such a collection of "sheet music, vocal gems, and dance arrangements would be unimaginable for a Schoenberg, Stravinsky, Bartók, or Hindemith, though perhaps not inconceivable for a Mozart, Rossini, or Verdi."[11]

To reach this classic status, Weill attempted to find an equally timeless— and in some sense, placeless—musical language. Even before arriving in the United States, Weill drew from the many styles in his compositional toolbox: European jazz, expressionism, operetta, baroque oratorio, and so forth. Upon arriving in the United States, he simply added more compositional tools to the box: Tin Pan Alley, U.S. folksong, vaudeville, minstrelsy, and many more. At times, Weill badly miscalculated. The Germanized jazz and obvious politics of *Die Dreigroschenoper* failed to impress in the United States. Fifteen years later, *Love Life's* combination of cynicism and Americana left U.S. audiences similarly cold. He could also miscalculate in the other direction, as evidenced by the failure of the light-hearted and Offenbachian *The Firebrand of Florence* (1945). But more often, Weill struck a nerve. The frothy operetta and popular ballads in *Lady in the Dark* and *One Touch of Venus* proved well-matched for those productions' exploration of modern femininity; and the amalgam of melodrama, Italian opera, and popular song in *Street Scene* conveyed both the pathos and the bathos of mid-century urban communities in ways that have continued to resonate with modern opera audiences.

This effort to connect with the broadest possible audience is perhaps the most contentious part of Weill's legacy. Even during his lifetime, it left him open to accusations of pandering and empty eclecticism. After *Lost in the Stars*, Harold Clurman, who had worked with Weill on *Johnny Johnson* (1936), wrote "Weill is so much the adaptable artist," that "if he were forced to live among the Hottentots [South Africans] he would in the shortest possible span of time become the leading Hottentot composer." But for Clurman, that adaptability was the composer's Achilles heel: "Weill's career since *Johnny Johnson*, despite excellent work now and again—always on a high level of craftsmanship—has been an adaptation toward an increasingly facile,

---

[10] Weill, "Commitment to Opera," 459.

[11] Stephen Hinton and Kim H. Kowalke, Introduction to *Kurt Weill: Popular Adaptations 1927–1950*, ed. Charles Hamm, Elmar Juchem, and Kim H. Kowalke, KWE, Series IV, Volume 2 (New York: Kurt Weill Foundation for Music/European American Music Corporation, 2009), 13.

I might say, artistically nondescript goal," with the result of "a decline in real quality, and an increase in journalistic praise as well as box office receipts." In the end, Clurman saw Weill as a victim of his own success, concluding that "to develop real roots," a composer should "shape some definite ideal for himself of the kind of world toward which he can aspire."[12] Elia Kazan, who also parted with Weill on less than amiable terms after the failure of *Love Life*, echoed Clurman, writing, "I found him always swinging toward whoever had the most power," even though he admired his adaptability: if "he'd landed in Java instead of the United States, within a year he'd have been writing Javanese temple music."[13]

Clurman's self-serving and somewhat anti-Semitic appraisal of Weill's artistic development notwithstanding, this attitude informed much of Weill's reception in the twentieth century. While *The Threepenny Opera* remained in the repertory, particularly after the 1954 off-Broadway revival, most of Weill's U.S. works were dismissed as merely commercial. Even critics who have observed continuities in Weill's career have characterized his popular success in ambivalent terms. In the preface to the volume of *Kurt Weill: Popular Adaptations*, Kowalke and Hinton take care to distance Weill from these popular adaptations, noting that Weill often authorized professional arrangers to make these songs "conform as much as possible to the norms of the marketplace," which "often proved problematic." During this process, aspects of the songs that challenged "conventions, often to dramatic, ironic or socio-critical effect" vanished.[14] But Weill did not see this process as "problematic"; he actively participated in it and courted popular audiences. Charles Hamm goes even farther, writing that "Kurt Weill did not, strictly speaking, compose popular songs," and that the composer "obviously needed a dramatic context to create a song; otherwise he simply couldn't, or wouldn't, write one," ignoring most of the World War II songs, and the fact that Weill often composed with a performer, rather than dramatic context, in mind.[15] This kind of language betrays a lingering ambivalence with Weill's commercial success and its effect on his legacy. Howard Pollack noted that the edition of popular adaptations highlights "the conflicts between commerce and art" that "posed

[12] Harold Clurman, "Lost in the Stars of Broadway," in *The Collected Works of Harold Clurman: Six Decades of Commentary on Theatre, Dance, Music, Film, Arts and Letters*, ed. Marjorie Loggia and Glenn Young (New York: Applause, 1994), 226, 227.

[13] Elia Kazan, *Elia Kazan: A Life* (New York: Alfred A. Knopf, 1988), 72.

[14] Kowalke and Hinton, Introduction to *Kurt Weill: Popular Adaptations 1927–1950*, 13–14.

[15] Charles Hamm, critical commentary for *Kurt Weill: Popular Adaptations 1927–1950*, 39.

an ever-going dilemma for many if not all composers of the popular musical stage with serious intentions."[16]

But for Weill, and for many opera composers from Handel to Verdi to Gershwin, there was no conflict between commerce and art. This was key to Weill's understanding of his own works. When Olin Downes wrote to Weill that he enjoyed *Lost in the Stars*, but eagerly anticipated "the day when you get exactly the subject which you can treat without the faintest consideration of public taste," the composer replied that the audience was key to "the nature of my experiment—to do a 'musical tragedy' for the American theatre so that the typical audience (not a specialized audience) can accept it; and the real success of the piece to me is the fact that the audience did accept it without hesitation."[17] The distinction between "art" and "commerce" springs from the nineteenth-century ideal of autonomous music, an ideal Weill explicitly rejected throughout his career.

Another narrative has emerged surrounding Weill's legacy among Broadway professionals, for whom Weill's operatic ambitions and formal experiments form a profound influence. In 1957, Leonard Bernstein, the initial musical director of the 1952 Brandeis University production of *The Threepenny Opera*, gave Broadway *West Side Story*, a show that draws on *Street Scene*'s combination of opera and popular song, and similarly depicts a tragic day in the life of a working-class New York City neighborhood. The influence of *Lady in the Dark* can be seen in shows like *Coco* (1969) and *Applause* (1970), both of which center around female stars (Katharine Hepburn and Lauren Bacall, respectively) trying to balance romance with a glamorous career (fashion designer, actress), each with the help of a queer sidekick in the vein of Danny Kaye's Russell Paxton. The queer dream sequences in Kander and Ebb's *Kiss of the Spider Woman* (1993), featuring the chameleonic diva Aurora, also likely owe something to *Lady in the Dark*. *Love Life* in particular has become a reference point for a number of Broadway creators, with its oft-noted connections to Kander and Ebb's *Cabaret* (1966) and *Chicago* (1975). In 1976, Alan Jay Lerner (*Love Life*'s librettist) teamed up with Bernstein for *1600 Pennsylvania Avenue*, which has the same actors playing different presidents in different historical eras. The early musicals of Stephen Sondheim, particularly *Company* (1970) and *Follies* (1971), also resemble

---

[16] Howard Pollack, "Weill's Popular Adaptations," *Notes* 69, no. 3 (2013): 628.

[17] Olin Downes to Kurt Weill, 9 December 1949; Kurt Weill to Olin Downes, 14 November 1949, both in ODP, Series 2 Box 63 Folder 32. Clearly, one of the them mistook the date.

*Love Life* in the ways they explore the challenges of marriage through the medium of vaudeville.[18] Hal Prince, who produced and directed the original *Cabaret*, *Company*, and *Follies*, acknowledged his debt to *Love Life* (and Rodgers and Hammerstein's *Allegro*) as the first "concept musicals." *Cabaret*'s lyricist Fred Ebb called *Love Life* a "a marvelous piece of theatre and a major influence."[19] Sondheim has also acknowledged his debt to *Love Life*.[20] For Broadway, Weill has become a symbol of experimentation, sophistication, and political engagement. His shows are part of a genealogy for those looking to distance themselves from the "Golden Age" model.[21]

One further evaluation of Weill's career perhaps best captures what Weill hoped to accomplish. Following the German premiere of *Street Scene* in 1955, the lyricist Langston Hughes wrote a tribute to Weill, "a great folk artist" who "could capture in his art the least common denominator uniting all of humanity." For Hughes, this was Weill's greatest advantage:

> Being an artist, in the true sense of the word, he understood all human beings, and all their songs—for good songs are but the dreams, the hopes, and the inner cries deep in the souls of all the peoples of the world. Kurt Weill did not scorn even the least of these songs—for he knew that the least might well be the most.

Hughes summed up the composer's career in what has become the most overriding cliché of Weill during his lifetime: "Had he immigrated to India instead of to the United States, I believe he would have written wonderful Indian musical plays." But, he concluded, "Only the universal man and the universal artist could do this."[22] That Weill so often succeeded in reaching that broader audience, even if it was not universal, is a remarkable feat.

---

[18] David Kilroy, "Kurt Weill's Musical Theatre: The Postwar Years (1945–1950)" (PhD diss., Harvard University, 1992), 327–29.

[19] Foster Hirsch, *Kurt Weill on Stage: From Berlin to Broadway* (New York: Knopf, 2002), 297.

[20] On Weill's influence on Sondheim, see Chapter 1 of Lara Housez, "Becoming Stephen Sondheim: *Anyone Can Whistle*, *A Pray by Blecht*, *Company*, and *Sunday in the Park with George*" (PhD diss., University of Rochester, 2013), especially 62–70.

[21] Mitchell Morris, "*Cabaret*, America's Weimar, and Mythologies of the Gay Subject," *American Music* 22, no. 1 (2004): 146.

[22] Langston Hughes, "Happy New Year Harbors Happy Happenings and Hopes," *Chicago Defender*, 31 December 1955, 7.

# Bibliography

## Works Cited

"1939 World's Fair—Railroad Exhibits." YouTube video. 10:59. Posted 24 September 2012. https://www.youtube.com/watch?v=NySKJczYKUQ.

"Address before the Inter-American Conference for the Maintenance of Peace, Buenos Aires, Argentina." 1 December 1936. Available online at Gerhard Peters and John T. Woolley, *The American Presidency Project*. http://www.presidency.ucsb.edu/ws/?pid=15238.

Adorno, Theodor W. "Kurt Weill." Originally published in 1950. In *Theodor W. Adorno: Gesammelte Schriften*. Edited by Rolf Tiedemann and Klaus Schutz, Vol. 18: 544–47. Frankfurt am Main: Suhrkamp, 1984.

Adorno, Theodor W. *Minima Moralia: Reflections of a Damaged Life*. Originally published in 1951. Translated by E.F.N. London: Verso, 2005.

Adorno, Theodor W. "On the Social Situation of Music." Originally published in 1932. Translated in Theodor W. Adorno, *Essays on Music*. Edited by Richard Leppert, 391–437. Berkeley: University of Los Angeles Press, 2002.

Alan Jay Lerner Papers. Library of Congress, Music Division, Washington, DC.

Allen, Holly. *Forgotten Men and Fallen Women: The Cultural Politics of New Deal Narratives*. Ithaca, NY: Cornell University Press, 2015.

Allen, Ray. "An American Folk Opera? Triangulating Folkness, Blackness, and Americanness in Gershwin and Heyward's *Porgy and Bess*." *Journal of American Folklore* 117, no. 465 (2004): 243–61.

Allen, Ray, and George P. Cunningham. "Cultural Uplift and Double-Consciousness: African American Responses to the 1935 Opera *Porgy and Bess*." *Musical Quarterly* 88 (2005): 342–69.

Alston, Lee J. "Farm Foreclosure Moratorium Legislation: A Lesson from the Past." *American Economic Review* 74, no. 3 (1984): 445–57.

Anderson, Maxwell, and Kurt Weill. *Knickerbocker Holiday: A Musical Comedy in Two Acts*. Washington, DC: Anderson House, 1938.

Anderson, Maxwell, and Kurt Weill. *Lost in the Stars: A Dramatization of Alan Paton's Novel*. Garden City, NY: Country Life, 1950.

Arndt, Jürgen. "Tango und Technik: Kurt Weills Rezeption des 'Amerikanismus' der Weimar Republik." In *Musik der zwanziger Jahre*. Edited by Werner Keil, with Kerstin Jaunich and Ulrike Kammerer, 42–58. Hildesheim: Georg Olms, 1996.

Avery, Lawrence G., ed. *Dramatist in America: Letters of Maxwell Anderson, 1912–1958*. Chapel Hill: University of North Carolina Press, 1977.

Bach, Steven. *Dazzler: The Life and Times of Moss Hart*. New York: Alfred A. Knopf, 2001.

Baer, Abraham, ed. *Baal Tefillah: Oder der practische Vorbeter*. 2nd edition. Frankfurt am Main: J. Kauffmann, 1883.

Bahr, Ehrhard. *Weimar on the Pacific: German Exile Culture in Los Angeles and the Crisis of Modernism*. Berkeley: University of California Press, 2007.

Baresel, Alfred. *Das Jazz-Buch*. Leipzig, 1926.

Barranger, Milly S. *A Gambler's Instinct: The Story of Broadway Producer Cheryl Crawford*. Carbondale: Southern Illinois University Press, 2010.

Bauer, Marion, and Claire R. Reis. "Twenty-Five Years with the League of Composers." *Musical Quarterly* 34, no. 1 (1948): 1–14.

Baumgartner, Michael. *Exilierte Göttinnen: Frauenstatuen im Bühnenwerk von Kurt Weill, Thea Musgrave, und Othmar Schoeck*. Hildesheim: Georg Olms, 2012.

Benson, Renate. *German Expressionism: Ernst Toller and Georg Kaiser*. London: Macmillan, 1984.

Bick, Sally. *Unsettled Scores: Politics, Hollywood, and the Film Music of Aaron Copland and Hanns Eisler*. Urbana: University of Illinois Press, 2019.

*Bill of the Play: Railroads on Parade; a Pageant Drama of Transport*. 1939. Author's personal collection.

*Bill of the Play: Railroads on Parade; a Pageant Drama of Transport*. 1940. Author's personal collection.

Bishop, Robert Lee. "The Overseas Branch of the Office of War Information." PhD diss., University of Wisconsin, 1966.

Block, Geoffrey. *Enchanted Evenings: The Broadway Musical from* Show Boat *to Sondheim and Lloyd Webber*. 2nd edition. Oxford, UK: Oxford University Press, 2009.

Bombola, Gina. "'Can't Help Singing': The 'Modern' Opera Diva in Hollywood Film, 1930–1950." PhD diss., University of North Carolina at Chapel Hill, 2017.

Botkin, B.A. ed. *A Treasury of American Folklore: Stories, Ballads, and Traditions of the People*. New York: Crown, 1944.

Botstein, Leon. "German Jews and Wagner." In *Richard Wagner and His World*. Edited by Thomas Grey, 151–200. Princeton, NJ: Princeton University Press, 2009.

Bradley, Laura. *Brecht and Political Theatre: The Mother Onstage*. Oxford, UK: Oxford University Press, 2006.

Brett, Philip. "Britten's Dream." In *Musicology and Difference: Gender and Sexuality in Music Scholarship*. Edited by Ruth A. Solie, 259–80. Berkeley: University of California Press, 1993.

Brodkin, Karen. *How Jews Became White Folks and What That Says about Race in America*. New Brunswick, NJ: Rutgers University Press, 2002.

Brooks, Van Wyck. "On Creating a Usable Past." In *American Literature, American Culture*. Edited by Gordon Hunter. Oxford, UK: Oxford University Press, 1999.

Brüstle, Christa. "Bach-Rezeption im Nationalsozialismus: Aspect Und Stationen." In *Bach und die Nachwelt III: 1900–1950*. Edited by Michael Heinemann and Hans-Joachim Hinrichsen, 115–53. Laaber: Laaber, 2002.

Buhle, Mari Jo. *Feminism and Its Discontents: A Century of Struggle with Psychoanalysis*. Cambridge, MA: Harvard University Press, 1998.

Burke, Kenneth. "Revolutionary Symbolism in America: Speech by Kenneth Burke to American Writers' Congress, April 26, 1935." In *The Legacy of Kenneth Burke*. Edited by Herman W. Simons and Trevor Melia, 267–73. Madison: University of Wisconsin Press, 1989.

Cantwell, Robert. *When We Were Good: The Folk Revival*. Cambridge, MA: Harvard University Press, 1996.

Carter, Tim. "Celebrating the Nation: Kurt Weill, Paul Green, and the Federal Theatre Project (1937)." *Journal of the Society for American Music* 5, no. 3 (2011): 297–334.

Carter, Tim. *Oklahoma! The Making of an American Musical*. New Haven, CT: Yale University Press, 2007.

Carter, Tim. Review of *Lady in the Dark: Biography of a Musical*, by bruce d. mcclung. *Kurt Weill Newsletter* 25, no. 1 (2007): 13–14.

Carter, Tim. *Rodgers and Hammerstein's Carousel*. Oxford, UK: Oxford University Press, 2017.

Chauncey, George. *Gay New York: Gender, Urban Culture, and the Making of the Gay Male World, 1890–1940*. New York: BasicBooks, 1994.

Chinoy, Helen Krich. *The Group Theatre: Passion, Politics, and Performance in the Depression Era*. Edited by Don B. Wilmeth and Milly S. Barranger. New York: Palgrave Macmillian, 2013.

Clum, John. *Something for the Boys: Musical Theater and Gay Culture*. New York: St. Martins, 1999.

Clurman, Harold. *The Collected Works of Harold Clurman: Six Decades of Commentary on Theatre, Dance, Music, Film, Arts and Letters*. Edited by Marjorie Loggia and Glenn Young. New York: Applause, 1994.

Cohen, Brigid. *Stefan Wolpe and the Avant-Garde Diaspora*. Cambridge, UK: Cambridge University Press, 2012.

Cook, Susan C. *Opera for a New Republic: The Zeitopern of Krenek, Weill, and Hindemith*. Ann Arbor: UMI, 1988.

Coontz, Stephanie. *The Way We Never Were: American Families and the Nostalgia Trap*. Revised edition. Philadelphia: Perseus, 2016.

Core Collection. Margaret Herrick Library, Academy of Motion Picture Arts and Sciences, Beverly Hills, CA.

Crawford, Cheryl. *One Naked Individual: My Fifty Years in the Theatre*. Indianapolis, IN: Bobbs-Merrill, 1977.

Crawford, Dorothy Lamb. *A Windfall of Musicians: Hitler's Émigrés and Exiles in Southern California*. New Haven, CT: Yale University Press, 2009.

Crist, Elizabeth B. *Music for the Common Man: Aaron Copland during the Depression and War*. Oxford, UK: Oxford University Press, 1999.

D'Andre, Mark. "The Theatre Guild, *Carousel*, and the Cultural Field of American Musical Theatre." PhD diss., Yale University, 2000.

Daniels, Rogers. "American Refugee Policy in Historical Perspective." In *The Muses Flee Hitler: Cultural Transfer and Adaptation, 1930–1945*. Edited by Jarrell C. Jackman and Carla M. Borden, 61–78. Washington, DC: Smithsonian Institution Press, 1983.

Danuser, Hermann, and Hermann Gottschewski, eds. *Amerikanismus, Americanism, Weill: Die Suche nach kultereller Identität in der Moderne*. Schliengen: Edition Argus, 2003.

Davidson, David. "Depression America and the Rise of the Social Documentary Film." *Chicago Review* 34, no. 1 (1983): 68–88.

Decker, Todd. *Show Boat: Performing Race in an American Musical*. Oxford, UK: Oxford University Press, 2013.

de la Croix, St. Sukie. *Chicago Whispers: A History of LGBT Chicago before Stonewall*. Madison: University of Wisconsin Press, 2012.

D'Emilio, John, and Estelle B. Freedman. *Intimate Matters: A History of Sexuality in America*. Chicago: University of Chicago Press, 2012.

de Mille, Agnes. *And Promenade Home*. Boston: Little, Brown, 1958.

Denning, Michael. *The Cultural Front: The Laboring of American Culture in the Twentieth Century*. London: Verso, 1997.

Diner, Hasia. *In the Almost Promised Land: American Jews and Blacks, 1915–1935*. Westport, CT: Greenwood, 1977.

Dinnerstein, Leonard. *Antisemitism in America*. Oxford, UK: Oxford University Press, 1994.

Doherty, Thomas. *Projections of War: Hollywood, American Culture, and World War II*. New York: Columbia University Press, 1999.

Downes, Olin. *Olin Downes on Music: A Selection of His Writings during the Half-Century 1906–1955*. Edited by Irene Downes. New York: Simon and Schuster, 1957.

Downes, Olin, and Elie Siegmeister. *A Treasury of American Song*. 2nd edition. New York: Alfred A. Knopf, 1943.

Drew, David. "Kurt Weill." In *The New Grove Dictionary of Music and Musicians*. Edited by Stanley Sadie, Vol. 20: 300–10. London: Macmillan, 1980.

Dunaway, David King, and Molly Beer. *Singing Out: An Oral History of America's Folk Revivals*. Oxford, UK: Oxford University Press, 2010.

Duranti, Marco. "Utopia, Nostalgia and World War at the 1939–40 New York World's Fair." *Journal of Contemporary History* 41, no. 4 (2006): 663–83.

Eisler, Garrett. "'This Theatre Is a Battlefield': Political Performance and Jewish-American Identity, 1933–1948." PhD diss., City University of New York, 2012.

Eisner, Lotte. *The Haunted Screen: Expressionism in the German Cinema and the Influence of Max Reinhardt*. Translated by Roger Greaves. Berkeley: University of California Press, 1973.

Elsaesser, Thomas. *Weimar Cinema and After: Germany's Historical Imaginary*. London: Routledge, 2000.

Espagne, Michel, and Michaël Werner. "Deutsch-Französischer Kulturtransfer im 18. und 19. Jahrhundert: Zu einem neuen interdisziplinären Forschungsprogramm des. C.N.R.S." *Francia* 13 (1985): 502–10.

Espagne, Michel, and Michaël Werner. "La Construction d'une Référence Culturelle Allemande en France Genèse et Histoire (1750–1914)." *Annales, Histoire, Science Sociales* 42, no. 4 (1987): 969–92.

Faderman, Lillian. *Odd Girls and Twilight Lovers: A History of Lesbian Life in 20th Century America*. New York: Columbia University Press, 1991.

Fauser, Annegret. *Sounds of War: Music in the United States during World War II*. Oxford, UK: Oxford University Press, 2013.

Fauser, Annegret, and Mark Everist, eds. *Music, Theatre, and Cultural Transfer: Paris 1830–1914*. Cambridge, UK: Cambridge University Press, 2009.

Feisst, Sabine. *Schoenberg's New World: The American Years*. Oxford, UK: Oxford University Press, 2011.

Flanagan, Hallie. *Arena: The History of the Federal Theatre*. New York: Blom, 1940.

Friedan, Betty. *The Feminine Mystique*. 50th anniversary edition. New York: W.W. Norton, 2013.

Gabbard, Krin. *Black Magic: White Hollywood and African American Culture*. New Brunswick, NJ: Rutgers University Press, 2004.

Gardner, Kara Ann. *Agnes de Mille: Telling Stories in Broadway Dance*. Oxford, UK: Oxford University Press, 2016.

Garrett, Charles Hiroshi. *Struggling to Define a Nation: American Music and the Twentieth Century*. Berkeley: University of California Press, 2008.

Gaston, Healan. *Imagining Judeo-Christian America: Religion, Secularism, and the Redefinition of Democracy*. Chicago: University of Chicago Press, 2019.

Gay, Peter. *Weimar Culture: The Outsider as Insider*. 1968. Reprint, New York: W.W. Norton, 2001.

Gemünden, Gerd. *Continental Strangers: German Exile Cinema, 1933–1951*. New York: Columbia University Press, 2014.

Gentry, Philip M. *What Will I Be: American Music and Cold War Identity*. Oxford, UK: Oxford University Press, 2017.

Giovacchini, Saverio. *Hollywood Modernism: Film and Politics in the Age of the New Deal*. Philadelphia: Temple University Press, 2001.

Glassberg, David. *American Historical Pageantry: The Uses of Tradition in the Early Twentieth Century*. Chapel Hill: University of North Carolina Press, 1990.

Goehr, Lydia. "Music and Musicians in Exile: The Romantic Legacy of a Double Life." In *Driven into Paradise: The Musical Migration from Nazi German to the United States*. Edited by Reinhold Brinkmann and Christoph Wolff, 66–91. Berkeley: University of California Press, 1999.

Gordon, Albert Claude. "A Critical Study of the History and Development of the Playwrights Producing Company." PhD diss., Tulane University, 1965.

Graber, Naomi. "Colliding Diasporas: Kurt Weill's *Ulysses Africanus* and Black–Jewish Relations during the Great Depression." *Musical Quarterly* 99, no. 3–4 (2017): 321–55.

Graber, Naomi. "Kurt Weill's *The River Is Blue*: 'Film-Opera' and Politics in 1930s Hollywood." *Journal of the Society for American Music* 11, no. 3 (2017): 313–53.

Graziano, John. "Musical Dialects in *Down in the Valley*." In *A New Orpheus: Essays on Kurt Weill*. Edited by Kim H. Kowalke, 217–319. New Haven, CT: Yale University Press, 1986.

Green, Paul. *Drama and the Weather: Some Notes and Papers on Life and the Theatre*. New York: French, 1958.

Green, Paul. *Dramatic Heritage*. New York: Samuel French, 1953.

Green, Paul. *The Lost Colony: A Symphonic Drama of American History*. Edited by Lawrence G. Avery. Chapel Hill: University of North Carolina at Chapel Hill Press, 2001.

Green, Paul. *A Southern Life: Letters of Paul Green, 1916–1981*. Edited by Lawrence G. Avery. Chapel Hill: University of North Carolina Press, 1994.

Green, Paul, and Kurt Weill. *Johnny Johnson: A Play with Music in Three Acts*. Edited by Tim Carter. Kurt Weill Edition, Series I, Volume 13. New York: Kurt Weill Foundation for Music/European American Music Corporation, 2012.

Grieve, Victoria. *The Federal Art Project and the Creation of Middlebrow Culture*. Urbana: University of Illinois Press, 2009.

Grosch, Nils. *Der Musik der Neue Sachlichkeit*. Stuttgart: J.B. Metzler, 1999.

Grosch, Nils. "Facetten des Amerikanismus in *Die Sieben Todsünden*." In *Amerikanismus, Americanism, Weill: Die Suche nach kultureller Identität in der Moderne*. Edited Hermann Danuser and Hermann Gottschewski, 271–82. Schliengen: Edition Argus, 2003.

Grosch, Nils. "'Gewohntes zu überdenken': Der andere Blick auf Musik in der Migration und im Exil." *Österreichische Musikzeitschrift* 72, no. 2 (2017): 30–35.

Gunning. Tom. *The Films of Fritz Lang: Allegories of Vision and Modernity*. London: British Film Institute, 2000.

HaCohen, Ruth. *The Music Libel against the Jews: Vocal Fictions of Noise and Harmony*. New Haven, CT: Yale University Press, 2011.

Hamm, Charles. "The Firebrand of New York: Kurt Weill and His Broadway Operetta." *Music & Letters* 85, no. 2 (2004): 239–54.

Hanson, Miriam. "The Mass Production of the Senses: Classical Cinema as Vernacular Modernism. *Modernism/Modernity* 6, no. 2 (1999): 59–77.

Harbert, Elissa. "Remembering the Revolution: Music in Stage and Screen Representations of Early America during the Bicentennial Years." PhD diss., Northwestern University, 2013.

Harris-Warrick, Rebecca. "*Lucia* Goes to Paris: A Tale of Three Theaters." In *Music, Theatre, and Cultural Transfer: Paris 1830–1914*. Edited by Annegret Fauser and Mark Everist. 195–227. Cambridge, UK: Cambridge University Press, 2009.

Harsh, Edward, Jürgen Selk et al. "Guide for Volume Editors of the Kurt Weill Edition." 2002. Available online at https://www.kwf.org/media/edguide.pdf.

Harsh, Edward, and Dave Stein, compilers. *Kurt Weill Songs: A Centennial Anthology*, Volume 2. Los Angeles: Alfred Publishing, 1999.

Hart, Moss, Kurt Weill, and Ira Gershwin. *Lady in the Dark*. New York: Random House, 1941.

Hart, Moss, Kurt Weill, and Ira Gershwin. *Lady in the Dark: Musical Play, Vocal Score*. Edited by Albert Sirmay. New York: Chappell Music, 1941.

Hart, Moss, Kurt Weill, and Ira Gershwin. *Lady in the Dark: A Musical Play in Two Acts*. Edited by bruce d. mcclung and Elmar Juchem. Kurt Weill Edition, Series I, Volume 16. New York: Kurt Weill Foundation for Music/European American Music Corporation, 2017.

Hartmann, Susan M. "Women's Employment and the Domestic Ideal." In *Not June Cleaver: Women and Gender in Postwar America, 1945–1960*. Edited by Joanne Meyerowitz, 86–100. Philadelphia: Temple University Press, 1994.

Hatten, Robert S. *Interpreting Musical Gestures, Topics, and Tropes: Mozart, Beethoven, Schubert*. Bloomington: Indiana University Press, 2004.

Hegarty, Marilyn E. *Victory Girls, Khaki-Wackies, and Patriotutes: The Regulation of Female Sexuality during World War II*. New York: New York University Press, 2008.

Heilbut, Anthony. *Exiled in Paradise: German Refugee Artists and Intellectuals in America from the 1930's to the Present*. New York: Viking, 1983.

Herzinger, Richard. "Der 'Amerikanismus' in den Deutungsmustern linker und rechter Modernekritik." In *Amerikanismus, Americanism, Weill: Die Suche nach kultureller Identität in der Moderne*." Edited by Hermann Danuser and Hermann Gottschewski, 91–105. Schliengen: Edition Argus, 2003.

Heuchemer, Dane. "American Popular Music in Weill's *Royal Palace* and Krenek's *Jonny Spielt Auf*: Influences and Usage." In *Jazz and the Germans: Essays on the Influence of "Hot" American Idioms on 20th-Century German Music*. Edited by Michael J. Budds, 99–140. Hillsdale, NY: Pendragon, 2002.

Higham, Charles, and Joel Greenberg, "Interview with Fritz Lang." 1969. Reprinted in *Fritz Lang Interviews*. Edited by Barry Keith Grant, 101–26. Jackson: University of Mississippi Press, 2003.

Hindemith, Paul. *Paul Hindemith: Aufsätze, Vorträge, Reden*. Edited by Giselher Schubert. Zürich: Atlantis Musikbuch, 1994.

Hindemith, Paul. *Selected Letters of Paul Hindemith*. Edited and translated by Geoffrey Skelton. Binghamton, NY: Vail-Ballou, 1995.

Hinton, Stephen. "Aspects of Hindemith's *Neue Sachlichkeit*." *Hindemith Jahrbuch* 14 (1985): 22–80.

Hinton, Stephen. "Hindemith and Weill: Cases of 'Inner' and 'Other' Direction." In *Driven into Paradise: The Musical Migration from Nazi German to the United States*. Edited by Reinhold Brinkmann and Christoph Wolff, 261–78. Berkeley: University of California Press, 1999.

Hinton, Stephen. *The Idea of Gebrauchsmusik: A Study of Musical Aesthetics in the Weimar Republic (1919–1933) with Particular Reference to the Works of Paul Hindemith*. New York: Garland, 1989.

Hinton, Stephen. "*Lehrstück*: Aesthetics of Performance." In *Music and Performance during the Weimar Republic*. Edited by Bryan Gilliam, 59–74. Cambridge, UK: Cambridge University Press, 1994.

Hinton, Stephen. "Weill contra Wagner: Aspects of Ambivalence." In '. . . *Das alles auch hätte anders kommen können*': *Beiträge zur Musik des 20. Jahrhunderts*. Edited by Susanne Schaal-Gotthardt, Luitgard Schader, and Heinz-Jürgen Winkler, 155–74. Berlin: Schott, 2009.

Hinton, Stephen. "Weill: *Neue Sachlichkeit*, Surrealism, and *Gebrauchsmusik*." In *A New Orpheus: Essays on Kurt Weill*. Edited by Kim H. Kowalke, 61–82. New Haven, CT: Yale University Press, 1986.

Hinton, Stephen, ed. *Kurt Weill: The Threepenny Opera*. Cambridge, UK: Cambridge University Press, 1990.

Hirsch, Foster. *Kurt Weill on Stage: From Berlin to Broadway*. New York: Alfred A. Knopf, 2002.

Hobbs, Stuart D. *The End of the American Avant-Garde*. New York: New York University Press, 1997.

Hohendahl, Peter U. "The Displaced Intellectual? Adorno's American Years Revisited." *New German Critique* 59 (1992): 76–100.

Housez, Lara. "Becoming Stephen Sondheim: *Anyone Can Whistle, A Pray by Blecht, Company*, and *Sunday in the Park with George*." PhD diss., University of Rochester, 2013.

Hungerford, Edward. *Setting History to Music*. Princeton, NJ: Princeton University Press, 1939.

Innes, Christopher. "Piscator's *Rasputin*." *Drama Review* 22, no. 4 (1978): 83–98.

Jacobson, Matthew Frye. *Whiteness of a Different Color: European Immigrants and the Alchemy of Race*. Cambridge, MA: Harvard University Press, 1998.

Jay, Martin. *Permanent Exiles: Essays on the Intellectual Migration from Nazi Germany*. New York: Columbia University Press, 1986.

Jones, John Bush. *Our Musicals, Ourselves: A Social History of the American Musical*. Waltham, MA: Brandeis University Press, 2004.

Juchem, Elmar. *Kurt Weill und Maxwell Anderson: Neue Wege zu einem amerikanischen Musiktheater, 1938–1950*. Stuttgart: J.B. Metzler 1999.

Kaes, Anton. "A Stranger in the House: Fritz Lang's *Fury* and the Cinema of Exile." *New German Critique* 89 (2003): 33–58.

Kaes, Anton, Martin Jay, and Edward Dimendberg, eds. *The Weimar Republic Sourcebook*. Berkeley: University of California Press, 1994.

Kalaidjian, Walter. *American Culture between the Wars: Revisionary Modernism and Postmodern Critique*. New York: Columbia University Press, 1993.

Kater, Michael H. *Composers of the Nazi Era: Eight Portraits*. Oxford, UK: Oxford University Press, 2000.

Kazan, Elia. *Elia Kazan: A Life*. New York: Alfred A. Knopf, 1988.

Kennedy, David M. *Freedom from Fear: The American People in Depression and War, 1929–1945*. Oxford, UK: Oxford University Press, 1999.

Kilroy, David. "Kurt Weill on Broadway: The Postwar Years (1945–1950)." PhD diss., Harvard University, 1992.

Kirle, Bruce. *Unfinished Business: Broadway Musicals as Works-in-Progress*. Carbondale: University of Illinois Press, 2005.

Knapp. Raymond. *American Musical Theatre and the Formation of National Identity*. Princeton, NJ: Princeton University Press, 2005.

Knapp, Raymond, Mitchell Morris, and Stacy Wolf, eds. *The Oxford Handbook of the American Musical*. Oxford, UK: Oxford University Press, 2015.

Koch, Frederick H. "The Drama of Roanoke Island." 1938. Excerpted in *History into Drama: A Source Book on Symphonic Drama including the Complete Text of Paul Green's* The Lost Colony." Edited by William J. Free and Charles B. Lower, 136–37. New York: Odyssey, 1963.

Koch, Frederick H., ed. *American Folk Plays*. New York: D. Appleton-Century, 1939.

Koegel, John. *Music in German Immigrant Theatre: New York City, 1840–1940*. Rochester, NY: University of Rochester Press, 2009.

Kowalke, Karin. *"Ein Fremder ward ich im fremden Land . . ." Max Reinhardts Inszenierung von Franz Werfels und Kurt Weills* The Eternal Road (Der Weg der Verheissung*) 1937 in New York*. Volume 1. Munich: Hieronymus, 2004.

Kowalke, Kim H. "Formerly German: Kurt Weill in America." In *A Stranger Here Myself: Kurt Weill Studien*, ed. Kim H. Kowalke and Horst Edler, 35–57. Hildescheim: Georg Olms, 1993.

Kowalke, Kim H. "'I'm an American!' Whitman, Weill, and Cultural Identity." In *Walt Whitman and Modern Music: War, Desire, and the Trials of Nationhood*. Edited by Lawrence Kramer, 109–32. New York and London: Garland, 2000.

Kowalke, Kim H. "Kurt Weill's *Amerika*/America." *Amerikanismus, Americanism, Weill: Die Suche nach kultereller Identität in der Moderne*. Edited by Hermann Danuser and Hermann Gottschewski, 9–15. Schliengen: Edition Argus, 2003.

Kowalke, Kim H. "Kurt Weill, Modernism, and Popular Culture: *Öffentlichkeit als Stil*." *Modernism/Modernity* 2, no. 2 (1995): 27–69.

Kowalke, Kim H. "Singing Brecht vs. Brecht Singing: Performance in Theory and in Practice." In *Music and Performance during the Weimar Republic*. Edited by Bryan Gilliam, 74–93. Cambridge, UK: Cambridge University Press, 1994.

Kowalke, Kim H. "*The Threepenny Opera* in America." In *Kurt Weill*: The Threepenny Opera. Edited by Stephen Hinton, 78–119. Cambridge, UK: Cambridge University Press, 1990.

Kowalke, Kim H. Jürgen Schebera, Christian Kuhnt, and Alexander Ringer. "*The Eternal Road*, and Kurt Weill's German, Jewish, and American Identity." *Theater* 30, no. 3 (2000): 83–95.

Krammer, Arnold. *Undue Process: The Untold Story of America's German Alien Internees*. Lanham, MD: Rowman and Littlefield, 1997.

Krenek, Ernst. "America's Influence on Its Émigré Composers." 1959. Translated in *Perspectives of New Music* 8, no. 2 (1970): 27–69.

Krohn, Claus-Dieter. *Intellectuals in Exile: Refugee Scholars and the New School for Social Research.* Translated by Rita and Robert Kimber. Amherst: University of Massachusetts Press, 1993.

Kuhnt, Christian. "Drei 'pageants'—ein Komponist: Anmerkungen zu *The Eternal Road, We Will Never Die* und *A Flag Is Born.*" In *Kurt Weill: Auf dem Weg zum Weg der Verheissung.* Edited by Helmut Loos and Guy Stern, 219–36. Freiburg im Breisgau: Rombach, 2000.

Kuhnt, Christian. *Kurt Weill und das Judentum.* Saarbrücken: Pfau, 2002.

Kuhnt, Christian, "Approaching the Music for *A Flag is Born.*" *Kurt Weill Newsletter*, 20, no. 1 (2002): 8–10.

Kurt Weill Foundation For Music. "Further Reading." Available online at https://www.kwf.org/pages/kw-further-reading.html. Accessed 29 October 2020.

Laird, Paul R. "How to Create a Musical: The Case of *Wicked.*" In *The Cambridge Companion to the Musical.* 3rd edition. 11–45. Cambridge, UK: Cambridge University Press, 2017.

Lareau, Alan. "Jonny's Jazz: From *Kabarett* to *Krenek.*" In *Jazz and the Germans: Essays on the Influence of "Hot" American Idioms on 20th-Century German Music.* Edited by Michael J. Budds, 19–61. Hillsdale, NY: Pendragon, 2002.

Leibman, Elizabeth A. "Catherine Littlefield's Bicycle Ballet and the 1940 World's Fair." *Dance Chronicle* 36 (2013): 326–51.

Lerner, Alan Jay. *The Street Where I Live: A Memoir.* 1978. Reprint, New York: Norton, 2018.

Lerner, Neil. "The Classical Documentary Score in American Films of Persuasion: Contexts and Case Studies, 1936–1945." PhD diss., Duke University, 1997.

Lessem, Alan. "The Émigré Experience: Schoenberg in America." In *Constructive Dissonance: Arnold Schoenberg and the Transformation of Twentieth Century Culture.* Edited by Julianne Brand and Christopher Hailey, 58–67. Berkeley: University of California Press, 1997.

Levitz, Tamara. "Either a German or a Jew: The German Reception of Kurt Weill's *Der Weg der Verheißung.*" *Theater* 30, no. 3 (2000): 97–105.

Levitz, Tamara. *Modernist Mysteries: Perséphone.* Oxford, UK: Oxford University Press, 2012.

Levitz, Tamara. "Putting Kurt Weill in His Historical Place: The *New Grove* Articles." *Kurt Weill Newsletter* 20, no. 2 (2002): 4–9.

Levitz, Tamara. "Teaching New Classicality: Busoni's Master Class in Composition, 1921–24." PhD diss., University of Rochester, Eastman School of Music, 1994.

Levy, Beth E. *Frontier Figures: American Music and the Mythology of the American West.* Berkeley: University of California Press, 2012.

Levy, Eugene. "'Is the Jew a White Man?' Press Reaction to the Leo Frank Case." In *Strangers & Neighbors: Relations Between Blacks & Jews in the United States.* Edited by Maurianne Adams and John Bracey, 261–70. Amherst: University of Massachusetts Press, 1999.

Locke, Ralphe P. *Musical Exoticism: Images and Reflections.* Cambridge, UK: Cambridge University Press, 2009.

Loeffler, James. "Richard Wagner's 'Jewish Music': Antisemitism and Aesthetics in Modern Jewish Culture." *Jewish Social Studies* 15, no. 2 (2009): 2–36.

Logan, Josh. *Josh: My Up and Down, In and Out Life*. New York: Delacorte, 1976.

Lomax, John A. and Alan Lomax. *American Folk Songs and Ballads*. New York: Macmilllan, 1934.

Lomax, John A. and Alan Lomax. *Our Singing Country: Folk Songs and Ballads*. New York: Macmillan, 1941.

Loos, Helmut. "Kurt Weill: *Der Weg der Verheissung*—Geistliche Oper und Oratorium." In *Kurt Weill: Auf der Weg zum* Der Weg der Verheissung. Edited by Helmut Loos and Guy Stern, 189–202. Freiburg im Breisgau: Rombach, 2000.

Love, Lauren. "Performing Jewish Nationhood: *The Romance of a People* at the 1933 Chicago World's Fair." *Drama Review* 55, no. 3 (2011): 57–67.

Lovensheimer, Jim. *South Pacific: Paradise Rewritten*. Oxford, UK: Oxford University Press, 2010.

Lugowski, David M. "Queering the (New) Deal: Lesbian and Gay Representation and the Depression-Era Cultural Politics of Hollywood's Production Code." *Cinema Journal* 38, no. 2 (1999): 3–34.

Lyons, James K. *Bertolt Brecht in America*. Princeton, NJ: Princeton University Press, 1980.

MacKaye, Percy. *Community Drama: Its Motive and Method of Neighborliness*. Boston: Houghton Mifflin, 1917.

Magee, Jeffrey. *Irving Berlin's American Musical Theatre*. Oxford, UK: Oxford University Press, 2012.

Martin, Mary. *My Heart Belongs*. New York: Morrow, 1976.

Mason, Daniel Gregory. *Tune In, America: A Study of Our Coming Musical Independence*. New York: Alfred A. Knopf, 1931.

May, Elaine Tyler. *Homeward Bound: American Families in the Cold War Era*. Revised edition. New York: Basic Books, 2008.

Mayer, Edwin Justus, Kurt Weill, and Ira Gershwin. *The Firebrand of Florence: Broadway Operetta in Two Acts*. Edited by Joel Galand, Kurt Weill Edition, Series I, Volume 18. New York: Kurt Weill Foundation for Music/European American Music, 2002.

McEuen, Melissa A. *Making War, Making Women: Femininity and Duty on the American Homefront, 1941–1945*. Athens: University of Georgia Press, 2010.

McHugh, Dominic. "'I'll Never Know Exactly Who Did What': Broadway Composers as Musical Collaborators." *Journal of the American Musicological Society* 68, no. 3 (2015): 605–52.

McHugh, Dominic, ed. *Alan Jay Lerner: A Lyricist's Letters*. Oxford, UK: Oxford University Press, 2014.

McLaughlin, Robert L., and Sally E. Parry. *We'll Always Have the Movies: American Cinema during World War II*. Lexington: University of Kentucky Press, 2006.

mcclung, bruce d. *Lady in the Dark: Biography of a Musical*. Oxford, UK: Oxford University Press, 2007.

mcclung, bruce d. "Liner Notes to *Kurt Weill's Lost Recording of Railroads on Parade*." Transcription Records, 2012.

Melnick, Jeffrey Paul. *Black–Jewish Relations on Trial: Leo Frank and Jim Conley in the New South*. Jackson: University of Mississippi Press, 2000.

Melnick, Jeffrey Paul. *A Right to Sing the Blues: African Americans, Jews, and American Popular Song*. Cambridge, MA: Harvard University Press, 1999.

Meredith, Burgess. *So Far, So Good: A Memoir*. Boston: Little, Brown, 1994.

Metzer, David. "The League of Composers: The Initial Years." *American Music* 15, no. 1 (1997): 45–69.

Moricz, Klára. *Jewish Identities: Nationalism, Racism, and Utopianism in Twentieth-Century Music*. Berkeley: University of California Press, 2008.

Morley, Michael. "'Suiting the Action to the Word': Some Observations on *Gestus* and *Gestische Musik*." In *A New Orpheus: Essays on Kurt Weill*. Edited by Kim H. Kowalke, 183–202. New Haven, CT: Yale University Press, 1986.

Morris, Mitchell. "*Cabaret*, America's Weimar and Mythologies of the Gay Subject." *American Music* 22, no. 1 (2004): 145–57.

Morrison, Toni. *Playing in the Dark: Whiteness and the Literary Imagination*. New York: Vintage, 1993.

Most, Andrea. *Making Americans: Jews and the Broadway Musical*. Cambridge, MA: Harvard University Press, 2004.

Mundy, Rachel. "The 'League of Jewish Composers' and American Music." *Musical Quarterly* 96, no. 1 (2013): 50–99.

Murphy, Brenda. "Plays and Playwrights: 1915–1945." In *The Cambridge History of American Theatre, Volume Two: 1870–1945*. Edited by Don B. Wilmeth and Christopher Bigsby, 289–343. Cambridge, UK: Cambridge University Press, 1999.

Muscio, Guiliana. *Hollywood's New Deal*. Philadelphia: Temple University Press, 1997.

Nahshon, Edna. "From Geopathology to Redemption: *A Flag Is Born* on the Broadway Stage." *Jewish Quarterly* 47, no. 2 (2000): 55–58.

New York World's Fair 1939 Incorporated. *Official Guidebook: New York World's Fair: The World of Tomorrow, 1939*. New York: Exposition, 1939.

New York World's Fair 1940 Incorporated. *Official Guide Book: The World's Fair of 1940 in New York: For Peace and Freedom*. New York: Rogers-Kellogg-Stillson, 1940.

Noonan, Ellen. *The Strange Career of* Porgy and Bess: *Race, Culture, and America's Most Famous Opera*. Chapel Hill: University of North Carolina Press, 2012.

Norich, Anita. *Discovering Exile: Yiddish and Jewish American Culture during the Holocaust*. Stanford: Stanford University Press, 2007.

Oenslager, Donald M. *The Theatre of Donald Oenslager*. Middletown, CT: Wesleyan University Press, 1998.

Oja, Carol. *Bernstein Meets Broadway: Collaborative Art in the Time of War*. Oxford, UK: Oxford University Press, 2014.

Oja, Carol. *Making Music Modern: New York in the 1920s*. Oxford, UK: Oxford University Press, 2000.

Osato, Sono. *Distant Dances*. New York: Knopf, 1980.

Palmier, Jean-Paul. *Weimar in Exile: The Antifascist Emigration in Europe and America*. Translated by David Fernbach. London: Verso, 2006.

Paramount Pictures Scripts. Margaret Herrick Library, Academy of Motion Picture Arts and Sciences. Beverly Hills, CA.

Parish, James Robert, with Steven Whitney. *The George Raft File: The Unauthorized Biography*. New York: Drake Publishers, 1973.

Parmelee, Patty Lee. *Brecht's America*. Columbus: Ohio State University Press, 1981.

Patterson, James T. *Grand Expectations: The United States, 1945–1974*. Oxford, UK: Oxford University Press, 1996.

Paul, Heike. "Cultural Mobility Between Boston and Berlin: How Germans Have Read and Reread Narratives of American Slavery." In *Cultural Mobility: A Manifesto*. Edited by Stephen Greenblatt, 122–72. Cambridge, UK: Cambridge University Press, 2010.

Perelman, S.J., and Ogden Nash. *One Touch of Venus*. Boston: Little, Brown, 1944.

Pisani, Michael V. *Imagining Native America in Music*. New Haven, CT: Yale University Press, 2005.

Plumb, Steve. *Neue Sachlichkeit 1918–1933: Unity and Diversity of an Art Movement*. Amsterdam: Brill Academic, 2006.

Pollack, Howard. *Marc Blitzstein: His Life, His Work, His World*. Oxford, UK: Oxford University Press, 2012.

Pollack, Howard. "Weill's Popular Adaptations." *Notes* 69, no. 3 (2013): 625–28.

Potter, Pamela M. *Most German of the Arts: Musicology and Society from the Weimar Republic to the End of Hitler's Reich*. New Haven, CT: Yale University Press, 1998.

Potter, Pamela M. "The Politicization of Handel and His Oratorios in the Weimar Republic, the Third Reich, and the Early Years of the German Democratic Republic." *Musical Quarterly* 85, no. 2 (2001): 311–41.

Prevots, Naima. *American Pageantry: A Movement for Art & Democracy*. Ann Arbor, MI: UMI, 1990.

Rehding, Alexander. "On the Record." *Cambridge Opera Journal* 18, no. 1 (2006): 59–82.

Riesman, David, with Nathan Glazer and Reuel Denny. *The Lonely Crowd: A Study of the Changing American Character*. 1950. Reprint, New Haven, CT: Yale University Press, 2001.

Reuss, Richard A., with JoAnne C. Reuss. *American Folk Music and Left-Wing Politics, 1927–1957*. Lanham, MD: Scarecrow, 2000.

Roarty, Robert C. "Lunchtime Follies: Food, Fun, and Propaganda in America's Wartime Workplace." *Journal of American Drama and Theatre* 11, no. 1 (1999): 29–48.

Robinson, J. Bradford. "Jazz Reception in Weimar Germany: In Search of a Shimmy Figure." In *Music and Performance during the Weimar Republic*. Edited by Bryan Gilliam, 107–34. Cambridge, UK: Cambridge University Press, 1994.

Rogin, Michael. *Blackface, White Noise: Jewish Immigrants in the Hollywood Melting Pot*. Berkeley: University of California Press, 1998.

Ronald Sanders Papers. NYPL.

Roosevelt, Eleanor. "My Day," 14 April 1943. Available online at *The Eleanor Roosevelt Papers Digital Edition* (2017), https://www2.gwu.edu/~erpapers/myday/displaydoc.cfm?_y=1943&_f=md056470.

Roper, John Herbert. *Paul Green: Playwright of the Real South*. Athens: University of Georgia Press, 2003.

Saal, Ilka. "Vernacularizing Brecht: The Political Theatre of the New Deal." In *Interrogating America through Theatre and Performance*. Edited by William W. Demastes and Iris Smith Fischer, 101–19. New York: Palgrave Macmillan, 2007.

Salehi, Eric. "No Brecht-fest in America: Revisiting the Theatre Union's 1935 Production of *The Mother*." *Onstage Studies* 21 (1998): 75–97.

"A Salute to France." YouTube video. 35:47. Posted 10 June 2017. https://www.youtube.com/watch?v=LdhHJM5hDL4.

Sandburg, Carl. *The American Songbag*. New York: Harcourt, Brace, 1927.

Sanders, Ronald. *The Days Grow Short: The Life and Music of Kurt Weill*. New York: Holt, Rinehart, and Winston, 1980.

Sanjeen, Eric J. "Anti-Nazi Sentiment in Film: *Confessions of a Nazi Spy* and the German-American Bund." *American Studies* 20, no. 2 (1979): 69–81.

Sarna, Jonathan D. *American Judaism: A History*. New Haven, CT: Yale University Press, 2004.

Sartwell, Crispin. *Political Aesthetics*. Ithaca, NY: Cornell University Press, 2010.

Savran, David. *Highbrow/Lowdown: Theater, Jazz, and the Making of the Middle Class.* Ann Arbor: University of Michigan Press, 2009.

Scarborough, Dorothy. *On the Trail of Negro Folk Songs.* Cambridge, UK: Harvard University Press, 1925.

Schebera, Jürgen. "'Awakening America to the European Jewish Tragedy . . .' Sechs Jahre nach *The Eternal Road*: Ben Hecht/Kurt Weills Massenspiel *We Will Never Die* von 1943—Vorgeschichte und Wirkung." In *Kurt Weill: Auf dem Weg zum Weg der Verheissung.* Edited by Helmut Loos and Guy Stern, 255–64. Freiburg im Breisgau: Rombach, 2000.

Schebera, Jürgen. "Der 'alien American' Kurt Weill und seine Aktivitäten für den *War Effort* der USA 1940-1945." In *A Stranger Here Myself: Kurt Weill Studien.* Edited by Kim H. Kowalke and Horst Edler, 267–84. Hildesheim: Georg Olms, 1993.

Schebera, Jürgen. *Kurt Weill: An Illustrated Life.* New Haven, CT: Yale University Press, 1995.

Schebera, Jürgen. "Zur Wirkungs Geschichte bis 1933." In *Brecht/Weill Mahagonny.* Edited by Fritz Hennenberg and Jan Knopf, 219–45. Frankfurt am Main: Suhrkamp, 2006.

Scheunemann, Dietrich. "Activating the Differences: Expressionist Film and Early Weimar Cinema." In *Expressionist Film: New Perspectives.* Edited by Dietrich Scheunemann, 1–32. Rochester, NY: Camden House, 2003.

Schmidt-Gernig, Alexander. "'Amerikanismus' als Chiffres des modernen Kapitalismus: Zur vergleichenden Kulturkritik in Deutschland der Weimarer Republic." In *Amerikanismus, Americanism, Weill: Die Suche nach kultureller Identität in der Moderne.* Edited by Hermann Danuser and Hermann Gottschewski, 49–68. Schliengen: Edition Argus, 2003.

Scott, Derek B. "Other Mainstreams: Light Music and Easy Listening, 1920–70." In *The Cambridge History of Twentieth-Century Music.* Edited by Nicholas Cook and Anthony Pople, 307–35. Cambridge, UK: Cambridge University Press, 2004.

Shickel, Richard. *Elia Kazan: A Biography.* New York: HarperCollins, 2005.

Silk, Mark. "Notes on the Judeo-Christian Tradition in America." *American Quarterly* 36, no. 1 (1984): 65–85.

Simmons, Christina. *Making Marriage Modern: Women's Sexuality from the Progressive Era to World War II.* Oxford, UK: Oxford University Press, 2009.

Smedley, Nick. *A Divided World: Hollywood Cinema and Émigré Directors in the Era of Roosevelt.* Bristol, UK: Intellectual, 2011.

Smith, Judith E. *Visions of Belonging: Family Stories, Popular Culture, and Postwar Democracy, 1940-1960.* New York: Columbia University Press, 2004.

Smith, Wendy. *Real Life Drama: The Group Theatre and America, 1931-1940.* New York: Vintage, 1990.

Spring, Katherine. *Saying It With Songs: Popular Music and the Coming of Sound to Hollywood Cinema.* Oxford, UK: Oxford University Press, 2013.

Steinbeck, John. *Their Blood Is Strong.* San Francisco: Simon J. Lubin Society of California, 1938.

Stempel, Larry. "*Street Scene* and the Problem of Broadway Opera." In *A New Orpheus: Essays on Kurt Weill.* Edited by Kim H. Kowalke, 321–42. New Haven, CT: Yale University Press, 1985.

Stern, Guy. "The Road to *The Eternal Road*." In *A New Orpheus: Essays on Kurt Weill*, edited by Kim H. Kowalke, 269–84. New Haven, CT: Yale University Press, 1986.

Stover, John F. *American Railroads.* 2nd ed. Chicago, IL: University of Chicago Press, 1997.

Susman, Warren I. *Culture as History: The Transformation of American Society in the Twentieth Century*. New York: Pantheon, 1984.

Susman, Warren I. "The People's Fair: Cultural Contradictions of a Consumer Society." In *Dawn of a New Day: The New York World's Fair, 1939/40*. Edited by Helen A. Harrison, 17–28. New York: New York University Press, 1980.

Symonette, Lys, ed. *The Unknown Kurt Weill: As Sung by Teresa Stratas*. New York: European American Music Corporation, 1982.

Taylor, Ronald. *Kurt Weill: Composer in a Divided World*. Boston: Northeastern University Press, 1992.

Taylor-Jay, Claire. "The Composer's Voice? Compositional Style and Criteria of Value in Weill, Krenek, and Stravinsky." *Journal of the Royal Musical Association* 134, no. 1 (2009): 85–111.

Terkel, Studs. *Hard Times: An Oral History of the Great Depression*. 1970. Reprint, New York: New Press, 2005.

Tirro, Frank. "Jazz Leaves Home: The Dissemination of 'Hot' Music to Central Europe." In *Jazz and the Germans: Essays on the Influence of "Hot" American Idioms on 20th-Century German Music*. Edited by Michael J. Budds, 61–82. Hillsdale, NY: Pendragon, 2002.

U.S. Department of Health, Education, and Welfare. "100 Years of Marriage and Divorce Statistics United States, 1867–1967." December 1983. Available online at https://www.cdc.gov/nchs/data/series/sr_21/sr21_024.pdf.

Valgemae, Mardi. *Accelerated Grimace: Expressionism in the American Drama of the 1920s*. Carbondale: Southern Illinois University Press, 1972.

Villamil, Victoria Etnier. *From Johnson's Kids to Lemonade Opera: The American Classical Singer Comes of Age*. Boston: Northeastern University Press, 2004.

Wagner, Richard. "Judaism in Music." In *Richard Wagner's Prose Works, Volume III: The Theatre*. Translated by William Ashton Ellis, 75–123. London: Kegan Paul, Trench, Trübner, 1907.

Walker, Julia A. *Expressionism and Modernism in the American Theatre: Bodies, Voices, Words*. Cambridge, UK: Cambridge University Press, 2005.

Watkins, Glenn. *Pyramids at the Louvre: Music, Culture and Collage from Stravinsky to the Postmodernists*. Cambridge, MA: Harvard University Press, 1994.

Weill, Kurt. *Music with Solo Violin*. Edited by Andreas Eichhorn. Kurt Weill Edition, Series II, Volume 2. New York: Kurt Weill Foundation for Music/European American Music Corporation, 2010.

Weill, Kurt. *Popular Adaptations 1927–1950*. Edited by Charles Hamm, Elmar Juchem, and Kim H. Kowalke. Kurt Weill Edition, Series IV, Volume 2. New York: Kurt Weill Foundation for Music/European American Music Corporation, 2009.

Weill, Kurt. *Zaubernacht*. Edited by Elmar Juchem and Andrew Kuster. Kurt Weill Edition, Series I, Volume 0. New York: Kurt Weill Foundation for Music/European American Music Corporation, 2008.

Weill, Kurt, and Maxwell Anderson. *Lost in the Stars*. New York: Chappell, 1950.

Weiner, Marc A. *Undertones of Insurrection: Music, Politics, and the Social Sphere in the Modern German Narrative*. Lincoln: University of Nebraska Press, 1993.

Weisgal, Meyer. *Meyer Weisgal . . . So Far: An Autobiography*. New York: Random House, 1971.

Weisstein, Ulrich. "Brecht's Victorian Version of Gay: Imitation and Originality in the *Dreigroschenoper*." In *Critical Essays on Bertolt Brecht*. Edited by Siegfried Mews, 45–62. Boston: G.K. Hall & Co., 1989.

Weitz, Eric D. *Weimar Germany: Promise and Tragedy*. Princeton, NJ: Princeton University Press, 2007.

Werfel, Franz. *The Eternal Road: A Drama in Four Parts*. Translated by Ludwig Lewissohn. New York: Viking, 1936.

Wharton, John F. *Life among the Playwrights: Being Mostly the Story of the Playwrights Producing* Company. New York: Quadrangle/New York Times Book Co., 1974.

White, Newman I. *American Negro Folksongs*. Cambridge, MA: Harvard University Press, 1928.

Whitfield, Sarah. "Kurt Weill: The 'Composer as Dramatist' in American Musical Theatre Production." PhD diss., Queen Mary College, University of London, 2010.

Whitfield, Sarah. "'Next You're Franklin Shepard Inc.?' Composing the Broadway Musical—A Study of Kurt Weill's working Practices." *Studies in Musical Theatre* 10, no. 2 (2016): 163–76.

Willett, John. *Art and Politics in the Weimar Period: The New Sobriety: 1917–1933*. New York: Pantheon, 1978.

Willett, John. *The Theatre of Erwin Piscator: Half a Century of Politics in the Theater*. London: Eyre Methuen, 1978.

Winkler, Allan M. *Home Front, U.S.A.: America during World War II*. 3rd edition. Wheeling, IL: Harlan Davidson, 2012.

Wipplinger, Jonathan O. *The Jazz Republic: Music, Race, and American Culture in Weimar, Germany*. Ann Arbor: University of Michigan Press, 2017.

Woll, Allen L. *The Hollywood Musical Goes to War*. Chicago: Nelson-Hall, 1983.

World's Fair Collection. NYPL.

Wylie, Philip. *Generation of Vipers*. New York: Ferris, 1942.

Zenck, Claudia Mauer. "Challenges and Opportunities of Acculturation: Schoenberg, Krenek, and Stravinsky in Exile." In *Driven into Paradise: The Musical Migration from Nazi Germany to the United States*. Edited by Reinhold Brinkmann and Christoph Wolff, 172–93. Berkeley: University of California Press, 1999.

# Permissions

# Index

Tables and figures are indicated by *t* and *f* following the page number.